MUSEUMS IN MOTION

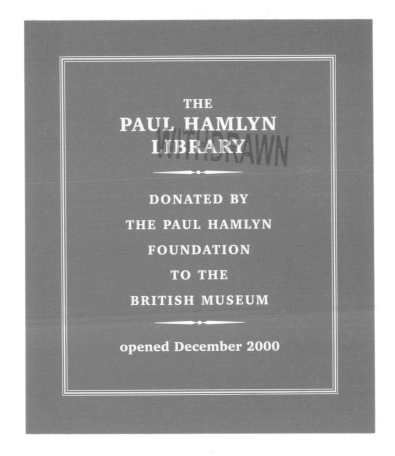

ABOUT THE SERIES
The American Association for State and Local History Book Series publishes technical and professional information for those who practice and support history, and addresses issues critical to the field of state and local history. To submit a proposal or manuscript to the series, please request proposal guidelines from AASLH headquarters: AASLH Book Series, 1717 Church St., Nashville, TN 37203. Telephone: (615) 320-3203. Fax: (615) 327-9013. Web site: www.aaslh.org.

ABOUT THE ORGANIZATION
The American Association for State and Local History (AASLH) is a nonprofit educational organization dedicated to advancing knowledge, understanding, and appreciation of local history in the United States and Canada. In addition to sponsorship of this book series, the Association publishes the periodical *History News*, a newsletter, technical leaflets and reports, and other materials; confers prizes and awards in recognition of outstanding achievement in the field; and supports a broad education program and other activities designed to help members work more effectively. To join the organization, contact: Membership Director, AASLH, 1717 Church St., Nashville, TN 37203.

MUSEUMS IN MOTION

An Introduction to the History and Functions of Museums

Second Edition

Edward P. Alexander and Mary Alexander

A Division of
Rowman & Littlefield Publishers, Inc.
Lanham • New York • Toronto • Plymouth, UK

ALTAMIRA PRESS
A division of Rowman & Littlefield Publishers, Inc.
A wholly owned subsidary of The Rowman & Littlefield Publishing Group, Inc.
4501 Forbes Boulevard, Suite 200, Lanham, MD 20706
www.altamirapress.com

Estover Road, Plymouth PL6 7PY, United Kingdom

British Library Cataloguing in Publication Information Available

Library of Congress Cataloging-in-Publication Data

Alexander, Edward P. (Edward Porter), 1907–
  Museums in motion : an introduction to the history and functions of
museums / Edward P. Alexander and Mary Alexander. — 2nd ed.
    p. cm. — (American Association For State and Local History book series)
  Includes bibliographical references and index.
  ISBN-13: 978-0-7591-0508-9 (cloth : alk. paper)
  ISBN-10: 0-7591-0508-1 (cloth : alk. paper)
  ISBN-13: 978-0-7591-0509-6 (pbk. : alk. paper)
  ISBN-10: 0-7591-0509-X (pbk. : alk. paper)
  1. Museums. 2. Museums—History. 3. Museums—Philosophy.
I. Alexander, Mary. II. American Association for State and Local History.
III. Title.

  AM5.A38 2008   069.09 ALE
  069—dc22
                        2007022412

Printed in the United States of America

∞™ The paper used in this publication meets the minimum requirements of
American National Standard for Information Sciences—Permanence of Paper
for Printed Library Materials, ANSI/NISO Z39.48-1992.

To the memory of Edward P. Alexander and to all students of museums, especially Norman Schou and George Hein

Contents

In Memoriam: Edward P. Alexander, 1907–2003   ix

Preface   xi

Acknowledgments   xiii

1 What Is a Museum?   1

Part I:
HISTORY

2 The Art Museum   23

3 Natural History and Anthropology Museums   53

4 Science and Technology Museums and Centers   85

5 The History Museum   113

6 Botanical Gardens and Zoos   139

7 Children's Museums   167

Part II:
FUNCTIONS

8   To Collect   187

9   To Conserve   217

10 To Exhibit   235

11 To Interpret   257

12 To Serve   281

13 The Museum Profession   305

Readings   323

Index   333

About the Authors   351

In Memoriam:
Edward P. Alexander, 1907–2003

On a snowy January day in Madison, Wisconsin, members of the State Historical Society gathered to say good-bye to Alice and Ed Alexander as they prepared to move to Williamsburg, Virginia, to join the staff of Colonial Williamsburg (CW). The party was planned, presents wrapped, and speeches written, but there was one hitch. Alice was blocks away at University Hospital where daughter Mary Sheron was making her entrance. That spring, the Alexanders, including Anne, John, and Mary (in a laundry basket) drove south to Williamsburg, Virginia.

Edward Alexander seems to have done it all in terms of history museums. In the 1930s and 1940s he led the New York and Wisconsin state historical societies. He brought to Colonial Williamsburg a commitment to intellectual rigor in public interpretation, relying on his academic background in U.S. history. He was elected president of the American Association of State and Local History (AASLH), the third in the association's history, and he was the American Association of Museums' (AAM) president in the 1960s. On his retirement from CW in 1972, he described his departure this way: "I left my office at the Goodwin Building on a Friday and the next Monday I faced my Museum Studies students in a classroom at the University of Delaware." He was sixty-five years old and was establishing a new museum studies program.

As I wrote and rewrote additions to this volume, I was striving to be the engaging storyteller that Dad was. One of his former students described reading his text as "having a chat with Dr. Alexander." His books *Museums in Motion: An Introduction to the History and Functions of Museums* (1979), *Museum Masters: Their Museums and Their Influence* (1983), and *The Museum in America: Innovators and Pioneers* (1997) remain basic texts on museum professionals' shelves. The last was published when he was ninety years old.

In his lifetime, Edward P. Alexander was appropriately honored for his contributions to museum practice with the Katherine Coffey Award (Northeast Museums Conference), the Award of Distinction (AASLH), and the Distinguished Service Award (AAM). He is listed on the AAM's Centennial Honor Roll.

—Mary Alexander

Preface

The first edition's foreword by Bill Alderson, longtime director of the American Association of State and Local History (AASLH) and Dad's successor at the University of Delaware, included this description of its significance: "This is an especially important book, because it reflects the analytical skills of the trained historian, the insights of an experienced leader of the profession, and the dedication of a teacher who wishes us to learn and to grow. The result is a pioneering effort that is informative, wise, and useful. Add to those virtues the fact that it is also highly readable, and you have a book that becomes 'must' reading, not only for museum professionals, but for everyone who is interested in the museum world." In creating this revision, I sought to retain the qualities of the original while updating the information on museum practice and providing readers with more current references. What follows is fundamentally Edward P. Alexander's book with emendations.

I am not a historian, nor do I have the breadth of my dad's experience. Therefore, I retained much of his text, adding to it based on broad reading and research. As I read and learned more and more about museum practice, I found that I could not judge the significance of some museum activities, but I knew they could be important. I began to collect elements to add to each chapter that I call "challenges." Here readers will find perhaps more questions than answers, but I hope that I've raised issues (and provided sources) to guide them to learn more. Some of the challenges recur with modifications based on the chapter's focus.

As I did my research, I came upon statements that caught my attention and suggested something important about the subject I was studying. As

I noted these, I began to copy them as possible openings for each chapter. Sometimes they startled me with their insights voiced so long ago; others seemed more provocative, almost "teasing" readers to begin the chapter. Both the quotes and the challenges may be useful for museum studies class discussions.

Two people played a central role in the revision process. The first is my husband, Norman Schou, who read every word and edited many of them. He reminded me again and again to retain "Ed's stories." Once Norman approved the draft, it went to my friend George Hein for review. George and I wrote *Museums: Places of Learning* for the American Association of Museums (AAM) some years ago and remain close friends. He agreed to serve as "first reader," adding his experience and worldwide network of colleagues. Where my experience is with history museums, George's is with science centers and children's museums, and so much more. He seems to know everyone and, as important, how to reach them.

I began this project in earnest in 2003; my dad lived less than a mile away. He was ninety-six and, unfortunately, no longer able to understand what I was doing. He died that summer. It seems appropriate that the final stages of republishing *Museums in Motion* are happening in Dad's centennial year.

—Mary Alexander

Acknowledgments

As a Maryland Historical Trust staff member, I have been humbled by the support from Wayne Clark, Rodney Little, Elizabeth Hughes, and Miriam Hensley. Their flexibility allowed me to complete this work. The Smithsonian libraries' staff has been incredibly helpful and friendly to me as I sought out references and tracked down obscure publications; Amy Levin and Anna Brooke are just the best librarians and neighbors. Thanks to the Smithsonian Center for Education and Museum Studies for a 2005 Fellowship in Museum Practice that allowed me to focus on my writing.

Four years of research and writing results in lots of indebtedness to colleagues and friends. The list that follows cannot reflect the level of thanks required. Jeffery Abt, Mitch Allen, Ellen Allers, Susan Breitkopf, Anna Brooke, Jeff Buchheit, Mary Case, Leticia Perez Castellanos, Claire Catron, Phil Deters, Nicole Diehlmann, Elaine Eff, Doug Evelyn, Jane Farmer, Eric French, Nancy Fuller, Robert Goler, Tom Hennes, Pam Henson, Richard Hughes, Rosemary Krill, Amy Levin, Kristen Laise, Kathy Maxwell, Elizabeth Merritt, Susan Nichols, Debbie Hess Norris, Leni Preston, Melanie Quin, Brian Ramer, Marsha Semmel, Kathy Speiss, Bryant Tolles, Bonnie Van Dorn, Ginny Vroblesky, Clara von Waldthausen, Susan Walter, Steve Weil, and Scott Whipple. Special thanks to AltaMira's reviewers "A" and "B," who offered terrific suggestions; you know who you are.

1

What Is a Museum?

A hospital is a hospital. A library is a library. A rose is a rose. But a museum is Colonial Williamsburg, Mrs. Wilkerson's Figure Bottle Museum, the Museum of Modern Art, the Sea Lion Caves, the American Museum of Natural History, the Barton Museum of Whiskey History, The Cloisters, and Noell's Ark and Chimpanzee Farm and Gorilla Show.

—Richard Grove, 1969[1]

The museum is an "empowering" institution, meant to incorporate all who would become part of our shared cultural experience. Any citizen can walk into a museum and appreciate the highest achievements of his culture. If he spends enough time, he may be transformed. This is precisely what the museum founders had in mind when they brought great collections to their own cities.

—Mark Lilla, 1985[2]

By thinking of their missions as contact work—decentered and traversed by cultural and political negotiations that are out of any imagined community's control—museums may begin to grapple with the real difficulties of dialogue, alliance, inequality, and translation.

—James Clifford, 1997[3]

The 1979 edition of this volume began with these words: "Museums in the United States are growing at an almost frightening rate. If we count the smallest ones with only one person on the staff and he or she without professional training, about five thousand of them exist today, and recently a new one has appeared every 3.3 days. People are crowding into them in droves, and the annual visits made to museums are now estimated at 600 million, give or take 100 million." Current estimates of the number of U.S. museums hover around sixteen thousand and the pace of additions, so noticable in the 1970s, according to the American Association of Museums (AAM) has slowed. U.S. museum attendance continues to be high, outstripping major sporting events. These numbers neglect the growing impact of "visiting" museum programs or exhibitions in cyberspace, or virtual museums with only World Wide Web addresses.[4]

Museum Definitions: Friendly and Unfriendly

A museum is a complex institution, and defining it is not easy. Whether one likes or dislikes museums will influence one's definition. Douglas Allan, former director of the Royal Scottish Museum in Edinburgh, said that "a museum in its simplest form consists of a building to house collections of objects for inspection, study and enjoyment."[5] Except for the confining of the museum to a single building, perhaps most of us would agree with that generalization.

The American Association of Museums, in developing a nationwide museum accreditation program, defines a museum as "an organized and permanent non-profit institution, essentially educational or aesthetic in purpose, with professional staff, which owns and utilizes tangible objects, cares for them, and exhibits them to the public on some regular schedule."[6] That definition met some objection from art centers, children's museums, science centers, and planetariums that have little or no collection. In 1988 the accreditation commisson changed the term from "owns and utilizes" to "owns or utilizes" to accommodate those institutions without collections. The International Council of Museums (ICOM) in 1995 defined a museum as "a non-profit making, permanent institution in the service of society and of its development, and open to the public, which acquires, conserves, researches, communicates and exhibits for the purposes of study, education and enjoyment, material evidence of people and their environment."[7]

Thomas P. F. Hoving, former director of the Metropolitan Museum of Art, declared that the museum possesses "a great potential, not only as a stabilizing, regenerative force in modern society, but as a crusading force for quality and excellence."[8] S. Dillon Ripley, former secretary of the Smithsonian Institution, which operates the huge national museum megalopolis in Washington, D.C., opined that "a museum can be a powerhouse," though only if "museum people and the public get away from the 'attic' mentality."[9] A lively German writer described an art museum as a place "where every separate object kills every other and all of them together the visitor."[10]

Barry Gaither, director of the Museum of the National Center of African American Artists, in a *Museum News* roundtable discussion of cultural diversity suggests:

> The struggle [for museums] . . . has to do with hegemony over the interpretation of one's own experience, and how to give institutional form to that hegemony. If I saw any mission as the appropriate mission of newer museums, evolving museums, museums associated with a specific heritage within the American story, I would say it's finding the courage "to be." And that "to be" is open-ended, because the "to be" is an evolving understanding of self and culture and its dynamic relationship. That's our real work. Other institutions can respond to us in a more concrete way, whether willingly or not, when we are more clearly ourselves.[11]

Perhaps this is attempt enough at definition for the moment, and we should leave the subject while enjoying the quip of an anonymous Englishman who considers the museum "a depository of curiosities that more often than not includes the director."

Ancient and Medieval Prototypes

The Latin word *museum* (Greek: *mouseion*) has had a variety of meanings through the centuries. In classical times it signified a temple dedicated to the Muses, those nine sprightly and pleasantly amoral young goddesses who watched over the welfare of the epic, music, love poetry, oratory, history, tragedy, comedy, the dance, and astronomy. The most famous museum of that era was founded at Alexandria about the 3rd century BC by Ptolemy Soter ("Preserver") and was destroyed during various civil disturbances in the 3rd century AD. The Mouseion of Alexandria had some objects, including statues of thinkers, astronomical and surgical instruments, elephant trunks and animal hides, and a botanical and zoological park, but it was chiefly a university or philosophical academy—a kind of institute of advanced study with many prominent scholars in residence and supported by the state. The museum and the great international library of papyrus rolls and other writings collected by Alexander the Great were housed in the royal quarter of the city known as the Bruchium. Euclid headed the mathematics faculty and wrote his *Elements of Geometry* there. Archimedes, Appolonius of Perga, and Eratosthenes were only a few of the noted scientists and scholars who lived in the king's household and made use of the library, lecture halls, covered walks, refectory, laboratories for dissection and scientific studies, and botanical and zoological gardens.[12] Bearing in mind that musing and amusement are interrelated and reflect pondering and deep thought as well as diversion and entertainment, it is no surprise that museums have long been considered to be places of study as well as repositories of collections. Didier Maleuvre's engaging description of a museum emphasizes the pondering of objects in an exhibit or collection quite apart from a museum's didactic program: "[T]he museum does give free time—freedom to loiter and tarry, to indulge the long double-take, the retracing of steps, the dreamy pause, the regress and ingress of reverie, the wending progress that is engagement. It is a tempo of consciousness disarming to modern audience conditioned to fear open-ended silence as a forerunner to boredom."[13] Some scholars of the museum movement, who emphasize its research function and prefer to define the museum as a community of scholars, look back on the Alexandria institution with real affection and nostalgia.

Though the Greeks and Romans thought of the museum in different terms from those we use today, the ancient world did possess public collections of objects valued for their aesthetic, historic, religious, or magical importance. The Greek temples had hoards of votive offerings of gold, silver, and bronze objects, statues and statuettes, paintings, and even bullion that could be expended in case of public emergency. The paintings were on planks (Greek: *pinas*), and thus a collection of them was called *pinakotheke*. In the 5th century the Acropolis at Athens had such paintings in the Prophylae, placed above a marble dado, lighted by two windows from the south, and protected individually by shutters. The Romans displayed paintings and sculpture, often the booty of their conquests, in forums, public gardens, temples, theaters, and baths. Roman generals, statesmen, and wealthy patricians often appropriated such objects for their country homes. The emperor Hadrian in the 2nd century at his villa near Tibur (today Tivoli) reconstructed some of the landmarks he had seen in his travels through the empire, for example, the Lyceum and Academy of Athens, the Vale of Tempe in

Thessaly, and the Canopus of the Egyptian delta. In a sense he created an open-air or outdoor museum.[14]

The museum idea was barely kept alive in western Europe during the Middle Ages. Churches, cathedrals, and monasteries venerated alleged relics of the Virgin, Christ, the apostles, and the saints and embellished them with gold, silver, and jewels, manuscripts in sumptuous metal bindings, and rich oriental fabrics. The Crusades brought back fabulous art objects to add to these treasures or to the palace collections of princes and nobles, thus illustrating what the late Francis Taylor wittily called the "magpiety" of mankind.[15]

From Private Collection to Public Museum

"The modern museum," says J. Mordaunt Crook, in his architectural study of the British Museum, "is a product of Renaissance humanism, eighteenth-century enlightenment and nineteenth-century democracy." The humanist, with keen interest in the classical past and the world about him, began to throw off the reins of superstition and take halting steps toward a scientific method. Two new words appeared in the 16th century to express the museum concept. The gallery (Italian: *galleria*), a long, grand hall lighted from the side, came to signify an exhibition area for pictures and sculpture. The cabinet (Italian: *gabinetto*) was usually a square-shaped room filled with stuffed animals, botanical rarities, small works of art such as medallions or statuettes, artifacts, and curios; the Germans called it *Wunderkammer*. Both types of collections rarely were open to the public and remained the playthings of princes, popes, and plutocrats.[16]

The ancient world had had its great gardens, and medieval monasteries cultivated and cherished plants and flowers, but true botanical gardens began to appear at universities—Pisa (1543), Padua (1545), Bologna (1567), Leiden (1587), Heidelberg and Montpellier (1593), and Oxford (1620). Scholarly botanists used them for scientific plant study; physicians, for testing remedies. Herbalists, barber surgeons, apothecaries, and physicians also established physic gardens as sources for medicinal treatments rather than simply for study, for example, at Holburn and Chelsea in London.[17]

The museum began to go public in the late 17th century. Basel opened the first university museum in 1671, and the Ashmolean Museum appeared at Oxford a dozen years later. The 18th century concerned itself with discovering the basic natural laws that formed a framework for the universe and humanity, and intellectuals of the day wished to preserve in museums natural specimens as well as human artistic and scientific creations. Supposedly they would help educate humankind and abet its steady progress toward perfection. The Vatican established several museums about 1750, and the British Museum was formed in 1753 when Parliament purchased Sir Hans Sloane's great collection devoted chiefly to natural science.[18] In 1793 France opened the Palace of the Louvre as the Museum of the Republic. Napoleon confiscated art objects by conquest and devised a grand plan for a unified French museum system as well as subsidiary museums elsewhere. The scheme collapsed with his defeat, but his conception of a museum as an instrument of national glory continued to stir the imagination of Europeans.[19]

Museums of the United States

As British colonies in North America merged and became the United States, museums evolved alongside the political process. The Charleston Museum, founded in 1773, collected natural history materials.[20] Along the Atlantic, small groups of enthusiasts met together to discuss and study objects emerging from the explorations of the new continent. Like their European predecessors, the institutions—philosophical societies, antiquarian groups, museums—began with "members." But quickly, the members offered public hours for visitors to gaze upon the rare and exotic. In addition to providing public access, these groups sought financial support from a variety of sources, including paid admissions, making the "entrepreneurial" spirit a special American contribution to museum practice.[21] Charles Willson Peale was the first great American museum director. Peale's Museum in Philadelphia began in his home, moved to Independence Hall, and had branches in Baltimore and New York. He mounted specimens of animals, birds, and insects with realistic backgrounds and displayed portraits of nearly three hundred Founding Fathers, painted chiefly by himself or members of his family.[22] In the captial city, the Smithsonian Institution, started in 1846 with the Englishman James Smithson's bequest to the United States "for the increase and diffusion of knowledge," for a time was loath to accept collections and remained chiefly a research institution of pure science. When George Brown Goode joined the Smithsonian in 1873, it began to become a national museum devoted to science, the humanities, and the arts.[23] The founding in about 1870 of three great museums—the American Museum of Natural History, the Metropolitan Museum of Art in New York, and the Museum of Fine Arts in Boston—marked the entry of the United States into the museum mainstream.[24]

By 1900 American museums were becoming centers of education and public enlightenment. This development was natural in a country that prided itself on its democratic ideals and placed deep faith in public education both as a political necessity and as a means of attaining technological excellence. Benjamin Ives Gilman, secretary of the Museum of Fine Arts in Boston, considered this conception proper for science museums, but not for art museums. He thought "a museum of science . . . in essence a school; a museum of art in essence a temple." Works of art communicated directly with their beholders and needed little labeling; art museums were "not didactic but aesthetic in primary purpose." But Gilman wanted art museums to have interpreters to help their visitors see the beauty of their collections. Thus in 1907 the Boston museum appointed a docent to its staff. Gilman dreamed up this new title that avoided any reference to "education"; he explained that "a museum performs its complete office as it is at once gardant, monstrant, and docent." The American Museum of Natural History, the Metropolitan Museum, and even the British Museum appointed such guides.[25] American museums have continued their leadership in educational programs. They frequently refer to the kind of education they provide as "interpretation" or teaching through the use of original objects, emotionally engaging the visitor and complementing learning through words and verbalization. American museums developed close relationships with schools, welcoming thousands of students with their teachers and in return sending both objects and museum staff to classrooms. The Brooklyn Children's Museum, founded in 1899, continues to serve young people today.

Museum Functions

The development of museums has been intensely personal and haphazard in plan. The emphasis had been upon collection of the beautiful and curious. The objects gathered were chiefly works of art, historical rarities, or scientific specimens and equipment; some objects were animate, and the botanical garden, arboretum, menagerie, and aquarium as living collections were essentially museums. Collecting seems to be instinctive for many human beings. It may be based upon the desire for physical security (today collections often are considered good investments), social distinction (Thorstein Veblen would call it "conspicuous consumption"), the pursuit of knowledge and connoisseurship (genuine love for objects and desire to find out everything about them), and a wish to achieve a kind of immortality, as witness the great number of named collections in museums. Collectors also sometimes display neurotic symptoms that may result in obsession or a kind of gambling fervor. Sir Kenneth Clark suggested that "collecting is like a biological function, not unrelated to our physical appetites."[26]

Collectors traditionally have turned their hoards over to museums, and museums have often caught the raging collecting fever. Museums have spent fortunes for paintings or objects while neglecting institutional needs from salaries to operating expenses. Conservative museum directors sometimes consider collecting far and away the most important museum function. One museum authority has suggested that it is the sole reason for museums and that exhibition, education, culture, and the social good are only rationalizations and window dressing used to justify the basic collecting passion.[27]

Closely connected with collection was the function of conservation. Collectors have always taken care of their hoards, oftentimes with miserly devotion. The techniques of conservation were at first little understood, as a result nearly all the panel paintings of antiquity have disappeared. The Greeks made crude attempts to preserve votive shields by coating them with pitch to prevent rust, and they placed vats of oil at the feet of Phidias's Athena Parthenos to reduce excessive dryness. By the 16th century, paintings were being cleaned and revarnished, but not until nearly 1750 was the rebacking process perfected that could transfer the layer of paint from its original wall, panel, or canvas to a new surface.[28]

As long as a collection was private, it could be kept under lock and key and relatively safe. When the public was admitted to the museum, however, precautions had to be taken against theft or handling, and the Industrial Revolution brought high-intensity lighting, central heating, air pollution, and other unfavorable conditions that could speed the deterioration of collections. Yet the revolution also brought scientific study and knowledge of the composition, conservation, and restoration of objects. Good housekeeping methods, proper control of lighting and relative humidity, and ingenious repair and rehabilitation procedures have revolutionized the preservation of museum objects and added to museum staffs skilled conservators trained in physics and chemistry.[29]

Research into museum collections allowed objects to be accurately described and cataloged. In natural history museums, botanical gardens, zoos, and aquariums, this study resulted in important taxonomic contributions to biological studies. In all museums research often has led to additions to the collection. Today museum research ranges from basic research into the nature of objects to applied research that places those objects in their artistic, scientific, or historic context. In the 20th century, museum research expanded beyond collections to include museum practices and the museum's visitors themselves.[30]

Once the museum admitted the public, its exhibition function became predominant. Collecting, conservation, and research in the main supported the development of exhibitions. At first the displays were arranged to benefit the aesthete, the scholar, the collector, and the craftsman, a knowledgeable audience satisfied with a minimum of interpretation. The collection usually was arranged either aesthetically or according to the principle of technical classification in chronological or stylistic order—a kind of visible storage with crowded walls of paintings or heavy glass cases crammed with ceramics, textiles, metalware, or natural history specimens. Museums were housed in palatial or templelike structures that made the man on the street feel uncomfortable and discouraged his attendance. Here's Alma Wittlin's amusing description of early encounters between the collector and the public: "The situation proved to be a disappointment to many owners of collections and probably to much more numerous visitors. The collectors felt that they received ingratitude in return for their favors, and many visitors were frustrated and angered. They had endured humiliating interrogations to obtain admission to a place described to them as a land of wonders, and they discovered they were aliens in it. Some people found an outlet in inappropriate and rambunctious behavior."[31]

In the 19th century the exhibition function began to change from displays of objects, whether art, natural history specimens or historically significant artifacts, organized with some overarching system (taxonomy). German and Swiss museum directors experimented with culture history arrangement—placing objects in period rooms or halls that gave the visitor the feeling of walking through different stages of national history.[32] The wonders of technical and scientific accomplishments were put on view to be admired and to celebrate "progress." The series of international expositions or world's fairs that began with London's Crystal Palace in 1851 contributed to ever more spacious and dramatic systems of exhibition. In Scandanavia, history museums in parklike settings celebrated the rural, nonmechanized life that was so quickly vanishing with industrialization and urbanization. Artur Hazelius' Skansen (opened in 1891) on the outskirts of Stockholm became an international model.[33]

Exhibition, education, or interpretation—the conveyance of culture—and a commitment to community or social welfare have grown to be important aims for the museum in the last century. As public education expanded worldwide, museums joined schools as agencies for conveying cultural traditions. With the 20th century came ever more emphasis on attracting visitors, which has led to more of an emphasis on public service over the basic maintenance of collections. Stephen Weil has suggested that museums have moved beyond collections and collecting so dominant in the 19th and early 20th centuries, to become institutions rooted in interpretation in its broadest sense, actively seeking to provoke thought and the exchange of ideas between the museum and its visitors.[34]

This rapid sketch of museum development through the ages underlines the origins of the flexible nature of today's museum. Wander into any midsize town's museum nearly anywhere in the world and you may see a variety of activities underway. A school group sits on the gallery floor enjoying a lesson from a museum staff member. Musicians are rehearsing in another space for an evening performance. An exhibition planning team argues over which objects best convey an upcoming exhibit's messages. Or, exhibit installers are building elements of a temporary exhibit. A researcher meets with curatorial staff to see and better understand an object featured on the museum's webpage. Staff members are leaving the museum to meet with other community organizations to arrange literacy training classes either at the museum or elsewhere. Staff and visitors connect to researchers continents away through a projected Internet hookup to review current research findings. This description neglects the invisible work of museums to secure financial stability; work that may involve local philanthropies, politicians, or leaders of other cultural institutions. Early in the 20th century, Arthur Parker cautioned museum directors that museums that are not changing are in essence "dead institutions" and to him therefore unworthy of notice or support. Today, no museum adminstrator can ignore Parker's advice.[35]

Changing Definitions for Museums

The ancients visited museums or the "place of the muses" to look upon beauty; to discuss ideas with others; to experiment with natural phenomenon, in essence to be "amused"; and thereby to think deeply and to learn. The 18th-century setting for these activities might best be described as a university. From these roots as a center for learning, museums added specimens, historical objects, documents, and artworks, assuming the role as guardian or "keeper." Brooklyn Museum director Duncan Cameron published the notion that museums occupy two ends of a spectrum from a "temple" to a "forum" in the early 1970s. A review of museum development, especially in the United States at the beginning of the 21st century, reveals that the premodern form of a museum as a site for musing and for discourse or Cameron's forum seems to be on the rise again. The 19th-century dominance of collections, the objects within Cameron's temple, has been challenged by those who identify museums to be places for public discussion, engagement, and learning. Today, the balance between museum as a repository of objects and as a place for learning has tipped back to the ancient forum.[36]

What follows is a snapshot of definitions of museums and their roles, primarily from the United States, beginning in the early 20th century and ending with the opening of the 21st century. They suggest the complexity and changing nature of museumness, ending with two institutions that describe themselves as "a museum different," and another that highlights its "unmuseum."

Anthropologist Franz Boas—whose actual museum experience was very short-lived, but whose work affected the development of anthropology museums within the 20th century—wrote in 1907: "The value of the museum as a resort for popular entertainment must not be underrated . . . where every opportunity that is given to the people to employ their leisure time in healthy and stimulating surroundings . . . that counteracts the influence of the saloon and of the race-track is of great social importance."[37]

Cleveland Museum of Art educator Adele Silver opens a 1979 national report on U.S. art museum education practices by reminding readers: "In the beginning, there were no art museums. Innocent irreverence reminds us that museums are inventions of men [sic], not inevitable, eternal, ideal nor divine. They exist for the things we put in them, and they change as each generation chooses how to see and use those things."[38]

American art historian Carol Duncan's writings place museums within their broader social and political contexts. "A Museum is not the neutral and transparent sheltering space that it is often claimed to be. More like the traditional ceremonial monument that museum buildings frequently emulate—classical temples, medieval cathedrals, Renaissance palaces—the museum is a complex experience, involving architecture, programmed displays of art objects, and highly rationalized installations. And like ceremonial structures of the past, by fulfilling its declared purposes as a museum (preserving and displaying art objects) it also carried out broad, sometimes less obvious political and ideological tasks."[39]

"Museums place history, nature, and traditional societies under glass, in artificially constructed dioramas and tableaux, thus sanitizing, insulating, plasticizing, and preserving them as attractions and simple lesson aids; by virtue of their location, they are implicitly compared with and subordinated to contemporary established values and definitions of social reality. We 'museumify' other cultures and our own past." Canadian anthropologist and museum director Michael Ames argues that museums by their very nature limit their audiences' abilities to make sense of collections and place them in broader social contexts.[40]

Stephen Weil chides American museums to use their collections for "the public good," rather than simply placing them in protective custody. His hope for museums echoes Cameron's forum rather than the temple. "The American museum—notwithstanding the ringing educational rhetoric with which it was originally established and occasionally maintained—had become primarily engaged in 'salvage and warehouse business.' . . . To the extent that some further benefit might be generated by providing the public with physical and intellectual access to the collections and information thus accumulated, that was simply a plus."[41]

Museum educator Elaine Heumann Gurian describes museums this way:

> The museums' relationship to its collections and to the ownership and care thereof will change, and in some instances already have changed. The distinct edges of differing function among libraries, memorials, social ser-

vices centers, schools, shopping malls, zoos, performance halls, archives, theaters, public parks, cafes, and museums will (and in many cases have already begun to) blur. On the content side museums will become more comfortable with presentations that contain a multiplicty of viewpoints and with the interweaving of scientific fact and what is considered by some, but not by others, to be 'myth.' On the interpretive side, museums will rely less on collections to carry the story, and more on other forms of expressions, such as stories, song, and speech and the affective dramatic, and psychological power that their presentations can contain; and they will be less apologetic about including emotional and evocative messages. These changes will help museums become more effective storehouses of cultural information.[42]

New York City's Chinatown History Museum founder and historian, John Kuo Wei Tchen, goes beyond Gurian's advice and writes that museums and their exhibitions "must be done in tandem with the people the history is about . . . personal memory and testimony inform and are informed by historical context and scholarship. The museum reaches its communities through 'reunions' (especially of P.S. [Public School] 23 where the museum is located) to link the felt need for history directly with historical scholarship."[43] The Chinatown project reflects the expansion of the fundamental "authority" of museums from academically trained curators to the museum's own audiences. The project from its outset was a working partnership with the intended audience; it offered them Cameron's forum as their own.

Understanding the concept of museum has become even more complex with variations on the term. National Museum of the American Indian (NMAI) director, W. Richard West describes NMAI as "museum different" arguing that the museum is "most accurately described, and functions as, an international institution of living cultures . . . [it] is a civic space not just a cultural stop. I don't pretend our model is the destination for every museum. I am saying as a model we present potential for a different way of putting a museum together."[44] The newly reopened Cincinnati Arts Center uses the term "unmuseum" for its educational programming, which director Charles Desmarais describes: "One of the things we've thrown into the mix is to ask contemporary artists to join us in planning the UnMuseum . . . to create works of art that kids can manipulate and change. The idea is for kids to discover on their own how we get meaning from visual art."[45] Some museums accentuate their uniqueness as a "brand" with names designed to attract the public; Finland's Heureka and San Francisco's Exploratorium are two examples.

What to Expect in These Pages

This volume is divided into two sections; the first centers on the history of museums by type, art, natural history and anthropology, science, history, botanical gardens, zoos, and those dedicated to youth. The second addresses museum functions starting with collecting through public service, and ending with a look at the museum profession. The emphasis is on European and U.S. museums. Each chapter closes with a discussion of "challenges." They are intended to give readers a glimpse into the future; they often raise questions rather than offering answers.

At the end of this volume is a very selective bibliography of museum texts. The citations have been selected to provide the reader with general information about museums; however, for every topic of this volume, there is much more literature that may be of interest to those seeking to understand museums. The list is only an introduction to the complexities of museum history and practice. Chapter footnotes will guide readers to fuller information.

Challenges

Public or Private Support

The European model for museums is one of governmental support that often is centralized. However, as these institutions diversify and proliferate, how should they be supported? Nicholas Burt points out limitations of both public and private support: "In Europe the state or the city has always supported museums. . . . It is not at all obvious that U.S. government support would be the best answer. What are the alternatives? Massive popular support on a broad base means popularity contests. State or city support means politics and poverty. Support by the rich, if available, means control by the rich." In the United Kingdom in recent years, the Millennium Fund, supported by a national lottery, has blended public-private support for the nation's cultural institutions. There is fierce competition among museums for these funds.[46]

Measuring Success

Museum boards of directors and governmental oversight entities too often measure a museum's success by attendance through the doorway. As the Internet has added a new format for museums to use to reach their audiences, this measurement seems both too limited and limiting. But, what are the appropriate criteria for measuring the impact of museums? How does a museum quantify its visitors' quiet, reflective inspiration for its oversight boards, funders, and even the general public?

Research

Museums as reflections of the Enlightenment sought to add to humanity's understanding of the world through the most basic research functions—finding, naming, collecting, and categorizing—elements of the world's wonders. Museums, along with universities, played a central role in this process. Today that role has changed, expanding in some instances and falling away in others. What role should research play within today's museums? In the past, basic research distinguished museums from their competitors for public entertainment; what research role should museums assume today? How has technology changed the place of museums within the scholarly research communities?

Authority

As museums open their doors and create more audience-based experiences, who should be the "authors" of the museum's interpretive messages from exhibitions to public programs? As historian Neil Harris suggests: "The museum's position is no longer seen as transcendent. Rather it is implicated in the distributions of wealth, power, knowledge, and taste shaped by the larger social order." What are the messages that the museum should convey? Who determines those messages and gives one idea precedence over another? Should the audience be engaged in the process and how?[47]

Collections

Stephen Williams, who has charted how collections have diminished within museums, states emphatically: "An art museum without a collection is only a gallery. A children's museum or a science museum without a collection is only a discovery center. A historical society without a collection is only an affinity group. A historic site without a collection is only a local attraction. A zoological or botanical garden without a collection is only a nature center. A museum without a collection is not a museum."[48]

As the 21st century opens, the dominance of collections in museums is certainly fading (and has faded). What are the implications for this change? What is the impact on the fundamental definition of a museum absent collections? If museums abandon their commitment to collections, will it be necesssary to create another institution to assume that role; another "museum"?

Notes

1. Richard Grove, "Some Problems in Museum Education," in *Museums and Education*, ed. Eric Larrabee, Washington, DC: Smithsonian Institution, 1968, p. 79.

2. Mark Lilla, "The Great Museum Muddle," *New Republic*, April 8, 1985, pp. 25–29.

3. James Clifford, "Museums as Contact Zones," *Routes, Travel and Translation in the Late 20th Century*, Cambridge, MA: Harvard University Press, 1997, p. 192.

4. American Association of Museums, *America's Museums: The Belmont Report*, Washington, DC: American Association of Museums, 1969, pp. 3, 17–20; American Association of Museums staff, personal correspondence, 2006.

5. Douglas A. Allan, "The Museum and Its Functions," in *The Organization of Museums: Practical Advice*, Paris: United Nations Educational, Scientific and Cultural Organization, 1967, p. 13; Elaine Heumann Gurian, "Choosing among the Options: An Opinion about Museum Definitions," *Civilizing the Museum*, London: Routledge, 2006, pp. 48–56; Eilean Hooper-Greenhill, *Museums and the Shaping of Knowledge*, London: Routledge, 1994, pp. 1–22.

6. American Association of Museums, *Museum Accreditation: Professional Standards*, Washington, DC: American Association of Museums, 1973, pp. 8–9.

7. www.icom.museum.

8. Thomas P. F. Hoving, "Branch Out!" *Museum News* 47 (September 1968): 16.

9. Daniel S. Greenberg, "There's a Windmill in the Attic: S. Dillon Ripley Is Blowing Dust off the Smithsonian," *Saturday Review* 48 (June 5, 1965): 48.

10. Benjamin Ives Gilman, *Museum Ideals of Purpose and Method*, 2nd ed., Cambridge, MA, 1923, p. xvii.

11. Edmund Barry Gaither, "Voicing Varied Opinions," *Museum News* 68, no. 2 (March–April 1989): 52.

12. George Sarton, *A History of Science: Hellenistic Science and Culture in the Last Three Centuries B.C.*, Cambridge, MA, 1959, pp. 29–34; Germain Bazin, *The Museum Age*, New York: Universe Books, 1967, p. 16; Alma S. Wittlin, *Museums:*

In Search of a Usable Future, Cambridge, MA: MIT Press, 1970, p. 221; David E. H. Jones, "The Great Museum at Alexandria," *Smithsonian* 2 (December 1971): 53–60, (January 1972): 59–63.

13. Didier Maleuvre, "A Plea for Silence: Putting Art Back in to the Art Museum," in *Museum Philosophy for the 21st Century,* ed. Hugh H. Genoways, Lanham, MD: AltaMira Press, 2006, p. 167.

14. Bazin, *The Museum Age,* pp. 12–14, 18–23; Wittlin, *Museums: In Search,* pp. 4–7, 12–13; Niels von Holst, *Creators, Collectors and Connoisseurs: The Anatomy of Artistic Taste from Antiquity to the Present Day,* New York, 1967, pp. 21–40.

15. Bazin, *The Museum Age,* p. 29; Wittlin, *Museums: In Search,* pp. 7–8; Francis Henry Taylor, *Babel's Tower: The Dilemma of the Modern Museum,* New York, 1945, p. 11.

16. J. Mordaunt Crook, *The British Museum,* London: Praeger, 1972, p. 32; Kenneth Hudson, *Social History of Museums: What the Visitors Thought,* Atlantic Highlands, NJ: Humanities Press, 1975, p. 6; Bazin, *The Museum Age,* pp. 129–130; Holst, *Creators,* pp. 92, 94–96, 103–105; Taylor, *Babel's Tower,* pp. 12–17; Silvio A. Bedini, "The Evolution of Science Museums," *Technology and Culture* 5 (1965): 1–29; Helmut Seling, "The Genesis of the Museum," *Architectural Review* 141 (1967): 103–114.

17. Edward S. Hyams and William MacQuitty, *Great Botanical Gardens of the World,* New York: Macmillan, 1969, pp. 16–23, 34–43, 87, 102–103, 107; A. W. Hill, "The History and Functions of Botanic Gardens," *Annals Missouri Botanical Garden* 2 (1915): 185–240.

18. Edward P. Alexander, "Sir Hans Sloane and the British Museum," in *Museum Masters: Their Museums and Their Influence,* Nashville, TN: American Association of State and Local History, 1983, pp. 19–42.

19. Bazin, *The Museum Age,* pp. 141–191; Hudson, *Social History of Museums,* pp. 3–6.

20. Laura M. Bragg, "The Birth of the Museum Idea in America," *Charleston Museum Quarterly* 1 (1923): 3–13.

21. Joel J. Orosz, *Curators and Culture: The Museum Movement in America, 1740–1870,* Tuscaloosa: University of Alabama Press, 1990, pp. 1–67.

22. Alexander, "Charles Willson Peale and His Philadelphia Museum," in *Museum Masters,* pp. 43–78.

23. Alexander, "George Brown Goode and the Smithsonian Museum," in *Museum Masters,* pp. 277–310.

24. Geoffrey T. Hellman, *Bankers, Bones, Beetles: The First Century of the American Museum of Natural History,* Garden City, NY, 1969; Calvin Tomkins, *Merchants and Masterpieces: The Story of the Metropolitan Museum of Art,* New York, 1970; Walter Muir Whitehill, *Museum of Fine Arts, Boston: A Centennial History,* 2 vols., Cambridge, MA, 1970.

25. Gilman, *Museum Ideals,* pp. 80–81, 88–102, 279–316; Whitehill, *Museum of Fine Arts,* 1:293–294.

26. Douglas J. Preston, *Dinosaurs in the Attic: An Excursion into the American Museum of Natural History,* New York: St. Martin's, 1986, p. xii.

27. Douglas and Elizabeth Rigby, *Lock, Stock and Barrel*, Philadelphia, 1944; Maurice Rheims, *The Strange Life of Objects: 35 Centuries of Art Collecting and Collectors*, New York, 1961; Sherman E. Lee, "The Idea of an Art Museum," *Harper's Magazine* 237 (September 1968): 76–79; Hudson, *Social History of Museums*, pp. 2–6.

28. Bazin, *The Museum Age*, pp. 12–14, 89, 116–118, 176.

29. Paul Coremans, "The Museum Laboratory" in *The Organization of Museums*, pp. 83–118, plates 3–33; H. J. Plenderleith and A. E. A. Werner, *The Conservation of Antiquities and Works of Art*, 2nd ed., New York, 1972.

30. "Working Knowledge," "Research," in *Museum Practice*, London: Museums Association, Winter 2006, pp. 49–67; Bryant Tolles, ed., "Scholarship and Museums: Roles and Responsibilities," *Spring Conference Proceedings*, University of Delaware, 1988; Craig Black, "The Case for Research," *Museum News* 58, no. 5 (May–June 1980): 51–53; Hiroshi Daifuku, "Museums and Research," in *Organization of Museums*, pp. 68–72; American Association of Museums, *America's Museums: The Belmont Report*, pp. 6–8.

31. Bazin, *The Museum Age*, pp. 177–180, 230–234; Charles R. Richards, *Industrial Art and the Museum*, New York, 1927, pp. 10–12; Wittlin, *Museums: In Search*, p. 71.

32. Richards, *Industrial Art and the Museum*, pp. 12–19.

33. Mats Rehnberg, *The Nordiska Museet and Skansen: An Introduction to the History and Activities of a Famous Swedish Museum*, Stockholm, 1957, pp. 9–14; Kenneth W. Luckhurst, *The Story of Exhibitions*, London: Studio Publications, 1951.

34. Stephen E. Weil, "From Being about Something to Being for Somebody: The Ongoing Transformation of the American Museum," *Daedalus* (Summer 1999): 229–258.

35. Arthur C. Parker, *A Manual for History Museums*, New York: Columbia University Press, 1935, p. 19.

36. Duncan Cameron, "The Museum, a Temple or the Forum," *Journal of World History* 14, no. 1: 189–204; also in Gail Anderson, ed., *Reinventing the Museum: Historical and Contemporary Perspectives on the Paradigm Shift*, Walnut Creek, CA: AltaMira Press, 2004.

37. Franz Boas, "Some Principles of Museum Administration," *Science* (June 14, 1907): 921.

38. Barbara Y. Newsom and Adele Silver, *The Art Museum as Educator*, Berkeley: University of California Press, 1979, p. 13.

39. Carol Duncan, Ivan Karp, and Steven D. Lavine, *Exhibiting Cultures: The Poetics and Politics of Museum Display*, Washington, DC: Smithsonian Institution, 1991, p. 90.

40. Michael Ames, *Cannibal Tours and Glass Boxes: The Anthropology of Museums*, Vancouver, Canada: University British Columbia Press, 1992, p. 23.

41. Barbara Franco quoted in Weil, "From Being about Something to Being for Somebody," p. 229.

42. Elaine Heumann Gurian, "Blurring the Boundaries," *Curator* 38, no. 1 (1995).

43. Quoted by Roy Rosenzweig in "Afterthoughts," in *The Presence of the Past: Popular Uses of History in American Life*, by Roy Rosenzweig and David Thelen, New York: Columbia University Press, 1998, p. 182; Candace Floyd, "Chinatown," *History News* (June 1984): 7–11.

44. Jacqueline Trescott, "Indian Museum Director Stepping Down," *Washington Post*, October 27, 2006.

45. www.contemporaryartscenter.org, July 18, 2005.

46. Nathaniel Burt, *Palaces for the People: A Social History of the American Art Museum*, Boston: Little, Brown, 1977, p. 415; Patrick J. Boylan, "Current Trends in Governance and Management of Museums in Europe," in *Museum Philosophy*, pp. 201–220.

47. Neil Harris, "The Hidden Agenda," in *Cultural Excursions: Marketing Appetites and Cultural Tastes in America*, Chicago, IL: University of Chicago Press, 1990, p. 142.

48. Stephen I. Williams, "Critical Concepts Concerning Non-living Collections," *Collections: A Journal for for Museum and Archives Professionals* 1 (2004): 61; Charles Alan Watkins, "Fighting for Culture's Turf," *Museum News* 70, no. 2 (March–April 1991): 61–65.

I

HISTORY

2

The Art Museum

A collection of science is gathered primarily in the interests of the real, a collection of art in the interest of the ideal. The former is a panorama of fact, the latter a paradise of fancy. In the former we learn, in the latter we admire. A museum of science is in essence a school; a museum of art is in essence a temple. Minerva presides over the one, sacred to the reason; Apollo over the other, sacred to the imagination.

—Benjamin Ives Gilman, 1908[1]

The National Gallery [in London] enables people to feel in one way or another that the collection is for them, and that they belong there. It's a place where ordinary people and rich patrons alike can touch base and feel they are part of a lively, learning community, a place where they can know that they are not alone.

—a visitor's letter to the gallery director, 2003[2]

The moment of personal awe taken from the aura of genuine art rarely, if ever, occurs in the realm of entertainment, because art is aimed at individuals and entertainment focuses on collectives.

—Timothy W. Luke, 2002[3]

Love of beauty is a basic human trait that goes back to our earliest days on Earth. The primitive Ice Age artists who created the vigorous bison and bulls, fleet horses, graceful deer, and other animals of the Lascaux or Altamira caves may have been appealing to supernatural powers to grant them good hunting and fertility or observing some since-lost traditional rites, but at the same time they took delight in combining line and color so as to please the human eye. Thus, it was natural that humankind collect and treasure paintings, sculptures, and other art objects. The ancient civilizations, whether Middle Eastern, Oriental, African, pre-Columbian American, Greek, or Roman, put on display their finest productions in temples or palace treasuries. Even during the Dark Ages in Western Europe, the artistic tradition was kept alive, chiefly in cathedrals, castles, and monasteries. This chapter, as conceived by Edward Alexander, reflects a broad definition of "art" museums and his approach to their histories through biographies, and it retains his classifications. More recently, some of the museums described here would be categorized as "universal collection" museums for their collections range from paintings to Egyptian mummies. See the index to find information on specific museums.

European Collectors and Patrons

The collector was the force that made the art museum possible. Usually a prince, nobleman, high clergyman, rich merchant, or banker, he purchased or commissioned paintings, sculptures, and other beautiful and useful objects. As his collection grew, connoisseurship became his passion, and he added or discarded pieces, ever seeking the highest quality.

Jean de France, duc de Berry and brother of the French king Charles V, was a great medieval collector. At his death in 1416, he possessed a fine library, some of its bindings adorned with jewels and precious stones. His collection also included handsomely illuminated manuscripts, antique gold and silver coins, cameos and intaglios, rich embroideries and fabrics, sculptures, panel paintings, and miniatures. He could not resist curiosities, and he had a menagerie and a cabinet that contained ostrich eggs, shells, polar bear skins, and reputed antidotes against poison, such as bezoars—the concretions formed in the stomachs of wild goats—and unicorn horns (actually narwhal tusks).[4]

The coming of the Renaissance made Italy the center of the art world. Members of the Medici family in Florence were shrewd businessmen and bankers who for two centuries ruled city and state, erected handsome buildings, established a great library, and accumulated fabulous hoards of art objects. They tried to acquire the finest products of the Greek and Roman past, and sculptures and other antiquities, whether found above or below ground, henceforth became important collectors' items. The Medici (Riccardi) Palace in the 15th century was in a sense a private museum. The other Italian states competed with Florence in collecting art, and the popes gradually made Rome preeminent. It was a virtual museum city, and soon archaeologists were unearthing its buried treasures. Sixtus IV in 1471 established a Capitoline Museum to house ancient statuary; he also forbade the exportation of antiquities from the city. Julius II obtained many rarities, including the *Apollo Belvedere* and *Laocoon*. Leo X filled the Cortile Garden near the Vatican with statues and in 1515 made Raphael his superintendent of antiquities. A dozen years later, Rome fell to a Lutheran army, and for a time leadership in art collecting moved elsewhere.[5]

Perhaps the most renowned collector of the first half of the 17th century was Charles I of England. As Prince of Wales, he had visited the Spanish court and sat for Diego Velazquez. About 1627 he made an astonishing coup by purchasing for some eighty thousand pounds the collection that the Gonzaga family had accumulated at Mantua for more than a century. On the advice of Rubens, he bought Raphael's seven original cartoons for the Acts of the Apostles tapestries. At its height, Charles's collection contained 1,387 pictures and 399 sculptures, with works by Raphael, Correggio, Tintoretto, Titian, Leonardo, and many other Italian, German, and Flemish masters. He was also a patron of Rubens and Van Dyck. As the Reverend Mr. William Gilpin justly said: "Charles was a scholar, a man of taste, a gentleman and a Christian; he was everything but a king. The art of reigning was the only art of which he was ignorant." Two of Charles's friends and associates were also collectors—discerning Thomas Howard, earl of Arundel, and flamboyant George Francis Villiers, duke of Buckingham. But all their holdings were largely dissipated when Buckingham was assassinated, Arundel exiled to the continent, and Charles beheaded. The Puritan Parliament in the 1650s, by private sale and public auction, disposed of most of Charles's choice treasures, and many of them made their way into the possession of the king of France.[6]

The French royal art collection began to grow when the Queen Mother Marie de Medici called Rubens to Paris in 1622 to depict the most glorious scenes from her life in twenty-one great pictures. Two French prime ministers were passionate lovers of art and contended that a great collection was a valuable symbol of royal authority. Cardinal Richelieu not only helped his king acquire Italian and French art, but also constructed in Paris the Palais Cardinal (today the Palais Royal) to house his own jewels and religious plate, five hundred paintings, fifty statues, bronzes, historical tapestries, textiles, furniture, and Chinese lacquers and ceramics. He left the palace and collection to the king. Richelieu's secretary and successor, Cardinal Mazarin, was a knowing connoisseur, but had some miserly attributes; he used to let his jewels flow through his hands. He feared rival collector, Queen Christina of Sweden, and begged his business manager, Jean Baptiste Colbert, to "keep that crazy woman out of my cabinets . . . for one could so easily take some of my small paintings." When near death, Mazarin paced about his collection in his nightshirt, grieving: "I must leave all this. What trouble I had to acquire these things! I'll never see them again where I'm going." He left 546 paintings, the cream of which Louis XIV purchased. The Cologne banker Everhard Jabach, sole supplier of buff leather to royal armies, had a passion for drawings, but, during a financial crisis, sold the king 101 paintings and 5,542 drawings. Colbert himself, a skillful administrator, deserves great credit for building the royal art collection.[7]

The Habsburgs, as Holy Roman Emperors, could draw on the German and Italian states, Spain, and the Low Countries. Rudolph II, one of the greatest connoisseurs of his day, had a magnificent collection in his Hradcany Castle in Prague. This mentally ill emperor hid his paintings from public view. During the Thirty Years War, Gustavus Adolphus of Sweden, emulating the Roman conquerors and foreshadowing Napoleon, captured Prague and removed many of Rudolph's treasures to Stockholm. Gustavus's daughter, Queen Christina, in 1654 renounced her throne and took most of the finest Habsburg paintings with her when she embraced Catholicism and settled in Rome. In Spain, the Habsburgs acquired Italian, German, Flemish, and Spanish paintings for their palaces at the Prado, Escorial, and Alcazar. Charles V and Philip II had Titian as their court painter and art adviser, and Philip IV had Rubens and Velazquez. Archduke Leopold-Wilhelm at Brussels built an admirable collection of paintings (which he later took to Vienna) with David Teniers the Younger as keeper and adviser.[8]

During the 18th century, the tide of collecting shifted to England. Her commercial empire brought the profits that enabled her nobility to build great country houses and allowed titled young Englishmen to take the Grand Tour to the continent and Italy. The stately homes of England fused the best of architecture, landscape design, paintings and sculpture, and rich furnishings into a unified, artistic style. London outstripped Amsterdam as an art market and threatened the supremacy of Paris. On the continent, Saint Petersburg joined the list of great art centers. Peter the Great acquired some art, including the gold jewelry found in prehistoric Siberian tombs, but Catherine the Great was a compulsive collector, "a glutton," as she called herself. Represented at all important auctions and frequently buying collections en bloc, by 1785 she owned 2,658 paintings and, in order to house them, had begun building the Hermitage (1767) on the banks of the Neva in Saint Petersburg.[9]

Thus, during the 15th to 18th centuries, hundreds of rich and powerful collectors gathered and preserved objects that today are found in the great art museums of the Western World. In addition to paintings and sculpture, they amassed the "exotic" and mysterious, reflecting their fascination with what it means to be human. The flow of art objects from their creators through different ownerships to their present resting places has created many exciting chapters in the history of art museums.

The Earliest Museums

During the 17th and 18th centuries, private collections slowly developed into museums. Before that time, collectors had occasionally allowed visitors to see their treasures; the Medici, for example, did so at least as early as the 16th century. The arrangements usually were privately made and often required a large tip to a servant.[10] In Rome in 1773 Pope Clement XIV opened the Pio-Clementine Museum; it contained the Vatican collection largely as we know it today.[11] The famed Farnese collection accumulated by Cardinal Farnese (later Pope Paul III) was left to Charles of Bourbon, king of the Two Sicilies, in 1735 and formed the core of the National Museum in Naples; that museum also received much rich material excavated at Herculaneum and Pompeii.[12] The Uffizi Palace at Florence in 1743 secured the Medici collection of paintings under the will of Anna Maria Ludovica, the daughter of Cosimo III. By 1795 the Uffizi had become a true art gallery, with the paintings arranged by schools.[13]

The Habsburg collection in Vienna under Emperor Charles VI in the 1720s had been given elaborate frames and ordered according to overall symmetry and color, with individual paintings cut down or enlarged in size to conform to the arrangement. About 1776 the painter Rosa began to reinstall the collection in the Belevedere Palace. He called in Chretien de Mechel from Basel, who restored the paintings to their original sizes in simple frames, arranged them chronologically according to schools, and produced a catalog. In 1781 the public was admitted three times a week to view the collection.[14]

France was slow to show the royal holdings of pictures. Under Louis XIV, the gardens of Versailles were open to the public, and one could easily visit the palace and its paintings if equipped with a plumed hat and sword, which could be rented from the caretaker. Louis XV in 1750 exhibited 110 paintings and drawings in Paris at the Luxembourg Palace, to which the public was admitted twice a week. There was a constant agitation among the intellectuals of the Enlightenment to open a permanent picture gallery, and the Palace of the Louvre was usually suggested as the appropriate place. Diderot, in his *Encyclopedie* (1765), stated that the Louvre ought to rival the famed Mouseion of Alexandria.

Louis XVI in 1774 appointed Count d'Angiviller director general of Public Buildings. D'Angiviller moved at once to prepare the royal collection for exhibition and eventually chose for this purpose the great gallery of the Louvre that paralleled the Seine. He had the paintings cleaned, repaired, and reframed, filled in gaps—especially of the Flemish and Dutch schools—and appointed the painter Hubert Robert keeper of the royal collection. The count created a commission of experts on museum problems. The commission prescribed overhead lighting and, for fire protection, that brick and iron be used wherever possible, as well as fire-resistant walls and a lightning conductor, an innovation popular in that day. But d'Angiviller was indecisive in carrying out the recommendations, and the gallery was not yet open when the French Revolution started.[15]

There were other scattered prototype museums. Basel probably had the first university art collection; in 1661 the city bought the Amerbach Cabinet that contained some excellent Holbeins; they were exhibited a decade later in the university library.[16] German collections were opened at Dusseldorf, Munich, Kassel, and Dresden about 1750.[17] In 1683, the collection of the Tradescants became the first English museum in its own building, the Ashmolean, at Oxford University, but it was composed chiefly of natural history specimens with little art.[18] Sir Hans Sloane's collection, opened as the British Museum in 1759, contained some miniatures, drawings, and archaeological objects, but was devoted chiefly to natural history. The radical John Wilkes tried to join a national gallery to the British Museum in 1777 with the Walpole Collection from Houghton Hall as a nucleus, but Parliament refused, and the collection went to Catherine the Great.[19]

Revolution and the Louvre

The Palace of the Louvre in Paris, opened to the public during the Revolution, may be regarded as the first great national art museum. The cataclysm of revolution destroyed some art objects, which, of course, could be considered hated symbols of the aristocratic regime, but fortunately the leaders who overthrew the old order argued that the nation's art belonged to all the people of the new society created under the democratic ideals of liberty, equality, and brotherhood. The Louvre was to be the capstone of a system of museums to serve the common man and woman of the new Republic.

The National Museum, a "Monument Dedicated to the Love and Study of the Arts," was opened at the Louvre on August 10, 1793, the first anniversary of the fall of the monarchy. Its Grande Galerie exhibited 537 paintings on the walls and 184 art objects on tables in the middle of the hall. Most of these artworks came from the royal palaces, from churches and religious orders, and a scattering from the émigrés. In the new decade, in the ten-day period that had replaced the week, the museum reserved five days for artists and copyists, two for cleaning, and three for the general public. So popular were the public days that the crowds of visitors attracted swarms of enterprising prostitutes, and streetlights had to be installed at the approaches.

The pictures were hung frame to frame from floor to ceiling by schools (which were organized by French, Italian, and Northern (Dutch and Flemish) paintings) but within the schools, according to the old miscellaneous principle, there were no labels, so that the museum was a confusing labyrinth for the untutored visitor. Windows from two sides lighted the hall, and on bright days pictures were exposed to too much sunlight. Fortunately, Hubert Robert, former keeper of the royal collection, was respected in the new order and managed to maintain tolerable standards of housekeeping and conservation. The Louvre was in such bad structural condition that it had to be closed in May 1796, not to open fully again until July 14, 1801. The Grande Galerie was then more rationally arranged on a chronological principle; a few years later, marble columns and statues divided the long vista of the gallery, and overhead lighting was obtained.[20]

The victorious revolutionary armies brought art treasures to France. Many masterpieces were requisitioned from Antwerp, Brussels, and other cities when Belgium was overrun in 1794. The radical artist Luc Barbier, one of the requisitioning commissioners, melodramatically justified this pillage of "the immortal works left us by the brush of Rubens, Van Dyck and other founders of the Flemish school" because "it is in the bosom of free folk that the works of celebrated men should remain; the tears of slaves are unworthy of their glory."[21]

General Bonaparte's Italian campaign of 1796–1797 was even more successful in adding to the French national collections of the Louvre, the Bibliotheque Nationale, and the Jardin des Plantes. He took a commission of scholars with him—a mathematician, a chemist, a botanist, two painters, a sculptor, and an archaeologist—to appropriate "goods of artistic and scientific nature" that included books, paintings, scientific instruments, typefaces, wild animals, and natural curiosities from all over Italy. In July 1798 a triumphal procession brought the loot of the campaign to Paris, enormous chariots bearing the paintings in huge packing cases, labeled with large letters, and massive carts transporting statues decked with laurel wreaths, flowers, and flags. There were exotic animals in cages and camels led by their keepers. Military detachments, members of the Institut de France, museum administrators, art professors, and typesetters marched in the parade. The vehicles formed a circle on the Champs de Mars three lines deep around a monument to Liberty, amid the thundering cheers of the packed spectators. Among the choicest items were the famed four Bronze Horses from Saint Mark's Basilica in Venice; they were placed above the Arc de Triomphe of the Carousel in the Tuilleries Gardens. The Louvre received the *Apollo Belvedere*, *Laocoon*, *Dying Gaul*, Raphael's *Transfiguration*, and Correggio's *Saint Jerome*.[22]

One blessing may have arisen from this seizure of art by the French armies. Many of the paintings were in bad repair, not having been treated since their creation. In a conservation workshop in the Louvre, staff knew how to clean and restore paintings and understood the rebacking process that had been perfected in Italy and France about fifty years earlier. At any rate, the French authorities used conservation partially to justify their confiscation of the paintings.[23]

Napoleon and National Glory

Shortly before Napoleon decided to invade Egypt in 1798, he met Baron Dominique Vivant-Denon at a party.[24] Denon was a charmer, a favorite of Madame de Pompadour. He had held diplomatic posts in Russia at the Court of Catherine the Great, in Switzerland, and at

Naples. Napoleon and Denon became close friends, and Denon, though in his fifties, went on the Egyptian campaign. His scholarship helped Napoleon choose superb museum objects, including the Rosetta stone that was afterward captured on its way to France by Lord Nelson and sent to the British Museum. Denon also aroused general admiration by his reckless coolness under fire. In 1800 Napoleon visited the Louvre for the first time and soon insisted that Denon be placed in charge of the museums of France and of all artistic services. In 1803 the Louvre became the Musee Napoleon, a name it retained until the emperor's downfall.

Napoleon and Denon, between them, devised a comprehensive museum system for France and her conquered satellites. Denon always sought the greatest masterpieces for the Louvre, but Napoleon made the final decisions, based on political expediency. As early as 1800, he had agreed to place paintings in the provincial cities of France that then included Brussels, Mainz, and Geneva. Eventually twenty-two cities benefited from the distribution of 1,508 paintings. Several museums were planned for Italian cities, though only the Brera Gallery in Milan, opened in 1809, was successfully organized; it received confiscations from throughout northern Italy.

Sometimes, reaction against French looting led to the establishment of museums. Thus, Louis Napoleon, king of Holland, founded the Koninklijk Museum (forerunner of the present Rijksmuseum) at Amsterdam in 1808. In Madrid, Joseph Bonaparte, king of Spain, worked with the artist Goya to keep the finest Spanish paintings from the clutches of Napoleon and Denon; later, in 1819, the collection was installed in the Prado and opened to the public. In 1813 Wellington captured paintings from the royal collection taken by Joseph on his flight from Spain. The duke offered to return them, but the Spanish government gave the 165 paintings to him. Today they repose in London as the Wellington Museum at Apsley House.[25]

But those who live by the sword and the requisition shall perish by the sword and the requisition. When Napoleon was finally defeated at Waterloo in 1815, the paintings and art objects he had seized began to flow back to their previous owners. Not all of them returned; Denon's conveniently poor memory of their location saved a few for the Louvre, and most of those taken from churches and monasteries remained in France. But in all, the French museums gave up 2,065 pictures and 130 sculptures, including, of course, the Bronze Horses, *Apollo Belvedere*, and *Laocoon*. With tears of frustration in their eyes, the French people saw many treasures leave the acknowledged art capital of the world.

Never again would so many masterpieces of painting and sculpture be on view in a single institution. Napoleon indeed had made great art and the museum symbols of national glory. This concept would be taken to the extreme in the 20th century with Hitler and Goering looting the national collections as revenge for the humiliation of the Treaty of Versailles. They didn't stop with museum collections; they added those of private citizens.[26]

A Golden Age for Art Museums

The violent and democratizing changes in European life brought about by both political and industrial revolution were accompanied by a steady growth of public art museums, and the 19th century sometimes is considered the museum's golden age. Parallel with growing nationalism, nearly every country in Western Europe built a comprehensive collection of masterpiece art that extended from ancient times to the present. Usually a royal collection formed its nucleus, but often the determined efforts of industrial and commercial leaders with able museum directors resulted in a museum taking its place as an important element of urban centers.

In France the Louvre enjoyed rapid growth and soon filled the gaps in its galleries left by the return of the Napoleonic additions. In the international competition for archaeological discoveries, the Louvre got thousands of Greek vases and bronzes, the best Egyptian collection outside Cairo, and such striking individual masterpieces as the Venus de Milo and the Nike from Samothrace. Napoleon III completed the Louvre complex so as to provide badly needed exhibition, storage, and administrative space. He acquired a rich collection of paintings and art objects from the Marquis Campana in Rome, for a time shown as the Musee Napoleon III. Just before the fall of the empire in 1869, Dr. Louis La Caze of Paris left the Louvre the greatest gift it had ever received—802 paintings, of which he wished 302 distributed in the provinces. Public funds and private gifts—the organization called Friends of the Louvre was formed in 1897—continued to add to its comprehensive holdings.[27]

Great Britain did not establish its National Gallery in London until 1824. For forty years, efforts had been made to secure an art museum for the nation, and in the end the Royal Academy (1768) and the British

Institution (1805) marshaled enough sentiment to carry the day. The National Gallery was unusual in that it did not grow from a royal collection. The fact that thirty-eight great pictures collected by John Julius Angerstein were up for sale triggered the establishment of the gallery; Sir George Beaumont, himself a collector of note, persuaded the prime minister, Lord Dover, to have the nation pay fifty-seven thousand pounds for the Angerstein pictures. Soon, the present building of the National Gallery was under construction at Trafalgar Square, to be opened by Queen Victoria in 1838. Its very location at Trafalgar Square ("the very gangway of London") represented the founders' interests in making its galleries available to all London's citizens. The gallery admitted the public four days per week, but the rooms were often dark because no artificial light was provided; on two days, not more than fifty students were allowed to copy the pictures. The gallery also closed on Sundays and for six weeks each year for cleaning purposes. Until after World War I, the pictures were crowded together from floor to ceiling. All in all, British collectors and artists generously supported the National Gallery, which today represents a comprehensive history of European painting.[28] The British royal family's vast collections, which are purported to be among the finest collections in "private" hands, are exhibited in Buckingham Palace, allowing it to add "gallery" to its many descriptors.

In Germany, the Hohenzollerns of Prussia backed the creation of one of the world's greatest museum centers in Berlin on a peninsula formed by the Spree and Kupfergraben rivers. This Museum Island, as it was called, contained five museums: the Altes Museum (1830) built around the antiquities and modern painting collections of an eccentric English connoisseur, Edward Solly; the Neues Museum (1855) with Egyptian collections, antique ceramics, and national antiquities; the Nationalgalerie (1876) for modern German art; and the Kaiser Friedrich Museum of Western Art (1904), now the Bode Museum. Most impressive of all was a group of monumental buildings (1907–1930) that contained the Pergamon Museum, with its Great Altar of Pergamon, one wing devoted to the Museum of German Art and another to the Near East Museum. Covered footbridges connected many of the buildings of the island complex. Dr. Wilhelm von Bode joined the staff of the museums in 1872 and served for fifty years, after 1905 as general director.[29] A learned art historian with encyclopedic knowledge of the art market and great diplomatic and administrative talent, he raised the Berlin museums to the high levels attained by those of Paris and London.

The rise of Hitler brought several disasters to the Museum Island. Ludwig Justi, the long-respected director of the Nationalgalerie, was dismissed though he refused to leave and was named director of the art library, "degenerate" modern art was removed and in some cases destroyed, and many Jewish staff members were discharged. World War II attacks greatly damaged the Museum Island buildings and 1,353 paintings were lost. Under the leadership of the occupying Soviet Union, other objects were moved "east" and vanished from public view. The partition of Berlin after the war made the Museum Island a cultural showcase for East Berlin, the German Democratic Republic (GDR) and its chief sponsor, the Soviet Union. The GDR focused its attention and resources on restoring the island to its former glory as evidence of its rightful place in European culture. Justi came back to the Museum Island as director in 1948. The Kaiser Friedrich Museum was fittingly renamed the Bode Museum. Work on the Pergamon Museum, Nationalgalerie, and Altes Museum moved forward. With the fall of the Berlin wall in 1989, the island assumed its rightful place at the center of Germany's artistic culture. The moving of the national capital to Berlin a decade later added to the island's importance. Today, while restoration projects still continue, the Bode Museum's world-class paintings, sculpture, and decorative arts reveal the primacy of its Western European art collection. The island's archaeological treasures of the Facade of the Kassite Temple of Uruk (c. 1415 BC), the Processional Way, Ishtar Gate, the Old Palace Throne Room of Babylon (c. 580 BC), the Great Altar of Pergamon (180–160 BC), the Market Gate of Miletus (c. AD 165), the Facade of the Mshatta Desert Palace (743–744), and the Prayer Niche from the Maydan Mosque of Kashan (1226) provide visitors an even larger context for the Museum Island's reflection of man's commitment to artistic expression.

Munich, to the south, is another city filled with museums. King Louis I of Bavaria planned to make it a second Rome. The Glyptothek (1830) contains the Aeginetal pediments from the Temple of Aphaia; the Alte Pinakothek (1836), a rich collection of old masters; and the Neue Pinakothek (1853), the Schack Gallery, and New State Gallery, more modern art. The Bavarian National Museum (1867) has historical paintings, decorative art, and period rooms, and the Residence, the former palace opened as a museum in 1920 and restored to its elegance after World War II damage, possesses a rich treasury of exquisitely jeweled pieces. Although Dresden suffered the worst air raids of World War II, its extensive museum holdings, initiated in the 18th century by Augustus the Strong, king of Poland and the elector of Saxony, have been magnificently reinstalled. The Zwinger Palace contains the Gemaeldegalerie Alte Meister, one of the world's preeminent painting collections, an armory, a porcelain collection; the Albertinum contains the incomparable Green Vault treasury of jeweled and precious objects, and the Gemaeldegalerie Neue Meister, a rich collection of romantic German painting.[30]

Catherine the Great's huge collection in the Hermitage in Saint Petersburg was more properly housed in a great palace built by Czar Nicholas I in the 1840s. The Berlin museum director and art historian Gustav Waagen was called in to arrange the pictures and prepare a catalog (1863). Visitors were allowed, but up until 1866, they needed to wear full dress, on the theory that they were visiting the czar and only incidentally the museum. The czars continued to collect great masterpieces, and the coming of the 1917 revolution gave the new Soviet Union control of rich private art collections from throughout the old empire. Museums, historical monuments, and art treasures were nationalized. Some old masters were sold to raise much-needed funds for economic necessities, but the Hermitage remains one of the greatest art museums of the world. Its ornate galleries are replete with a comprehensive painting collection; significant impressionist and postimpressionist works; Scythian goldwork; Greek vases obtained from sites on the northern Black Sea coast; Oriental, Egyptian, Babylonian, Assyrian, Near East, and Russian antiquities.[31]

A specialized form of art museum collected and exhibited modern art, as, for example, the Luxembourg Palace (1818) in Paris, superseded by the National Museum of Modern Art (1937) that later moved to the Centre Georges Pompidou, or Beaubourg, in 1977; the Neue Pinakothek (1853) in Munich; the Nationalgalerie (1876) in Berlin; and the National Gallery of British Art (1897) in London, known today as Tate Britain Gallery with its annex south of the Thames, Tate Modern, opened in 2000.[32]

Another specialized museum was devoted to the decorative arts—architecture, furniture, metalwork, ceramics, glass, textiles, and the like. The Great Exhibition at South Kensington in London, the first true world's fair, in 1851 was enormously successful, and the profits (some 186,000 pounds) were used to acquire land for a group of museums in the South Kensington area. One of them finally evolved into the Victoria and Albert Museum in 1909. In France, a world's fair at Paris in 1855 inaugurated a similar interest in the decorative arts, and the Central Society of Decorative Arts established a museum in 1882, later moved to the Marsan Pavilion of the Louvre. Berlin and Vienna also had such museums.[33]

American Models

The earliest progenitors of the American Art Museum displayed portraits of historical figures (or events) as part of their historical or natural science focus. Pierre Eugene du Simitiere and Charles Willson Peale had portraits in their Philadelphia collections in the 1780s, but regarded them more as historical documents than as works of art. So also did the early historical societies, though the New-York Historical Society (1804) had secured the Luman Reed and Thomas J. Bryan collections of American paintings and European old masters by the 1860s. The society planned a museum of antiquities, science, and art, but failed to raise the necessary funds. The Pennsylvania Academy of the Fine Arts (1805) in Philadelphia not only conducted an art school and held annual exhibitions, but also acquired an outstanding collection of American paintings and sculpture. The Boston Athenaeum (1807), though essentially a library, collected paintings and sculptures that it later turned over to the newly established Museum of Fine Arts. In 1832 Yale built the pioneer American college gallery to house the historical paintings of Colonel John Trumbull. Perhaps the first true and continuing art museum in the country was the Wadsworth Atheneum (1842) at Hartford, Connecticut, which displayed about eighty works by Trumbull, Thomas Cole, and other Americans.[34]

The year 1870 was a landmark year for American art museums, with the establishment of the Metropolitan Museum of Art in New York and the Museum of Fine Arts in Boston. Within the decade, the Corcoran Gallery of Art in Washington, the Pennsylvania (now Philadelphia) Museum of Art, and the Art Institute of Chicago opened for public visitation. Other leading encyclopedic art collections in the United States today include the Detroit Institute of Art (1885), Brooklyn Museum (1893), in Ohio, the Toledo Art Museum (1901) and Cleveland Museum of Art (1913), and the National Gallery of Art (1937) in Washington, D.C. By the year 2000 there were thirty-five hundred art museums in the United States, half of which were established after 1970.[35] The combination of private beneficence, city maintenance, and federal tax laws that encouraged private support produced some of the greatest art museums of the world.

An examination of the Metropolitan and the Museum of Fine Arts reveals the chief forces in the development of comprehensive American art museums. The purposes of the Metropolitan, expressed in Joseph C. Choate's dedication speech of 1880, were to gather together a more or less complete collection of objects illustrative of the history of art in all its branches, from the earliest beginnings to the present time, which should serve not only for the instruction and entertainment of the people, but also show to the students and artisans of every branch of industry, in the high and acknowledged standards of form and color, what the past has accomplished for them to imitate and exceed.[36]

The Metropolitan was greatly influenced by the South Kensington (today the Victoria and Albert) Museum in London, as also was the Museum of Fine Arts, one of whose founders wrote: "The designer needs a museum of art, as the man of letters needs a library, or the botanist a herbarium." Both museums agreed that few masterpieces were available to them, and in the field of sculpture, they began to gather plaster casts of famed originals. A delay in the arrival by sea of fifty cases of casts and an amusing debate about the placement of fig leaves on nude statues accompanied the opening of the Museum of Fine Arts, and in 1883 the first large money bequest to the Metropolitan was earmarked for the purchase of architectural casts.[37]

The Metropolitan Museum and the American Museum of Natural History were responsible for a partnership arrangement between city government and a private board of trustees that has been followed by nearly one hundred American museums, though not by the Boston Museum of Fine Arts, which operated primarily on private support for nearly a century. The two New York museums in 1871 planned to erect a building together and secured the signatures of the owners of more than half of the real estate of the city on a petition asking the state legislature to authorize the city to tax itself five hundred thousand dollars for this purpose. The two boards sent emissaries to visit William Marcy Tweed, the city's representative in Albany. Impressed by the standing of the petitioners, "Boss" Tweed had Peter Barr Sweeney, the city chamberlain, reputed to be the brains of the Tweed Ring, work out a compromise under which the city agreed to erect and take title to the building (and later to maintain it), and the trustees would own and control the collections. As it turned out, the two museums built separate structures, but an important pattern of museum organization had been established.[38]

The Metropolitan and the Museum of Fine Arts have helped define the scope of a comprehensive art museum. General Louis P. di Cesnola, who became the first director of the Metropolitan in 1879, had been the U.S. consul on the island of Cyprus; he sold to the Metropolitan two collections of classical antiquities he had excavated and also sold a smaller accumulation to the Boston museum. J. P. Morgan became president of the Metropolitan in 1904, and by the time of his death in 1913, the museum had acquired important Greek art, made numerous archaeological expeditions to Egypt, secured an outstanding collection of armor, and received the Benjamin Altman bequest of about two thousand masterpiece paintings and Chinese porcelains valued at 15 million dollars. Morgan himself shocked the Metropolitan by failing to leave it his own collection, perhaps the greatest assembled in modern times, though his son eventually donated about 40 percent of its treasures.[39]

In 1924 the president of the Metropolitan, Robert W. de Forest, and Mrs. de Forest gave the museum its American Wing, which housed colonial and federal period rooms and a distinguished collection of decorative arts. The American Wing has had great influence upon both art and history museums, and this kind of collection reached new heights with the opening of the Henry Francis du Pont Winterthur Museum in Delaware in 1951. In 1938 the Metropolitan also added to its exhibits the Cloisters, on a lofty site in Fort Tryon Park facing the Hudson River. George Gray Barnard, the sculptor, had begun this collection of architectural elements and sculpture from medieval cloisters, and John D. Rockefeller Jr. presented the park to the city and paid for erecting, furnishing, and endowing the Cloisters. During World War II, a great collection of musical instruments, acquired as early as 1889, was rejuvenated and beautifully displayed at the Metropolitan; in 1946 the Metropolitan absorbed the ten-year-old Museum of Costume Art and installed it as the Costume Institute with sixteen thousand items dating from 1690. Since 1975, the Metropolitan has carried out major expansions of its building leading to what director Philippe de Montebello calls "museums within the Museum." These expansions began with the Temple of Dendur from Egypt (1978); a wing for the Robert Lehman Collection of three thousand paintings, tapestries, and bronzes; enlarging the American Wing (1980); adding the Michael Rockefeller collection of Asia and Oceania (1982); opening the Lila Acheson Wallace Wing for modern artworks (1987); and most recently opening the Henry R. Kravis Wing of sculpture and decorative arts. The museum has been well described as "a sort of cultural coral reef, always growing and changing."[40]

The Museum of Fine Arts in Boston did not have the great wealthy patrons of the Metropolitan but had a host of devoted, well-to-do collectors who worked with knowledgeable curators to build a strong collection. Its Oriental art is the most remarkable of its holdings and is one of the finest collections in the world. Edward S. Morse and Ernest Fenollosa of Salem and Dr. William Sturgis Bigelow of Boston in the

1870s and 1880s journeyed to Japan to collect ceramics, statuary, and paintings that eventually went to the museum, and Chinese, Korean, Indian, and other Near and Far Eastern art found an appreciative home there. The museum also acquired Egyptian materials, mainly through Harvard-Boston archaeological expeditions, and was for a time the leading purchaser of Greek, Roman, and Etruscan antiquities. In addition to a comprehensive collection of European and American paintings, the museum's holdings of textiles, American decorative arts, and prints are of high quality. Its building on the Fenway, opened in 1908, was planned with great care and constituted a noble experiment in trying to separate the more popular display of outstanding masterpieces from study collections accessible to scholars. Today, an effort is underway to expand the museum's footprint, adding an east wing for American art; expanding the education facilities, including increased auditorium space; and renovating the European galleries, visitors' services, and conservation laboratories. In all, the projected price tag is 425 million dollars to be sought from both public and private funds.[41]

What of a National Art Gallery in the United States? James Smithson's bequest to the nation in 1846 encompassed both a national collection of art and a research library. As the Smithsonian Institution took shape in Washington these elements of Smithson's vision became secondary to its science interests. In the 1920s when Pittsburgh financier and art collector Andrew W. Mellon joined the Coolidge administration as treasury secretary, Mr. Mellon's chagrin at the lack of a national art gallery in Washington inspired a personal crusade to build a gallery comparable to those in European capitals. Over the next two decades, in addition to building his own private collection to the highest artistic standards, Mellon developed and pursued the creation of a national gallery in Washington. The U.S. National Gallery of Art emerged from America's own "princely" collections, those of major industrialists. But, based on Mellon's insistence that no collection, including his own, be maintained as a separate entity within the gallery's collections, the National Gallery of Art, not the Mellon Art Museum, opened in 1941 as a true gift to the nation.[42]

In the 1930s New York City emerged as an important center for modern art with three museums; first, the Museum of Modern Art, familiarly known as MOMA (1929). Founded by Miss Lizzie Bliss, Mrs. John D. Rockefeller Jr., and Mrs. Cornelius J. Sullivan, it hired a dynamic director, Alfred H. Barr Jr. He sold New Yorkers on French postimpressionism (Cezanne, Seurat, Van Gogh, Gauguin, Picasso, and others) and on Bauhaus modernism, bringing together the visual arts, including architecture, industrial design, film, photography, graphics, and typography. At about the same time, Mrs. Gertrude Vanderbilt Whitney, assisted by the energetic and witty Mrs. Juliana Force, crowned their efforts to assist America's militantly modern painters by establishing the Whitney Museum of American Art (1930). Still another aspect of modern art—this one glorifying the abstract art of Vasily Kandinsky and others—was served with the opening of the Solomon R. Guggenheim Museum (1939), financed by Guggenheim and directed by Hilla Rebay, baroness von Ehrenwiesen. These three museums have been responsible for the enthusiasm of Americans for modern art. Their leadership continues to this day, with the Guggenheim's museums around the world (Soho in New York City, Las Vegas, Bilbao, Berlin, and in the planning stages, Rio de Janeiro) and the Whitney's influential biennial exhibitions that reflect the latest trends in contemporary art. In 2000 MOMA became the sole corporate member of P.S. (Public School) 1 Contemporary Art Center, founded in 1971 in Long Island City, to broaden its opportunities to support contemporary artists. P.S. 1 has rejuvenated the 19th-century school building and its vast spaces provide contemporary artists with intriguing spaces to show, construct, and build their works (in all dimensions, including sound). These three creative institutions remind one of Gertrude Stein's alleged remark that a museum can either be a museum or be modern, but it cannot be both.[43]

Today, many American art museums that focus on modern and contemporary art often are identified as art centers, suggesting that their interest in art may include not only paintings, video projections, and sculpture, but also performances with or without musical elements. An Internet search of "art centers" resulted in more than 105 million replies. However, both the Walker Art Center (1929) in Minneapolis and the Cincinnati Art Center (1939) are two examples of institutions that hold permanent collections. The Cincinnati's new building even includes an "Unmuseum" that provides educational programming aimed at young people from five to twelve years old. Another form of art museum emerging in the 21st century is one that allows for large-scale, even multimedia installations in nontraditional spaces. Mass-MOCA (Massachusetts Museum of Contemporary Art) inhabits more than twenty-five buildings along the streets and industrial alleys of North Adams, Massachusetts, transforming a dying industrial town into an innovative center for the arts (of all stripes). The Dia Foundation was founded in 1974 to play a role among visual arts organizations nationally and internationally by initiating, supporting, presenting, and preserving art projects, and by serving as a locus for interdisciplinary art and criticism. Dia presents its permanent collection at Dia: Beacon Riggio Galleries, in Beacon, New York, and supports long-term, site-specific projects in venues across the United States.[44]

Educational Purpose

In addition to the physical expression of national power and dominance, European art museums following the French Revolution served the public through their displays of beauty to "inspire and uplift" the lower classes. Public hours were expected. "The Louvre, once the palace of kings, was reorganized as a museum of the people, to be open to everyone free of charge."[45] The concept of Liberte, Egalite, and Fraternite extended to the Louvre's galleries, which were brimming with Napoleon's war booty, physical manifestations of French dominance. As the 19th century progressed, museums gained value not only as storehouses for artistic masterpieces but also as promoters of design exemplars to inform commerce and, in today's terminology, influence "product" development. These attitudes extended across the Atlantic to influence American art museums.

The charter or constitution of nearly every American art museum puts emphasis upon its educational aims—often specialized teaching for artists, craftsmen, and industrial designers but always, general instruction for the public. In the 1870s the contemplation of art was sometimes considered a means of fighting vice and crime by providing "attractive entertainment of an innocent and improving character." Classes for artists and craftsmen and lecture series for the public were established and comprehensive educational programs with emphasis upon co-operation with the public schools soon followed. Henry Watson Kent, appointed assistant secretary of the Metropolitan Museum in 1905, brought order and efficiency to its total operation, but was especially devoted to the educational program. Soon made supervisor of education, Kent organized gallery lectures, a lantern-slide collection, publications including a bulletin, programs for visiting school groups, traveling exhibitions to schools, Saturday morning story hours (sometimes with costumed clowns), and radio programs for disabled children.[46]

The Museum of Fine Arts in Boston, in carrying out its aim "of offering instruction in the Fine Arts," promptly opened a School of

Drawing and Painting in 1876, and then its secretary, Benjamin Ives Gilman, starting in 1906, established a lecture room, published a handbook, and appointed a docent who would take groups of ten persons on one-hour interpretive tours every Tuesday, Thursday, and Saturday morning. On Thursday afternoons curators and visiting scholars would hold conferences to discuss the collections, and storytelling sessions were provided for disadvantaged children. The nationwide study of art museum programs (1973–1976) that culminated in *The Art Museum as Educator* revealed a wide variety of education programs in art museums all across the United States with strong commitments to children and school students. Almost thirty years later, a national survey of 135 art museums (2003) reveals that more than 80 percent of respondents offer education programs, and plan on increasing them.[47]

Challenges

Art Museum Purpose(s)

American art museums have developed differing and sometimes conflicting philosophies about their aims. Benjamin Ives Gilman of Boston insisted that art museums differ from science and history museums in that their collections exist to allow their viewers to experience beauty rather than to convey information. This aesthetic emphasis in a sense meant "art for art's sake," not education. John Cotton Dana of Newark had a very different idea—to emphasize art in the everyday activities of the community, to make immigrant and minority groups as well as factory workers proud of their culture and their products, to show how even everyday household wares could be well designed; in short, to define the museum as an instrument for community betterment. One should notice that each of these museum innovators with their differing points of view still advocates for education as a basic museum purpose. Gilman, though insistent that art objects in themselves were aesthetic rather than educational, organized the first museum docents, offered lectures about art and artists, and generally offered programs for the public that today are part of standard offerings for museum education departments. Such discussions continue today: a fine example of the "arguments" and "perspectives" alive in art museums is revealed in *Whose Muse? Art Museums and Public Trust*, published in 2004.

Art Centers

The spread of community art centers throughout the United States has stretched the definition of the art museum to include institutions that focus on art instruction from crafts to traditional watercolor painting or photography. Many of these community institutions were founded in the 1930s thanks to Roosevelt's Works Progress Administration. In the 1970s these art centers often developed as elements of urban revitalization projects taking over unused buildings such as schools and, in Alexandria, Virginia, a torpedo factory, abandoned since the end of World War II. Organized by volunteer groups interested in art instruction (and frequently led by females), these centers do not generally care for collections, though in addition to classes they do offer public exhibitions based on juried competitions or visiting artists.

Art and Architecture

In the 19th century many U.S. cities built museums to house their artistic treasures to impress citizens and visitors with the community's culture. Often these buildings resembled banks, reflecting a commitment to protecting the objects. With the opening of the 21st-century building styles, Victoria Newhouse argues: "Art as entertainment is contested by many together with the related trend toward ever more spectacular museum architecture. While the latter suits some art, it does not suit all art, and in today's wide variety of museums there is often a lack of harmony between container and contents. The need to coordinate this relationship is all too often ignored—by those commissioning new museums, those renovating and/or expanding existing museums, and those in charge of museum programming."[48]

Art Collections

With the collapse of the Soviet empire and increased access to records relating to the Nazi era (1933–1945), holocaust victims (and families of victims) are seeking restoration of art objects once in their possession and expropriated by the Nazis. The American Association of Art Museum Directors reports that "among the 14 million objects held by American art museums in public trust, museum researchers have identified approximately one thousand works, which, though not necessarily stolen by the Nazis, require further study into their ownership during the Nazi period." This search for "lost" art has challenged museum record-keeping systems, forced art museums to address issues of the provenance of collections, and especially threatened international exhibitions where museums are fearful of confiscation of artworks lacking proper documentation.

Winter 2006 marked a change in attitude within the art museum community toward ancient archaeological collections. The Metropolitan Museum, in concert with the Italian government, crafted an agreement to return to Italy objects long on view at the museum, but subject to skeptical provenance. The *Euponeius krater*, mentioned in chapter 8, will be returned to Italy in 2008 in exchange for long-term loans for other ancient objects. Metropolitan director Philippe de Montebello "has conceded that, on occasion, in the past the museum had received artifacts that may have been obtained in an 'improper' way. . . . We're no longer in an era where you ask no questions, now we look before we buy; the world has changed."[49]

Deaccessions

"Deaccession" is the term used by the museum profession to describe the reduction of a museum's collections by sale, auction, or trade with other museums. The American Association of Museums' Code of Ethics requires income from collections sales to be restricted to acquisition or direct care of collections within the museum's mission. In the world of art museums, especially those with modern art collections, deaccessioning has created calls for more transparency of a museum's collecting policies. Recently, both the Guggenheim and the Museum of Modern Art have faced public outcries over their disposal of artworks, once featured as primary elements to the collections.[50]

Blockbusters

Blockbuster exhibitions have become central to the financial support for U.S. art museums, especially those in large urban centers. They not only attract visitors and increase admissions income and museum shop sales, but they also allow for "cross marketing" to increase tourism citywide. For example, the 1996 Cezanne retrospective exhibition at the Philadelphia Museum of Art attracted more than half a million people in three months. It stimulated "package tours to the city" that included discount airfares, hotel rooms, and even restaurant meals. The city's tourism office estimated that the exhibition had an economic impact on the city of 86.5 million dollars. A larger issue is one of balance for the museum to ensure that these exhibitions reflect the museum's core mission. Philippe de Montebello says, "the competitive hyperactivity of most museum programs is no longer the glow of health but the flush of fever."[51]

Controversies

Art museum exhibitions reflect interpretive, in addition to financial, choices. How do today's art museums balance scholarship, educational purpose—whether in the Gilman or Dana mode—and public service? In the early 1990s, the Smithsonian's National Museum of American Art's *The West as America: Interpreting Images of the Frontier* and in 2000 the Brooklyn Museum of Art's *Sensation: Young British Artists from the Saatchi Collection* each "challenged" visitors and raised questions about the museums' roles as public institutions. Each of these exhibitions created controversy from both their interpretive choices and their sources for funding, affecting future art museum exhibition planning. They leave us with the questions, especially in the United States of "who decides?" along with "who funds?"

Art That Shocks

In 19th-century Paris, the group of artists that came to be known (and loved) as impressionists challenged the "academy's" standards. Today artists such as Andres Serrano, Robert Mapplethorpe, and Judy Chicago have challenged artistic "norms," offended some exhibition visitors, and more significantly caused public calls for greater controls on the use of federal funds to support art (and artists). Museum director Franklin Robinson reminds us of the role of contemporary artists: "Contemporary artists, by the very nature of what they do, make new things, they push the accepted boundaries of art. They redefine that simple, immensely complex world and challenge our preconceptions of what it means. That process of redefinition is often a shock: what we had come to expect of "art" and "artists"—and "museums"—is sometimes turned on its head. A museum that seemed to be a bastion of tradition, a safe haven, a protector and preserver of the past, suddenly becomes a proponent of the new and the radical."[52]

Evaluation

How do art museums measure their success? Is it by attendance numbers, sales at their gift shops, or the amount of public funds contributed to art museums? Michael Kimmelman in the *New York Times* suggests: "The question should not be how many people visit museums, but how valuable are their visits? . . . [M]useums are equal opportunity elitists. But museums have not yet learned how to measure precisely the *quality* of the experience they offer." Measuring success is not just a task for professional evaluators, but of concern to directors and boards of trustees as they create exhibitions, develop programs, and seek funding.[53]

Notes

1. Stephen E. Weil, "Courtly Ghosts and Aristocratic Artifacts," *Museum News* 77, no. 6 (November–December 1998): 47.

2. James Cuno, ed., *Whose Muse? Art Museums and Public Trust*, Princeton, NJ: Princeton University Press, 2004, p. 47.

3. Timothy W. Luke, *Museum Politics: Power Plays at the Exhibition*, Minneapolis: University of Minnesota Press, 2002, p. 220.

4. Francis Henry Taylor, *The Taste of Angels: A History of Art Collecting from Rameses to Napoleon*, Boston, 1948, pp. 50–51; Germain Bazin, *The Museum Age*, New York: Universe Books, 1967, pp. 37–39; Germain Bazin, *The Louvre*, New York, 1958, p. 12; Alma S. Wittlin, *Museums: In Search of a Usable Future*, Cambridge, MA: MIT Press, 1970, pp. 8, 18.

5. Niels von Holst, *Creators, Collectors and Connoisseurs*, New York: Putman, 1967, pp. 58–66; Taylor, *The Taste of Angels*, pp. 55–72; Bazin, *The Museum Age*, pp. 44–46, 58–62; Wittlin, *Museums: In Search*, p. 75; Helmut Seling, "The Genesis of the Museum," *Architectural Review* 141 (1967): 103; Jean Louis Deotte, "Rome, the Archetypal Museum, and the Louvre, the Negation of Division" in *Grasping the World: The Idea of the Museum*, eds. Donald Preziosi and Claire Farago, Hants, UK: Ashgate, 2004.

6. Holst, *Creators*, pp. 69–74; Taylor, *The Taste of Angels*, pp. 85–109; Bazin, *The Museum Age*, pp. 46–52; Wittlin, *Museums: In Search*, p. 101; Seling, "Genesis of the Museum," p. 103; Frank Herrmann, *The English as Collectors: A Documentary Chrestomathy*, London, 1972, pp. 57–68; Holst, *Creators*, pp. 116–129, 168; Taylor, *The Taste of Angels*, pp. 208–241; Bazin, *The Museum Age*, pp. 83–84, 90–91; Bazin, *The Louvre*, pp. 25–26; Wittlin, *Museums: In Search*, p. 101; Kenneth Hudson, *A Social History of Museums: What the Visitors Thought*, Atlantic Highlands, NJ: Humanities Press, 1975, pp. 11–12.

7. Taylor, *The Taste of Angels*, pp. 277–278, 324–337; Bazin, *The Museum Age*, pp. 92–95; Bazin, *The Louvre*, pp. 21–28; Holst, *Creators*, pp. 157–160; Wittlin, *Museums: In Search*, pp. 57–59.

8. Holst, *Creators*, pp. 86, 90, 107–116, 128–139, 157, 161–163, 169–177, 179, 187–189, 190–198, 202–203; Taylor, *The Taste of Angels*, pp. 140–182, 279–290; Bazin, *The Museum Age*, pp. 75–80, 101; Wittlin, *Museums: In Search*, pp. 10–11, 92–93.

9. Holst, *Creators*, pp. 144–146; Taylor, *The Taste of Angels*, pp. 403–409, 420–464, 511–531; Bazin, *The Museum Age*, pp. 118–126; Mikhail Piotrovsky, "The Hermitage: Museum of World Cultures," *Museum* 217 (May 2003).

10. Wittlin, *Museums: In Search*, pp. 92–93; Taylor, *The Taste of Angels*, p. 469; Bazin, *The Museum Age*, p. 89; Holst, *Creators*, pp. 153–154.

11. Bazin, *The Museum Age*, pp. 166–167; Taylor, *Taste of Angels*, pp. 382–383; Seling, "Genesis of the Museum," p. 105; Holst, *Creators*, pp. 209–214.

12. Bazin, *The Museum Age*, pp. 163–166.

13. Bazin, *The Museum Age*, pp. 162–163.

14. Bazin, *The Museum Age*, pp. 158–159; Seling, "Genesis of the Museum," p. 109; Holst, *Creators*, pp. 161–163, 206–209; Hudson, *Social History of Museums*, pp. 28–29.

15. Bazin, *The Museum Age*, pp. 150–156; Bazin, *The Louvre*, pp. 39–45; Taylor, *The Taste of Angels*, p. 371; Christiane Aulanier, *Histoire de Palais et du Musee du Louvre*, 9 vols., Paris, 1947, p. 64.

16. Bazin, *The Museum Age*, p. 144.

17. Bazin, *The Museum Age*, pp. 159–160; Taylor, *The Taste of Angels*, pp. 511–525; Holst, *Creators*, pp. 166–167, 169–178, 184–185.

18. Bazin, *The Museum Age*, pp. 144–145; Taylor, *The Taste of Angels*, pp. 414–416; Wittlin, *Museums: In Search*, p. 46.

19. Bazin, *The Museum Age*, pp. 145–150; Taylor, *The Taste of Angels*, pp. 417–420, 475–476; Holst, *Creators*, pp. 194, 205–206.

20. Bazin, *The Museum Age*, pp. 171–172; Bazin, *The Louvre*, pp. 46–48; Holst, *Creators*, pp. 215–217; Taylor, *The Taste of Angels*, p. 539; Seling, "Genesis of the Museum," p. 109; Linda Nochlin, "Museums and Radicals: A History of Emergencies," in *Museums in Crisis*, ed. Brian O'Doherty, New York, 1972, pp. 7–41; Cecil Gould, *Trophy of Conquest: The Musee Napoleon and the Creation of the Louvre*, London, 1965, pp. 13–29, 70–71; Wilhelm Treve, *Art Plunder: The Fate of Works of Art in War and Unrest*, New York, 1961, pp. 139–199; Russell Chamberlin, *Loot! The Heritage of Plunder*, New York: Facts on File, 1983.

21. Bazin, *The Museum Age*, p. 174; Bazin, *The Louvre*, p. 48; Taylor, *The Taste of Angels*, pp. 540–541; Nochlin, "Museums and Radicals," p. 11; Gould, *Trophy of Conquest*, pp. 30–40.

22. Bazin, *The Museum Age*, p. 174; Bazin, *The Louvre*, pp. 48–49; Holst, *Creators*, pp. 217–218; Taylor, *The Taste of Angels*, pp. 544–547; Nochlin, "Museums and Radicals," p. 13; Gould, *Trophy of Conquest*, pp. 41–66; Victoria Newhouse, *Art and the Power of Placement*, New York: Monacelli Press, 2005, pp. 77–82.

23. Bazin, *The Museum Age*, p. 176; Gould, *Trophy of Conquest*, pp. 67–69.

24. Edward P. Alexander, "Dominique Vivant Denon and the Louvre of Napoleon," in *Museum Masters: Their Museums and Their Influence*, Nashville, TN: American Association of State and Local History, 1983, pp. 81–112; Carol Duncan, "Art and the Ritual of Citizenship," in *Exhibiting Cultures, The Poetics and Politics of Museum Display*, eds. Ivan Karp and Steven D. Lavine, Washington, DC: Smithsonian Press, 1991, pp. 88–103.

25. Bazin, *The Museum Age*, pp. 180–185, 190; Bazin, *The Louvre*, pp. 52–56; Taylor, *The Taste of Angels*, pp. 561–562, 572–573; Holst, *Creators*, pp. 220–224; Gould, *Trophy of Conquest*, pp. 75–80.

26. Bazin, *The Museum Age*, pp. 185–191; Bazin, *The Louvre*, pp. 57–60; Taylor, *The Taste of Angels*, pp. 571–589; Gould, *Trophy of Conquest*, pp. 80–85, 116–135; David Roxan and Ken Wanstall, *The Rape of Art: The Story of Hitler's Plunder of the Great Masterpieces of Europe*, New York, Coward-McCann, 1965; Lynn H. Nicholas, *The Rape of Europa: The Fate of Europe's Treasures in the Third Reich and the Second World War*, New York: Vintage, 1994; Hector Feliciano, *The Lost Museum: The Nazi Conspiracy to Steal the World's Greatest Works of Art*, New York: Basic Books, 1997.

27. Bazin, *The Museum Age*, pp. 201, 204, 207, 209; Bazin, *The Louvre*, pp. 61–85; Holst, *Creators*, pp. 260–261; Marc Fumaroli, "What Does the Future Hold for Museums?" in *Masterworks from the Musee des Beaux-Arts, Lille*, New York: Metropolitan Museum of Art, 1992; Kenneth Hudson, *Museums of Influence*, Cambridge, UK: Cambridge University Press, 1987, pp. 39–64.

28. Frank Herrman, *English as Collectors: A Documentary Chrestomathy*, London: Chatto and Windus, 1972, pp. 263–273; Philip Hendy, "The National Gallery," in *Art Treasures of the National Gallery*, London, 1959, pp. 9–25; Holst, *Creators*, pp. 224–225; Neil MacGregor, "Scholarship and the Public," in *Collections Management*, ed. Anne Fahy, London: Routledge, 1995, p. 219; Gwen Wright, *The Formation of National Collections of Art and Archaeology*, Studies in the History of Art 47, Washington, DC: National Gallery of Art, 1996; Samson Spanier, "Return to Victorian Splendor," *International Herald Tribune*, September 29, 2005, p. 24; Christopher Whitehead, *The Public Art Museum in Nineteenth Century Britain: The Development of the National Gallery*, Aldershot, UK: Ashgate, 2005; Kate Hill, *Culture and Class in English Public Museums 1850–1914*, Aldershot, UK: Ashgate, 2005.

29. Bazin, *The Museum Age*, pp. 195–197, 270; Herrman, *English as Collectors*, pp. 202–209, plate 61; Seling, "Genesis of the Museum," pp. 112–114; Holst, *Creators*, pp. 231–232, 257, 279; A. Mahr, "The Centenary Celebrations of the Prussian State Museums," *Museums Journal* 30 (March 1931): 253–260; Berlin State Museums Curatorial Staff, *Art Treasures of the Berlin State Museums*, New York:, 1964, pp. 7–22, 91, 99–104, 122–126, 130–131, 133; Edward P. Alexander, "Wilhelm Bode and Berlin's Museum Island," in *Museum Masters*, pp. 207–238; Rudiger Klessmann, *The Berlin Museum*, New York: Abrams, 1983; James J. Sheehan, *Museums in the German Art World from the End of the Old Regime to the Rise of Modernism*, New York: Oxford University Press, 2000.

30. Bazin, *The Museum Age*, pp. 198–199, 270; Seling, "Genesis of the Museum," pp. 111–112, 114; Holst, *Creators*, pp. 227–230; *Munich Art Galleries* Staff and University of Munich Art Historians, Munich, South Brunswick, NJ, 1969, pp. 1–60.

31. Bazin, *The Museum Age*, pp. 214–215, 269; B. B. Piotrovsky, ed., *Art Treasures of the Hermitage*, Leningrad, 1969, pp. 15–16; Geraldine Norman, *The Hermitage: The Biography of a Great Museum*, New York: Fromm International, 1997; "The State Hermitage Museum, Leningrad," *Museum* 10 (1957): 97–113; *Museum* 217, May 2003 issue dedicated to future plans for Hermitage.

32. Bazin, *The Museum Age*, pp. 217–218; Raymond Charmet, *The Museums of Paris*, New York, 1967, pp. 5–6; *National Gallery, Millbank [Tate Gallery], Illustrated Guide: British School*, London, 1928, pp. viii–ix; Philip Hendy, "National Gallery," in *Art Treasures of the National Gallery*, London, 1959, pp. 9–25; Newhouse, *Art and the Power of Placement*.

33. Bazin, *The Museum Age*, 230–234; Kenneth W. Luckhurst, *The Story of Exhibitions*, London: Studio Publications, 1951, pp. 83–116; Eugene S. Ferguson, "Technical Museums and International Exhibitions," *Technology and Culture* 6 (1965): 30–46; Winslow Ames, "London or Liebnitz?" *Museum News* 43 (October 1964): 27–35; Charmet, *The Museums of Paris*, p. 11; Victoria and Albert Museum, *Masterpieces in the Victoria and Albert Museum*, London: Victoria and Albert Museum, 1952, pp. iii–iv; Leigh Ashton, "100 Years of the Victoria and Albert Museum," *Museums Journal* 53 (May 1953): 43–47; Bruce Robertson, "South Kensington Museum in Context: An Alternative History," *Museum and Society* 2, no. 1 (March 2004).

34. Leo Lerman, *The Museum: One Hundred Years of the Metropolitan Museum of Art*, New York, 1969; Calvin Tomkins, *Merchants and Masterpieces: The Story of the Metropolitan Museum of Art*, New York, 1970, pp. 115–120; Stephen Mark Dobbs, "Dana and Kent and Early Museum Education," *Museum News* 50 (October 1971): 38–41; Barbara Y. Newsom, *The Metropolitan Museum as an Educational Institution*, New York, 1970; Nathaniel Burt, *Palaces for the People: A Social History of the American Art Museum*, Boston: Little, Brown, 1977 (a readable series of portraits of art museum "characters" from Charles Willson Peale to Thomas Hoving); Joel J. Orosz, *Curators and Culture: The Museum Movement in America, 1740–1870*, Tuscaloosa: University of Alabama Press, 1990; Steven Conn, *Museums and American Intellectual Life, 1876–1926*, Chicago, IL: University of Chicago Press, 1998; David Carrier, *Museum Skepticism: A History of the Display of Art in Public Galleries*, Durham, NC: Duke University Press, 2006; Richard Rossett, "Art Museums in the United States: A Financial Portrait," in *The Economics of Art Museums*, ed. Martin Feldstein, Chicago, IL: University of Chicago Press, 1991, pp. 129–177; William Hendon, *Analyzing an Art Museum*, New York: Praeger, 1979, pp. 18–33; Alan Wallach, *Exhibiting Contradictions: Essays on the Art Museum in the United States*, Amherst, MA: University of Massachusetts Press, 1998.

35. Barbara Y. Newsom and Adele Z. Silver, eds., *The Art Museum as Educator*, Berkeley: University of California Press, 1978 (a study of art museum practices

across the United States); Association of Art Museum Directors, *State of the Nation's Art Museums*, New York: Association of Art Museum Directors, March 2004; Cuno, *Whose Muse?*; Didier Maleuvre, "A Plea for Silence: Putting Art Back in to the Art Museum," in *Museum Philosophy for the 21st Century*, ed. Hugh H. Genoways, Lanham, MD: AltaMira Press, 2006, pp. 165–176.

36. Whitehill, *Museum of Fine Arts* 1:10, 41, 288–301.

37. Laurence Vail Coleman, *The Museum in America: A Critical Study*, 3 vols., Washington, 1939, 1:10, 11, 14–15, 112 and 2:230 and 3:429–432; Walter Pach, *The Art Museum in America*, New York, 1948, pp. 32, 33, 38, 40, 42; Tomkins, *Merchants and Masterpieces*, p. 38; Burt, *Palaces for the People*; Nancy Einreinhofer, *The American Art Museum: Elitism and Democracy*, London: Leicester University Press, 1997, pp. 144–149.

38. Pach, *Art Museum*, pp. 40–41; Eloise Spaeth, *American Art Museums and Galleries: An Introduction to Looking*, New York, 1960, pp. 217–229; Holst, *Creators*, pp. 257–259, 271–272.

39. Tomkins, *Merchants and Masterpieces*, p. 21.

40. Walter Muir Whitehill, *Museum of Fine Arts, Boston: A Centennial History*, 2 vols., Cambridge, MA, 1:9–13, 31; Tomkins, *Merchants and Masterpieces*, p. 23, 70; Weil, "Courtly Ghosts and Aristocratic Artifacts: The Art Museum as Palace," pp. 44–49 (a discussion of the role of casts at the Metropolitan and the Museum of Fine Arts, Boston); Winifred E. Howe, *A History of the Metropolitan Museum of Art*, 2 vols., New York, 1913, 1946, 1:138–139; Coleman, *The Museum in America*, 1:106–111; Tomkins, *Merchants and Masterpieces*, pp. 39–41.

41. Howe, *Metropolitan History*, 1:153–156, 180–181, 281–283 and 2:8–14; Tomkins, *Merchants and Masterpieces*, pp. 44, 47, 49–59, 95–182; Whitehill, *Museum of Fine Arts*, 1:chaps. 4, 5, 8 and 2:chaps. 14, 19, 21; Pach, *Art Museum*, pp. 65–68; "Museum of Fine Arts, Boston," *Newsweek*, 1969, pp. 9–15, 162–165; www.mfa.org.

42. David Edward Finley, *A Standard of Excellence: Andrew W. Mellon Founds the National Gallery of Art*, Washington, DC: Smithsonian Press, 1973 (Major donors to the National Gallery, in addition to Mellon, included: Joseph Widener, Samuel H. Kress, and Chester Dale.).

43. National Endowment for the Arts, *Museums USA: Art, History, Science, and Other Museums*, Washington, DC: National Endowment for the Arts, 1974, p. 5; Burt, *Palaces for the People*; Russell Lynes, *Good Old Modern: An Intimate Portrait of the Museum of Modern Art*, New York, 1975; Avis Berman, "Pioneers in American Museums: Juliana Force," *Museum News* 55 (November–December 1976): 45–49, 59–62; Edward P. Alexander, "Alfred Hamilton Barr, Jr.," in *The Museum in America: Innovators and Pioneers*, Walnut Creek, CA: AltaMira Press, 1997, pp. 67–83; Cuno, *Whose Muse?*; Calvin Tomkins, "How American Is It? The Whitney Museum Takes a New Direction," *New Yorker*, March 13, 2006; www.moma.org; www.ps1.org.

44. www.contemporaryartscenter.org; www.massmoca.org; www.walkerart .org; www.diacenter.org.

45. Gilman, *Museum Ideals*, pp. 86–87, 92; John Cotton Dana, *The New Museum*, Woodstock, VT, 1917; Francis Henry Taylor, *Babel's Tower: The Dilemma of the Modern Museum*, New York, 1945, pp. 23, 25–27; Sherman E. Lee, "The Idea of an Art Museum," *Harper's Magazine* 237 (September 1968): 76–79; W. G. Constable, "Museums in a Changing World," *Museums Journal* 55 (January 1956): 259–262; Cuno, *Whose Muse?*; Carol Duncan, *Civilizing Rituals: Inside Public Art Museums*, London: Routledge, 1995; Wright, *The Formation of National Collections*; Carol Duncan and Alan Wallach, "Universal Survey Museums," *Art History* 3 (1980): 447–469; Kenneth Hudson, "An Unnecessary Museum," *Museum* 41, no. 2 (1989): 114–116.

46. Lerman, *The Museum*, p. 14; Tomkins, *Merchants and Masterpieces*, pp. 115–120; Stephen Mark Dobbs, "Dana and Kent and Early Museum Education," *Museum News* 50 (October 1971): 38–41; Newsom, *The Metropolitan*; Edward P. Alexander, "Henry Watson Kent," in *The Museum in America*, pp. 51–66.

47. Newsom and Silver, *The Art Museum as Educator*; Cuno, *Whose Muse?*; Association of Art Museum Directors, *State of the Nation's Art Museums*, p. 5.

48. Newhouse, *Art and the Power of Placement*, p. 215.

49. Association of Art Museum Directors, *Art Museums and the Identification and Restitutions for Works Stolen by the Nazis*, New York: Association of Art Museum Directors, 2001; Elizabeth Povoledo, "Italy and U.S. Sign Antiquities Accord," *New York Times*, February 22, 2006; Anne McC. Sullivan, "Law and Diplomacy in Cultural Property Matters," in *Collections Management*, ed. Anne Fahy, London: Routledge, 1995, pp. 97–117.

50. Einreinhofer, *The American Art Museum: Elitism and Democracy*, pp. 145–147.

51. Quoted in Newhouse, *Art and the Power of Placement*, p. 23; Kevin F. McCarthy, Elizabeth H. Ondaatje, Arthur Brooks, and Andras Szanto, *A Portrait of the Visual Arts: Meeting the Challenges of a New Era*, Santa Monica, CA: RAND, 2005, p. 32 (Concludes that blockbusters don't increase audiences, they simply get current visitors to return.); Julia Beizer, Susan Breitkopf, and Amanda Litvinov, "Marketing the King: Tut 2 and the New Blockbuster," *Museum News* 84, no. 6 (November–December 2005).

52. Franklin Robinson, "The Moral Dilemma of American Art Museums" *Museum News* 74, no. 2 (March–April 1995).

53. Michael Kimmelman, "Museums in a Quandary: What Are the Ideals?" *New York Times*, August 26, 2001; Philip Wright, "The Quality of Visitors' Experiences in Art Museums," in *The New Museology*, ed. Peter Vergo, London: Reaktion, 1989, pp. 119–148.

3

Natural History and Anthropology Museums

I don't know what 'natural history' means, and 'museum' means dead, stuffed, and in the past to me.

> —public comment at a strategy session for the
> San Diego Museum of Natural History, 1997[1]

Whilst natural-science museums are concerned with the physical man as the apex of the tree of life they are also concerned with cultural man as the predator of the natural environment.

> —Georges-Henri Riviere, 1973[2]

Museums place history, nature, and traditional societies under glass, in artificially constructed dioramas and tableaux, thus sanitizing, insulating, plasticizing, and preserving them as attractions and simple lesson aids; by virtue of their location, they are implicitly compared with and subordinated to contemporary established values and definitions of social reality. When we "museumify" other cultures and our own past, we exercise conceptual control over them.

> —Michael Ames, 1992[3]

The early medieval and Renaissance collectors gathered natural curiosities thought to have magical powers to promote healing, longevity, fertility, and sexual virility. During the 16th and 17th centuries, the collections showed signs of becoming research centers, since they provided important documents for the scientist—rocks and minerals, fossils and shells, anatomical and botanical specimens, and stuffed animals and fishes from all over the world.[4] Taxonomic displays of collections, first amassed to aid in understanding God's plan, evolved under the influence of humanists and later the impact of naturalist Charles Darwin. Furthermore, in the United States anthropologists associated with natural history museums sought to reveal the origins of the original "American" peoples.[5] By the end of the 19th century, advances in taxidermy allowed for more "natural" displays of habitat groups (from birds to elephants), attracting the public to what Charles Willson Peale called "statues of animals with real skin to cover them."[6]

Collections of Natural Curiosities

Many of the holdings of the early museums seem strange indeed to the modern naturalist. The fabulous unicorn's horn, thought capable of foiling poisoners or assassins, was worth a fortune, though no such beast existed; horns of rhinoceros or other animals were used, as well as the sea unicorn (narwhal) or fossils. Giants' bones were found in many a collection, though they actually might be of mammoths, elephants, or fossil remains. Egyptian mummies were greatly prized, and mummy powder (sometimes a criminal's body treated with bitumen) was sold by apothecaries to staunch the flow of blood or heal bruises and fractures. Human skulls and human skin, the best grades supposedly came from unburied corpses, were used for medicinal cures, as were stag and elk antlers. Figured stones included fossils, thunderbolts (actually the ax heads of primitive man), and serpents' tongues (in reality, fossil teeth of sharks). Barnacles were observed to have the shape of small geese and were thought to be born in decayed wood; barnacle geese became another medicinal source used by apothecaries.[7]

And, of course, some collections manifested a mix of purposes. In 14th-century Mantua, the Gonzaga family took advantage of an insurrection to depose the Bonacolsi who had ruled for a century and amassed a large palace. Rinaldo, the last of the Bonacolsi, was killed by bravos who pursued him in flight to his palace. The vast palace contained many rooms with collections of natural curiosities: a room of petrified objects; a second of corals, shells, and marine wonders; and a third of rare objects, diamonds, and curiosities from the plant kingdom.

The fourth room housed curiosities from the animal kingdom, show-casing a stuffed hippopotamus. After the Gonzagas took control of Mantua and moved into the palace, they mounted and displayed the embalmed body of Rinaldo sitting bolt upright on the hippopotamus. In his honor, the room was renamed for him, the name it bears today, although the hippopotamus and its mount are gone.[8]

In the 16th and 17th centuries, an astonishingly large number of col-lections of curiosities were found in every western European country. Conrad Gesner, the Zurich physician sometimes called "the Father of Zoology," in about 1550 had one of the first museums devoted chiefly to natural history; his collection was combined with one belonging to Felix Platter, remnants of which are found today in the Natural History Museum in Basel. Ulisse Aldrovandi had a large museum at Bologna that early in the 17th century was joined to one of Ferdinando Cospi and acquired by the City of Bologna.[9]

The 17th century saw technical improvements in handling zoologi-cal specimens. The use of spirits of wine made preservation in liquid possible; cheap flint glass enabled wet specimens to be viewed more easily; and wax or mercury could be injected into vascular systems so as to exhibit specimens dry. Ole Worm, physician, scientist, and founder of prehistoric archaeology, had a museum at Copenhagen, as did King Christian V. The Amsterdam collections of Bernhardus Palu-danus, Frederick Ruysch, and Albert Seba found their way to the Im-perial Palace in Saint Petersburg.[10]

Important centers of scientific research developed in Italy. At Bologna the Aldrovandi-Cospi collection was joined by the Instituto delle Scienze of the Conte de Luigi Ferdinando Marsigli. The Medici in Florence collected natural science specimens as well as art. Ferrante and Francesco Imperati had a well-known museum at Naples, while the Jesuit Athanasius Kircher, who considered Noah's ark to have been the most complete natural history museum, was director of the Museo Kircheriano in Rome.[11]

The collectors gave considerable thought to the classification and arrangement of their treasures. Caspar F. Neickel in his *Museographia*, printed at Leipzig in 1727, recommended six shelves around the room. Natural objects should go on one side with human anatomy, including skeletons and mummies, on the top shelf, and quadrupeds, fishes, and minerals below. Another wall was to hold man-made objects with an-cient and modern productions separated. The short end of the room op-posite the entrance and lighted by three windows contained cabinets for coins. Portraits of famous men occupied the space above the shelves. Ole Worm's Museum in Copenhagen used three continuous shelves and suspended from the ceiling or mounted on the walls large objects such as stuffed crocodiles, a polar bear, skeletons, arms and armor, and an Eskimo kayak. The Imperati museum in Naples presented a similar appearance, while an Egyptian mummy at the entrance lured the visitor into the Museo Kircheriano.[12]

Displaying Collections

The displays of early natural history collections reflected the individual collector's interests and the growing "scientific" focus on identifying and classifying objects. Publications such as *Museographia* (1727) provided schematics for organizing collections. The actual displays evolved from simple shelves and cases of objects carefully laid out in some rational order into efforts to cluster and group items to explain their places in the increasingly complex world.[13] In Britain, museum founder and innovator William Bullock introduced realistic specimens to his displays, while the multitalented Charles Willson Peale added stuffed creatures to his Philadelphia museum displays. As tourists, collectors, and big game hunters scoured the far reaches of the world, the focus on displaying prized objects merged with museums' taxonomic systems. Collectors sought to show their collections in more realistic settings, placing the individual item within its natural context. In the United States, Ward's Natural Science Establishment (Rochester, New York) prepared specimens for hunters and as large metropolitan natural history museums began to open, technicians from Ward's applied their talents to museum displays. Popular agriculture fairs across the United States provided venues for displays of stuffed animals, adding to the demand for more realistic taxidermy and natural settings. American innovator Carl Akeley began his long career at Ward's.[14] Setting off these displays with backdrops—both realistic and fantastical—added to the visitors delight at "entering" the world of nature. The diorama made its entry into the museum exhibition space. "The recognition of the educational value of animal groups by such an acknowledged authority as a government museum (National Museum of Natural History of the Smithsonian) had much to do with their adoption by other institutes; once entrenched behind the bulwarks of high scientific authority, they began to find their way into all museums."[15]

British Antecedents

The Ashmolean Museum

The first public natural history museum was established at Oxford University in 1683. Two remarkable gardeners, the John Tradescants, father and son, may be considered its founders. The elder Tradescant laid out gardens for several English noblemen and journeyed to Flanders, France, Russia, Algeria, and the Mediterranean as far east as Turkey to bring back trees and plants chosen for their beauty and rarity rather than their medicinal qualities. In 1626 he moved to South Lambeth, outside London; his house, known as "Tradescant's Ark," was filled with his renowned Cabinet of Rarities and surrounded by a fine garden.

In 1656 the younger Tradescant issued *Musaeum Tradescantium*, a catalog of the collection that listed preserved birds, animals, fish, and insects; minerals and gems; fruits; carvings, turnings, and paintings; weapons; costumes; household implements; coins and medals; and beautiful and exotic plants, shrubs, and trees. The garden was especially strong in Virginia materials, many of them gathered by the son on three trips he made there. Typical rarities in the collection were "unicornu marinum" (narwhal); "dodar, from the Island Mauritius" (the famed, now-extinct dodo); "a cherry-stone, upon one side S. Geo: and the Dragon perfectly cut; and on the other side 88 Emperour's faces"; "Pohaton, King of Virginia's habit all embroidered with shells, of Roanoke"; "Henry the 8 his Stirrups, Haukeshoods, Gloves"; and "Anne of Bullens Night-vayle embroidered with silver."

Elias Ashmole, smooth-talking lawyer, amateur scientist, and collector, helped his friend Tradescant issue the catalog. When John died in 1662, the rarities passed to Ashmole and he gave the collection to Oxford but required the university to put up a special museum building to house the twenty cartloads of the Tradescant accumulation, to which he added books and coins of his own. The museum was on the upper floor, a school of natural science below it presided over by Dr. Robert Plot, keeper of the museum and professor of chemistry, and a chemistry laboratory in the basement. The whole was called the Ashmolean Museum, though some thought it might better have been named for the Tradescants. The museum printed regulations on its use in Latin in 1714. Only one group was admitted at a time, and entrance fees were in proportion to the time spent on the guided tours, though groups received a discount. Unfortunately, the Tradescant dodo, in moldy condition, was ordered removed and burnt in 1755, though the head and one foot were salvaged from the flames.

The old Ashmolean building (now the Museum of the History of Science) is still extant today beside the Sheldonian Theatre on Broad Street. Its contents have been scattered—the geological and physical collection to the Clarendon Building, the ethnographic specimens to the Pitt Rivers Museum, natural history material to the University Museum, and the books and manuscripts to the Bodleian Library. The new Ashmolean Museum of Art and Archaeology (1894) is a general collection of art, antiquities, and numismatics with a few items related to its predecessor, including portraits of the Tradescant family and of Ashmole, and the shell-embroidered mantle said to have belonged to Powhatan.[16]

The British Museum and Others

The British Museum, the first great national museum in the world, was founded by the House of Commons in 1753 as a combined national library and general museum that soon became especially strong in collections of antiquities, natural history, and ethnography. In fact, the British Museum might just as readily be included in the previous chapter as an "Art Museum." It appears here as a Natural History Museum based on its origins. Today it stands with a few other national institutions with universal collections: the Louvre, the Smithsonian, the Metropolitan Museum of Art, and the Hermitage. The man behind the museum part of the enterprise was Sir Hans Sloane, eminent physician and observant naturalist and scientist. Sloane served as president of the Royal Society in succession to Isaac Newton and of the Royal College of Physicians. He was best known for his collection that was a kind of private museum housed in his home. Sloane's collection attracted many distinguished visitors—among others, Voltaire, Benjamin Franklin, Linnaeus, and Handel. The great composer angered Sloane by putting down a buttered muffin on one of his rare volumes. At his death in 1753, Sloane's natural history collection was enormous—a herbarium of 334 large folio volumes of dried plants; 12,500 vegetable specimens; zoological objects; and stones, minerals, shells, and fossils—without doubt the finest in the world. Then there were fifty thousand volumes, including seven thousand manuscripts; twenty-three thousand coins and medals; classical, medieval, and oriental antiquities; drawings and paintings; ethnographic objects; and mathematical instruments. All together, there were more than eighty thousand objects in addition to the herbarium. Sloane had spent large sums on arranging and cataloging his collections, at least 100,000 pounds.

In his will, Sir Hans stated that he had made the collection for "the manifestation of the glory of God, the confutation of atheism and its consequences, the use and improvement of physic and other arts and sciences, and benefit of mankind." He wished it to "remain together and not be separate" in the vicinity of London with its "great confluence of people." Parliament decided to meet Sloane's terms and the British Museum opened in 1759 in Montagu House in Bloomsbury. No admission charge was made, but tickets were required that often took several weeks and at least two visits to obtain. Armed sentries guarded the entrance after the Gordon riots of 1780; children were not admitted; and tours were hurried, lasting no more than an hour. By 1810, however, "any person of decent appearance" was admitted without a ticket during restricted hours.[17]

At first there were three departments—Manuscripts, Medals, and Coins; Natural and Artificial Productions; and Printed Books, Maps, Globes, and Drawings. A fourth—Antiquities—was added in 1807 that contained such rarities as the Rosetta stone; the Towneley collection of Greek and Roman sculptures, bronzes, and terra-cottas; and later, the Portland Vase and the famed Elgin Marbles from the Parthenon. Both the library and the archaeological collections with outstanding Egyptian, Babylonian, and Assyrian rarities expanded enormously and remained together at Bloomsbury in the neo-Grecian building begun by Sir Robert Smirke in 1823 and expanded often since that day.[18] In 2000 the museum opened the Great Court that increased public space by almost 40 percent. It allows for greater public access to galleries, including the 1857 Reading Room carefully restored to its original design, and adds auditorium space, classrooms, even studios, along with an educational center for young visitors. In fact, the new space provides the largest covered public space in Europe.[19]

Captain James Cook and other explorers contributed many specimens to the British Museum, and the Royal Society turned over its collection in 1781. Sir Joseph Banks in 1820 left it a herbarium, natural history library, and botanical collection. Between 1880 and 1883 the natural history collection was transferred to a twelve-acre site in Kensington; the institution (which became independent in 1963) was known as the British Museum (Natural History). Sir William Flower, its innovative director from 1884 to 1898, divided the collections into a selected and meaningful public exhibition series and a vastly larger reserve or study series for those with special interests (and credentials).[20] Flower believed that scientific research and public instruction were parallel functions of the museum. To this end, he focused on exhibition techniques, especially naturalistic dioramas to display collections. His attention to improving the appeal of specimens led to improvements in basic taxidermy techniques that would further increase the public's interest. Today at the Museum's Darwin Centre, the museum remains true to Flower's parallel goals. The centre brings the researchers out of their labs to interact with visitors. Through World Wide Web connections, one can join these discussions.[21]

There were also several well-known private museums. Sir Ashton Lever began with a bird collection near Manchester, moved to London in 1775, and was knighted for his natural history museum. Though he charged one-half guinea admission, he could not make a go of it, and his collection was finally sold at auction in 1806. Scottish brothers William (1718–1783) and John (1728–1793) Hunter amassed large collections of specimens relating to their teaching of anatomy to aspiring doctors in London. Nearly thirty-five hundred items were on display in their London home. Upon the death of the younger brother, the Hunterian collections were left to the University of Glasgow and subsequently purchased by the Scottish government in 1799. They remain on view today. William Bullock formed a collection at Sheffield, moved to Liverpool, and then came to London in 1809. Two years later he had the Egyptian Hall built in Piccadilly with an appropriate facade. He was an innovator who, like American circus founder Phineas T. Barnum, did much to popularize museums; he devised crude habitat groups and displayed Napoleon's coach captured after Waterloo, parrots brought back by Captain Cook, Laplanders and their reindeer from Norway, and a distinguished Mexican exhibition that he had gathered on a trip there.[22]

Continental Natural History Museums

The Jardin des Plantes, originally part of the king's garden, was formed in Paris and opened to the public in 1739. Georges-Louis LeClerc, comte de Buffon, its superintendent from 1739 to 1788, used it in writing his thirty-six-volume *Histoire Naturelle*. During the French Revolution in 1793, the Museum National d'Histoire Naturelle was established there. Twelve professional chairs attached to the museum were held, over the years, by the leading French naturalists—Jussien,

Geoffroy Sainte Hillaire, Lamarck, Cuvier, Chevreul, Milne-Edwards, Quatrefages, and Marcellus Boule. The museum buildings situated in the sixty-acre Jardin des Plantes alongside the Seine provide today's visitors with the opportunity to experience two centuries of natural history museum exhibition techniques. Starting in the Galerie d'anatomie comparee near the park entrance, one can walk by case upon case of articulated skeletons from across the globe. At the other end of the park, however, stands the Grand Galerie de l'evolution opened in 1994. One enters the doors of this impressive 19th-century building (designed by Gustave Eiffel) at the lowest level of four floors and is surrounded by steel and glass 21st-century exhibition spaces.[23]

The Naturhistoriches Museum in Vienna was founded in 1748, when Emperor Francis I purchased a collection of J. de Ballou of Florence. The museum is housed today in an Italianate building (1881), situated with a twin art museum in a handsome garden. Its collections cover mineralogy, petrography, geology, paleontology, zoology, and botany. Rarities include the finest meteorites in Europe and outstanding prehistory exhibits. It has transferred superb ethnographic materials, including feather ornaments of the Aztecs, to the Museum fur Volkerkunde (1876).[24]

The closest approximation to a natural history museum in Italy today is La Specola, the zoological museum of the University of Florence. It goes back to the Medici, but was opened to the public by Grand Duke Peter Leopold in 1775. It contains wet specimens, live reptiles, and amphibians, mollusks, skeletons, dried bird and mammal skins, mounted specimens, and dioramas. Most unusual of all are wax anatomical models created between 1770 and 1840 in the museum laboratories. This collection may someday become the basis for an Italian national museum of natural history.[25]

American Beginnings

The first permanent museum in the American English colonies was started in 1773 when the Charleston Library Society decided "to collect materials for a full and accurate natural history of South Carolina." Gentlemen were asked to send natural products—animal, vegetable, or mineral—with careful descriptions to be looked after by four curators. The society ordered an orrery from David Rittenhouse of Philadelphia and acquired a telescope, camera obscura, hydrostatic balance, and a pair of elegant globes. Early accessions included an Indian hatchet, a Hawaiian woven helmet, a cassava basket from Surinam, and parts of a skull and other bones of the fossilized Guadaloupe man. In 1850 the College of Charleston agreed to house the collection, and the Charleston Museum, incorporated in 1915 with its own board of trustees, has maintained unbroken its historical primacy.[26]

Pierre Eugene du Simitiere, the Swiss painter of miniatures, preserved snakes and other natural history specimens in his Curio Cabinet or American Museum opened to the public at Philadelphia in 1782. Du Simitiere may have been "the nation's earliest museologist," but far more important was Charles Willson Peale, also of Philadelphia. An accomplished artist, ingenious craftsman, enthusiastic student of nature, and a kind of universal scholar, Peale acquired most of du Simitiere's collection in 1784 to add to some mastodon bones, a preserved paddlefish from the Allegheny River, and paintings of Revolutionary heroes on display in his home. In 1786 he announced that he was forming a museum there—"a Repository for Natural Curiosities" or "the Wonderful Works of Nature"—to be arranged according to Linnaean classification. Among other exhibits was a grotto showing snakes and reptiles in natural surroundings. By 1794 the museum had outgrown Peale's house and moved to the newly completed Philosophical Hall of the American Philosophical Society; in 1802 it acquired the Long Room and Tower of what is today Independence Hall, rent free by unanimous action of the Pennsylvania Legislature. The Philadelphia Museum or Peale's American Museum was one of the leading attractions of the city and indeed of the eastern United States.

Peale was an imaginative and skilled museum director. His enthusiasm and good nature brought many gifts, and the American Philosophical Society in 1801 financed his expedition to Ulster County, New York, to exhume the bones of three "mammoths" (actually mastodons). Peale originated a habitat arrangement with curved, tastefully painted backgrounds to exhibit birds and animals showing their customary environment. He developed his own methods of taxidermy and carved larger animals of wood in natural poses to receive the skins. He used arsenic (even though it made him ill) and bichloride of mercury to protect his mounted specimens from insects. The fangs of a rattlesnake were shown under a lens, and "insects too small to be examined with the naked eye" were "placed in microscopic wheels." He also housed living animals and reptiles in the yard at Independence Hall.[27]

Peale's interest in interpreting his "School of Nature" was equally great; he was one of the first to appeal to the general public as well as to the scholar. The Philadelphia Museum and the Baltimore branch developed pioneer systems of gas lighting so as to stay open at night. In addition to a framed catalog after the Linnaean system and an eight-page guidebook, there were lectures, magic-lantern shows, and demonstrations of chemistry and physics (including electricity). Peale's museum, however, received increasingly heavy competition from catchpenny museums and shows devoted solely to entertainment. The city of Philadelphia also took over Independence Hall and charged Peale twelve hundred dollars in annual rent. The result was that the museum began to sacrifice the "rational amusement" of its educational and scientific programs to become more entertaining. By 1820 it was featuring Signor Hellene, an Italian one-man band who played the Italian viola, Turkish cymbals, tenor drum, Pandean pipes, and Chinese bells. The Peale museums went downhill rapidly after Peale's death in 1827, and the Baltimore and New York ones were soon bankrupt.[28]

In Philadelphia, at the start of the 19th century, the Academy of Natural Sciences convened its first meeting. This group of a dozen or so apothecaries, chemists, and a dentist, came together first to socialize and then to collect natural history specimens and to pursue research into natural phenomena. Though slow to open their study collections to the public, they sponsored lectures for members and friends and by 1839 their library maintained regular public hours. By the time the Philadelphia Peale Museum doors closed in 1850 the Academy of Natural Sciences was open to the public, and in 1866 it welcomed more than thirty-four thousand visitors. In 1868, it displayed the first American dinosaur *Hadrosaurus* from Haddonfield, New Jersey.[29]

In 1790 the patriotic, fraternal Tammany Society of New York conceived the notion of "The American Museum" to emerge from its own members-only cabinet. By 1815 the city's alms house was designated the home for the New-York Historical Society (previously in City Hall), the American Academy of Fine Arts, and the American Museum and the City Library. But, as important as the designation of a central location was the strengthening of the commitment of the city's power brokers to supporting a museum. John Scudder, who was a naturalist, taxidermist, and youthful curator at John Savage's City Museum, bought his former employer's ragtag collections and gave his own establishment the designation the "New American Museum" which opened its doors to the public in 1816.[30]

Phineas T. Barnum took over John Scudder's American Museum in New York late in 1841. This master showman was determined to make his fortune by amusing and even bamboozling the public. He never allowed scientific principles to stand in his way. By 1845 the Philadelphia Museum had failed, and Barnum eventually acquired much of its collection as well as the holdings of the Baltimore and New York branches. Barnum's American Museum, with more than six hundred thousand accessions, included "industrious fleas," three serpents fed their noonday meals in front of the crowds, two white whales swimming in tanks of salt water, a white elephant from Siam, two orangutans, a hippopotamus ("The Great Behemoth of the Scriptures"), grizzly bears, wolves, and buffalo. In addition there was a national portrait gallery, panoramas of the Holy Land, waxwork figures showing the horrors of intemperance, and an anatomical Venus (one shilling extra). Even more spectacular were General Tom Thumb and assorted midgets, giants, and bearded ladies; Barnum's traveling circus developed from this start.[31]

Despite the emphasis on entertainment and hokum, Barnum's American Museum had serious collections of shells, fish, animals, minerals, and geological specimens. When the museum was destroyed by fire in 1865, Barnum talked of building a great new national museum in New York, open to the public without charge. Henry Ward Beecher, Horace Greeley, William Cullen Bryant, and other leading New Yorkers backed the plan and urged President Andrew Johnson to instruct American ministers and consuls to help collect specimens. Nothing much came of the effort, though Barnum, in union with the Van Amburgh Menagerie Company, set up a New American Museum, which also burned, in 1868. His interest in natural history and museums continued, however, and he made gifts of animal skeletons, hides, and other materials chiefly to the Smithsonian Institution, the American Museum of Natural History, and Tufts College. His chief contributions to the museum movement, however, were on the popularization and entertainment side, where his promotional talent and sense of fun were most effective.[32]

Smithsonian Institution

James Smithson, illegitimate son of an English duke and keen student of chemistry and mineralogy, at his death left a contingent bequest to "the United States of America, to found at Washington, under the name of the Smithsonian Institution, an establishment for the increase and diffusion of knowledge among men." When his heir, a nephew, died unwed and childless, the contingent inheritance became a reality. In 1835, 110 bags of gold sovereigns worth $508,318.46

were shipped to the United States. Smithson had never visited there, and a somewhat startled Congress began to debate what to do with the unprecedented gift.

Proposals were made to use it for a national university, a large museum of natural science, an astronomical observatory, an agricultural experiment station, a normal school for training teachers of natural science, a school for orphan children, or an agricultural bureau to aid farmers. John Quincy Adams, the grand old former president then serving selflessly in the House of Representatives, fought hard to keep the fund intact as an endowment for the promotion of science. In 1846 Congress created the Smithsonian Institution with a board of regents composed of the chief justice of the United States, the vice president, three congressmen, three senators, and six private citizens. The dispute over the use of the money (the income then amounted to about thirty thousand dollars per year) was reflected in the provision that the board erect a building to house a museum with a study collection of scientific materials, a chemical laboratory, a library, an art gallery, and lecture rooms.[33]

The regents chose as their executive or secretary Joseph Henry, probably the leading American scientist of the day, who had done distinguished research in electromagnetism and discovered the principle of the telegraph. Henry thought the increase of knowledge more important than its diffusion; there were "thousands of institutions actively engaged in the diffusion of knowledge in our country," he wrote, "but not a single one which gives direct support to its increase. Knowledge can only be increased by original research, which requires patient thought and laborious and often expensive experiments."[34]

Henry passionately argued the merits of pure science and resisted as much as he dared putting Smithsonian income into erecting a large building, acquiring a library, establishing a museum and art gallery, and offering a series of public lectures. He set up a system of meteorological observations throughout the country that became the United States Weather Bureau; cautiously backed Smithsonian participation in exploring expeditions to the western states, Alaska, and elsewhere; inaugurated an international exchange of scientific publications; and began to publish *Smithsonian Contributions to Knowledge*. He managed to defeat efforts to make the Smithsonian a general copyright library, firing the librarian and transferring the accumulated books to the Library of Congress. He placed the Smithsonian art holdings on permanent loan with the Corcoran Gallery of Art.[35]

Henry could not, however, stop the growth of a natural history museum. Spencer Fullerton Baird, a first-rate biologist who became Henry's assistant secretary in 1850, was too clever and too patient for him. Baird thought a United States National Museum would both increase public knowledge of flora and fauna and provide scholars with comparative materials for biological research. Pressure for such a museum came from the exploration of natural resources in the western United States and from Smithsonian participation in international expositions. Both activities brought a stream of specimens and artifacts to Washington.[36]

Baird employed a promising young ichthyologist, George Brown Goode, to arrange Smithsonian and United States Fish Commission exhibits for the Philadelphia Centennial Exposition of 1876. Goode became the leading American museum professional of his day and in his short career (he died in 1896 at age forty-five) placed Smithsonian museum activities on a sound scientific basis. He brought back forty-two freight carloads of specimens and objects from the Philadelphia centennial, and after Baird succeeded Henry as secretary, Congress established the United States National Museum in 1879 and provided it with a new home, the present redbrick Arts and Industries Building. Goode argued that they were creating a museum of record to preserve material foundations of scientific knowledge, a museum of research to further scientific inquiry, and an educational museum to illustrate "every kind of material object and every manifestation of human thought and activity. " In other words, Goode was determined to collect not only natural history specimens but also art, historical, and technological objects. The centennial haul included sculpture and graphics, machinery, and decorative arts materials of wood, metal, ceramics, glass, and leather.[37]

Since then the Smithsonian has grown enormously and today contains more than 143.5 million objects (including artworks and specimens), about 80 percent of them in the National Museum of Natural History. It has been housed in its own building since 1911 and has sections devoted to anthropology (including what was once the famed Bureau of American Ethnology), botany, entomology, invertebrate and vertebrate zoology, mineral sciences, and paleobiology. The museum has for more than a century led the world in the study, classification, and publication of descriptions of new forms of animals, plants, and fossils. Its huge collections of specimens from all over the globe have permitted systematists to conduct outstanding taxonomic research.[38]

The Smithsonian Institution is a complex mixture of scientific and museum programs. It has been called the "university on the National Mall." Though not entirely an agency of the national government, it receives more than six hundred million dollars per year of federal funds that covers 70 percent of its expenses. Individual, foundation, and corporate support, along with Smithsonian business ventures, provide the remaining 30 percent. The Smithsonian regards itself as "an independent establishment devoted to public education, basic research, and national service in science, the humanities, and the arts."[39] Dichotomies such as Smithson's "increase and diffusion of knowledge" or Henry's pure science and Baird's taxonomic research still exist, but Congress has been willing to support their different approaches. The Smithsonian Institution as a whole echoes European museums because of its governmental support, and its Museum of Natural History stands as a world leader in its field.

American Museum of Natural History

Albert S. Bickmore studied with Louis Agassiz, founder of the Museum of Comparative Zoology at Harvard, and was determined that New York City should have a museum of natural history second to none, "affording amusement and instruction to the public" and "teaching our youth to appreciate the wonderful works of the Creator." Bickmore's enthusiasm enlisted the aid of the financial titans of the city, and the state of New York chartered the American Museum of Natural History on April 9, 1869. Bickmore became superintendent of the new institution, which the Commissioners of Central Park provided with quarters and exhibit cases on the upper floors of the Arsenal Building in the park.[40]

The American Museum joined with the Metropolitan Museum of Art to secure an arrangement under which New York City provided museum buildings and paid for maintenance and guards, while the boards of trustees furnished collections and the curatorial and educational staffs. President Ulysses S. Grant in 1874 laid the cornerstone of the American Museum's new building on Central Park West, which President Rutherford B. Hayes dedicated three years later. On that occasion, Professor Othniel C. Marsh, of the Peabody Museum at Yale, made a singularly accurate prophecy. "These vast collections," he said, "will spread the elements of Natural Science among the people of New York and the surrounding region, but the quiet workers in the attic, who pursue Science for its own sake, will bring the museum renown throughout the world." Professor Bickmore resigned as superintendent in 1884 to become curator of a new department of public instruction, for a time paid for by the state of New York. He offered schoolteachers a special course in natural history, devised high-quality lantern slides (known as "Bickmore slides"), and soon had reached more than one million persons with his public lectures.[41]

Morris K. Jesup, multimillionaire banker, became president of the museum in 1881. He was actually what today would be called the director—a working administrator who concerned himself with the smallest operating decisions. Though no scientist, Jesup attracted wealthy men to support the museum, appointed scholarly curators, personally financed museum expeditions, helped send Robert E. Peary on expeditions to the North Pole, and supported Frank M. Chapman in developing his bird-habitat groups. Jesup liked to see young people in the museum, which he considered a most effective agency "for furnishing education, innocent amusement, and instruction to the people."[42]

Jesup was followed in the museum presidency in 1908 by paleontologist Dr. Henry Fairfield Osborn. Osborn sensed the public appeal of large fossils, especially those of dinosaurs and when museum expeditions to the West brought back dinosaur bones, he had the huge skeletons articulated and placed on display. Many scientists considered this innovation radical and vulgar showmanship and insisted that the bones ought to be sorted into drawers and reserved for scientific study. Osborn got Carl E. Akeley, brilliant taxidermist, sculptor, explorer, and inventor, to obtain specimens from which a Hall of African Mammals developed with twenty-eight habitat groups placed around eight mounted elephants. Roy Chapman Andrews (memorialized as Indiana Jones in the film *Raiders of the Lost Ark*) was dispatched on a series of explorations of the Gobi Desert in Mongolia and in 1923 he brought back dinosaur eggs.[43] He developed a well-balanced program of exploration, scientific laboratory work, and exhibition techniques that attracted a large popular audience, including numerous school groups. Publications were of great importance, both the numerous series of scientific reports and the popular, copiously illustrated *Natural History* magazine. Dynamic reactions took place between patrons contributing financial backing and a quality program that attracted new patrons. The Smithsonian museums often contrasted governmental penury with this private generosity.[44]

After Osborn's retirement in 1932, the museum secured less flamboyant but more professional administration. Its departments were devoted to astronomy, minerals and gems, paleontology, forestry and conservation, living invertebrates, insects, living fishes, living reptiles, living birds, living mammals, and man and his origins. The museum continued to attract strong financial support from the wealthy and installed the much-appreciated Hayden Planetarium. The team of curators and designers provided ever more authentic and telling exhibits, and school programs broadened in their appeal. Still, the museum's chief function remained research; its 23 million specimens were under study by a large staff of scientists, while its expeditions constantly brought in more materials.[45]

The late Margaret Mead, the museum's well-known anthropologist, thought that the museum existed for the children and ideally should be planned for twelve-year-olds. But she valued its research function also when she said: "The Museum is an old-fashioned institution, though up-to-date in relation to the media. Nobody is here just to make money. . . . Most of the curators could get better paying jobs elsewhere, and some of them have, but the ethos is so good that not many are tempted. The Museum gives you great intellectual independence."[46]

Visiting the museum today, Mead might not recognize some exhibition halls such as the Hall of Biodiversity that surrounds visitors with evidence of the earth's diversity and the impact of evolution on development. Rather than the narrative messages of the exhibit halls dedicated to particular places, exhibitions now transcend those designations and provide visitors with evidence of the world's complexities and interconnectedness. In addition to reinstallations of the "old halls" the museum offers visitors IMAX theater presentations, a "walk-in" butterfly conservatory, and changing exhibits from across the globe. In 2000 the building itself expanded to the north with the glass cube surrounding the sphere of the Hayden Planetarium in the new Rose Center for Earth and Space to provide visitors with the largest, most powerful virtual reality simulator experience of the universe and Earth's role within it. The "natural" in the museum's name has expanded exponentially from the 18th-century Enlightenment notions of classifying and creating rational order for the universe.[47]

Museum director Ellen Futter describes the museum's commitment this way: "[B]iodiversity . . . is foursquare what natural history museums are all about: the natural world and humanity's place within it. . . . Natural history museums . . . support enormous collections and large scientific staffs that are not typically fostered elsewhere. The formidable scientific research produced by the scientists from those collections and their allied field work provide both a standard for assessing the scale of historical changes affecting habitats and insights into the use of species as indicators of the health of the environment. This research has immediate relevance to many conservation measures and policies."[48]

Field Museum of Natural History

A third great American natural history museum is the result of another world's fair—the World's Columbian Exposition of 1893 in Chicago. Frederick Ward Putnam, curator of the Peabody Museum at Harvard, in 1891 was appointed to head the Department of Anthropology for the exposition, and he urged that the collections shown there become a permanent museum to be known as the Columbian Museum of Chicago. For two years Putnam and his assistants carried out excavation, collecting, and research from Greenland to Tierra del Fuego that brought anthropological and ethnographic materials to the exposition. Putnam also secured a great collection of minerals, skeletons, mastodon bones, and mounted mammals and birds from Ward's Natural Science Establishment of Rochester, New York.

When Marshall Field, the merchant prince, was asked to give money for the proposed museum, he said: "I don't know anything about a museum and I don't care to know anything about a museum. I'm not going to give you a million dollars." But Edward E. Ayer, an incorporator and the first president, convinced Field that his gift would bring him a kind of immortality, so that he changed his mind and gave 1 million dollars; other wealthy patrons contributed nearly five hundred thousand dollars. The articles of incorporation of 1893 defined the museum's purpose as "the accumulation and dissemination of knowledge, and the preservation and exhibition of objects illustrating Art, Archaeology, Science and History." Putnam secretly hoped to become the director, but was passed over in favor of Dr. Frederick J. V. Skiff, who had been chief of the exposition's Department of Mines and Mining.[49]

The new museum, opened in 1894 in the Palace of Fine Arts building of the exposition in Jackson Park, has been generously supported by the elite of Chicago, and the Park District paid maintenance and security expenses through taxation. Marshall Field eventually gave the museum 9 million dollars; his nephew Stanley Field was its president for fifty-six years and contributed 2 million dollars; and his grandson Marshall Field III bestowed another 9 million dollars. The museum's name was changed to the Field Museum of Natural History in 1905 and moved into a mammoth white marble building in Grant Park along the lakeshore in 1921.

The museum has four main departments—anthropology, botany, geology, and zoology—and issues scholarly research publications known as *Fieldiana* in each area. Its scientific expeditions are outstanding and numerous; in 1929, for example, seventeen expeditions included Eastern Asia (with Theodore Roosevelt Jr. and Kermit Roosevelt), the Pacific (on Cornelius Crane's yacht, the *Elyria*), West Africa, the South Pacific, the Amazon, Mesopotamia (the Field Museum–Oxford University Expedition to Kish), Abyssinia, the Arctic, British Honduras, and the Bahamas.

Many of the museum's exhibits are world famous, as, for example, Malvina Hoffman's 1930s life-size bronze sculptures of the races of mankind and the more recently exhibited *Tyrannosaurus rex*, "Sue," the most complete such skeleton on view. Today one can visit the museum's exhibitions online, "traveling" through the museum's halls by type of collection or by geographic location. And, one may even check in on the museum's expeditions and their current research "finds" through Web connections. Beginning in 1997, the museum created the "Center for Cultural Understanding and Change" following the popular *Living Together Exhibition* that addressed contemporary cultural attitudes. The center's programs focus on Chicago and its environs as venues for cultural understanding. Together with twenty-one cultural organizations ranging from the Chicago Historical Society to the Korean American Cultural Resource Center, the Field has built up a Cultural Diversity Network for both research and public programs. The center's Urban Research Initiative (URI) employs college-age interns to research issues of cultural diversity and change, using the tools of "urban anthropology" in the Field Museum's own neighborhoods. These efforts confirm one of the museum's mottoes that "a living museum is never finished." As its website declared in 2005: "The Museum invites its visitors, and all the other communities it serves, to use these rich [anthropology] collections not only as a window on the past but also as a framework for imaginative yet practical solutions to the challenges of the future."[50]

Anthropological Museums

A word should be said here about the placement of collections of anthropology, archaeology, and ethnology in museums. Sometimes encyclopedic or universal museums such as the British Museum, the

Louvre, the Metropolitan Museum of Art, and the Museum of Fine Arts, Boston, possess important antiquities and ethnological materials. Many natural history museums contain such objects, as, for example, the three American museums we have just discussed. Other museums are devoted primarily to the anthropological field. Outstanding among them are the National Museum of Ethnology in Leiden, the Musee de l'Homme in Paris, and the National Museum of Anthropology in Mexico City.

The Leiden museum was founded in 1837 by Dr. F. B. von Siebold, who had lived in Japan and gathered an ethnographic collection of some five thousand objects. The museum suffered for a century because of inadequate housing, but slowly accumulated an important collection of materials from outside the European and classic regions. Transfers from the Royal Cabinet of Rarities, the International Colonial Exhibition held at Amsterdam in 1883, and the National Museum of Antiquities greatly strengthened the museum's holdings. In 1939 it was able to expand its exhibits as a result of acquiring the former building of the University Hospital. Its chief strengths lie in materials from Japan, China, Indonesia, Oceania, India, the Near East, Africa (including Benin bronze heads), America (Peruvian pottery and the Mayan so-called Leiden plate), Java, Tibet, and Siberia. Its dramatic presentation of Buddha on display in a stark gallery is most noteworthy. As the 21st century opened, the museum was fully renovated and adopted a global perspective seeking not only to link with the Indonesian National Museum but also to host a computer-based network of Asian-European Museums (ASEMUS) to encourage collections information sharing. In addition to its long tradition of exhibitions, the museum has extended its reach to cultural minorities throughout Europe through "global experiences" that combine the museum's exhibitions with art, literature, theater, and music events.[51]

The Musee de l'Homme in Paris is an offshoot of the Museum National d'Histoire Naturelle. Its founder, anthropologist Paul Rivet coined the name for the new museum; he believed that "humanity is an indivisible whole, in space and in time," and that scholarship should break down the barriers of political geography and synthesize the artificial classifications of physical anthropology, prehistory, archaeology, ethnology, folklore, sociology, and philology. The Musee de l'Homme opened in 1938 in the Palais de Chailot that had been built for the world's fair of 1937. The museum has been innovative in its exhibits, using sound ethnography and aesthetic display but subordinating them to the exposition of anthropological theory. It seeks to illustrate the function of the objects against the total background of the culture. The museum has been undergoing major renovations of its physical plant and exhibitions. The African, Oceanic, and Asian artworks and collections from the Musee de l'Homme and the Musee des Arts Africains et Oceaniens moved across the Seine in 2006 to the architecturally striking Musee du Quai Branly. The installation has been criticized as focusing more on the aesthetic appeal of the objects as spotlit artworks than on their ethnographic content and context, although the installation does reflect context through evocative scenic backdrops and dramatic lighting.[52]

One of the greatest museums of the world is the National Museum of Anthropology in Mexico City, opened at Chapultepec Park in 1964 and recently renovated, an architectural triumph reminiscent of the ancient Mayan governor's Palace in Uxmal with an imposing interior patio and pool dominated by a vast umbrella fountain from which falls a curtain of water. The building is set in a handsome park, and from the interior visitors can see gardens and exciting outdoor exhibits that they may inspect, such as a colossal Olmec stone head from LaVenta or the reconstructed Mayan temple of Hochob. Near the entrance is an imposing twenty-three-foot-high ancient statue of the rain god Tlaloc that weighs 168 tons.

The museum has two floors of display rooms, the first devoted to anthropology and archaeology. In the Mexica Room, for example, are Coatlicue ("Goddess of the Serpent Skirt"); the Sun Stone ("Aztec Calendar"), twelve feet in diameter; and the Stone of Tizoc. These three huge monoliths, found in Mexico City about 1790, inspired official collection of antiquities. In addition to original artifacts, the museum has ingenious and artistic displays, such as the spectacular diorama of the Market of Tlatelolco with hundreds of authentically modeled miniature figures in an area measuring thirty by twelve feet or the setting of the Pakal tomb in the Mayan Room. Also on the first floor visitors see all kinds of archaeological remains, from prehistoric times to the most recent cultures before Columbian times, and representing all regions of the country.

The second floor of the museum is devoted to ethnology with buildings, furnishings, tools, and costumes of the different cultures of Mexico as they exist today. Not only did the anthropologists, archaeologists, architects, and artists co-operate in the creation of this museum, but humble skilled craftsmen from different cultures also came to build the ethnographic displays—until they were complete, actually living in the museum. The result of all this scientific, artistic, and practical effort is a museum of breathtaking beauty that serves as a scientific anthropological center for all of Mexico.[53]

Whither Natural History and Anthropology Museums?

Museum scholar and critic Paula Findlen writes: "The openness of eighteenth-century cultural institutions contributed significantly to the redefinition of natural history. As museums became more of a public phenomenon, learned practitioners took greater pains to differentiate themselves from the unlearned audience who exhibited only curiosity and not virtuosity. . . . Curiosity was no longer a valued premise for intellectual inquiry but rather the mark of an 'amateur.' . . . Lamarck differentiated the 'cabinet of curiosity' from the 'cabinet of natural history' to underscore their diverse purposes; the former for amusement and the latter for the progress of sciences."[54] To close this discussion, can the late 19th century be considered the heyday of natural history and anthropology museums? At that time imperialism and colonialism brought to these museums objects for study and exhibition. Add to these phenomena growing urbanism and the "back to nature" movement that sought to promote nature to protect citizens from the negative effects of cities. The popularity of world's fairs and their use of dioramas meant that these museums adapted these techniques to their exhibition halls and, often located in city centers, emerged as institutions able to both entertain and educate the public.

Since that time, the world has continued to shrink. Travel, communication, and growing empowerment of the world's peoples have meant that the authority once proclaimed in natural history and anthropological museums has become at best dated and to some offensive. One example of this sea of change can be found at the Smithsonian Institution on the National Mall in Washington, D.C. On the mall's northern boundary stands the 1911 National Museum of Natural History and less than a quarter of a mile southeast is the 2004 National Museum of the American Indian. The former contains all the elements of a 21st-century natural history museum with 19th-century roots, including galleries that represent the continent's earliest inhabitants. Across the mall, the American Indian Museum is described by its director as a "museum different," stepping away from previous forms. The museum's formal mission statement begins: "[The Museum] shall recognize and affirm to Native communities and the non-Native public the historical and contemporary culture and cultural achievements of the Natives of the Western Hemisphere by advancing—in consultation, collaboration, and cooperation with Natives—knowledge and understanding of Native cultures."[55]

As the 18th-century cabinet collections changed from the "curious" and "exotic" to scientific specimens to be studied, the ethnographic museum form, at least at the National Museum of the American Indian, strove to give voice to its subjects in a manner unprecedented. The objects' owners and their heirs participated in interpretive decision making, changing the nature of the museum's relation between its collections and audiences. The installations supplied functional context for native objects with multimedia narratives supplied by collaborating National American sources supplementing large photographic backdrops. Today, although there are few displays of numerous objects of similar type, there is more emphasis on visual excitement than on an investigation of function, as in an array of projectile points with identifying information on a nearby touch screen, but without a comparison among examples from, for example, Plains or Eastern Woodland types. Even the museum's name suggests this new balance. And across the Atlantic, the Musee du Quai Branly offers a similar approach to public exhibition of ethnographic objects, but without the involvement of relevant communities.[56]

Challenges

Scientists in Museums

When the early natural history museums were established, they served as centers of scientific work. Their expeditions added to human knowledge of the natural world and brought in vast collections of specimens. Their staffs described and classified these ever-increasing materials, and Darwin's theory of evolution provided a rational framework to explain the whole. Today, however, the study of nature and life has moved in many directions and technology has altered the scientists' reliance on museum specimens. The same is true for students of cultural anthropology. These scientists have a greater need for field studies and laboratories than for museum collections and tend to work for scientific agencies or universities. Michael Ames offers three reasons for the lack of scholarly involvement with museums (and their collections): "First, many items are not worth studying anyway, either because they are intrinsically uninteresting or because they lack sufficient data concerning provenance, function, or meaning. Second, many museums, ironically, offer meager facilities to researchers and some seem to discourage visiting scholars. . . . Third is the absence of important theoretical issues in material culture studies."[57]

Nineteenth-century Forms in Twenty-first-century Institutions

Scholar Carol Yanni writes: "Since biologists tend to study living organisms in the laboratory or in the field, they do not need museums as nineteenth-century paleontologists and taxonomists did. . . . Scientists determined the way their discipline was presented to the public and, not surprisingly, museums represented the interests of science. Rather than admit their obsolescence (or possible estrangement from the biological sciences), natural history museums have shifted their focus to educating the public about conservation. Their role in research has been pushed, literally, to the back room." And, National Museum of Natural History former assistant director for public programs Robert Sullivan confirms: "In the same way that the vertical, evolutionary paradigm became the skeletal framework for natural history museums in the 19th and 20th centuries, the horizontal, interconnected, 'ecosystem' paradigm may serve the 21st-century natural history museum. We must reconnect our collections, exhibitions, and interpretive programs and take steps to synthesize the fragmented, isolated and specialized knowledge that characterized preceding natural history museums."[58]

Museum Expeditions for Science and Profit?

Nineteenth-century natural history museums sponsored expeditions to "the holy lands" and other exotic venues, returning with objects to enrich their exhibition halls. Today, that process has evolved into a growing tourism opportunity where everyday citizens can dig in the mountains of Peru or join groups tracking migration patterns of animals of all stripes. The natural history museum literally opens the doors of its research laboratories and invites the public to participate in its research efforts (and the public pays the museum to join the process). "Eco-tourism" is good marketing, but is it good science for the museum?

Public Science and Public Entertainment

Visit any natural history museum in a midsize city around the world and most likely you will find multimedia programming (IMAX theaters; screeching, moving dinosaurs; and virtual reality headsets). These new "entertainment" opportunities add to the visitor's museum experience in ways that extend museums' missions and services but should be assessed for their value (as museum programming, educational opportunity, and marketing expense). How do they enhance the natural history museum and its role as a cultural and scientific institution?

Evolution versus Creationism

European and American collectors' early cabinets sought to explain science and beauty, God's plan, and the order of the universe. Darwin's theory of evolution altered the message, but not the desire for order. Today, interpretations of evolution continue to affect natural history museum displays and interpretation. American "creationists" have raised their voices within community discussions, pressuring natural history museums to represent evolution as simply one theory. The American Museum of Natural History catalog states [n.d.]: "The view of evolutionary history seen in these halls represents the best interpretation of the available evidence according to researchers at the American Museum of Natural History. These views like all scientific ideas are subject to change and refinement. Further research and the discovery of new fossils may well modify our present understanding."[59]

American Museum of Natural History astrophysicist and director of the Hayden Planetarium Neil deGrasse Tyson writes: "Science is a philosophy of discovery. Intelligent design is a philosophy of ignorance. You cannot build a program of discovery on the assumption that nobody is smart enough to figure out the answer to a problem. Once upon a time, people identified the god Neptune as the source of storms at sea. Today we call these storms hurricanes. We know when and where they start. We know what drives them. We know what mitigates their destructive power."[60]

Notes

1. "Forum," *Museum News* 76, no. 6 (November–December 1997): 48.

2. Georges-Henri Riviere, *Museum International* 53, no. 4 (2001): 33.

3. Michael M. Ames, *Cannibal Tours and Glass Boxes: The Anthropology of Museums*, Vancouver, Canada: University of British Columbia Press, 1992, p. 23.

4. Paula Findlen, *Possessing Nature: Museums, Collecting and Scientific Culture in Early Modern Italy*, Berkeley: University of California Press, 1994, p. 398; Eilean Hooper-Greenhill, *Museums and the Shaping of Knowledge*, London: Routledge, 1994.

5. Don D. Fowler and David R.Wilcox, eds., *Philadelphia and the Development of American Archaeology*, Tuscaloosa: University of Alabama Press, 2003, p. xii; David Hurst Thomas, "The First American Archaeologist," chap. 3 in *Skull Wars: Kennewick Man, Archaeology and the Battle for Native American Identity*, New York: Basic Books, 2000.

6. Charles Willson Peale, *A Walk through the Philadelphia Museum*, Philadelphia, 1892, pp. 6–7.

7. David Murray, *Museums: Their History and Their Use*, 3 vols., Glasgow, 1904, 1:45–73 (includes a bibliography and list of museums in the UK); Alma S. Wittlin, *Museums: In Search of a Usable Future*, Cambridge, MA: MIT Press, 1970, pp. 17–22; P. J. P. Whitehead, "Museums in the History of Zoology," *Museums Journal* 70 (1970–1971): 51.

8. Renato Berzaghi, *The Palazzo Ducale in Mantua*, Milan, Italy: Electa, 1992, pp. 7, 49–50.

9. Murray, *Museums*, 1:25, 27, 78–80; Wittlin, *Museums: In Search*, pp. 39–53; Whitehead, "Museums in the History of Zoology," pp. 51–52; Silvio A. Bedini, "The Evolution of Science Museums," *Technology and Culture* 5 (1965): 2–6, 11–12; Germain Bazin, *The Museum Age*, New York: Universe Books, 1967, pp. 62, 144; Willy Ley, *Dawn of Zoology*, Englewood Cliffs, NJ, 1968, pp. 121–161, 268–273; Giuseppe Olmi, "Science-Honor-Metaphor: Italian Cabinets of the 16th and 17th Centuries," in *Grasping the World: The Idea of the Museum*, eds. Donald Preziosi and Claire Farago, Hants, UK: Ashgate, 2004.

10. Murray, *Museums*, 1:95–96, 103–104, 115–117; Whitehead, "Museums in the History of Zoology," p. 52; Bedini, "The Evolution," pp. 2–6; Holger Jacobaeus, *Museum Regium, seu Catalogus rerum*, Hafniae, 1696.

11. Bedini, "The Evolution," pp. 4–6, 11–17; Murray, *Museums*, 1:2, 106–107; Findlen, *Possessing Nature*, p. 407.

12. Bazin, *The Museum Age*, p. 115; Wittlin, *Museums: In Search*, pp. 64–65; Bedini, "The Evolution," pp. 25–26; Murray, *Museums*, 1:205–230.

13. Stephen Asma, *Stuffed Animals and Pickled Heads: The Culture and Evolution of Natural History Museums*, Oxford, UK: Oxford University Press, 2001.

14. Edward P. Alexander, "Carl Ethan Akeley," in *The Museum in America: Innovators and Pioneers*, Walnut Creek, CA: AltaMira Press, 1997, pp. 33–49; James Kelly, "Gallery of Discovery," *Museum News* 70, no. 2 (March–April 1991): 49–52.

15. F. A. Lucas, *Fifty Years of Museum Work*, in *Habitat Dioramas: Illusions of Wilderness in Museums of Natural History*, by Karen Wonders, Uppsala, Sweden: Acta Universitatis Upsaliensis, 1993, p. 123; Diorama defined by *Encyclopedia Britannica* (1981, p. 15): "A diorama is an adaptation of the panorama; an illusionistic spectacle of reality consisting of real objects that blend into a large painted landscape."

16. Robert Theodore Gunther, *Early Science in Oxford*, 15 vols., Oxford, 1923–1967, 1:43–47 and 3:280–333, 346–366, 391–447; Mea Allan, *The Tradescants: Their Plants, Gardens and Museum, 1570–1662*, London, 1964; Bazin, *The Museum Age*, pp. 141, 144–145; Whitehead, "Museums in the History of Zoology," pp. 54–55; Murray, *Museums*, 1:107–111; Ley, *Dawn of Zoology*, pp. 202–203; Ashmolean Museum, University of Oxford, *Treasures of the Ashmolean Museum: An Illustrated Souvenir of Art, Archaeology and Numismatics*, Oxford, 1970, pp. ii–iii, no. 24; F. J. North, "On Learning How to Run a Museum," *Museums Journal* 51 (April 1951): 4–5; (June 1951): 63–66; D. B. Harden, "The Ashmolean Museum—Beaumont Street," *Museums Journal* 52 (February 1952): 265–270.

17. Edward P. Alexander, "Sir Hans Sloane and the British Museum," in *Museum Masters*, pp. 19–42; G. R. de Beer, *Sir Hans Sloane and the British Museum*, London, 1953, pp. 13–49, 50–95, 108–134, 138–139, 143–153, 160–161; E. St. John Brooks, *Sir Hans Sloane: The Great Collector and His Circle*, London, 1954, pp. 13–77, 78–118, 176–201, 209–210, 218–223; Edward Miller, *That Noble Cabinet: A History of the British Museum*, Athens, OH, 1974, pp. 26, 36–39, 41, 42–46, 70–71, 74, 77–79, 86–87, 92; J. Mordaunt Crook, *The British Museum*, London: Praeger, 1972, pp. 42–49, 52–54, 65–66; Murray, *Museums*, 1:127–144, 171–172; Kenneth Hudson, *A Social History of Museums: What the Visitors Thought*, Atlantic Highlands, NJ: Humanities Press, 1975, pp. 8–10, 18–21, 38, 40; Frank Charlton Francis, *Treasures of the British Museum*, London, 1967, p. 10; James Britten, *The Sloane Herbarium*, rev. and ed. J. E. Dandy, London: British Museum, 1958; Henry C. Shelley, *The British Museum: Its History and Treasures*, Boston, 1911, pp. 59–62; Wittlin, *Museums: In Search*, pp. 102–105; Kelly Elizabeth Yasaitis, "Collecting Culture and the British Museum," *Curator* 49, no. 4 (October 2006).

18. Miller, *That Noble Cabinet*, pp. 74–76, 85–86, 96–108, 111–115, 191–223, 299–320, 327, 336–339, 355–356; Crook, *British Museum*, pp. 62, 66–71, 118, 128, 216, 226–229; Francis, *Treasures of the British Museum*, pp. 22, 25; Hermann Justus Braunholtz, *Sir Hans Sloane and Ethnography*, London, 1970, pp. 19–20, 37–45; Hudson, *Social History of Museums*, pp. 39–40.

19. www.thebritishmuseum.ac.uk.

20. Miller, *That Noble Cabinet*, pp. 224–244; Crook, *British Museum*, pp. 199–200; Edward Edwards, *Lives of the Founders of the British Museum: With Notices of Its Chief Augmentors and Other Benefactors, 1570–1870*, 1870, reprint, New York, 1969, pp. 333–336, 487–510, 601–607; Francis, *Treasures of the British Museum*, pp. 14–15, 20–21; Karl P. Schmidt, "The Nature of the Natural History Museum," *Curator* 1 (January 1958): 23; William Henry Flower, *Essays on Museums and Other Subjects Connected with Natural History*, New York, 1898, pp. 15–22, 37–41; James A. Bateman, "The Functions of Museums in Biology," *Museums Journal* 74 (March 1975): 159–164; William T. Stearn, *The Natural History Museum at South Kensington*, London: Heinemann, 1981.

21. www.nhm.ac.uk.

22. W. H. Mullens, "Some Museums of Old London: I. The Leverian Museum; II. William Bullock's London Museum," *Museums Journal* 15 (1915–1916): 120–129,

162–172; 17 (1917–1918): 51–56, 132–137, 180–187; Hugh Honour, "Curiosities of the Egyptian Hall," *Country Life* 115 (1954): 38–39; Whitehead, "Museums in the History of Zoology," pp. 156–159; Murray, *Museum*, 1:175–179; Hudson, *Social History of Museums*, pp. 17–18, 24–26.

23. Whitehead, "Museums in the History of Zoology," p. 156; Flower, *Essays on Museums*, pp. 41–47; Rene Taton, ed., *History of Science*, 3 vols., New York, 1963–1965, 3:325–326; *Museums of the World: A Directory of 17,000 Museums in 48 Countries*, compiled by Eleanor Braun, New York, 1973, pp. 78–79; *Guide des Musees de France*, Fribourg, 1970, pp. 136–137; *Blue Guide: Paris*, London, 1968, pp. 108–110; *Libraire Larousse, Dictionnaire de Paris*, Paris, 1964, pp. 285–286, 358; Murray, *Museums*, 2:93; Hermann Heinrich Frese, *Anthropology and the Public: The Role of Museums*, Leiden: E. J. Brill, 1960, pp. 20, 26–29; Paul Lemoine, "National Museum of Natural History . . . Paris," *Natural History Magazine* (London) 5 (January 1935): 4–19; Bateman, "Museums in Biology," p. 161; Asma, *Stuffed Animals and Pickled Heads*, pp. 82–86, 170–178; Jacques Maigret, "Aesthetics in the Service of Science: The Grande Galerie de l'Evolution in Paris," *Museum* 48, no. 2 (1996); Michael A. Osborne, "Zoos in the Family," Robert J. Hoage and William A. Deiss, eds., *New Worlds, New Animals: From Menagerie to Zoological Park in the Nineteenth Century*, Baltimore, MD: Johns Hopkins University Press, 1996, pp. 33–38.

24. Flower, *Essays on Museums*, pp. 41–47; *Museums of the World*, p. 21; Murray, *Museums*, 2:245–246; Karl Baedeker, *Austria Handbook for Travelers*, 12th ed., Leipzig, 1929, pp. 103–108.

25. Maria Luisa Azzarol Puccetti, "La Specola, the Zoological Museum of the University of Florence," *Curator* 15 (1972): 93–112; Bazin, *The Museum Age*, p. 163.

26. Laura M. Bragg, "The Birth of the Museum Idea in America," *Charleston Museum Quarterly* 1 (First Quarter 1923): 3–13; Paul M. Rea, "A Contribution to Early Museum History in America," *American Association of Museums Proceedings* 9 (1915): 53–65; William G. Mazyck, *The Charleston Museum: Its Genesis and Development*, Charleston, 1908, pp. 5, 28; Hudson, *Social History of Museums*, pp. 31–33.

27. Steven Conn, *Museums and American Intellectual Life, 1876–1926*, Chicago: University of Chicago Press, 1998, pp. 35–37, 38–43, 45–47; Joel J. Orosz, *Curators and Culture: The Museum Movement in America, 1740–1870*, Tuscaloosa: University of Alabama Press, 1990, pp. 119–127, 187–195; Fowler and Wilcox, *Philadelphia*; Patricia M. Williams, *Museums of Natural History and the People Who Work in Them*, New York: St. Martins, 1973.

28. William E. Lingelbach, "An Early American Historian," in *Bookmen's Holiday: Notes and Studies Written and Gathered in Tribute to Harry Miller Lydenberg*, New York: New York Public Library, 1943, pp. 355–361; Hans Huth, "Pierre Eugene du Simitiere and the Beginnings of the American Historical Museum," *Pennsylvania Magazine of History and Biography* 69 (October 1945): 315–325; Charles Coleman Sellers, *Charles Willson Peale*, New York: Scribner, pp. 203–211; Edward P. Alexander, "Charles Willson Peale," in *Museum Masters*, pp. 43–78; E. P. Alexander, "Bringing History to Life: Philadelphia and Williamsburg," *Cu-*

rator 4 (1961): 61; Hudson, *Social History of Museums*, pp. 33–36; Sellers, *Peale*, pp. 212–217, 219, 221–222, 230, 241, 264–265, 281, 293–301, 303, 333, 335, 340–341.

29. Sellers, *Peale*, pp. 245, 256, 331, 337, 350–351, 380, 386, 394, 401, 408.

30. Orosz, *Curators and Culture*, pp. 75–80.

31. P. T. Barnum, *Struggles and Triumphs: Or, Forty Years' Recollections of P. T. Barnum Written by Himself*, [1869] New York, 1930, pp. 66–73, 74, 84, 102–103, 105–106, 180–181, 251–252, 392, 406–409; John Rickards Betts, "P. T. Barnum and the Popularization of Natural History," *Journal of the History of Ideas* 20 (1959): 353–368; Morris Robert Werner, *Barnum*, New York, 1923, pp. 43–50, 235–252; Neil Harris, *Humbug: The Art of P. T Barnum*, Boston, 1973, pp. 33–57.

32. Barnum, *Struggles and Triumphs*, pp. 465–475, 514–517; Werner, *Barnum*, pp. 302–303; Betts, "Barnum and Popularization," pp. 357–368.

33. Paul H. Oehser, *The Smithsonian Institution*, New York, 1970, pp. 3–25; Walter Karp, *The Smithsonian: An Establishment for the Increase and Diffusion of Knowledge among Men*, Washington, DC, 1965, pp. 7–19; Geoffrey T. Hellman, *The Smithsonian: Octopus on the Mall*, Philadelphia: Lippincott, 1967, pp. 26–55; Wilcomb E. Washburn, "Joseph Henry's Conception of the Purpose of the Smithsonian Institution," in *A Cabinet of Curiosities: Five Episodes in the Evolution of American Museums*, by Whitfield J. Bell Jr. et al., Charlottesville, VA, 1967, pp. 106–166; Curtis M. Hinsley, "Magnificent Intentions: Washington, DC and American Anthropology in 1846," in *Museum Studies: An Anthology of Contexts*, ed. Bettina Messias Carbonell, London: Blackwell, 2004; Ellis E. Yochelson, *The National Museum of Natural History: 75 Years in the New Museum*, Washington, DC: Smithsonian Press, 1985.

34. Washburn, "Joseph Henry's Conception," pp. 106–108.

35. Oehser, *The Smithsonian*, pp. 26–40; Karp, *The Smithsonian*, pp. 19–27; Hellman, *The Smithsonian*, pp. 56–58; Washburn, "Joseph Henry's Conception," pp. 108–166.

36. Oehser, *The Smithsonian*, pp. 40–44; Karp, *The Smithsonian*, pp. 29–43; Hellman, *The Smithsonian*, pp. 89–116; Washburn, "Joseph Henry's Conception," pp. 129–152; James M. Goode, "A View from the Castle," *Museum News* 54 (July–August 1976): 38–45.

37. Oehser, *The Smithsonian*, pp. 44–47; Karp, *The Smithsonian*, pp. 76–80; Hellman, *The Smithsonian*, pp. 94–95, 97, 198; G. Carroll Lindsay, "George Brown Goode," in *Keepers of the Past*, ed. Clifford L. Lord, Chapel Hill, NC, 1965, pp. 127–140 (see also "A Memorial of George Brown Goode" in *Annual Report of the Board of Regents of the Smithsonian Institution for the Year Ending June 30, 1897: Report of the U.S. National Museum, Part II*, Washington, DC: Smithsonian Institution, 1901); Robert C. Post, ed., *National Museum of History and Technology, 1876: A Centennial Exhibition*, Washington, DC, 1976, pp. 11–23; Edward P. Alexander, "George Brown Goode and the Smithsonian Museums," in *Museum Masters*, pp. 277–310.

38. Ellis L. Yochelson, "More than 150 years of Administrative Ups and Downs for Natural History in Washington," *Proceedings of California Academy of Sciences*, vol. 55, supp. I, art. 6, pp. 113–176; Oehser, *The Smithsonian*, pp. 87–95;

Karp, *The Smithsonian*, pp. 44–49; Hellman, *The Smithsonian*, pp. 198–201, 207–208, 215–216; 2003 Collections Statistics, National Collections Program, Smithsonian Institution Archives. Today there are seventeen Smithsonian museums located in the Washington, D.C., area (there are two in New York): the National Museum of American History (1964 as Museum of History and Technology); the National Air and Space Museum (1976); the Steven Udvar-Hazy Center (2004); the National Zoological Park (1887); the Freer Gallery of Art (1906); the National Collection of Fine Arts (1846), today the Smithsonian American Art Museum; the National Portrait Gallery (1962); the Joseph H. Hirshhorn Museum and Sculpture Garden (1966); the Arthur M. Sackler Gallery (1989); the National Museum of African Art (1989); the National Postal Museum (1993); the Anacostia Neighborhood Museum (1967), today the Anacostia Museum and Center for African American History and Culture. The Cooper-Hewitt Museum (1967) is in New York City and the National Museum of the American Indian has buildings in both New York (1990) and Washington (2004). Nominal bureaus of the Smithsonian, but with their own boards and financing, are the National Gallery of Art (1941) and the John F. Kennedy Center for the Performing Arts (1958); www.si.edu.

39. Oehser, *The Smithsonian*, pp. 72–86, 203–217, 225–232; Karp, *The Smithsonian*, pp. 119–125.

40. Tony Bennett, *Pasts beyond Memory: Evolution, Museums and Colonialism*, London: Routledge, 2004, chap. 5; Geoffrey T. Hellman, *Bankers, Bones and Beetles: The First Century of the American Museum of Natural History*, New York: Natural History Press, 1969, pp. 9–28; *Natural History: The Journal of the American Museum* 30 (September–October 1930): 452; Donna Haraway, "Teddy Bear Patriarchy: Taxidermy in the Garden of Eden, New York City, 1908–1936," in *Primate Visions: Gender, Race and Nature in the World of Modern Science*, London: Routledge, 1989.

41. Hellman, *Bankers, Bones, and Beetles*, p. 28; pp. 35–36; *Natural History* 27 (July–August 1927): 309–391.

42. Hellman, *Bankers, Bones and Beetles*, pp. 57–115.

43. Douglas J. Preston, *Dinosaurs in the Attic: An Excursion to the American Museum of Natural History*, New York: St. Martin's, 1986; Alexander, "Henry Fairfield Osborn," pp. 19–31; Alexander, "Carl Ethan Akeley," in *The Museum in America*, pp. 42–45.

44. Hellman, *Bankers, Bones, and Beetles*, pp. 117–206; *Natural History* 30 (September–October 1930): 451–525.

45. Hellman, *Bankers, Bones, and Beetles*, pp. 207–244; Geoffrey T. Hellman, "The Hidden Museum," *New Yorker*, May 19, 1975, pp. 42–74.

46. Hellman, *Bankers, Bones, and Beetles*, p. 256.

47. www.amnh.si.edu.

48. Ellen V. Futter, "Toward a Natural History Museum for the 21st Century," *Museum News* 76, no. 6 (November–December 1997): 41.

49. Ralph W. Dexter, "The Role of F. W. Putnam in Founding the Field Museum," *Curator* 13 (1970): 21–26; George A. Dorsey, "The Department of An-

thropology of the Field Columbian Museum—A Review of Six Years," *American Anthropologist*, n.s., 2 (1900): 247–265; Field Museum of Natural History, *Annual Report of the Director to the Board of Trustees*, 1960, Chicago: Field Museum of Natural History, 1961; Donald Collier, "Chicago Comes of Age: The World's Columbian Exposition and the Birth of the Field Museum," *Field Museum Bulletin* (May 1969): 2–7; "The Museum's First Million," *Field Museum Bulletin* (August 1970): 13–15.

50. Chesly Manly, "One Billion Years on Our Doorstep" Six Articles on the Chicago Natural History Museum Reprinted from the *Chicago Tribune*, Chicago, 1959, pp. 17–22; Field Museum, *Annual Report of Director* (for the years 1911, 1926, 1929, 1940), Chicago, IL: Field Museum, 1912, 1927, 1930, 1941; John R. Millar, "1921–1961: 40 Years Recalled," *Field Museum Bulletin* (May 1961): 6–7; "Stanley Field, 1875–1964," *Field Museum Bulletin* (December 1964): 2–3, 8; E. Leland Webber, "Field Museum Again: Name Change Honors Field Family," *Field Museum Bulletin* (March 1966): 203; Joyce Zibro, "About Field Museum," *Field Museum Bulletin* (October 1971): 2–8; www.thefieldmuseum.org.

51. Frese, *Anthropology and the Public*, pp. 7, 12, 24, 28, 134–136, 163, 183–186; P. H. Pott, *National Museum of Ethnology, Leiden, 1837–1962*, The Hague, 1962, pp. 1–15; Hudson, *Social History of Museums*, pp. 52–53, 74–75; Robert Goldwater, "The Development of Ethnological Museums," in *Museum Studies*; James Clifford, *The Predicament of Culture: Twentieth-Century Ethnography, Literature, and Art*, Cambridge, MA: Harvard University Press, 1988, pp. 135–141; Fabrice Grognet, "Ethnology: A Science on Display," *Museum* 53, no. 1 (2001): 51–56; Ames, *Cannibal Tours and Glass Boxes*, pp. 165–168; Stanley Freed, "Everyone Is Breathing on Our Vitrines: Problems and Prospects of Museum Anthropology," *Curator* 34, no. 1 (1991): 58–80.

52. Paul Rivet, "Organization of an Ethnological Museum," *Museum* 1 (1948): 113; Clifford, *The Predicament of Culture*; James Clifford, "Museums as Contact Zones," in *Routes, Travel and Translation in the Late 20th Century*, Cambridge, MA: Harvard University Press, 1997; Asma, *Stuffed Animals and Pickled Heads*, p. 167; Goldwater, "The Development of Ethnological Museums"; Alan Riding, "Imperialist? Moi? Not the Musee du Quai Branly," *New York Times*, June 22, 2006; Nicholas Ouroussoff, "For a New Paris Museum, Jean Novel Creates His Own Rules," *New York Times*, June 27, 2006; Michael Kimmelman, "A Heart of Darkness in the City of Light," *New York Times*, July 2, 2006; Caroline Brothers, "For Some, a Museum Hits Close to the Heart," *International Herald Tribune*, August 18, 2006; www.quaibranly.fr.

53. Ignacio Bernal, "The National Museum of Anthropology of Mexico," *Curator* 9, no. 1 (1966); Ignacio Bernal et al., *The Mexican National Museum of Anthropology*, London, 1968; Pedro Ramirez Vasquez et al., *The National Museum of Anthropology, Mexico: Art, Architecture, Anthropology*, New York, 1968; personal correspondence, Lourdes Arizpe and Azedine Beschaouch, "Dialogue on Museum of Civilization," *Museum* (May 2002): 144–148.

54. Findlen, *Possessing Nature*, p. 348; Frese, *Anthropology and the Public*; Ames, *Cannibal Tours and Glass Boxes*, pp. 165–168.

55. www.nmai.si.edu.

56. Edward Rothstein, "Who Should Tell the Story—Indian Tribes or Museums?" *New York Times*, December 21, 2004; Curtis M. Hinsley, "Magnificent Intentions: Washington, DC and American Anthropology in 1846," in *Museum Studies*; George F. MacDonald and Stephen Alsford, *Canadian Museum of Civilization: A Museum for the Global Village*, Canadian Museum of Civilization, 1989; *The Public Historian, A Journal of Public History* 28, no. 2 (Spring 2006) includes a comprehensive review of the National Museum of the American Indian. Commentators include museum staff and museum professionals; Riding, "Imperialist? Moi?"; Helen Rees Leahy, "A World Apart: Musee Quai Branly," in *Museum Practice*, London: Museums Association, Winter 2006, pp. 12–17.

57. Frese, *Anthropology and the Public*; Stephen E. Nash and Gary M. Feinman, eds., "Curators, Collectors and Contexts: Anthropology at the Field Museum 1893–2002," *Fieldiana: Anthropology*, n.s. 36 (2003); Ames, *Cannibal Tours and Glass Boxes*, p. 40.

58. K. Elaine Hoagland, "Socially Responsible" *Museum News* 68, no. 5 (September–October 1989): 50–52; Leonard Krishtalka, "At Natural History Museums, the Ox Is Gored," *Museum News* 82, no. 4 (July–August 2003); Carla Yanni, *Nature's Museums: Victorian Science and the Architecture of Display*, Baltimore, MD: Johns Hopkins University Press, 1999, p. 156; Robert Sullivan, "Trouble in Paradigms," *Museum News* 71, no. 1 (January–February 1992): 41; Peter Davis, *Museums and the Natural Environment: The Role of Natural History Museums in Biological Conservation*, New York: Leicester University Press, 1996.

59. Quoted in Asma, *Stuffed Animals and Pickled Heads*, p. 190.

60. Bennett, *Pasts beyond Memory*; "The Perimeter of Ignorance," *Natural History Magazine*, November 2005; For an overview of current museum trends relating to evolution discussions see *Informal Learning Review* no. 69 (November–December 2004) and Robert "Mac" West, "The Lay of the Land—The Current Context for Communicating Evolution in Natural History Museums," and "Creationism v. Evolution: Origins of a Controversy," *Museum News* 84, no. 4 (July–August 2005): 38–45; Martin Weiss, "Beyond the Evolution Battle: Addressing Public Misunderstanding," *ASTC Dimensions*, March–April 2006; Discussion of *Ktizmiller v. Dover Area School* (2005), *Reports, National Center for Science Education* 26, nos. 1–2, (January–April 2006).

4

Science and Technology Museums and Centers

Technological artifacts . . . suffer from having been wrenched out of contexts that cannot be restored. The structure within which they were used has vanished. Kits of tools have been separated from the men and the shops in which they were used and from the products fabricated, machines from their operators and factories.

—Brooke Hindle, 1983[1]

Explaining science and technology without props can resemble an attempt to tell what it is like to swim without letting a person near the water.

—Frank Oppenheimer, 1968[2]

Showplace for the idea of technological progress, "value free" playground for scientific exploration, or lively forum for learning, controversy and the search for solutions—each of these is a scenario for a contemporary science museum.

—Alice Carnes, 1986[3]

Artificial curiosities in the early collections included a broad spectrum of practical and scientific technology—tools and utensils; locks and keys; lighting devices; clocks and watches; arms, armor, and apparatus of warfare; musical instruments; globes, astrolabes, and navigational devices; machines, automatons, engines, and mechanical models; telescopes, microscopes, and other optical apparatus; magnetic and electrical equipment; and scientific or philosophical apparatus and instruments devoted to mathematics, medicine, astronomy, chemistry, and physics. With the coming of the Industrial Revolution in the 18th century and the advent of the world's fair in the 19th, increased recognition came to the products of man's inventive mind, and museums of technology and science arose. In contrast to natural history museums, science museums sought and exhibited collections relating to technology and the physical sciences.

Some of these museums evolved into science centers, with less emphasis on preserving collections for study and for future generations and more attention on educating the public about science and its principles. Melanie Quin outlines four forms of science centers: "scientists' workshop," "technological trade fair," "historical storehouse," and "adventure playground." She suggests that many centers are a combination of these forms.[4] Others suggest that the term *science center* is more appealing to potential visitors as the word *museum* suggests stodgy halls with static collections while centers are seen as sites for activity and engagement.[5]

The discussion that follows addresses first those museums that have emerged from collections-based institutions, followed by those that originated as science centers, with the emphasis on interactive exhibitions rather than historical collections. Readers should be aware that both of these "types" of institutions are evolving and using techniques from both historical traditions, sometimes in the same galleries.[6]

European Collections of Artificial Curiosities

Medieval and Renaissance collectors usually owned abundant artificial curiosities. Jean de France, duc de Berry, had clocks, mechanisms, and scientific apparatus. Emperor Rudolph II brought to Prague great instrument makers like Erasmus Habermel and Tycho Brahe, as well as the distinguished mathematician Johannes Kepler. Landgrave Wilhelm IV at Kassel collected instruments and studied mathematics and astronomy, while August I in Dresden used his collection to form a scientific research center in the famed Green Vaults of his palace.[7]

Most of the 17th-century Italian scientific centers mentioned in chapter 3 had artificial as well as natural curiosities—Aldrovandi, Cospi, and Marsigli at Bologna; the Medici brothers, Grand Duke Ferdinand

II and Leopold, with their Academia del Cimento (of the Experiment) in Florence; Ludovico and Manfredo Settala, father and son, in Milan; and the Jesuit Kircher in Rome.[8] So did Ole Worm and Christian V in Denmark and the Tradescants and the Royal Society (1662) in London. The Society for the Encouragement of Arts, Manufactures, and Commerce (now the Royal Society of Arts), founded in 1754, eventually placed its collection of models in the Science Museum. The Teyler Stichting (Foundation) established at Haarlem in 1778 had the chemist and electrical experimenter Martin van Marum as its first director and still contains his great electrostatic machine of 1784.[9]

Conservatoire National des Arts et Metiers

In the 17th century René Descartes suggested that the French government collect models of inventions for the instruction of artisans, but it was not until 1794 that the revolutionary National Assembly established the Conservatoire National des Arts et Metiers (CNAM). This public depository of machines, inventions, models, tools, drawings, descriptions, and books on the applied arts and trades was housed in the buildings of the old Priory of Saint-Martin-des-Champs in Paris. The machines and models collected by the great engineer and inventor Jacques Vaucanson and by the Academie Royale des Sciences (1666) were the core of the collection that grew rapidly during the last half of the 19th century and received much material from the various universal exhibitions. The chief divisions of the collection were physics, electrical industries, geometry, weights and measures, mechanics and machines, transportation, chemical industries, mining and metallurgy, graphic arts, textile arts, arts of construction, and agriculture, and later industrial accident prevention and industrial hygiene. As early as 1819, the conservatoire hired professors to give courses on applying science to arts and industries that in one year in the 1860s enrolled 177,000 persons. About 1900, laboratories were established to test scientific apparatus, building materials, machines, and vegetable substances. The conservatoire also published a six-volume catalog of its holdings, between 1905 and 1910.

This educational emphasis remains today with CNAM providing courses for students whether enrolled in formal educational programs or simply adults—especially workers—interested in learning about technology. Additionally the conservatoire maintains a central Paris museum and a library rich with materials relating to technology and industrial design. The modern museum, artfully fitted into the ancient Merovingian site, features early aircraft, including the first helicopter; automobiles; the origins of photography; motion pictures; radio and television; radar and the laser; and modern technology. It reports a collection of eighty thousand objects and 150,000 industrial designs. Its displays complement older rarities such as the ornamental turning lathes Peter the Great presented to the Academie des Sciences, materials on the evolution of the Jacquard loom, apparatus from Lavoisier's laboratory, and Daguerre's early equipment. For today's visitors to Paris, the Musee des Arts et Metiers offers the most traditional approach to displaying scientific and technological objects. That is not to say that there are not computer monitors and other up-to-date exhibition techniques in evidence. Of special interest is the program that brings working scientists into the galleries for the purpose of explaining their research work to visitors. The youthful "explainers" of the past have "grown up." The transformed setting, renovated in 2000, in the ancient priory adds to the overall sense of historical interpretation of industry, technology, and science. In fact the museum boasts the title "the Louvre des techniques" reinforcing its traditional roots.[10]

National Museum of Science and Industry, London

British manufacturers and businessmen were concerned to see that workingmen received practical technical education so as to produce more and better goods. Mechanics' institutes and government schools of design were established in the 1820s and 1830s, and sporadic trade exhibitions were held to show how art and science could be applied to industrial products. The Royal Society of Arts held several such exhibits, imitating those started in France. Henry Cole, versatile artist, musician, litterateur, and civil servant, became convinced that the society should sponsor an international exhibition so as to compare the industrial progress of many nations.[11] Prince Albert, consort of Queen Victoria and president of the society, eagerly embraced the idea, and his support was chiefly responsible for bringing into actuality the Great Exhibition of the Industry of All Nations at London in 1851. The "Crystal Palace" exhibition building—1,851 (the date that year) feet long and some 450 feet broad—enclosed eighteen acres that included several large trees. The exposition was an enormous success; in 120 days it attracted more than 6 million visitors. When it closed in October, unlike later world's fairs, it had a surplus—186,000 pounds. The exhibition had beneficial effects on British industrial design and international trade and inspired a series of world's fairs including a New York Crystal Palace (1853) and the Philadelphia Centennial Exhibition (1876). Many of these expositions influenced the museum movement; their collections and, in some instances, their buildings were used to house museums.[12]

The royal commissioners, at the urging of Prince Albert, invested the earnings of the Great Exhibition in South Kensington real estate that adjoined the exposition site and eventually helped build a museum complex there. In 1857 the South Kensington Museum of Science and Art opened; it contained much material from the Crystal Palace. Bennet Woodcroft, patent commissioner, who gathered mechanical models in the Patent Office Museum, brought the collection to South Kensington. Woodcroft preserved important historic equipment, including a Necomen type of atmospheric engine (1791); the Boulton and Watt rotative beam engine (1788); Arkwright's cotton-spinning machine (1769); Symington's marine engine (1788); and the locomotives *Puffing Billy* (1813) and Stephenson's *Rocket* (1829). The collection eventually went to the South Kensington Museum. In 1909, when the building for the Victoria and Albert Museum was completed, the National Museum of Science and Industry (NMSI)—the Science Museum—became independent, opening in its own buildings across Exhibition Road in 1928.

The Science Museum developed into one of the greatest museums of science and technology. It collected important historical material relating to power technology, transportation, communication, and manufacturing creating large "taxonomic" collections of 19th-century industrial practices. In the 1960s the museum added important elements of biomedicine to its collecting roster. The museum offers lectures, demonstrations, films, and special exhibits that treat topics of contemporary research interest; today the museum's Dana Centre provides visitors— real and virtual—access to live scientific debates about the impact of science and technology on today's world. As the museum's website states: "The Centre offers a place for experimental dialogue events, blending the best from science, art, performance and multimedia to 'provoke' discussion and real engagement with the key issues of the day." Through the Internet, the Dana Centre offers scientists a worldwide venue for discussion and public debate. Using a home computer, the public can register to join the discussions.

The museum also has excellent children's programs, including a children's gallery that opened in 1931 with participatory exhibits and engaging programs, both at the museum and today through the Internet. Today's version of that gallery, the Launch Pad—offers children interactive programming both in the museum and through computer connections, at home or school. Children's programs, whether for kids with their parents or school classes, encompass thematic tours, special exhibition spaces, dramatic presentations within exhibitions, IMAX theater presentations, and even supervised sleepovers. These children's programs are especially significant as they reflect current research into how young people learn. They balance current research and children's interests with historical artifacts relating to science and technology.

The NMSI has expanded in the last thirty years. In 1975 the museum added a new venue to its public spaces, the National Railway Museum in York reflecting the nation's leadership in the development of rail transportation. Acquiring Wroughton Airfield in Swindon in 1983 allowed space to store eighteen thousand "large" objects, such as airplanes. Wroughton opens its five airplane hangars for special tours. Three years later the museum welcomed the National Museum of Photography, Film and Television in Bradford, adding a new form of technology and 3 million objects to the industrial elements already on view. And, most recently, in 2000, the Science Museum at Kensington opened the Wellcome Wing expanding its space by 30 percent and allowing more focus on contemporary science and technology. The Wellcome collection is one of the largest collections of medical materials in the world. The three-story museum wing's ground floor exhibitions begin with a focus on the human body, while the top floor exhibition centers on how the future of medical technology may affect our daily lives. Here, the museum engages the visitor by using science center techniques to involve them in decision making and drawing conclusions from scientific evidence.

In 1989 NMSI extended its national reach with a program to assist British regional and local science and technology museums in their collecting and preservation functions. The Preservation of Industrial and Scientific Materials (PRISM) offers important guidance to small institutions in how to organize and care for their collections. This effort has been further expanded with funding from the Heritage Lottery Fund administered by NMSI. So, in addition to professional advice, the museum provides funding for museum activities relating to collecting science and technology around Britain.[13]

The Deutsches Museum, Munich

The French and British established the first technical museums, but the Germans devised an even more striking and influential one. Oskar von Miller, an outstanding engineer largely responsible for the Bavarian grid electrical system, was the founder of the Deutsches Museum von Meisterwerken der Naturwissenschaft und Technic (of Outstanding Achievements in Natural Science and Technology). As a young man in 1879, von Miller visited the conservatoire in Paris and the Patent Office Museum in South Kensington. A man of massive frame and boundless drive, in 1903 he presented a plan for a museum to illustrate the development of natural science and technology and the vivid influence of invention and mechanical progress on society.[14] It was endorsed enthusiastically by leading industrialists and scientists, engineering and scientific organizations, the National and Bavarian governments, and the city of Munich. The museum was housed for many years in an old building of the Bavarian National Museum and expanded into a disused infantry barracks. In 1903 the city gave it an island, formerly used as a coal dump, in the river Isar, where the kaiser observed the laying of the building's cornerstone in 1906. The city, Bavarian state, and German empire contributed millions of marks for construction. Industries furnished building materials free or at cost, organizations of workers donated labor, and the German railroads contributed transport; von Miller enjoyed his reputation as "the biggest highwayman and sturdiest beggar in Christendom." By 1913 the reinforced concrete structures were complete, but war delayed moving the collections, and the new museum island building did not open its 250,000 square feet of displays to the public until May 6, 1925, the seventieth birthday of its founder.

The Deutsches Museum introduced many innovations in its effort to make science and technology understandable for the general public. At the entrance was a Science Hall of Fame with likenesses of Germans such as Leibniz, Siemens, Krupp, and Kepler, as well as world scientists and inventors from Arkwright and Stephenson to Thomas Edison. Full-scale original or reproduced equipment was on display—for example, replicas of the *Puffing Billy* and *Rocket* locomotives in the Science Museum, the first Siemens electric locomotive (1899), early automobiles by Benz (1885) and Daimler (1886), and Edison's electric-lighting apparatus (1879). A museum visitor pushing buttons or turning cranks could animate many ingenious scale models. The principles of physics and chemistry were demonstrated, and a dramatic electrical surge generator (1.3 million volts) produced lightning flashes two meters long. The first Zeiss planetarium was installed, as well as realistic reconstructed mines for coal, iron, and salt with full-sized shafts, drifts, and galleries. The museum used period settings, such as an alchemist's laboratory and Galileo's study, as well as dioramas that included a glassblower's workshop and a high-tension power plant.

After extensive post–World War II reconstruction was completed in 1965, the Deutsches Museum retained the traditional chronological presentation of objects of historical interest but pioneered in offering ingenious and exciting exhibits and demonstrations of scientific laws of nature and their application through contemporary technology. It encouraged technological research with a fine scientific library of eight hundred thousand volumes, but its chief purpose was informal education for the masses. A well-equipped auditorium accommodated two thousand persons at public lectures. Attracting more than 1 million visitors every year, the Deutsches Museum still has the highest attendance figures of any museum in Germany. In terms of exhibition area, the number and importance of its objects and collections, the breadth of its stated aims and the multiplicity of its activities, it is among the internationally leading scientific and technological museums.[15]

The influence of the Deutsches Museum has been pervasive and extensive. Its display techniques for modern technology emphasize how science works today, and many smaller technical museums have concentrated on this aspect, largely giving up the goal of exhibiting historical development. In the United States, the Smithsonian's Museum of History and Technology (later the Museum of American History); Chicago's Museum of Science and Industry; Henry Ford's Museum in Dearborn, Michigan; and San Francisco's Exploratorium all trace their origins not only to the Deutsches Museum, but also to its founder, Oskar von Miller. His interest in educating the public about science and technology within the museum setting continues to this day in these North American institutions. The Technical Museum of Vienna used materials accumulated during the International Exposition held there in 1873 and the 1908 Jubilee of Emperor Franz Joseph to build support for the museum. It was greatly influenced by the Deutsches Museum and when it finally opened in 1918, it used many of von Miller's vivifying exhibition techniques. Its dynamic director, Ludwig Erhard, used consultants from most of Austria's trade organizations to build the museum's collections.[16]

Franklin Institute Science Museum, Philadelphia

Philadelphia's Franklin Institute, named to honor Benjamin Franklin, was founded in 1824 as a mechanics' institute to dispense information on the useful arts. Located in Independence Hall, it held important industrial exhibitions, awarded prizes, conducted classes and lectures, accumulated a library and a small technological museum with models and natural history specimens, and published a journal. In 1918 it began to develop laboratories, where scientists carried on chemical, biological, physics, and space research. The Franklin Institute opened its Fels Planetarium (only the second planetarium in the United States) in 1933 and a year later its Science Museum. In the Deutsches Museum tradition, the institute offered visitors interactive exhibitions. The institute's giant-sized, walk-through human heart complete with sound effects, opened in 1953, providing visitors, especially young ones, an appreciation for the role of that organ in the health of us all. Today, the Franklin Institute Science Museum's exhibitions, including a recently refurbished planetarium with exhibitions relating to space and space exploration, focus on technology, science, and medicine, and, in the tradition of Benjamin Franklin, human inventiveness.[17]

The Smithsonian Institution's Technology Museums

The Philadelphia Centennial Exposition of 1876 was a six-month extravaganza paying tribute to the hundredth anniversary of the Declaration of Independence. Five huge main buildings devoted to industrial exhibits, machinery, agriculture, horticulture, and art, together with 250 smaller structures, were scattered through 233 acres of the broad reaches of Fairmount Park. There were some thirty thousand exhibitors, including those from forty-one foreign governments. Machinery Hall was especially impressive with its great seven-ton

Corliss engine started up by President Grant and Dom Pedro II, emperor of Brazil, and furnishing power to fourteen acres of clattering machinery that included printing presses, typecasting machines, envelope makers, and pin-forming machines amid huge Krupp cannons, car wheels, water pumps, boats, and locomotives. One enthusiastic reporter wrote: "Surely here, and not in literature, science, or art, is the true evidence of man's creative power; here is Prometheus Unbound." Federal, state, and city funds underwrote the cost of the fair to supplement concession fees and admission revenue from more than 8 million visitors.[18]

Many foreign and state governments donated their centennial exhibits to the Smithsonian, and this flood of materials led to the erection of a new redbrick National Museum Building (today the Arts and Industries Building) completed in 1881. The Smithsonian regents in 1924 appealed to Congress unsuccessfully for a "Museum of Engineering and Industry." At last, in 1955, Leonard Carmichael, the institution's seventh secretary, persuaded Congress to appropriate funds for a new National Museum of History and Technology that opened in 1964 (its name changed to the National Museum of American History in 1980). At the Museum of History and Technology, the chief science and technical displays included military ordnance, graphic arts, photography, musical instruments, farm machinery, road vehicles, American merchant shipping, bridges and tunnels, heavy machinery, electricity, tools, timekeepers, record players, typewriters, locks, physical sciences, medical sciences, manufactures, textiles, petroleum, nuclear energy, coal, iron, and steel. Full-scale original objects—including a railroad engine built into the building—meticulously built scale models, period rooms and shops, visitor-activated demonstrations, and motion pictures are used in interpreting these subjects.

This U.S. hybrid science and technology museum sought to address the gulf between history and technology making manifest the American notion that technology is a "civilizing force" in the nation's development. The museum balances exhibitions of technology with historical topics, sometimes combining the two with temporary exhibitions such as *Science in American Life*. Today the museum's mission states that it "dedicates its collections and scholarship to inspiring a broader understanding of our nation and many peoples. We create learning opportunities; stimulate imaginations, and present challenging ideas about our country's past." Opened in 1994, the Lemelson Center for Invention and Innovation creatively continues the museum's commitment to technology through its exhibitions, both in-house and traveling, and its programs to stimulate the inventive sprit among young people. The web allows the center to extend its reach worldwide.[19]

National Air and Space Museum

Before the creation of the Smithsonian's Museum of History and Technology, the institution's Arts and Industries Building displayed the famed Wright Brother's *Flyer* (1903), Langley's *Aerodrome Six*, Charles Lindbergh's *Spirit of St. Louis*, Dr. Robert Goddard's first successful rocket, and numerous other examples of air and space equipment until the National Air and Space Museum on the National Mall was completed in 1976. A single story will illustrate the difficulties that sometimes attended the accumulation of the air and space materials. Samuel P. Langley, the third secretary of the Smithsonian, experimented with heavier-than-air machines, but in December 1903 his piloted *Aerodrome Six* failed to take off when catapulted over the Potomac. Nine days later, the Wright Brothers, Orville and Wilbur, made their successful flight at Kitty Hawk in North Carolina. Smithsonian secretary Charles D. Walcott, Langley's successor at the Smithsonian, asserted that the *Aerodrome Six* had made the first successful flight. This claim so angered Orville Wright, the surviving brother, that in 1928 he deposited the Kitty Hawk *Flyer* in the Science Museum, London. The Smithsonian finally made apologies satisfactory to Wright, and the *Flyer* came to the Smithsonian in 1948, to be placed on display in the Arts and Industries Building on December 17, the forty-fifth anniversary of its first flight.

The National Air and Space Museum today houses many of the icons of flight, including the Wright *Flyer*, *Spirit of St. Louis*, Chuck Yeager's *Bell X-1*, John Glenn's *Friendship 7* spacecraft, and the *Apollo 11* command module. In addition to this aeronautical and space hardware are materials that relate to man's centuries-old fascination with traveling in and through the air around us. There's even a "moon rock" for visitors to touch. On the National Mall visitors enjoy engaging permanent and temporary exhibitions, a children's gallery on flight, and an IMAX theater, along with a planetarium show. The museum's Center for Earth and Planetary Studies collects and displays photographs and images of Earth made by satellites and space missions. The Air and Space Museum's

Steven F. Udvar-Hazy Center near Dulles International Airport in Virginia opened in December 2003. Its hangar-sized building permits the display of many more artifacts including a Lockheed SR-71 Blackbird, a Concorde, the Boeing B-29 Superfortress *Enola Gay*, the "Dash 80" prototype for the 707, the sole-surviving Boeing 307 Stratoliner, and the space shuttle *Enterprise*. One wing of the center is devoted entirely to spacecraft. Attendance at these two facilities tops 9 million visitors each year.[20]

The Museum of Science and Industry, Chicago

Julius Rosenwald, head of Sears, Roebuck and Company in Chicago, took his family to Munich in 1911. His eight-year-old son William was fascinated with the Deutsches Museum in the old Bavarian National Museum there; by pushing buttons or working levers, he could do all sorts of exciting things—see the bones in his hand on an X-ray screen, generate static electricity, or make the wheels of a gigantic locomotive spin. Rosenwald, who met the enthusiastic Dr. von Miller and continued visiting him through the years, in 1921 told the Chicago Commercial Club "that Chicago should have . . . a great Industrial Museum or Exhibition" with "machinery and working models illustrative of as many as possible of the mechanical processes of production and manufacture."[21] By 1926 the museum was incorporated, Rosenwald had given it 3 million dollars, and the Chicago South Park Board had earmarked 3.5 million dollars of a bond issue to renovate for its use the crumbling Palace of Fine Arts, a building left from the Columbian Exposition of 1893 and once used by the Field Museum of Natural History. In June 1933, during the Chicago centennial world's fair, "A Century of Progress," the museum managed to open partially, featuring a simulated coal mine complete with operating mine "cage elevator," shaft, mine train, and working face of a coal seam.

By 1940, the museum board elected as its president Major Lenox R. Lohr, who had successfully managed "A Century of Progress" and had since been serving as president of the National Broadcasting Company. Major Lohr combined the qualities of the hard-driving, tough businessman and the imaginative promoter. He did everything he could to build attendance, which in 1939 was about 470,000; he believed that if it could reach a million, then more industry would be attracted to design and install significant technological displays. He thought 90 percent of the exhibits should be devoted to the present, only 10 percent to the past, and that 10 percent of the total should change each year. In exchange for a company's planning and erecting an exhibit, the museum would guarantee to show it for at least five years, would charge the company a fixed yearly fee that would reimburse the museum for operating, maintaining, and demonstrating it, and would give the company credit with an appropriate and discreet label. The museum would have full control of the exhibit to see that it met its standards of truthfulness, clarity, and educational purpose. This was, essentially, a world's-fair approach to the technical museum and required no curators, but much imaginative showmanship and excellent public relations and promotion.

Today the museum website boasts that it's the largest and oldest interactive science and technology museum in the Western Hemisphere. With attendance of more than 2 million visitors each year, it certainly ranks near the top of America's science and technology museums. The museum's mission "to inspire the inventive genius in everyone by presenting captivating and compelling experiences that are real and educational" places it in the mainstream of history and technology institutions both in the United States and elsewhere.[22]

The Henry Ford, Dearborn, Michigan

At the start of the 20th century, automobile industrialist Henry Ford began to accumulate vast stores of cultural and industrial Americana, including historic American buildings. He arranged his collections at Dearborn, Michigan, into two sections—an outdoor or open-air historical village similar to the Scandinavian folk museums, and an indoor museum extending behind a reproduction of Philadelphia's Independence Hall, Carpenter's Hall, and Old City Hall. In 1929 Thomas Alva Edison, Ford's close friend and idol, came to Dearborn with President Herbert Hoover to open Greenfield Village and Edison Institute, known since 2003 as the Henry Ford. Ford wished to show "the history of our people as written into things their hands made and used," and he argued that "a piece of machinery, or anything that is made is like a book, if you can read it." Though his museums contained many historical, architectural, and decorative arts materials, they were especially rich in important American and British items of industrial development. Greenfield Village included craft and early machine shops, as well as the cycle shop of the Wright brothers, three Edison laboratories in the Menlo Park compound, and birthplaces or other buildings connected with the Wrights, Edison, Luther Burbank, Charles Steinmetz, and Ford himself.

Most important of all in showing technological development was the Mechanical Arts Hall, an eight-acre teakwood expanse with serried rows of machines and apparatus devoted to agriculture, domestic arts, lighting, power, machinery, communications, and transportation. Ford was well acquainted with the London and Munich technical museums, and the power and machinery sections are especially strong. All objects are full-scale, most of them original, but with a few reproductions. This vast hodgepodge of largely uninterpreted artifacts may have given the ordinary visitor visual and intellectual indigestion, but we are indebted to Ford for recognizing their value as historical evidence. Today, modern exhibition techniques have transformed the setting and its objects into comprehensible and valuable evidence of mainly British and American inventiveness. This section of the Henry Ford is most like a traditional science and technology museum, while the village area reflects history museum traditions and practices. The Henry Ford is a blend of museum types, enjoying the highest attendance of all Michigan museums.[23]

Science Museum, Boston

Emerging from a 19th-century natural history society in Boston, the Science Museum, Boston, today takes its place as a leader in science museums. Following World War II, the museum's leaders expanded the scope of the "society" to encompass science and technology in addition to natural history. This change was made manifest when the museum relocated from Boston's Back Bay to the shores of the Charles River, forming a science park. And progress continued throughout the decades. With its 1951 expansion, the museum sought to address all the sciences within a single building. Subsequent additions—including an IMAX theater—and the location of a stop on Boston's mass transit system secured the museum as a major element of the city's cultural and educational offerings. Today the Science Museum offers visitors a wide variety of hands-on experiences, focuses on school visitors, and promotes both its facilities and programs as accessible to all, regardless of scientific background, intellectual capabilities, or physical limitations. The museum's Current Science and Technology Center (CSTC) with its multiaccess Internet approach to up-to-date scientific investigations allows visitors (onsite and virtual) to learn about science from its practitioners and through a variety of mediums to interact with them. Like London's Dana Centre, the CSTC expands the museum's reach through interactive programming, but in this case those interactions are virtual.[24]

Science Centers

Museums of science and technology emerged from the traditional enlightenment museum form, simply changing the exhibitions from those of natural objects to man-made phenomenon but continuing the overall purpose to aid visitors in understanding the world around us. The earliest science centers opened their doors in the 1930s at the height of public appreciation for the contributions of science (and technology) to daily comforts. These centers, in many instances, emerged from international expositions where a nation's technological muscle was on display. It was the Russian's early rocket and the subsequent U.S. focus on science education that spawned the surge of centers in the 1960s. As John Beetlestone et al. write: "A visit to a science center is an experience . . . Science centers aim to create an environment that stimulates learning: a relaxed, open atmosphere, conveying the message that 'there is something special and worthy of attention here, while remaining friendly and unintimidating." In 1962 the Pacific Science Center, one of the first to use the term *science center*, opened in the Seattle World's Fair building. Today, the Association of Science and Technology Centers (ASTC) reports that there are fourteen hundred centers worldwide. And, don't be confused by their names, which do not necessarily mention science, technology, or even museum or center; they can be as innovative as the centers' programming.[25]

Palais de la Découverte, Paris

Perhaps the first science center is the Palais de la Découverte in the Grand Palais in Paris. Built for the International Exposition of 1937 and attached to the University of Paris, the Palais contains relatively few original objects but uses ingenious mock-ups, some of them automated, as well as photographs, artwork, and demonstrators to teach the principles of pure science and scientific research as applied to the fields of mathematics, astronomy, physics, chemistry, biology, and medicine. Designed chiefly for young students, its exhibits focus on the physical sciences, and it has been "staffed" with young people within the galleries to help visitors (young and old) to understand the scientific principles of the exhibitions. These young people inspired the teenage "explainers" who staff the San Francisco's Exploratorium today. Today, the museum's public programs extend the definitions of exhibitions, seeking to directly engage visitors in experiences within the museum's galleries.[26]

Ontario Science Centre, Canada

A thoroughly 20th-century science center, the Ontario Science Centre opened in Toronto in 1969 to celebrate Canada's centennial. Housed in an architectural complex of three extremely innovative buildings, it has welcomed more than 39 million visitors since its opening. Though it has a few historical technological exhibits, its director declares its purpose is "to take science out of the laboratory and put it where casual browsers could observe and experience some of its challenge for themselves." The center, sometimes described as a push-button science adventure land, treats not only physical science and technology, but also natural history, medicine, music, and the theater, and operates an arboretum, an indoor rain forest exhibition, and an aquarium. With more than six hundred exhibits, it enjoys an annual attendance exceeding a million and accommodates two hundred thousand schoolchildren each year. In 2003 the centre opened a "Kidspark" for children under eight years old that proved so popular, plans are in place to double its space. Under the principle of "agents of change," the centre is just completing a three-year renovation revitalizing a third of the public spaces.[27]

Exploratorium, San Francisco

Oskar von Miller, the mastermind and impresario behind Munich's Deutsches Museum, personally influenced founders of other science and technology museums (as mentioned here, Henry Ford and Julius

Rosenwald) and more recently physicist Frank Oppenheimer, creator and founder of the Exploratorium in San Francisco. From his position as a professor at the University of Colorado, Oppenheimer envisioned a new sort of museum that addressed the interests of learners and their curiosity about the world around them. He called it a Museum of Science, Art, Industry and Craft (MOSAIC), generically, "an exploratorium," a place where visitors could understand the world by exploring it themselves. Oppenheimer acknowledged that a visit to the Deutsches Museum sparked his thinking about how museums could "teach" their visitors. In 1968 the Exploratorium opened in the abandoned buildings of the Pan-American Exposition in San Francisco. The early exhibitions were "works in progress" that captured the imagination of the few visitors that found their way to the door. Youthful explainers within the exhibit spaces offered explanations and guidance to visitors when asked. Oppenheimer stated the Exploratorium's purpose: "It should be a place where people come both to teach and to learn."[28] Today, the Exploratorium and Dr. Oppenheimer's vision of the dynamic role museums can play in engaging their visitors are models for other institutions worldwide. In addition to Oppenheimer's personal wit and humanity, the museum's legacy has been conveyed through its "cookbook" publications that provide museums across the world with simple ways to illustrate scientific principles, whether in community-based children's museums or larger regional science centers. Its website, live webcasts, and online material are recognized as among the most extensive and finest among science museums. The Exploratorium also houses the world's largest group of museum-based researchers on visitor studies, who contribute both to exhibition development and to a broader understanding of how visitors behave and what they learn in museums. As museum planners, von Miller and Oppenheimer are perhaps the broadest shoulders that today's science centers stand upon.[29]

Cite des Sciences et de l'Industrie

Today on the outskirts of Paris stands the Cite des Sciences et de l'Industrie (CSI) on the site of a small village, La Villette, that served as the central slaughterhouse for the Paris district from 1867 until the last cow met its end in 1974. Under the leadership of President d'Estaing, the former industrial complex of La Villette grew into a 136-acre multiuse cultural facility. In addition to a Museum of Science, Technology and Industry, La Villette encompasses performance stages, meeting halls, and public parkland. La Villette's first museum opened to the public on March 13, 1986, the centennial of the appearance of Halley's comet. The exhibitions, which have been described as "islands" that allow visitors to choose their own paths, are organized around four themes: "Earth to Universe," "Adventure of Life," "Matter and the Work of Man," and "Languages and Communication." All the cultural venues at La Villette have welcomed 3.5 million visitors each year. La Villette expands the meaning of science center with its goal as "a place of civilization, its task to assist its contemporaries in entering the intelligence of today's world to better manage the future." One European describes La Villette and CSI as "a cool place to be, there's masses going on beyond exhibitions."[30]

Teknorama, Heureka, and Experimentarium

Victor Danilov suggests that science centers have become popular institutions in American cities of medium size, for example, in Columbus, Ohio, and Baltimore, Maryland. The same can be said for Europe, especially in Scandinavia. Three warrant special attention for their innovations and contributions to the changing nature of science centers as a class of museum organizations. The privately financed Tekniska Museet (National Museum of Science and Technology) of Stockholm, opened in 1936, and followed Deutsches Museum practices. With government support, its goal is to use its collections and knowledge about industrial society, technology, and technological development to engage and satisfy people's interest and to generate a belief in the future. Its 1985 Teknorama galleries are designed especially to engage children with the world around them. In Finland in 1984, the Finnish Science Center Foundation brought together academics, scientists, government officials, and trade unions to create a center that would display and demonstrate achievements in science and technology. The foundation selected the City of Vantaa as the site for the new center. The city invested in establishing the center as a part of its effort to attract tourists. In 1989 "Heureka" opened to the public with two hundred interactive exhibitions, programming for schoolchildren, and traveling exhibitions. In its first year, it welcomed 250,000 visitors, and reached an additional 650,000 with its traveling exhibits. These exhibits have been transported to ten different countries and serve as an important source of revenue for the center. As with Teknorama, Heureka is committed to serving the needs and interests of young visitors, whether in school classes or visiting with their families. To the south in Denmark, the Center for Information about Natural Science and Modern Technology began, in 1986, as a study of "[a national] institution of learning where concrete experience was in the fore." For nearly five years, traveling pilot exhibits attracted visitors to this approach to learning. In 1991, the center opened to the public under the name Experimentarium in an abandoned Tuborg brewery, just north of Copenhagen. The center described its purpose this way: "Danish science has been given a new window to the world as well as a new channel of communication. The center was to be a bridge between experts and lay people." Of special note are the Experimentarium's close ties to school curriculum and teachers, many of whom work with the center in developing school materials.[31]

Science Museums as Partners

Whereas France's La Villette site with its many public amenities seeks to be comprehensive in its approach, other science museums have expanded their scopes and audiences with alliances with related institutions in different venues. For example, the Science Museum, London, combines York's National Railway Museum and Bradford's National Museum of Photography, Film and Television all under the administration of the National Museum of Science and Industry. The Deutsches Museum in 1996 opened Verkehrszentrum (Transportation Museum) nearby in Munich and in cooperation with the City of Bonn, a branch museum, the Deutsches Museum Bonn, a year earlier. Historical exhibitions within these institutions have become more and more rare, most often as temporary exhibitions, with the emphasis on engaging visitors in the techniques of science and technology rather than their histories. La Villette's CSI has taken the notion of partnerships even further, supporting the European Collaborative for Science, Industry and Technology Exhibitions (ECSITE) that provides channels for professional exchange and seeks to take full advantage of Internet collaborations among its 385 members in thirty European countries.

Challenges

Caring for Collections in Science and Technology Museums

Machinery is most meaningful to observers when it is in operation, complete with movement, noise, and fumes. In the museum setting, it is too often shown in sculptured repose. Few museums can command the resources required to keep machines operating. Problems also may arise in providing adequate safety devices to protect both the public and machine operators. And, there are declining numbers of operators familiar with the operations of some machines, especially those of the 19th century.[32]

Simon Knell describes the conservation issues this way: "[T]he Science Museum has seen its primary objective as explaining how things work rather than maintaining an encyclopaedic archive of artifacts, it has adopted a different strategy for the treatment of objects. . . . For the technical museum it is not a matter of principle as to whether or not to operate objects; some objects will inevitably be operated. The 'principle' has become the more pragmatic . . . decision as to which objects to operate, and the balance to be struck between the medium-term needs of exposition and the long-term needs of preservation." Each individual, museum, or center must address this tension; some have separated "working" and "archival" collections with each one requiring different conservation approaches.[33]

Who Defines Progress?

Industrialization and the machine have, of course, brought much progress; a large portion of humankind no longer works from sunup to sundown to obtain the bare necessities of life. There can be no doubt that most museums of science and technology glorify machines. But industrialization also creates problems—harm to the environment and ecology; neglect of social, cultural, and humanistic values; depletion of resources; and even threats of human extinction. Science and technology museums often have been "partners" with industry (and even government agencies). In his book *Museums of Influence*, Kenneth Hudson closes his chapter on science, technology, and industry museums with this admonition: "In today's world, a museum of science and technology which does not encourage its visitors to think of the human and social consequences of new developments is acting in a singularly irresponsible and out-of-date fashion. To worship Progress uncritically may suit the manufacturers and advertisers but it is not in the best interests of humanity."[34] Environmental advocacy is not within the missions of most science and technology museums or centers, so how does an institution confront the impact of science and technology on the earth? What are the boundaries between representation of current environmental conditions and advocacy? And, who sets them?

Scientific "Literacy"

How do science and technology museums address the gap between rapidly changing science and a diverse public audience with little knowledge of basic scientific principles? Where should interpretation begin in this process and how can the museum or science center balance engaging visitors with conveying scientific concepts? These questions are especially challenging for the science center with its reputation for "hands-on" activities that are comprehensible to visitors of all ages and interests. A 2000 study of science centers suggests that the experiences in centers can affect changes in both adults and children; however, the study's authors point out a disturbing finding. "[A]s a result of the visit [to the science center], visitors became stronger in their opinion that scientists agree with each other and that science provides definite answers—views that do no reflect increased understanding of the way that progress in scientific knowledge is made."[35]

Those science centers that evolved from older institutions emerged from two museum branches: natural history (i.e., Boston) and technology (i.e., Chicago and London). Today's centers seem to reflect "science" as physics, chemistry, geology, and mathematics. Biology and botany, the so-called live sciences, seem to be neglected. Graham Farmelo argues: "[S]cience centers do scant justice to basic science and the overwhelming majority of them concentrate on topics that are most amenable to public presentation—notably, applied physics and technology. It is possible to argue that the term 'science centers' is a really a misnomer—perhaps they should have been called 'technology centers?'"[36]

Science as Public Activity

With the demands of ever-increasing attendance, how do science centers satisfy visitors who have come to see "science in action" when scientific processes rarely engage spectators? As educator Melanie

Quin writes: "Science is a slow, often tedious, business, with most experiments being controls designed to show that in certain conditions nothing happens. . . . Is it simply that science museums seldom attempt explanations because explaining is not their traditional aim? Or have they found it impossible to present ideas in a museum context? Are the concepts and principles underlying appearances just too hard to present without the kind of background knowledge instilled over years, in courses in schools and universities? We may need somewhat separated, more thoughtful 'Explanatories.'"[37]

Public Perceptions of Science Centers

Science centers are lively places filled with visitors engaged with exhibitions and demonstrations. They are sometimes noisy in contrast to traditional museum galleries where visitors only speak with hushed voices. Some adults dismiss them as places to visit with children rather than institutions that serve to convey complex scientific principles to both children and adult visitors. Demonstrating their renowned flexibility, science centers are designing programming to reach out to adult audiences, especially grandparents with their grandchildren in tow. Ann Mintz points out that because science centers focus on children, they lose some of their capacity to attract funding from the community. If adults (parents) focus on science center visits when children are young, often under twelve, their interests and contributions may be diverted to other cultural institutions as they age (and their incomes increase).[38]

Science Centers and Cyberspace

In 1993 the Exploratorium launched its website, www.exporatorium.edu. Since then the opportunities for Internet access have exploded. Two Association of Science Technology Centers (ASTC) *Dimensions* articles only five years apart reveal the changes. In 2001, Rob Semper wrote of the Internet as a valuable extension of a science center's visitor's "browsing" behavior. He reported that science centers were using their websites for connecting with audiences and to support membership, admissions, public information, and exhibition promotion. He described the Exploratorium as becoming a "giant production studio for the web." In 2006, Jim Spadaccini explained how those Exploratorium beginnings remain unfulfilled. He suggested that the museums must "embrace user-created content . . . the science center 'audience' could be seen as potential collaborators and, in some cases, even content experts." But, to do so museums have to embrace two-way communications through the web, which challenges the museums "as authoritative sources of information." To return to the notion of "browsing" behavior, these two authors suggest that science centers especially need to approach the web as they do their onsite exhibition spaces and programming; simply stated, it's browsing in a different venue.[39]

Notes

1. Brooke Hindle, "Technology through the 3-D time Warp," *Technology and Culture* 24, no. 3 (1983): 453.

2. Frank Oppenheimer, "A Rationale for a Science Museum," *Curator*, (1968): 206.

3. Alice Carnes, "Showplace, Playground or Forum," *Museum News* 64, no. 4 (April 1986): 29–35.

4. Melanie Quin, "Aims, Strengths, and Weaknesses of the European Science Centre Movement," in *Towards the Museum of the Future: New European Perspectives*, eds. Roger Miles and Lauro Zavala, London: Routledge, 1994, p. 40.

5. Victor Danilov, *America's Science Museums*, New York: Greenwood Press, 1990, p. 291; Howard Learner, *White Paper on Science Museums*, Washington, DC: Center for Science in the Public Interest, 1979; Victor J. Danilov, *Science and Technology Centers*, Cambridge, MA: MIT Press, 1982.

6. John G. Beetlestone, Colin H. Johnson, Melanie Quin, and Harry White, "The Science Center Movement: Contexts, Practice, New Challenges," *Public Understanding of Science* 7, no. 1 (January 1998): 5–26; Kenneth Hudson, *Museums of Influence*, Cambridge, UK: Cambridge University Press, 1987, pp. 88–112.

7. Silvio A. Bedini, "The Evolution of Science Museums," *Technology and Culture* 6, no. 1 (Winter 1965): 1–29, esp. the table on pp. 2–6; Germain Bazin, *The Museum Age*, New York: Universe Books, 1967, pp. 37–39, 75–76, 86–87, 144.

8. Martha Ornstein, *The Role of Scientific Societies in the Seventeenth Century*, 3rd ed., Chicago, 1938, pp. 77–90, 219.

9. Bedini, "The Evolution," pp. 18–20; Ornstein, *The Role*, pp. 112–115; Eugene S. Ferguson, "Technical Museums and International Exhibitions," *Technology and Culture* 6 (1965): 30–46, esp. pp. 32, 45; Bazin, *The Museum Age*, 144–145.

10. Charles R. Richards, *The Industrial Museum*, New York, 1925, pp. 7–11; "Imperial Conservatory of Arts and Trades at Paris," *American Journal of Education* 21 (1870): 439–449; H. W. Dickinson, "Museums and Their Relation to the History of Engineering," *Transactions* 16 (1933–1934): 4–6; Bedini, "The Evolution," pp. 20–21; Ferguson, "Technical Museums," p. 31; Ornstein, *The Role*,

p. 155; *Museums of the World: A Directory*, compiled by Eleanor Braun, New York, 1973, pp. 78–79; *Guide des Musees de Paris*, Fribourg, Switzerland, 1970, p. 135; Alexis Blanc, "The Technological Museum of the Conservatoire des Arts et Metiers, Paris," *Museum* 20 (1967): 208–213; Victor J. Danilov, "European Science and Technology Museums," *Museum News* 54, no. 4 (July–August 1976): 34–37, 71–72; Daniel Beysens, "1 Researcher, 1 Exhibit," *ECSITE Newsletter*, no. 65 (Winter 2006): 6; www.arts-et-metiers.net.

11. Edward P. Alexander, "Henry Cole and the South Kensington Museum," *Museum Masters: Their Museums and Their Influence*, Nashville, TN: American Association of State and Local History, 1983, pp. 141–175.

12. Kenneth W. Luckhurst, *The Story of Exhibitions*, New York: Studio Publications, 1951, pp. 83–116; Christopher Hobhouse, *1851 and the Crystal Palace*, New York, 1937, 1–9, 24–40, 43–61, 150–165; Hector Bolitho, *Albert, Prince Consort*, Indianapolis, IN, 1964, pp. 117, 119–120, 125–128; Ferguson, "Technical Museums," pp. 30, 32–33, 35–39; Lord Amulree, "The Museum as an Aid to the Encouragement of Arts, Manufactures, and Commerce," *Museums Journal* 39 (November 1939): 350–356; Kenneth Hudson, *A Social History of Museums: What the Visitors Thought*, Atlantic Highlands, NJ: Humanities Press, 1975, pp. 41–47.

13. Dickinson, "Museums," pp. 1–12; Ferguson, "Technical Museums," pp. 38–39; Richards, *The Industrial Museum*, pp. 12–19; W. T. O'Dea, "The Science Museum, London," *Museum* 7 (1954): 154–160 and "New Galleries at the Science Museum, London," *Museum* 16 (1963): 198–204; W. T. O'Dea and L. A. West, "Editorial: Museums of Science and Industry," *Museum* 20 (1967): 150–157, 190–193; H. W. Dickinson, "The New Buildings of the Science Museum," *Museums Journal* 27 (May 1928): 336–341; "The Children's Gallery at the Science Museum," *Museums Journal* 31 (January 1932): 442–444; E. E. B. Mackintosh, "Special Exhibitions at the Science Museum," *Museums Journal* 37 (October 1937): 317–327; Herman Shaw, "Science Museums," *Museums Journal* 46 (December 1946): 169–173 and "The Science Museum and Its Public," *Museums Journal* 49 (August 1949): 105–113; F. Sherwood Taylor, "The Physical Sciences and the Museum," *Museums Journal* 51 (October 1951): 169–176 and "Children and Science in the Museum," *Museums Journal* 55 (November 1955): 202–207; Frank Greenaway, "A New Chemistry Gallery at the Science Museum," *Museums Journal* 64 (June 1964): 59–7; *International Committee, Museums of Science and Technology, Guidebook*, 1974, pp. 373–381; Neil Cossons, ed., *Making of the Modern World: Milestones of Science and Technology*, Science Museum, London: John Murray, 1992; www.danacentre.org.uk; www.sciencemuseum.org.uk.

14. Alexander, "Oskar von Miller and the Deutsches Museum," in *Museum Masters*, pp. 341–375.

15. Richards, *Industrial Museum*, pp. 20–32, 70–110; Ferguson, "Technical Museums," pp. 30, 41–42; Karl Bassler, "Deutsches Museum: Museum of Science and Technology," *Museum* 2 (1949): 171–179; "Heavy Current Electrotechnology: A New Department of the Deutsches Museum," *Museum* 7 (1954): 161–166; three articles by Hermann Auer: "The Deutsches Museum, Munich," *Museum* 20 (1967): 199–201; "Problems of Science and Technology Museums: The Experience of the Deutsches Museum, Munich," *Museum* 21 (1968):

128–139; and "Museums of the Natural and Exact Sciences," *Museum* 26 (1974): 68–75. See also "Oskar von Miller," *Museums Journal* 34 (June 1934): 76–79; Richards, *Industrial Museum*, pp. 33–45, 111; Gunter Knerr, "Technology Museums: New Publics, New Partners," *Museum International* 288, no. 4 (October–December 2000): 8–13; www.deutsches-museum.de.

16. "Technisches Museum fur Industrie und Gwerbe, Wien," *Museum* 5 (1952): 98; www.tmw.at.

17. Bruce Sinclair, *Philadelphia's Philosopher Mechanics: A History of the Franklin Institute, 1824–1865*, Baltimore, MD, 1974, pp. 39–41, 93–96, 100–103, 259–261; I. M. Levitt, "The Science Teaching Museum of the Franklin Institute, Philadelphia," *Museum* 20 (1967): 169–171; Robert W. Neatherby, "Education and the Franklin Institute Science Museum," *Museums Journal* 64 (June 1964): 50–58; Ferguson, "Technical Museums," pp. 34–35; Brooke Hindle, "Museum Treatment of Industrialization: History, Problems, Opportunities," *Curator* 15 (1972): 216; Victor J. Danilov, "Under the Microscope," *Museum News* 52 (March 1974): 37–38; *International Committee, Museums of Science and Technology, Guidebook*, 1974, pp. 145–154; www.fi.edu.

18. Charles S. Keyser, *Fairmount Park and the International Exhibition at Philadelphia*, Philadelphia, PA, 1876, pp. 1–82; Lynne Vincent Cheney, "1876: The Eagle Screams," *American Heritage* 25 (April 1974): 15–35, 98–99; Luckhurst, *Story of Exhibitions*, pp. 52, 124–125, 136–137, 175, 190, 202, 206; Paul H. Oehser, *The Smithsonian Institution*, New York, 1970, pp. 49–57, 189–190, 193–194, 196–197; Geoffrey T. Hellman, *The Smithsonian Institution: Octopus on the Mall*, Philadelphia: Lippincott, 1967, pp. 97–98; Walter Karp, *The Smithsonian Institution: An Establishment for the Increase and Diffusion of Knowledge among Men*, Washington, DC, 1965, pp. 55–69, 75–93; Gene Gurney, *The Smithsonian Institution: A Picture Story of Its Buildings, Exhibits and Activities*, New York, 1964, pp. 7–22, 62–97, 99–102; *National Museum of History and Technology, Exhibits in the Museum of History and Technology: An Illustrated Tour*, Washington, DC, 1968, pp. 40–41, 45–51, 60–63, 74–127; O'Dea and West, "Editorial," pp. 150–157; Frank A. Taylor, "The Museums of Science and Technology in the United States," *Museum* 20 (1967): 158–163; *Museums Journal* 27 (April 1927): 327; *Museums Journal* 28 (December 1928): 204; *Museums Journal* 48 (November 1948): 174; Robert P. Multhauf, "A Museum Case History: The Department of Science and Technology of the United States Museum of History and Technology," *Technology and Culture* 6 (Winter 1965): 47–58; Bernard S. Finn, "The Science Museum Today," *Technology and Culture* 6 (Winter 1965), pp. 74–82. One centennial park visitor was Dom Pedro II, last emperor of Brazil. He loved museums, technology, and education. He was a collector and spent a good deal of time at the Smithsonian.

19. Arthur P. Molella, "Tilting at Windmills," *Technology and Culture* 36, no. 4 (1995): 1,000–1,006; Arthur P. Molella, "The Museum That Might Have Been: The Smithsonian's National Museum of Engineering and Industry," *Technology and Culture* 32, no. 2 (1991): 237–263; www.americanhistory.si.edu.

20. Michal McMahon, "The Romance of Technological Progress: A Critical Review of the National Air and Space Museum," *Technology and Culture* 22, no. 2

(1981): 281–296; Michael Wallace, *Mickey Mouse History and Other Essays on American Memory*, Philadelphia, PA: Temple University Press, 1996, pp. 288–291; www.nasm.si.edu.

21. Herman Kogan, *A Continuing Marvel: The Story of the Museum of Science and Industry*, Garden City, NY, 1973, pp. 9–11, 18–19, 30, 43, 45–55, 71, 87, 89, 95, 98–101, 111–113, 115, 117–120, 124–129, 131–133, 134, 138–143, 145–157, 162–163, 174, 185, 194–195, 197–199, 205.

22. Lenox Riley Lohr, "Publicity and Public Relations," *Museum* 4 (1951): 229–233; Daniel M. MacMaster, "The Museum of Science and Industry, Chicago," *Museum* 20 (1967): 167–168; Hindle, "Museum Treatment," pp. 206–219; Ferguson, "Technical Museums," pp. 42–46; Danilov, "Under the Microscope," pp. 37–44; *International Committee, Museums of Science and Technology, Guidebook*, 1974, pp. 169–176; www.msichicago.org.

23. Henry Ford Museum Staff, *Greenfield Village and Henry Ford Museum*, New York, 1972, pp. 6–25, 46, 50–53, 70–91, 98–103, 142–217; *Greenfield Village and Henry Ford Museum, Selected Treasures*, Dearborn, MI, 1969, pp. 4, 6; William Greenleaf, *From These Beginnings: The Early Philanthropies of Henry and Edsel Ford, 1911–1936*, Detroit, MI, 1964, pp. 71–112; Allan Nevins and Frank Ernest Hill, *Ford: Expansion and Challenge, 1915–1933*, New York, 1957, pp. 497, 500–506; Ferguson, "Technical Museums," p. 42; Hindle, "Museum Treatment," pp. 210–211; www.hfmgv.org.

24. www.mos.org.

25. Archie F. Key, *Beyond Four Walls: The Origins and Development of Canadian Museums*, Toronto, 1974, pp. 263–265; Archie F. Key, "Canada's Museum Explosion," *Museums Journal* 67 (June 1967): 26–27; O'Dea and West, "Editorial," pp. 150–157; *International Committee, Museums of Science and Technology, Guidebook*, 1974, pp. 121–128; Beetlestone et al., "The Science Center," p. 10; Sheila Grinell, *A New Place for Learning Science: Starting Science Centers and Keeping Them Running*, Association of Science Technology Centers, 1992; Alice Carnes, "Showplace," pp. 29–35; G. Farmelo and J. Carding, *Here and Now: Contemporary Science and Technology in Museums and Science Centers*, 1996; Proceedings, Science Museum, London; Per-Edvin Persson, "The Changing Science Center: Sustaining Our Mission into the 21st Century," *ASTC Dimensions*, January–February 2000, pp. 3–6.

26. *Guide des Musees de Paris*, p. 135; Key, *Beyond Four Walls*, pp. 46–47; Louis de Broglie, "Scientific Museology and the Palais de la Découverte," *Museum* 2 (1949): 141–149; Andre Leveille, "The History of Sciences in the Palais de la Découverte," *Museum* 7 (1954): 195–201; A. J. Rose, "The Palais de la Découverte, Paris," *Museum* 20 (1967): 204–207; Danilov, "European Science and Technology Museums," p. 37; *International Committee, Museums of Science and Technology, Guidebook*, 1974, pp. 201–208.

27. Douglas N. Ormand, "The Ontario Science Centre, Toronto," *Museum* 26, no. 2 (1974): 76–85; Susan M. Pearce, ed., *Exploring Science in America*, London: Athlone, 1996; John Beetlestone et al., "The Science Center," pp. 5–26; Ronen Mir, "Natural Attractions: Implementing Your Science Park," *ASTC Dimensions*, March–April 2001, pp. 3–5; www.ontariosciencecentre.ca.

28. Frank Oppenheimer, "A Rationale for a Science Museum," *Curator* 11, no. 3 (1968): 206.

29. Edward P. Alexander, "Frank Friedman Oppenheimer," in *The Museum in America: Innovators and Pioneers*, Walnut Creek, CA: AltaMira Press, 1997, pp. 117–132; Hilde S. Hein, *The Exploratorium: The Museum as Laboratory*, Washington, DC: Smithsonian Press, 1990; Sally Deunsing, "Exporting the Exploratorium: Creating a Culture of Learning," *ASTC Dimensions*, November–December 1999, pp. 3–7. Linda Dackman, "Invisible Aesthetic: A Somewhat Humorous, Slightly Profound Interview with Frank Oppenheimer," *Museum* 150 (1986): 120–122.

30. Anne Decrosse, Johanne Landry, and Jean-Paul Natali, "Explora: The Permanent Exhibition of the Centre for Science and Industry at La Villette, Paris," *Museum* 155 (1987): 176–191; personal correspondence; www.cite-science.fr; Kenneth Hudson, "An Unnecessary Museum," *Museum* 41, no. 2 (1989); www.ECSITE.net.

31. H. Philip Spratt, "Tekniska Museet; A New Science Museum Opened in Stockholm," *Museums Journal* 36 (September 1936): 243–245; "The Technical Museum, Stockholm," *Museums Journal* 45 (April 1945): 4–6; Thorsten Althin, "The Automarium of the Tekniska Museum, Stockholm," *Museum* 7 (1954): 167–173; S. Strandh, "The Museum of Science and Technology, Stockholm," *Museum* 20 (1967): 188–190; *International Committee, Museums of Science and Technology, Guidebook*, 1974, pp. 81–104, 253–276; www.experimentarium.dk; www.tekniskamuseet.se; www.heureka.fi.

32. Hindle, "Museum Treatment," pp. 206–219; George Basalla, "Museums and Technological Utopianism," *Curator* 17 (1974): 105–118; N. W. Bertenshaw, "Museums of Science and Industry—Whither?" *Museums Journal* 64 (June 1964): 68–78; Finn, "Science Museum Today," pp. 74–82; Victor J. Danilov, "Science/Technology Museums Come of Age," *Curator* 16 (1973): 183–219; Danilov, "Under the Microscope," pp. 37–44 and Danilov, "European Science and Technology Museums," pp. 34–37, 71–72.

33. Simon Knell, ed., *Care of Collections*, UK: Routledge, 1994, p. 45.

34. Kenneth Hudson, *Museums of Influence*, Cambridge, UK: Cambridge University Press, 1987, p. 112.

35. L. J. Rennie and G. F. Williams, "Science Centres and the Image of Science," annual meeting of the American Educational Research Association, New Orleans, LA, 2000; Quoted in *The Impact of Science Centers/Museums on Their Communities: Summary Report*, Association of Science Technology Centers and European Network of Science Centers and Museums, 2001; Colin Johnson, "Science Centers as Learning Environments," *ASTC Dimensions*, November–December 2005, pp. 3–5; David Anderson, "Factors That Shape Vivid Long-Term Memories: Issues for Science Centers to Ponder," *ASTC Dimensions*, November–December 2005, pp. 8–9; Colin Johnson, "Science Centers as Learning Environments," Association of Science Technology Centers Resource Center, Education, pp. 1–14.

36. Beetlestone et al., "The Science Center," p. 24.

37. Melanie Quin, "The European Science Centre Movement," in *Towards the Museum of the Future*, p. 47.

38. Ann Mintz, "Science, Society and Science Centers," *Informal Learning Review* 71 (March–April 2005): 282; Emlyn Koster, "In Search of Relevance: Science Centers as Innovators in the Evolution of Museums," *Daedalus* 128, no. 3 (Summer 1999): 277–296.

39. Rob Semper, "Nodes and Connections: Science Museums in the Networked Age," *ASTC Dimensions*, November–December 2001; Jim Spadaccini, "Museum and the New Web: The Promise of Social Technologies," *ASTC Dimensions*, July–August 2006; Leo Tan and R. Subramaniam, *E-Learning and Virtual Science Centers*, Hershey, PA: Information Science Publishing, 2004.

5

The History Museum

According to some estimates, history museums and historic sites account for two of every three museums in this country; they are also the most widespread and accessible museum type, from the great public collections down to the small town's roomful of memorabilia. . . . It is no stretch . . . that museums actually deliver more history, more effectively, more of the time to more people than historians do.

—Randolph Starn, 2005[1]

The museum of history in your community should not be a tomb wherein the bones of antiquity silently rest. Your Museum of History, rather, must be a power station sending out a current that illumines the community and gives a clearer vision of social values.

—Arthur C. Parker, 1935[2]

The *Washington Post* reported the closing of the Museum of American History's numismatics hall this way: "The Hall of Money and Medals won't be much missed because the sort of people who go to good museums, who used to love to pore over coins and medals, don't anymore. Flash, electric speed, eyegrabbers and narrative— that's what we want now." Museum Director Brent Glass is quoted: "We're at the end of a major chapter in the history of museums. I hope we're opening a new one."

—Paul Richard, 2004[3]

Since classical days, humankind has taken some interest in the past and gradually learned to separate myth from actual happening. History museums emerged in the 18th century from natural history museums aping their focus on taxonomic collections that revealed man's progress in controlling and designing the environment. In the 19th century, the history museum adapted exhibit styles from art museums and presented objects from the past as exemplars of design and human accomplishment. Today, history museums collect and preserve three-dimensional objects of the past and use them to convey historical perspective and inspiration as well as a sense of what it was like to live in other ages. These objects supplement literary and oral records and thus are revealing documents for the historian, if he or she will only learn to use them. History museums encompass small local museums that commemorate the contributions of a city father (or mother) or an important organization; historical societies that, in addition to museum exhibition spaces, may include libraries, historic houses, historic sites, and open air or outdoor museums. As Ellis Burcaw notes: "All museums are history museums in the sense that all preserve objects pertaining to past events and situations."[4]

History museums in the United States enjoyed a mid-20th-century renaissance with the academic social history movement that sought to better understand the American past from the perspective of "the bottom up," those participants who were unlettered and left behind little physical evidence of their existence. An abundance of young academically trained historians seeking employment outside the academy added to the impact of these intellectual changes on history museums.

Museum Jovianum

The history museum emerged from those devoted to natural history and art. It was, at first, a spin-off from the art collection. Paolo Giovio, bishop, humanist, and scholar, was the best known of the early collectors of likenesses of famous men. At his residence in Como about 1520, he began to assemble 280 portraits in four categories—deceased poets and scholars, living poets and scholars, artists, and political leaders, including military commanders, statesmen, popes, and monarchs. The living members of this cult of glory were represented by portraits painted from life (Hernando Cortez, for example, hastened to send Giovio his likeness), but the others were represented by busts one and one-half feet high painted on canvas and based upon what sources Giovio could find. The Museum Jovianum (Giovio revived and brought into general use the word *museum*) was considered one of the marvels of the age, and when Giovio died, Cosimo de Medici sent Christofano dell' Altissimo to Como to make copies of its portraits for the Medici collection in Florence. Even more important in keeping alive the idea of this type of historical collection were the books of engravings of the portraits that appeared in Florence (1551), Paris (1552), and Basel (1557).[5]

This kind of history museum became enormously popular with noble and wealthy collectors in the 16th and 17th centuries. Catherine de Medici, wife of the French Dauphin (later Henri II), in her Paris residence had 551 portrait drawings, many of them set in paneled walls. Her Enamel Cabinet paired 32 portraits with 32 Limoges enamels, and her Mirror Cabinet contained another 83 portraits mounted with 119 Venetian-looking glasses.[6] Paul Ardier, lawyer and secretary of defense, filled a long gallery of his Chateau de Beauregard in the Loire Valley with 327 portraits organized and displayed around the kings of France; his collection can still be viewed in the chateau today. Bussy-Rabutin, soldier and philanderer, exiled to his chateau in Burgundy, developed a museum of historical portraits that included a rotunda exhibiting likenesses of the beautiful women of court; the collector boasted that he had slept with most of them. About 1600, the Gonzagas had a special room containing the likenesses of "the most beautiful women in the world," and Catherine the Great later bought *Cabinet of Muses and Graces* for her Peterhof palace.[7]

The concept of the Museum Jovianum may have appealed to antiquarians, but rows of portraits, often uniform in size, did not constitute an exciting exhibition technique. Nevertheless, it had American versions. Du Simitiere's small museum at Philadelphia in 1782 exhibited many of his drawings of Revolutionary military leaders and statesmen; some of his works were engraved and published in French, Spanish, and English editions. Peale's Philadelphia Museum displayed 269 portraits and paintings, most of them by Peale and his family and of Revolutionary leaders and Founding Fathers. From 1817 until his death in 1834, John H. I. Browere sought unsuccessfully to establish a national gallery by modeling busts of famous Americans, most of their faces delineated from life masks made by a secret process of applying thin coats of quick-drying grout to the greased subject. Alexander Hamilton, Thomas Jefferson, Marquis de Lafayette, John Adams, John Quincy Adams, James and Dolley Madison, James Monroe, Martin Van Buren, and Henry Clay are some of the twenty-three busts or masks that have survived, most of them at the New York State Historical Association in Cooperstown. The early American historical societies also collected portraits, and as late as the 1850s, Lyman Copeland Draper of the State Historical Society of Wisconsin was forming a frontier historical art gallery composed chiefly of portraits of pioneers and Indians; he thought "the noblest aim of Art . . . the illustration or perpetuation of great events in history." Many of the Peale portraits, together with others of the signers of the Declaration of Independence, are shown today by the National Park Service in the old Second Bank of the United States in Philadelphia, while the National Portrait Gallery of the Smithsonian Institution in Washington has become a modern American Museum Jovianum.[8]

Panorama Craze

A specialized form of the history museum employed the panorama or cyclorama—a huge circular painting of a battle or other extensive scene with the observer placed at the center and, sometimes, three-dimensional objects in the foreground. The painting often was housed in a rotunda and lighted from above. Robert Barker, a young Edinburgh painter in prison for debt, conceived the idea of the panorama and in London in 1792 exhibited one of the English fleet anchored between Portsmouth and the Isle of Wight. A panorama craze developed in both Europe and America. In 1823 Louis J. M. Daguerre and Charles Marie Bouton invented the diorama; by painting on translucent gauze and using moving lights, they could give an impression of movement and changing scenes. No more spectacular panorama ever existed than Colonel Jean-Charles Langlois's Battle of Navarino, shown in Paris in 1830. One entered between decks of a fighting ship and came out on the poop deck to view the conflict. Wax representations of maimed and dying sailors and realistic sound supplied by hidden men heightened the effect. Cadets entering the Naval Academy of Brest were taken to see the panorama to experience what it was like to be aboard a warship during battle.[9]

   The true panorama reached New York in 1797 with a complete view of London, twenty feet high and nearly 130 feet in circumference. Yet as early as 1784, Charles Willson Peale had shown in his Philadelphia residence a primitive type of small moving pictures titled *Perspective*

Views with Changeable Effects; or, Nature Delineated and in Motion. An assistant with screens and lights made the scenes appear to move, and they were accompanied by sound effects. The system was invented by Philippe de Loutherbourg in London in 1781, and Peale spent eighteen months perfecting a two-hour program that included portrayals of Walnut Street at dawn and at nightfall; a view of hell itself, its evil mood enhanced by appropriate music; and the naval battle between *Le Bonhomme Richard* and *Serapis.* Peale charged one shilling, or twenty-five cents, to see his moving pictures, and during the summer of 1787, the delegates to the Constitutional Convention were amazed and entertained by the show. American artists continued to experiment with such art forms for nearly a century. In 1849 Henry Lewis completed a panorama of the Mississippi River from Saint Paul to New Orleans; it was 1,975 feet long and unrolled from one creaking upright spool to another amid the spiel of an interpreter and musical accompaniment. Two panoramas of the 1880s can still be seen in the United States today—*Pickett's Charge*, by the Frenchman Philippoteaux, at Gettysburg National Historical Park and the *Battle of Atlanta*, painted by German artists in Milwaukee, at the Cyclorama in Atlanta.[10]

Culture History Arrangement

Still another precursor of the history museum was the museum of industrial or decorative arts. After the Great Exhibition of 1851 in London, the South Kensington Museum (today the Victoria and Albert Museum, the V&A) was founded with industrial and decorative art from the Crystal Palace. Its exhibits were organized under the technical classification system, by which ceramics, glassware, metalwork, enamels, and the like were placed together, often in separate rooms, arranged chronologically or by patterns. Nearly everything was on display (today we call this system "visible storage"). This kind of exhibit may have satisfied scholars and connoisseurs intent upon examining large numbers of examples and craftsmen looking for sources of inspiration for their own work, but crowded paintings on walls and heavy glass cases crammed with objects did little to engage or educate the general public. At the end of the 20th century, the V&A began a major reinstallation of its collections, organizing them around topics believed to be of interest to visitors. The "British Galleries" cluster the vast collections around themes and offer video and audio components that provide visitors with "deep" context for individual objects and ideas. There are even gallery performances with actors reading from historical texts or interpreting an element of British life that adds to a visitor's understanding of the objects on view.[11] See chapter 2 for further discussion of the Victoria and Albert Museum origins.

A group of German museum curators conceived a new arrangement for such material. The Germanisches Museum at Nuremberg in 1856 purchased an old Carthusian monastery and installed there six original rooms ranging from one of a Tyrolean peasant (15th century) to those of Nuremberg patricians (17th century). By 1888 the museum had many such rooms following this culture history arrangement, so that one could imagine that he was walking through several centuries of German history. At the turn of the century, the Swiss Landesmuseum in Zurich had sixty-two such rooms, and the Bavarian Museum in Munich offered seventy-six period galleries and rooms.

The role and attitude of the 19th-century-museum visitor in relation to museum objects changed in a dramatic way, especially in history museums (and to some degree in natural history museums, too). No longer did visitors expect to stroll past portraits of the famous and cases of precious objects. The actual setting of the experience fundamentally changed a museum visit. Ethnographic clusters of "folk," displays of costumes on mannequins, and even whole room settings of objects removed the separation of the viewer from the object in significant ways. As will be revealed, the outdoor museum changed the dynamic further. First, visitors encountered spaces "inhabited" by wax figures. And museums in Holland, Denmark, and Sweden welcomed visitors into display spaces, complete with a person to add to the visitor-object exchange.[12]

U.S. Historical Societies and General History Museums

The historical society has been a staunch backer of the history museum in the United States. The founders of the first societies—Massachusetts Historical Society (1791) at Boston, New-York Historical Society (1804), and American Antiquarian Society (1812) at Worcester, Massachusetts—were driven by zeal for learning and love of country. As true disciples of the Enlightenment, they had unlimited faith in the power of knowledge and reason. They also were determined to preserve the story of their defeat of the powerful British

Empire and to point out the factors that caused the American genius for self-government to flower.

With their broad aspirations and enthusiastic energy, the early historical societies often embarked upon programs too ambitious and too widely dispersed. Thus, the New-York Historical Society collected animal, vegetable, and mineral specimens; productions of "the American Continent and the adjacent Islands"; coins and medals; European old-master paintings; artifacts of the Plains and South American Indians; Nineveh sculptures; Egyptian rarities, including three large mummies of the sacred bull Apis; as well as documents, paintings, and objects of New York origin and interest. Eventually, the society narrowed its field of collection to New York and began to dispose of materials outside that scope.[13]

By 1876, the centennial of American independence, seventy-eight historical societies existed in the country, about half of them with museums. Today there are some fifteen thousand societies. Some of the earliest societies, for example, the Massachusetts Historical Society and the American Antiquarian Society, had limited membership; still, the general trend has been to admit anyone with the proper interest and willingness to pay dues. The earliest societies were all entirely private in finance and control, but starting in the 1850s, Wisconsin and others in the Midwest received state appropriations. Their ideal became to serve everyone in the state, and programs broadened; the imaginative efforts of Reuben Gold Thwaites of the State Historical Society of Wisconsin to reach both learned and popular audiences well illustrate this development.[14] Many societies no longer limit themselves to the scholarly activities of library, research, and publication; instead they now also promote museums, the marking of historic sites, historic preservation, school tours and clubs, and a host of other programs appealing to all ages. Their central museums often have expanded to include a chain of historic houses, preservation projects, and outdoor museums. As part of its central function, the historical society sometimes institutes educational, cultural, and outreach programs similar to those carried on directly by art or science museums, and state historical societies have often helped promote and assist local historical societies in counties and municipalities.

Historical societies are not the only form of history museum in the United States. Some U.S. cities—often spearheaded by their founding families or a prominent collector—created another form of history museum, not associated with the society. These general history museums often stand as imposing edifices within the city's central business district or in nearby parkland. The historical and cultural interests of their founders impact the scopes of their collections. In Michigan alone, the Detroit Historical Museum and the Grand Rapids Public Museum celebrate those cities' past accomplishments. Some of these institutions emerged from an individual's collection and expanded to serve the broader community. The Valentine Museum in Richmond, Virginia, was the residence of collector Mann Valentine II and opened to the public in 1898. In the 1980s the board changed its name to the Valentine Richmond History Center seeking to extend its public appeal.[15]

What of a national history museum in the United States? Chapter 3 describes the establishment of the Smithsonian Institution's Museum of History and Technology in 1964. The museum's name changed to the National Museum of American History in 1980, broadening its emphasis from science and technology, although those collections remained primary. Here's how the Smithsonian's annual report describes the basis for the change: "The fundamental mission is clear: to interpret histories of the peoples of the United States primarily through evidence inherent in material artifacts. Science and technology has provided many of those artifacts, the ways in which they reflect social history is an important part of their story. Therefore, without diminishing our traditional emphasis upon technology, we have been reordering our staff not only to elucidate the recent effloresence of research into America's social history but also to participate actively in expanding the frontiers of such knowledge." Today the museum is well known for its general history exhibitions ranging from the inaugural gowns of the First Ladies to thematic exhibits such as *America on the Move* that addressed issues of transportation and its impact on American life. In the 1980s the museum assumed a leadership role in expanding its programs to new audiences, reaching out to the disabled and disadvantaged and offering programing outside the museum. In recent years, to extend the impact of its exhibits, the museum has used the Internet to allow visitors to see and interact with its collections from the comfort of their own homes.[16]

Open-Air or Outdoor Museums

European international expositions in the 19th century featured national displays that promoted technological achievements, agricultural products, and unique qualities; for example, Swedish museum impresario Artur Hazelius brought a group of Laplanders (Sami people) to the 1878 Paris Exposition. The Paris World's Fair of 1889 showcased members of twelve African tribes, as well as Javanese, Tonkinese, Chinese, and Japanese living in reconstructed native houses, wearing traditional dress, practicing native arts, and playing native music. A Colonial Exhibition at Amsterdam in 1883 displayed an Indonesian Kampong, and, two years later, this outdoor village was given to the Rijksmuseum voor Volkenkunde at Leiden, where it attracted large crowds before damage from the harsh winters led to its closing in 1891. These popular exhibitions used ethnographic techniques, linking history museums to natural history and anthropological museum practices and providing viewers with an engaging sense of culture and history. The Smithsonian Institution's folklife festival reflects these same practices each summer on the mall in Washington.

In the last quarter of the 19th century, the Scandinavians developed another form of cultural expression, giving the world a new kind of museum devoted to folk culture, ethnography, and social history. Artur Hazelius of Stockholm was father of the idea. Hazelius was distressed to see the Industrial Revolution threaten the pleasant, coherent, and distinctive ways of living found in the different regions of Sweden and, indeed, all Scandinavia. He determined to collect and preserve the furniture, furnishings, implements, costumes, and paintings of the old days. In 1873 he opened in Stockholm his Museum of Scandinavian Folklore (later called Nordiska Museet). As his collection grew, he was offered entire buildings and other materials too bulky to show indoors. As a result, he acquired seventy-five acres on a rocky bluff at an old fortification (Skansen) overlooking Stockholm Harbor and started an open-air or outdoor museum there in 1891.

At Skansen, Hazelius amassed buildings moved from various parts of Scandinavia—today, some 150 structures dating from medieval times to the 20th century that include farm houses, a manor house, barns, outbuildings, cottages, shops, a church, and craftsmen's workshops. Hazelius and his successors added attractive gardens and typical farm crops to set off the buildings, as well as authentic furniture and furnishings for the interiors. Costumed guides interpret the culture, traditions, and life of the former inhabitants. Divine services and numerous weddings use the 18th-century wooden church from Seglora. Musicians play and sing old melodies, and folk dancers trace ancient steps with vigor. Glassblowers and other craftsmen make traditional products by hand; animals, domestic and exotic, enliven the park; orchestras and the best musicians of Europe perform in an outdoor auditorium; an excellent theater presents Shakespeare, Selma Lagerlof's comedies, and other favorite plays; and restaurants and bars serve period food and cater to every taste. More than 1.3 million visitors come to this outdoor history museum each year.

Hazelius used the idea of heritage and understanding of the past as a steadying influence in the face of the violent changes of modern life. He offered a new approach in museum exhibition, for he wished "to place the historical objects in their functional context . . . against the background of their entire cultural environment." He re-created the life of older periods, stimulating the sensory perceptions of the visitors and giving them a memorable experience. As they walk about the carefully restored environment of another day, their thoughts and emotions help bring the place to life. "Hazelius's achievement," says Iorwerth C. Peate, director of the Welsh Folk Museum, "was that of taking a sudden leap in museum technique and so transforming the museum from a curiosity shop into a home of national inspiration."[17]

Hazelius's museum idea inspired other Scandinavian versions. Bernhard Olsen, former director of the Tivoli amusement park in Copenhagen, saw Hazelius's period tableaux in 1878 at the world's fair in Paris. He organized folk collections that became part of the Danish National Museum and in 1901 opened Frilandsmuseet that now has more than one hundred farmhouses, barns, cottages, craft shops, and wind and water mills situated in a lush ninety-acre rural park about eight miles from Copenhagen. Dr. Anders Sandvig, a dentist in Lillehammer, Norway, was so indignant at seeing five wagonloads of furniture and furnishings of the region on their way to Hazelius in Stockholm that he began collecting folk materials. They were finally placed in 1904 at Maihaugen (May Hill), where Norwegian National Day is observed every May 17. Lillehammer's Sandvig Collection at Maihaugen is one of the loveliest outdoor museums. Clustered about five lakes, it includes a tiny log cabin (built about 1440), the Garmo Stave Church (begun in the early 12th century), an 18th-century farm estate, Seters or summer farm buildings from the mountains, and some fifty workshops. As the 21st century opens, Maihaugen expanded its agricultural environment to include a 19th-century village street, complete with commercial establishments and residences arrayed along a "main street." The museum's 20th-century collection of houses reflects Norwegian urban design as it has changed decade by decade.[18] In Norway's capital city, Oslo, Dr. Hans Aal founded the Norsk Folkemuseum, which in 1902 moved to Bygdoy, a peninsula extending into Oslo Harbor. Its Stave Church from Gol dates from 1200. Peter

Holm, a charismatic schoolteacher, established Den Gamle By (the Old Town) at Aarhus in Jutland in northern Denmark in 1909. Its emphasis is on the folklife of a town instead of a peasant community.

U.S. Outdoor Museums

Colonial Williamsburg, the preserved and restored capital of 18th-century Virginia, is probably the best-known outdoor museum in the United States. Other examples that combine historic preservation with outdoor museum functions include: Historic Deerfield (Massachusetts), a New England village; Old Salem (North Carolina), a Moravian community; Conner Prairie (Indiana), a Midwest frontier settlement; and Columbia (California), a mining town.[19] As a history museum, Colonial Williamsburg expanded the historic-house concept to include the major part of a colonial city, some 175 acres and about thirty buildings with carefully furnished interiors open to the visiting public. As a living historic district, it also has about one hundred properties occupied by residents of Williamsburg or rented to tourists.

Colonial Williamsburg was founded in 1926, when John D. Rockefeller Jr. decided to finance the dream of the Reverend W. A. R. Goodwin, rector of Bruton Parish Church, to bring the colonial capital back to life. The town plan was virtually intact, and some eighty-five original buildings still stood. They were provided with authentic outbuildings; gardens based on American and English precedents were developed; and some important buildings were reconstructed when enough evidence was available. Historical, architectural, archaeological, and curatorial researchers worked together to obtain a high degree of authenticity. As the project matured, careful attention was given to its education program or interpretation. Well-trained costumed guides, working craftsmen, life on the scene (carriages, oxcarts, and livestock), period dining, military drills, music, dancing, plays, fireworks, and many other activities appeal to the visitor and encourage his participation, while a varied list of publications and audiovisual productions as well as reproduced furniture and furnishings spread the Williamsburg story outside the restored city. Special attention is given to school groups, with emphasis placed on using the historical environment with the new inquiry method of teaching history. A forum series employed the Williamsburg background for in-depth study of furniture and furnishings, gardens, principles of government, and other areas.

The first large American outdoor museum organized on the Scandinavian model and moving historical structures to a central location was Greenfield Village at Dearborn, Michigan, dedicated by Henry Ford in 1929. Ford thought that historians emphasized politics and wars too much, and he was sometimes contemptuous of book learning, big ideas, and windy generalizations. His anti-intellectual attitude led him to assert: "Most history is more or less bunk." Still, he was interested in his own kind of history, and he said about Greenfield Village:

> When we are through, we shall have reproduced American life as lived; and that, I think, is the best way to preserve at least a part of our history and tradition. For by looking at things people used and that show the way they lived, a better and truer impression can be gained than could be had in a month of reading.[20]

By 1936 the 240-acre "village" contained more than fifty buildings that included a traditional New England green with a church, town hall, courthouse, post office, and general store; the Scotch Settlement schoolhouse Ford attended as a boy; the Plymouth, Michigan, carding mill to which Ford's father took wool; Noah Webster's house; William Holmes McGuffey's (of McGuffey's Readers fame) Pennsylvania log-cabin birthplace; a five-hundred-ton stone Cotswold Cottage; and the Sir John Bennet jewelry shop from Cheapside, London, with its clock graced by statues of Gog and Magog. Ford did not intend that his village would actually represent the life of a specific historical place. Rather he conceived of the village in toto as a museum, and the buildings that make it up as specimens. Ford turned the buildings of Greenfield Village into enormous museum objects and thus created a new context for them.[21] Historian Steven Conn writes: "Ford wanted his museum to have a much broader sweep, nothing less than a comprehensive record of America's preindustrial past. Though it too is heavy with its own historical fictions, Williamsburg stands as a monument to the techniques of scientific and historical recreation in a way that Greenfield Village does not."[22]

Many outdoor museums of this general type developed in the first half of the 20th century, including Old Sturbridge Village in Massachusetts; Mystic Seaport in Connecticut; Farmers Museum in Cooperstown, New York; Shelburne Museum in Vermont; and Stonefield and Old World Wisconsin in Wisconsin. The best of these projects work hard to define a clear concept of purpose and do painstaking historical research to re-create an authentic, historically justifiable community.

For example, Plimoth Plantation, a recreation of the 17th-century set-tlement in Massachusetts, opened in 1947. While consisting of repro-duction dwellings and public buildings based on careful research into both the site and the era, the plantation's major contribution to history museum practice is its intepretive approach of using staff to represent the actual early inhabitants of the colony. The research efforts led by an-thropologist James Deetz included not only understanding what the site should look like, but also seeking to reproduce for visitors the adaptations of the English language that emerged in 17th-century Massachusetts. As the Scandinavian precursors welcomed visitors into the display spaces, Plimoth Plantation sought to engage them with "characters" from the past to further intensify the experience. Plimoth's "first-person" interpretive approach would affect interpre-tive practices in all museums regardless of subject matter. The scholarly approach makes the outdoor museum much more useful for teaching social history and advances it several steps beyond the idea of moving disparate old buildings into a pleasant parklike setting.[23]

The outdoor museum concept has spread around the world, and its influence seems to be constantly increasing. Some scholars regard it chiefly as a folk museum or ethnographic park, but separating folklore and ethnography from social history is a difficult task. Most American outdoor museums fit as history museums, including political, eco-nomic, and social history topics in their offerings. The outdoor mu-seum was "more than a new idea of museum arrangement," more than combining the pleasant atmosphere of the picnic with the serious mu-seum visit. Its most important contribution "was the conception that the greatness of a country, the strength of its industries, the beauty of its art, have firm roots in that country's own history."[24] Georges-Henri Riviere, cofounder of the Musee de l'Homme in Paris, led yet another museum first in conceiving the ecomuseum. This museum form sought to create museums around actual communities rather than removing materials from their contexts. The museum relied on citizens to present their community to visitors as a "living entity," complete with cultural resources, social issues, and economic relations. Just as the 19th-cen-tury outdoor museums brought visitors "into" the museum space, the ecomuseum concept placed residents of an area (both urban and rural) in roles as museum "administrators" and "interpreters." French minis-ter of culture, Jack Lang, described the ecomuseum in this way: "a new generation of museums in which the object retains its context, bearing witness to a specific culture, population and physical environment."[25] While there are about two hundred ecomuseums worldwide, with most in Europe, it has not prospered for reasons ranging from lack of funding to changing governmental policies.

U.S. Historic Houses, Sites, and Preservation

Americans developed their own distinctive version of historic preservation while Europeans were restoring their churches and castles or gathering vernacular architecture and folk objects into outdoor museums. The founders viewed the historic house museum as a vehicle to teach love of country. The committee seeking to save the Hasbrouck House, George Washington's headquarters in Newburgh, New York, for example, argued that no traveler in the area would hesitate to make a pilgrimage to this beautiful spot, associated as it is with so many delightful reminiscences of our early history. "And if he have an American heart in his bosom, he will feel himself to be a better man; his patriotism will kindle with deeper emotion; his aspirations for his country's good will ascend from a more devout mind, for having visited the 'Head-Quarters of Washington.'"[26]

The State of New York bought Hasbrouck House for about ten thousand dollars in 1850, agreed to maintain and operate it, and appointed the Newburgh Village Board of Trustees custodian "to keep it as it was during General Washington's occupancy." This was the first historic house museum opened in the United States, but another one, much better known, is Mount Vernon, Washington's plantation in Virginia. It is a monument to the first outstanding American historic preservationist, Ann Pamela Cunningham of South Carolina.[27]

Various proposals had been made for Mount Vernon—that it serve as a summer residence for the president, that it be an old soldiers' home, a model farm, or an agricultural college. Private speculators suggested converting the mansion into a resort hotel or using the estate as a factory site. Neither the federal government nor the commonwealth of Virginia would agree to acquire it, but Miss Cunningham was determined to "save American honor from a blot in the eyes of the gazing world" and to establish a shrine where "the mothers of the land and their innocent children might make their offering in the cause of greatness, goodness, and prosperity of their country." The commonwealth of Virginia in 1856 chartered the Mount Vernon Ladies' Association of the Union. The Ladies' Association raised two hundred thousand dollars to buy the plantation and began preservation work on the mansion on February 22, 1860. Extravagant schemes were suggested, such as taking the house down piece by piece and replacing it with a marble-faced replica, but Miss Cunningham, with good common sense, declared that the Ladies' Association would "preserve with sacred reverence" Washington's house and grounds "in the state he left them."

Mount Vernon illustrates American reliance on private voluntary organizations. Amateur efforts could count, especially when led by clever, energetic women. The Ladies' Association, as an early example of effective organization, helped advance the cause of women's rights. Mount Vernon inspired many imitators. General Andrew Jackson's Hermitage near Nashville, Tennessee; George Mason's Gunston Hall and the Lees' Stratford Hall in Virginia; and Valley Forge in Pennsylvania are only a few of them. The fashion was for historic-house projects to refer to themselves as "second only to Mount Vernon."[28]

Another great contribution to saving historic houses was made by William Sumner Appleton through the Society for the Preservation of New England Antiquities (SPNEA), which he organized in Boston in 1910. Appleton had a much broader concept of historic preservation than the women who worked on Mount Vernon and on other early projects. To them, historical and patriotic purposes were dominant, and they regarded historic houses as shrines. They thought it best to develop the houses as museums devoted to great personalities and important historical events. Appleton, on the other hand, played up the architectural or aesthetic worth of historic houses. He wished to save them as useful documents of the past, and he saw clearly that many valuable houses would be lost if only those connected with great leaders and significant historical events were preserved. He also realized that not every historic house was suitable for, or could be supported as, a museum.

Thus, Appleton's society tried to save houses by continuing them as residences or by finding some suitable adaptive use (as offices, antiques shops, community centers, tearooms, and the like) that would not harm their fabric and would prolong their usefulness. This approach emphasized the mellow and pleasing aura of an old building for modern living. It also had the practical advantage of keeping the house on the tax roll. Appleton was so enthusiastic, inspiring, and ingenious that, at his death in 1947, his society possessed fifty-one historic structures scattered throughout New England outside of Vermont. Since then, SPNEA has continued its leadership in the preservation field.[29] In 2005 SPNEA changed its name to Historic New

England, offering many ways to experience the lives and stories of New Englanders, including access to thirty-five historic properties across the region, traveling exhibitions of New England treasures, an archive of over one million items, educational programs and events that use history to reach adults and students, and a tradition of partnership with owners of historic properties.[30]

Today there are six to eight thousand historic house museums in the United States, and new ones open every year.[31] The national bicentennial in 1976 stimulated preservation activities in communities across the country. Many houses and sites opened as public museums in the years surrounding the bicentennial celebrations.

In contrast to most U.S. historic houses and sites that celebrate the contributions of the owner or occupier of the site, at the end of the 20th century, representatives of a small group of historic sites began a dialogue in Italy that resulted in the formation of the International Coalition of Historic Site Museums of Conscience. Their purpose is to preserve sites "that stimulate dialogue on pressing social issues and promote humanitarian and democratic values as our primary function."[32] Several of their members are the Eastside Tenement Museum in New York, the Gulag Museum as Perm 36 in Russia, Slave House Museum in Senegal, and the Terezin Memorial in the Czech Republic. With this international organization, the 19th-century traditions of filiopietism and celebration have broadened to teaching the lessons of the past and actively promoting humanitarianism and social justice. See chapter 12 for further discussion of the Coalition.

Rather than preserving individual sites for museum purposes, leaders of U.S. historic preservation movements defined future growth in historic districts—areas of residential and adaptive uses in our cities. The first of these districts developed in Charleston and New Orleans in the 1930s, and there are about twenty-three hundred of them in existence today. This U.S. practice falls short of the French ecomuseum model. Though the districts usually designate some buildings as museums, the emphasis is on using the architectural past as a pleasant, inspiring background for modern living much in Appleton's tradition.[33]

The National Park Service, created in 1916 as part of the U.S. Department of the Interior, brought the federal government fully into the history museum and historic preservation movement with the Historic Sites Act of 1935. It declared the act "a national policy to preserve for historic use historic sites, buildings, and objects of national significance for the inspiration and benefit of the people of the United States." This policy was greatly expanded by the Historic Preservation Act of 1966, which established the National Register of Historic Places, created the Advisory Council on Historic Places to protect registered landmarks, and authorized the Park Service to administer a matching grants-in-aid program. The Park Service also developed trailside museums and visitor centers for its numerous archaeological and historical properties. A central coordinating but nongovernmental preservation agency appeared in 1949 in the National Trust for Historic Preservation, which operates a few properties of its own and advises and assists numerous member organizations.

Theme Parks and Interactive History Exhibitions

In 1955 cartoonist and moviemaker Walt Disney opened Disneyland in southern California. This amusement park included, in addition to carnival-type activities, exhibitions extolling Disney's products, American ingenuity, and patriotism. Throughout the mid–20th century, similar parks emerged. Some were merely for play but others provided experiences—reproduced European streetscapes complete with restaurants offering appropriate fare, small-scale Effiel Towers, and exhibitions that used technology to put visitors within historical tableaux. In a sense they reflected the atmosphere of the 19th-century international expositions in a permanent setting. In 1971 Disney added Disney World in Florida and subsequently, Experimental Prototype Community of Tomorrow (EPCOT) Center in 1982 focused on exposing visitors to technological innovations.[34] These parks, especially those operated by the Disney Corporation, focused on customer service, managing staff dress, manners, and even required smiles. These visitor-centered parks raised the standards for public service for all museums, especially those in the United States, and impacted exhibition techniques as well. In England, the Jorvik Center in York re-created underground the ancient Viking village on that site. Visitors travel in moving "cars" that pass re-created scenes of inhabitants living their lives in the town's ancient days, complete with the rank odors of the streets.[35] In 2005 the Abraham Lincoln Presidential Library and Museum opened to the public in Springfield, Illinois, featuring an interactive hologram theatrical experience that brings visitors into "contact" with Lincoln and other historical figures. In another setting, visitors are encouraged to "Ask Mr. Lincoln" and their questions are answered by an actor reading from Lincoln's words.[36] Twenty-first-century technology has bettered Charles Willson

Peale's Philadelphia Museum's "Perspective Views," but the notion is the same, to make history "come alive" for visitors.

Challenges

What's in a Name?

U.S. historical societies originated in socially exclusive groups and societies and today that exclusivity raises questions for institutions seeking to "serve the public." Some societies have literally changed their names (Western Pennsylvania Historical Society to Pittsburgh History Center, and Society for the Preservation of New England Antiquities to Historic New England) to signify their openness to new audiences. Others have changed their emphasis from museum activities to library services (Pennsylvania Historical Society) closing their museum exhibition spaces and disposing of three-dimensional collections, while others have closed their doors completely (Historical Society of Washington, D.C.). These changes, while scattered regionally and subject to local conditions, suggest that these societies need to adapt to changing interests and needs. See *The New-York Historical Society: Lessons from One Nonprofit's Long Struggle for Survival* by Kevin M. Guthrie for an instructive review and assessment of one society's institutional challenges (and failures?).[37]

Historical Collections Rule

Many U.S. history museums' collections center around 19th-century materials from upper middle-class, often white, citizens. This concentration and its concomitant financial obligation, limits the ability of many museums to illustrate the stories of all Americans in their exhibitions. As history museums seek to extend their audiences, this basic "limitation" of their collections complicates that process. The 1980s Scandinavian SAMDOK (samtidsdokumentation which means same-day documentation) project that sought to build contemporary collections from all elements of society has not been adopted in the United States.[38]

Collections and Collecting

Anders Sandvig, founder of Maihaugen in Norway, when interviewed in 1903, was asked if it was easy to acquire objects for his outdoor museum. He replied: "Oh, no . . . on the contrary people are in-clined to believe that everything . . . has quite enormous value."[39] The British and American television programs *Antiques Roadshow* and the Internet auction site eBay have affected history museum collecting in significant ways. The publicity of the potential value of everyday ob-jects has made collecting for history museums even more competitive and, perhaps more significantly, costly. While museums monitor eBay for desired objects for their collections and exhibitions, they also note that increased competition has raised prices for some items, even for those to be used in exhibitions as props.

History in Museums: Good, Bad, and Ugly?

How should community history museums that open to the public as a result of civic pride include the more disturbing elements of the past? What is the proper place for topics that might contradict conventional wisdom or mythology? How should visitors be informed of interpre-tation that includes subjects that may be offensive? Sociologist James Loewen in *Lies across America* suggests that in the United States there is an excessive number of "lies" perpetrated by history museums. "[His-toric house] guides almost always avoid negative or controversial facts, and . . . omit any blemishes that might taint the heroes they commem-orate, making them larger and less interesting than life." Historian David Lowenthal goes further, distinguishing history from heritage this way: "History tells all who will listen what has happened and how things came to be as they are. Heritage passes on exclusive myths of origin and continuance, endowing a select group with prestige and common purpose . . . History is for all, heritage for ourselves alone. . . . Heritage reverts to tribal rules that makes each past an exclusive, secret possession."[40]

Controversy and Public Funding

The National Air and Space Museum's exhibition on the end of World War II that became known simply as *The Enola Gay*; the Museum of American History's exhibit of sweatshops, *Between a Rock and a Hard Place*; and the Museum of the City of New York's *Gaelic Gotham: A His-tory of the Irish in New York City* are all exhibitions that echo public con-troversy over interpretation and public funding of museums, not simply history museums. History museums are especially vulnerable to public outcry when "interest" groups believe that their perspective has been "neglected," "ignored," "misrepresented," or fundamentally misinterpreted. These public controversies and the financial implications of funding cuts have chilled the atmosphere for edgy, provocative exhibitions. The opening label for *Between a Rock and a Hard Place* stated the issue well: "Why Do Museums Mount This Kind of Exhibition? History museums interpret difficult, unpleasant, or controversial episodes, not out of any desire to embarrass, be unpatriotic, or cause pain, but out of a responsibility to convey a fuller, more inclusive history. By examining incidents ripe with complexities and ambiguities, museums hope to stimulate greater understanding of the historical forces and choices that shaped America." The label was signed by Spencer Crew, director, and Lonnie Bunch, associate director of Curatorial Affairs, National Museum of American History, Smithsonian Institution.[41]

Proliferation of Historic Houses

Articles and conference presentations with titles such as "New Uses for Old Houses: Rethinking the Historic House Museum" and "Does America Need Another Historic House Museum?" are beginning to appear. And yet, communities continue to preserve the homes of their founding families to celebrate their past. As the *New York Times* reports: "Simply put, there may be too many antique houses, with too many similarly furnished living rooms, too few docents to show them all, and too many families taking advantage of cheaper airfares to show their children places like Versailles, where tourism is increasing." Who will provide the long-term operating funds for the museum? Volunteers often "staff" these museums, who will play that role? As communities change, will newer and more diverse residents have the interest and commitment to support the organization?[42]

Heritage Tourism

Heritage areas (regional clusters of historical and cultural organizations that combine, often with state or local government support, to promote tourism) are a growing phenomenon across Europe and the United States. These entities combine museums, tourist attractions, hotels, restaurants, and other tourism services into "marketing clusters." The challenges that attend them range from competitive marketing practices to issues of authenticity of interpretation. With the ongoing needs of museums to secure funding for their operating expenses, heritage areas are seen as a viable solution to that challenge.[43]

History in the Museum and in the Classroom

Academic historians and history museum professionals enjoy separate career paths. The former flourish in classrooms and in print, while the latter are engaged in interpreting the past through its physical evidence for museum visitors. In the late 1980s the Common Agenda for History Museums—a project of the American Association for State and Local History and the National Museum of American History with support from the National Endowment for the Humanities—addressed issues relating to these two professions and sought greater cooperation between them. Securing this cooperation is especially important as history museums strive to be authentic while competing with commercial leisure-time attractions for audiences. In *The Presence of the Past*, Roy Rosenzweig closes his "Afterthoughts" essay on this optimistic note: "The most significant news of this study is that we [historians] have interested, active, and thoughtful audiences for what we want to talk about. The deeper challenge is finding out how we can talk to—and especially with—those audiences." Historian Eric Foner, in an interview in *Museum News*, echoes Rosenzweig's position from the perspective of history exhibitions and scholarship: "But I think they [museums] don't give enough credit to the audience for being able to tackle complicated ideas, so there is frequently a tendency towards oversimplication. . . . I think that we owe it to visitors to give them the most up-to-date, complex history that we can, and that's where museums have sometimes fallen down in the past. The history presented has been oversimplified and too bland."[44]

Notes

1. Randolph Starn, "A Historian's Brief Guide to New Museum Studies," *American Historical Review* 110, no. 1 (February 2005): 68.
2. Arthur C. Parker, *A Manual for History Museums*, New York: Columbia University Press, 1935, p. 19.
3. Paul Richard, "Taking the Nation's Coin Collection Out of Circulation," *Washington Post*, April 30, 2004.
4. G. Ellis Burcaw, *Introduction to Museum Work*, 3rd ed., Walnut Creek, CA: AltaMira Press, 1997, p. 63.
5. Niels von Holst, *Creators, Collectors and Connoisseurs*, New York: Putman, 1967, pp. 92, 106; Francis Henry Taylor, *The Taste of Angels: A History of Art Collecting from Rameses to Napoleon*, Boston, 1948, pp. 77–78; Germain Bazin, *The*

Museum Age, New York: Universe Books, 1967, pp. 56–58; Alma S. Wittlin, *Museums: In Search of a Usable Future*, Cambridge, MA: MIT Press, 1970, p. 37.

6. Taylor, *The Taste of Angels*, p. 193; Bazin, *The Museum Age*, pp. 65–67.

7. Bazin, *The Museum Age*, pp. 102–104; Holst, *Creators*, p. 92.

8. Bazin, *The Museum Age*, p. 230; Hans Huth, "Pierre Eugene du Simitiere and the Beginnings of the American Historical Museum," *Pennsylvania Magazine of History and Biography* 69 (October 1945): 315–325; Charles Coleman Sellers, *Charles Willson Peale*, pp. 213, 264–265, 303, 334–344; John H. Demer, "The Portrait Busts of John H. I. Browere," *Antiques* 110 (July 1976): 111–117; E. P. Alexander, *The Museum: A Living Book of History*, Detroit, 1959, pp. 4–5, 7–8; E. P. Alexander, "An Art Gallery in Frontier Wisconsin," *Wisconsin Magazine of History* 29 (March 1946): 281–300.

9. Bazin, *The Museum Age*, p. 225; Ned J. Burns, "The History of Dioramas," *Museum News* 17 (February 15, 1940): 8–12; E. V. Gatacre, "The Limits of Professional Design," *Museums Journal* 76 (December 1976): 95; Sellers, *Peale*, pp. 205–211; Oliver W. Larkin, *Art and Life in America*, New York, 1949, pp. 112–113.

10. Larkin, *Art and Life*, p. 13; Sellers, *Peale*, pp. 204–211; Porter Butts, *Art in Wisconsin*, Madison, WI, 1936, pp. 53–63, 178–181; Edward P. Alexander, "Charles Willson Peale and His Philadelphia Museum," in *Museum Masters: Their Museums and Their Influence*, Nashville, TN: American Association of State and Local History, 1983, pp. 43–78.

11. www.vam.ac.uk; Victoria Newhouse, *Art and the Power of Placement*, New York: Monacelli Press, 2005, p. 267.

12. Mark B. Sandberg, *Living Pictures, Missing Persons: Mannequins, Museums and Modernity*, Princeton, NJ: Princeton University Press, 2003, pp. 208–231.

13. Kevin M. Guthrie, *The New-York Historical Society: Lessons from One Nonprofit's Long Struggle for Survival*, San Francisco, CA: Jossey-Bass, 1996.

14. Edward P. Alexander, "Ruben Gold Thwaites," in *The Museum in America: Innovators and Pioneers*, Walnut Creek, CA: AltaMira Press, 1997, pp. 85–100.

15. Michael Frisch, "The Presentation of Urban History in Big-City Museums," *History Museums in the United States: A Critical Assessment*, eds. Warren Leon and Roy Rosenzweig, Urbana: University of Illinois Press, 1989, pp. 38–63; Lonnie Bunch, "Fueled by Passion," in *Ideas and Images: Developing Interpretive History Exhibits*, eds. Kenneth L. Ames, Barbara Franco, and L. Thomas Frye, Nashville, TN: American Association of State and Local History, 1992, pp. 283–311.

16. *Smithsonian Year, 1980*, Washington, DC: Smithsonian Institution, 1981, p. 208; Arthur P. Molella, "Tilting at Windmills," *Technology and Culture* 36, no. 4 (1995): 1000–1006; Arthur P. Molella, "The Museum That Might Have Been: The Smithsonian's National Museum of Engineering and Industry," *Technology and Culture* 32, no. 2 (1991): 237–263.

17. Hermann Heinrich Frese, *Anthropology and the Public: The Role of Museums*, Leiden: E.J. Brill, 1960, pp. 11, 12; P. H. Pott, *National Museum of Ethnology, Leiden, 1837–1962*, The Hague, 1962, pp. 4–5; Mats Rehnberg, *The Nordiska Museet and Skansen*, Stockholm, 1957; Bo Lagercrantz, "A Great Museum Pio-

neer of the Nineteenth Century," *Curator* 7 (1964): 179–184; Lorwerth C. Peate, *Folk Museums*, Cardiff, 1948, pp. 15–21; Peter Michelsen, "The Outdoor Museum and Its Educational Program," in *Seminar on Preservation and Restoration*, Williamsburg, VA, 1963; *Historic Preservation Today*, Charlottesville, VA, 1966, pp. 201–217 and also comment by E. P. Alexander, pp. 218–224; F. A. Bather, "The Triumph of Hazelius," *Museums Journal* 16 (December 1916): 136; Holger Rasmussen, ed., *Dansk Folkemuseum und Frilandsmuseet*, Copenhagen, 1966, pp. 7–10; *The Sandvig Collections: Guide to the Open Air Museum*, Lillehammer, 1963; Reidar Kjellberg, "Scandinavian Open Air Museums," *Museum News* 39 (December 1960–January 1961): 18–22; Peter Holm, "The Old Town: A Folk Museum in Denmark," *Museums Journal* 37 (April 1937): 1–9; Adelhart Zippelius, *Handbuch der europaischen Freilichtmuseen*, Koln, 1975; Alexander, "Artur Hazelius and Skansen," in *Museum Masters*, pp. 239–276; Sandberg, *Living Pictures, Missing Persons*, pp. 123, 148–153; Tony Bennett, *The Birth of the Museum: History, Theory and Politics*, London: Routledge, 1995, pp. 110–114; Kenneth Hudson, *Museums of Influence*, Cambridge, UK: Cambridge University Press, 1987, chap. 6 (Skansen).

18. www.maihaugen.no.

19. Raymond B. Fosdick, *John D. Rockefeller, Jr.: A Portrait*, New York, 1956, pp. 272–301; E. P. Alexander, *The Interpretation Program of Colonial Williamsburg*,Williamsburg, VA, 1971, pp. 1–46; E. P. Alexander, "Restorations," in *In Support of Clio: Essays in Memory of Herbert A. Kellar*, eds. William B. Hesseltine and Donald R. McNeil, Madison, WI, 1958, pp. 195–214; Richard Handler and Eric Gable, *The New History in an Old Museum: Creating the Past in Colonial Williamsburg*, Durham, NC: Duke University Press, 1997; Henrietta Wexler, "The Way Things Really Were," and Tracey Linton Craig, "A Hard Row to Hoe," *Museum News* 69 no. 1 (January–February 1988); Michael Wallace, "Mickey Mouse History: Portraying the Past at Disney World," in *Mickey Mouse History and Other Essays on American Memory*, Philadelphia, PA: Temple University Press, 1996, pp. 13–16; Irvin Haas, *America's Historic Villages and Restorations*, New York: ARCO Publishing, 1974; Jay Anderson, *Time Machines: The World of Living History*, Nashville, TN: American Association of State and Local History, 1986; Candace Tangorra Matelic, "Through the Historical Looking Glass," *Museum News* 59, no. 2 (March–April 1980): 36–45; James Deetz, "A Sense of Another World: History Museums and Cultural Change," *Museum News* 59, no. 3 (May–June 1980): 40–45; David Peterson, "There Is No Living History, There Are No Time Machines," *History News* (September–October 1988): 28–30; Hudson, *Museums of Influence*, chap. 7 (Colonial Williamsburg).

20. William Greenleaf, *From These Beginnings: The Early Philanthropies of Henry and Edsel Ford, 1911–1936*, Detroit, MI, 1964, pp. 71–112; Allan Nevins and Frank Ernest Hill, *Ford: Expansion and Challenge, 1915–1933*, New York, 1957, pp. 497–506, 614; *Guidebook of Greenfield Village*, Dearborn, MI, 1957, p. 1; Greenfield Village and the Henry Ford Museum; Alexander, "Restorations," pp. 201–204; "The Henry Ford, America's Greatest History Attraction Brings the American Experience to Life," press release, January 28, 3003;

www.hfmgv.org; Wallace, *Mickey Mouse History*, pp. 9–13; See chapter 4 discussion of the Henry Ford name change 2003.

21. Steven Conn, *Museums and American Intellectual Life, 1876–1926*, Chicago, IL: University of Chicago Press, 1998, p. 158.

22. Conn, *Museums and American Intellectual Life*, p. 159.

23. www.Plimoth.org; Warren Leon and Margaret Piatt, "Living-History Museums," in *History Museums in the United States*, pp. 64–97.

24. Bather, "The Triumph of Hazelius."

25. Georges-Henri Riviere, "Role of Museums of Art and of Human and Social Sciences," *Museum* 25 no. 1–2 (1973): 38–44; Dominique Poulot, "Identity as Self-Discovery: The Ecomuseum in France," in *Museum Culture: Histories, Discourses and Spectacles*, eds. Daniel J. Sherman and Irit Rogoff, p. 73; Hudson, *Museums of Influence*, 163; Francois Monoit, "The Ecomuseums of Marqueze, Sabres, Part of Regional National Park of the Landes de Gascogne," *Museum* 25, no. 1–2, pp. 79–84; Kevin Walsh, *The Representation of the Past: Museum and Heritage in the Post-Modern World*, New York: Routledge, 1992, pp. 160–164.

26. New York State Legislature, *Assembly, Select Committee on the Petition of Washington Irving and Others to Preserve Washington's Headquarters in Newburgh*, No. 356, March 27, 1839, pp. 1–5.

27. Richard Caldwell, *A True History of the Acquisition of Washington's Headquarters at Newburgh, by the State of New York*, Salisbury Mills, NY, 1887, pp. 7–41; Charles B. Hosmer Jr., *Presence of the Past: A History of the Preservation Movement in the United States before Williamsburg*, New York: Putnam, 1965, pp. 35–37; Alexander, "Anne Pamela Cunningham," in *Museum Masters*, pp. 177–204; Michael Wallace, "Preserving the Past: Historic Preservation in the U.S.," in *Mickey Mouse History*; John A. Herbst, "Historic Houses," in *History Museums in the United States*, pp. 98–114; Patricia West, *Domesticating History: The Political Origins of America's House Museums*, Washington, DC: Smithsonian Institution Press, 1999, pp. 1–37; Rosanne Pavoni, "Towards a Definition and Typology of Historic House Museums," *Museum International* 53, no. 2 (2001): 16–21; Karen Zukowski, "The Importance of Context," in *Conservation in Context: Finding a Balance for the Historic House Museum*, ed. Wendy Claire Jessup, Washington, DC: National Trust for Historic Preservation, 1995, pp. 5–19.

28. Gerald W. Johnson, *Mount Vernon: The Story of a Shrine*, New York, 1953, pp. 8–11; Hosmer, *Presence of the Past*, pp. 44–62.

29. Hosmer, *Presence of the Past*, pp. 255–257; E. P. Alexander, "Sixty Years of Historic Preservation: The Society for the Preservation of New England Antiquities," *Old-Time New England* 61 (1970–1971): 14–19; Alexander, "William Sumner Appleton," in *The Museum in America*, pp. 101–115.

30. www.historicnewengland.org; Wallace, "Preserving the Past," in *Mickey Mouse History*.

31. William O. Dupuis, "The Hillside Solution: Readapting an Historic House for the Community," *History News*, Summer 2005, pp. 12–16.

32. www.sitesofconscience.org; see *Worklab Newsletter* no. 3 (2000).

33. William C. Everhart, *The National Park Service*, New York, 1972, pp. 33, 74–79, 249–260; U.S. Council of Mayors, *With Heritage So Rich: A Report on Historic Preservation*, New York, 1966, pp. 204–208; American Association of Museums, *The Official Museum Directory, 1977: United States and Canada*, Washington, DC: American Association of Museums, 1976, pp. 849–871; National Alliance of Preservation Commissions, www.napc.uga.edu.

34. Wallace, "Mickey Mouse History," in *Mickey Mouse History*; Gary Kulik, "Designing the Past: History-Museum Exhibitions from Peale to the Present," in *History Museums in the United States*, pp. 3–37.

35. www.jorvik-viking-centre.co.uk.

36. Edward Rothstein, "Strumming the Mystic Chords of Memory," *New York Times*, April 29, 2005; Daniel Spock, "Lincolns in Latex: Exploring Lincoln's Legacy at the Abraham Lincoln Library and Museum," pp. 95–104 and Beverly Serrell, "The Abraham Lincoln Library and Museum: The Civil War in Four Minutes," pp. 105–108, *Curator* 49, no. 1 (2006), two thoughtful reviews of the Lincoln Museum and one of its films; Myron Marty, "The Abraham Lincoln Presidential Library and Museum," *Public Historian* 28, no. 3 (Summer 2006): 185–189.

37. Guthrie, *The New-York Historical Society*.

38. Bengt Nystrom and Gunilla Cedrenius, "Spread the Responsibility for Museum Documentation—A Programme for Contemporary Documentation at Swedish Museums of Cultural History," Stockholm: SAMDOK Council, 1982; Thomas Schlereth, "Defining Collecting Missions: National and Regional Models," in *A Common Agenda for History Museums*, ed. Lonn W. Taylor, Nashville, TN: American Association of State and Local History, 1987; Anne Applebaum, "Give 'Attic' a Story to Tell," *Washington Post*, June 21, 2005.

39. Sandberg, *Living Pictures, Missing Persons*, p. 184.

40. James W. Loewen, *Lies across America: What Our Historic Sites Get Wrong*, Touchstone, 2000, p. 17; David Lowenthal, *Possessed by the Past*, New York: Free Press, 1996, p. 128; Thomas J. Schlereth, "Causing Conflict, Doing Violence," *Museum News* 63, no. 1 (October 1984): 45–52; Julia Clark, "Talking with Empty Rooms," Island of Vanishment Conference, Port Arthur, Tasmania, June 2002; Jennifer Eichstedt, "Museums and (In)Justice," in *Museum Philosophy for the Twenty-first Century*, ed. Hugh H. Genoways, Lanham, MD: AltaMira Press, 2006, pp. 127–138.

41. Martin Harwit, *An Exhibit Denied*, New York: Copernicus, 1996; Mary Alexander, "Do Visitors Get It? A Sweatshop Exhibit and Visitors' Comments," *Public Historian* 22, no. 3 (Summer 2000): 85–94; Bob Thompson, "Who Owns History?" *Washington Post Magazine*, January 20, 2002, pp. 14–29; Edward Linenthal, *History Wars: The Enola Gay and Other Battles for the American Past*, New York: Metropolitan Books, 1996; Wallace, *Mickey Mouse History*, pp. 269–318; Loewen, *Lies across America*, pp. 443–447; Steven C. Dubin, *Displays of Power: Memory and Amnesia in the American Museum*, New York: New York University Press, 1999.

42. Carol B. Stapp and Kenneth C. Turino, "Does America Need Another Historic House Museum?" *History News* 59, no. 3 (Summer 2004): 7–11; Dupuis,

"The Hillside Solution," pp. 12–16; Tracie Rozhon, "Homes Sell, and History Goes Private," *New York Times*, December 31, 2006.

43. Lowenthal, *Possessed by the Past*; Timothy W. Luke, *Museum Politics: Power Plays at the Exhibition*, Minneapolis: University of Minnesota Press, 2002, p. 224.

44. Taylor, *A Common Agenda for History Museums*; Roy Rosenzweig and David Thelen, *Presence of the Past: Popular Uses of History in American Life*. New York: Columbia University Press, 1998, p. 189; Eric Foner, "The Historian in the Museum," *Museum News* 85, no. 2 (March–April 2006): 46–47; Susan A. Crane, "Memory, Distortion and History in the Museum," in *Museum Studies: An Anthology of Contexts*, ed. Bettina Messias Carbonell, London: Blackwell, 2004: Starn, "A Historians Brief Guide," pp. 68–98.

6

Botanical Gardens and Zoos

The [botanical garden's] challenge and aim is to make the visitor's first impression one of entering a garden where science reigns.

—Mary Soderstrom, 2001[1]

Some people have the mistaken impression that botanical gardens are parks devoid of play, something like 19th century museums where plants bear labels with unpronounceable names. Modern botanical gardens, however, are global treasures in an age of ecological crisis.

—H. Bruce Rinker, 2002[2]

[Ninteenth-century zoos' three purposes]: to advance science, to promote public education, and to provide people with a refuge from the pressures of urban environments.

—Nigel Rothfels, 2002[3]

Throughout history, zoos have entertained and educated; now they have a staggering opportunity before them: to tip the global balance back in favor of nature. To work toward the restoration of harmony in the living world. Zoos, which have provided so much joy to people, can now breathe life back into moribund populations of wild creatures.

—Vicki Croke, 1997[4]

Botanical gardens, arboretums, zoos, and aquariums fit into the definition of a museum adopted by the American Association of Museums. They are organized, permanent, and nonprofit in form; essentially educational or aesthetic in purpose; have a professional staff; and own, utilize, and conserve tangible objects that they exhibit to the public on some regular schedule. The only difference between them and an ordinary museum is that their objects are alive. As the 21st century opens, each of these institutions strives both to serve their public visitors and to engage them in understanding the importance of biodiversity and its protection.

The botanical garden is a collection of labeled plants, the primary purpose of which is the advancement and diffusion of botanical knowledge. The garden studies taxonomy, the system of classification and nomenclature of plants, and experimental botany that deals with their anatomy, cytology, and metabolism. An arboretum is virtually the same as a botanical garden except that it specializes in woody plants. Over 1,800 botanical gardens and arboretums in 148 countries annually welcome over 200 million visitors.[5]

Similarly, a zoological garden (usually shortened to "zoo") or aquarium contains a collection of labeled animals to be protected and studied while incidentally providing enlightenment and enjoyment for the public. Animal physiology and psychology are the chief subjects for zoo research. Zoos, unlike museums, often include in their formal mission statements references to "recreation" as one of their primary purposes.

The First Botanical Gardens

Humankind has long enjoyed and appreciated the aesthetic, medicinal, and economic uses of plants and has mixed these purposes for organizing a garden with the purely scientific and botanical ones. While the gardens of the ancients, of the semimythical Emperor Shen Nung (2800 BC), of the King of Thebes or of Thutmose III at the Temple of Karnak in Egypt (both about 1500 BC), and of Aristotle in Athens or the Mouseion at Alexandria (4th century BC) may not have been true botanical gardens, they contained exotic plants, both beautiful and useful. Similarly the gardens of herbs and simples [medicinal plants] of the early monasteries such as Saint Gall (9th century) or even the Holburn Physic Garden at London (1575) had many botanical features. The

Mexican gardens of Istapalan and Chalco encountered by Cortez and his followers were closer to true botanical gardens, for the Aztecs had made considerable study of medical botany.[6]

There is a long-standing dispute over whether the first European botanic garden was situated in Padua or Pisa. The senate of the Venetian Republic ordered the garden at Padua in May 1545, and its original layout remains largely intact. Its rectangular plan shows elegance and taste, with a central circle eighty meters in diameter and beds arranged geometrically inside. Francesco Bonafede was its founder, Giovanni Moroni drew the plan, and Luigi Squalerno (commonly called Anguillara) was its first prefect. It was attached to the University of Padua, which had had a Chair of Simples (medicinal plants) since 1533, and in 1591 it issued the first garden catalog. The English botanist John Ray reported on his visit to Padua in 1644: "Here is a publick Physick garden, well stored with simples but more noted for its prefects, men eminent for their skill in Botanics." Goethe visited the garden before 1790 and especially admired a palm planted in 1585; "Goethe's Palm" still flourishes today in its unique greenhouse.[7]

The Pisa garden may have been in existence in July 1545, but was moved to the site it occupies today in 1595. It was founded by Luca Ghini, and its second prefect, Andrea Cesalpino, was a famed botanist. Its arrangement was geometric with separate sections for bulbs and poisonous, prickly, odoriferous, marsh plants, and an arboretum was added to the garden in 1841. The prefect gave lectures on simples and actual demonstrations on living plant specimens in the garden. It was attached to the University of Pisa.[8]

Another famed early botanic garden, Hortus Botanicus, was established in Leiden in 1587. The university there decided that a botanical, rather than an apothecary, garden was better suited for the development of its medical faculty and persuaded the great botanist Charles de l'Ecluse (Carolus Clusius) to become its second prefect, 1593–1609. The Leiden garden had a succession of able directors, including Hermann Boerhaave, 1709–1730, with whom Linnaeus studied. He published a catalog of the garden, but perhaps more significantly he introduced the tulip to Holland and the potato to Europe. In 1740 the garden was open every day (even on Sundays), though a small fee was charged and "couples openly in love are on no account admitted." Today Clusius' garden has been re-created, allowing visitors to experience the original plan of the garden. The garden merged with three university gardens in 1989 to form the Nationaal Herbarium Nederland (NHN). The consortium has oversight for the Clusis and Von Siebold gardens along with tropical greenhouses and an orangery. It is one of the largest herbariums in the world and its collections are accessible on the Internet.[9]

Other 16th-century gardens were established at Zurich, Bologna (1567); Leipzig, Montpellier (1593); Heidelberg (1597); and Copenhagen (1600), and by 1700 there were twenty such gardens in Europe, usually connected with universities. Interest in close observation and taxonomy caused scientific botany to thrive as an adjunct to the medical schools in the universities at a time when the development of other sciences was being hampered by medieval tradition. The Oxford Botanic Garden (1621) boasted a "Nursery of Simples" and "a Professor of Botanicey"; its conservatory was heated by a four-wheel fire basket of burning charcoal hauled back and forth by a gardener. In 1670 Dr. Robert Morison, professor of botany, took his class in the Medical School "to the Physic Garden where he read in the middle of it (with a table before him) on herbs and plants for five weeks space, not without a considerable Auditory." At Montpellier in 1773 a professor taught anatomy at the university in the winter and botany at the garden in the summer.[10]

The private garden of the Tradescants was contemporary with Oxford, and the Chelsea Physic Garden was founded at London in 1673 by the Society of Apothecaries. Sir Hans Sloane purchased a site for it in 1722 on the condition that it present fifty well-dried and preserved specimens of distinct plants to the Royal Society each year until two thousand had been given. Philip Miller, whom Linnaeus called "the Prince of Gardeners" and whose *Gardeners Dictionary* (1731) soon ran through eight editions, was head gardener at Chelsea in 1723. He trained William Aiton, first gardener of Kew, and Dr. Nathaniel Bagshaw Ward, the physician who, about 1833, invented the Wardian case, a small portable greenhouse (like today's terrarium) that made possible the successful transportation of plants. By Miller's day, botanical gardens were found throughout western Europe, including one on the Apothecary Island in Saint Petersburg (1714).[11]

European botanical gardens evolved into distinct types over the centuries. The 16th and 17th centuries saw medicinal gardens that provided university medical faculties with plant material. Colonial gardens emerged in the 17th and 18th centuries with growing fascination for the new plant materials from Europe's far-flung colonies. Linnaean gardens developed in the 18th century and affected 19th-century gardens as well with a focus on the taxonomy of plants, both native and colonial in origin. Civic gardens reflected the growing urbanization of Europe and the United States in the 19th and early 20th centuries. To complement civic gardens, specialist gardens focused on plant materials of specific types and emphasized research and conservation. And today, the sanctuary garden reflects the need to protect plant material from degradation and extinction.[12]

The Royal Botanic Gardens at Kew

In the 1750s Augusta Saxe-Gotha, dowager princess of Wales, began to develop her nine acres in Kew House west of London as a botanical garden. They had been laid out by William Kent, the landscape architect. She was assisted in this work by Lord Bute (John Stuart, third earl of Bute), a keen and knowledgeable botanist. The dowager princess commissioned Sir William Chambers, the distinguished architect, to embellish the grounds with various fanciful structures. Of these, the Alhambra, Mosque, and Gothic Cathedral have disappeared, but the Pagoda (1761–1762), Ruined Arch (1759), Orangery (1760), and several smaller temples remain. The garden was arranged scientifically under the Linnaean system and had a physic garden section. In 1759 William Aiton, upon Philip Miller's recommendation, became its head. Augusta's son George III, in 1772 inherited Kew and joined to it his Richmond Lodge garden; thus, the name, "the Royal Botanic Gardens of Kew." The king loved Kew and enjoyed playing the role of "Farmer George" there. He retained Aiton as "His Majesty's Principal Gardener of Kew" and also employed Lancelot ("Capability") Brown to landscape the gardens.[13]

The king's chief botanical adviser, however, was Sir Joseph Banks, just home from a round-the-world trip with Captain Cook on the *Endeavour*. Banks determined to make the little botanic garden a place where plants from every country could be seen and "a great exchange house of the Empire, where possibilities of acclimatising plants could be tested." He sent collectors across the empire. By the time the king and Sir Joseph died in 1820, some seven thousand new plants had come to Kew from overseas.

After the passing of George III and Banks, the Royal Gardens deteriorated, but an investigative committee report caused Parliament in 1840 to transfer them from the personal property of the Crown to the Commissioners of Woods and Forests. Thus, Kew became a national institution. In 1841 Sir William Jackson Hooker was named its first director. Sir

William had served for twenty years as regius professor of botany at Glasgow. In five years he expanded the fifteen acres of the gardens to 250 acres. With the help of architect Decimus Burton and engineer Richard Turner, he built the graceful and airy Great Palm House—363 feet long and 62 feet high, with 45,000 square feet of glass, the largest planthouse in the world. He added a herbarium and library, admitted the public on weekdays and published a guidebook. In 1848 he started a Museum of Economic Botany to exhibit plants useful for commerce, industry, and medicine.

Kew became the great center for botanical exchange. Plant exploration continued, and Sir William's son, Dr. Joseph Dalton Hooker, after going with Sir James Ross to Antarctica from 1848 to 1850, explored the Himalayas in India, Sikkim, Tibet, and Nepal and sent back many exotic plants, including beautiful rhododendrons. Cinchona plants (from which quinine is derived) came to Kew from Peru, to be grown and sent to India. Cork oaks from Portugal were developed for South Australia, tobacco for Natal, and China tea for Assam. Coffee, allspice, cinnamon, mango, tamarind, cotton, ginger, and indigo went around the world in Wardian cases from the nurseries and forcing houses of Kew.[14]

In 1865 Dr. Joseph Dalton Hooker became director at Kew on the death of his father. He continued the plant exploration and exchange. He greatly improved the research facilities. The herbarium begun in 1853 was enlarged when Parliament purchased his father's collection in 1866; today Kew has the largest herbarium in the world, with some 7 million dried specimens, adding thirty thousand specimens each year. The library counts 450,000 individual records including maps, manuscripts, photographs, and books on the history of Kew. In 1876 the Jodrell Laboratory was set up to study the structure and physiology of plants. In 1965 the gardens leased the great Wakehurst garden at Ardingly in Sussex from the National Trust—five hundred acres with fertile soil, abundant rainfall, long periods of sunshine, and mild climate that allowed for the surival of complementary collections from South America and Australasian locales. The Cell Physiology Laboratory and Millennium Seedbank Project are now located at Wakehurst. The seed bank seeks to collect the seeds of twenty-five thousand species from around the world.[15]

Kew also began to be known in this period as a nursery for botanists and gardeners. As early as 1860, lectures were given to foremen and gardeners, and more recently a one- or two-year student-gardener internship developed. Kew's Diploma in Horticulture welcomes twenty students annually for its three-year intensive training. Just as in the 19th century, through this training program Kew students influence botanic gardens worldwide.

Other European Botanical Gardens

The Royal Botanic Garden at Edinburgh is another important British horticultural institution. The fourth garden in that city since 1670, it moved to its present site at Inverleith (now seventy-five acres) in 1820. Again, family succession was important. William McNab, the principal gardener, was followed by his son James, a true landscape artist who also helped Edinburgh University develop an outstanding school of landscape gardening. John Hutton Balfour and his son Isaac Bailey were both regius keepers, and the son shifted the research focus to investigating the function and structure of living plants. George Forrest, of the garden's herbarium, made seven plant-exploring trips to China and brought back many of the rhododendrons for which the Royal Botanic is famous. In 2001 the garden formalized its links to three sites in China based at the Garden and Research Station in Yunnan, continuing the 19th-century connections. Its rock garden, rose garden, arboretum, herbaceous borders, and greenhouses are all outstanding.[16]

The Jardin des Plantes in Paris, founded in 1635 and opened to the public in 1640, began as a royal garden. It was renowned for its great botanists and their study of the chemistry of plants but was not influential in the development of either ornamental horticulture or economic botany. Georges Buffon directed the garden for forty-nine years, and in that time he doubled its size, organized the collections along Linnean principles, dispatched collectors worldwide, and published a thirty-six-volume *Histoire Naturelle*. After the Revolution, the garden's formal name was changed to the Museum of Natural History, reflecting its scientific focus. It also added a small group of animals to its collections at that time. The garden's seventy-acre central location in Paris makes it a favorite of Parisians and the city's international visitors.[17]

On the continent, Vienna has two botanical gardens that go back to the 18th century—the Belvedere, with the oldest Alpine collection in Europe, and Schonbrunn, with an elaborate set of greenhouses, not so important botanically, but demonstrating that a garden can survive economically by growing beautiful plants for commercial sale. The Berlin Botanical Garden (today the Berlin-Dahlem Botanical Museum) was founded by Carl Ludwig Willdenow in 1801, who also taught at the University of Berlin and had Alexander von Humboldt as a student. Heinrich Friedrich Link fused the botanical garden, royal herbarium, and library into a single powerful institution that placed scientific botany first but never forgot to attract and educate the general public. It opened to the public in 1910. Destroyed in 1945, the garden reopened to the public in 1950, but without its original conservatories (they were reconstructed in 1968). One of Europe's largest gardens, the Berlin Botanical Garden covers 126 acres and includes sixteen greenhouses that allow visitors to "travel" through tropical and subtropical plant life. Just as in its early years, it is committed to education "to deepen the [public's] knowledge necessary for the utilization and protection of plant diversity on earth."[18]

Uppsala University in Sweden has a botanical garden that goes back to the early 18th century. Its students stood in the center of a geometric plan looking toward the circumference of a circle; the labels faced out so that only the professor could see them. The university also properly maintains the little garden based on Linnaeus' plan of 1745.[19] The first Russian botanical garden (1714) was in Saint Petersburg, and with the National Herbarium, is today part of the Komarov Botanical Institute. It is a special challenge to maintain a garden in the city's harsh climate but it is famous for its 18th-century Siberian plants and conifers from North America and Asia. Despite losses in World War II, the garden exceeds its prewar conditions and research practices.[20]

Economic Botanical Garden Expansion

The British Empire was largely responsible for a worldwide expansion of botanical gardens, as it provided new crops and economic resources for its colonies. Other than the British Isles, its first tropical garden was at Pamplemousse in Mauritius (1735), which introduced nutmeg, pepper, cinnamon, and other spices from the East Indies and improved the production of sugar cane. Gardens were also established in the West Indies at Saint Vincent (1764), Jamaica (1774), and Trinidad (1819).[21]

What today is the Indian Botanic Garden at Calcutta was started by Robert Kyd in 1787 as a garden of acclimatization for food and spice plants, teak trees, and the like. Six years later, Dr. William Roxburgh, a distinguished botanist, became its superintendent and transformed it into a true botanical garden with plants from India, Southeast Asia, and the Far East. He introduced the mahogany tree from West Indian seeds, reputed progenitor of all Indian mahogany trees. In 1851 Superintendent Robert Fortune returned from China with seventeen thousand tea plants, forming the basis for India's tea industry.[22] Ten years later, Superintendent Thomas Anderson introduced cinchona for the production of quinine, for which he established a commercial plantation in Sikkim, and expanded the garden with an arboretum. After two disastrous tornadoes, Sir George King in 1871 rebuilt and expanded the garden to its present 270 acres. Its great banyan tree may be the largest plant living; it is about two hundred years old, one hundred feet high, one-fourth mile long, and with a canopy covering four acres.[23]

The botanic garden in Sri Lanka was started on Slave Island in 1812 by William Kerr, its chief gardener, and moved to its present location at Peradeniya ten years later by Alexander Moon. Its most famous superintendent was Henry George Kendrick Thwaites. In 1860 he established a satellite garden high in the mountains at Hakgala for the successful growing of cinchona and later at Henaratogoda for rubber. He fought a parasite disease attacking coffee plantations, developed the tea brought from China to Peradeniya in 1828, failed to establish cotton, but secured good results with cacao, coca (from which comes cocaine), camphor, nutmeg, clove, vanilla, croton, oil palm, mahogany, and eucalyptus.[24] Two beautiful botanical gardens are situated at Bogor in Java and at Singapore. Bogor (1817), developed by the Dutch, has two hundred acres with six thousand species of trees and shrubs and five thousand species of lesser flowering plants as well as a mountain garden of five thousand acres at Cibodas. Kew-trained Henry James Murton led the development of Singapore's garden (1822). He built a herbarium and library and introduced many plant exchanges; coffee and rubber being the most important. Australia has two botanical gardens with especially handsome sites at Sydney (1816) and Melbourne (1854).[25]

The South African National Botanical Garden at Kirstenbosch, a few miles from Cape Town, is descended from the Company's Garden or Town Garden (1750) and the Botanic Garden of Cape Town (1848). Cecil Rhodes bought four hundred acres at Kirstenbosch and left it to the state. In 1911 Harold Welch Pearson, trained at Kew, organized the wild site filled with Cape Province plants in the lee of Table Mountain into a botanical garden and served as its first director. Its function is to preserve South African flora. Today its success comes from government funds and resources from the Botanical Society of South Africa (founded in 1913).[26]

The Botanic Garden in Rio de Janeiro was founded largely for economic reasons. In 1808 Prince Regent John VI of Portugal bought an old sugar mill property to acclimatize useful plants from the East Indies. That same year Luiz de Abreu, a Portuguese naturalist, was captured by the French and interned in the West Indies on Ile de France, which had an acclimatization garden, Jardin Gabrielle. De Abreu escaped to Brazil, carrying seeds and roots that he planted in the royal garden. At his urging, Asiatic plants including tea and superior sugar cane were imported. Frei do Sacramento and Joao Barbosa Rodriguez were two of the garden's great directors. The garden contains marvelous avenues of royal palms two hundred feet high, descended from the seed smuggled from Jardin Gabrielle by de Abreu.[27]

American Botanical Gardens

During the colonial period, John Bartram, plantsman and plant explorer, collected native species at his farm near Philadelphia as early as 1728. John Bartram's cousin, Humphrey Marshall, in 1773 established a similar garden at West Bradford in Chester County near Philadelphia. Robert and William Prince started a nursery at Flushing, Long Island, in 1737, and four generations of their family continued the business until 1867; for a time they called part of it the Linnaean Botanic Garden. A most important early venture was the Elgin Botanic Garden of 1801 that occupied twenty acres in New York City on the present site of Rockefeller Center. Its founder was Dr. David Hosack, prominent physician and professor of botany and materia medica at Columbia College, who considered the garden a valuable adjunct to his teaching. By 1811, however, he was compelled to sell to the state of New York, which eventually turned the property over to Columbia College. The college allowed the garden to deteriorate and disappear.[28]

Today there are over five hundred botanical gardens in the United States. The oldest is the Missouri Botanical Garden of seventy-five acres, organized at Saint Louis in 1859. Henry Shaw, a native Englishman, came to Saint Louis in 1819 and made a fortune in merchandising. Dr. George Engelmann, a German immigrant physician and botanist, urged Shaw to transform his estate into a botanical garden, and Asa Gray of Harvard and Joseph Hooker, later director at Kew, supported that idea. Dr. Engelmann refused the directorship of the garden because it was too far out of town (now about twenty minutes from center city) and Shaw, from 1859 to 1889, served as director of what is often still called "Shaw's Garden."[29]

The Missouri Botanical Garden has a fine herbarium (including the Bernhardi collection of more than 5 million specimens), a library, an orangery (the Linnaean House which is the oldest continuously operating display conservatory in the United States) built in 1850, conservatories for American and South African desert plants, two rose gardens, outstanding collections of the flora of Panama and of water lilies (developed by George H. Pring), and good arrangements with local colleges and universities for training gardeners. Perhaps its most spectacular feature is the Climatron, a Buckminster Fuller geodesic dome, built in 1960, eighty feet high and 175 feet in diameter. The Climatron controls air and humidity so as to provide different climatic environments for the plants grown there. Today it is linked to the Shoenberg Temperate House and the Brookings Interpretive Center with changing public exhibitions. The Temperate House has established long-term inventories of South American plants, providing online access to its extensive database. The William Kemper Center for Home Gardening answers home gardener's questions and training needs and keeps biodiveristy issues before the public.[30]

The Arnold Arboretum of 265 acres, situated at Jamaica Plain, just outside Boston, contains the greatest collection of woody plants in the United States. James Arnold left Harvard University money to establish the arboretum in 1872, and Charles Sprague Sargent, brother of the artist John Singer Sargent, served as its director for fifty-four years, from 1873 to 1927. He was a remarkable botanical administrator who carried out well his charge to grow "all the trees, shrubs, and herbaceous plants, either indigenous or exotic, which can be raised in the open air" at that location. Sargent and Frederick Law Olmsted, the distinguished landscape architect, persuaded the city of Boston to include the arboretum in its park plan and to construct driveways and help with its maintenance. It was planted according to Olmsted's plan in 1885 and soon acquired a fine herbarium and library. The Arnold combined serving Boston's population with scientific study and worldwide exploration activities.[31]

Today, the New York Botanical Garden in the Bronx is the country's largest, with two thousand acres (including its Cary Arboretum at Millbrook) and an annual budget of just under 8 million dollars serving nearly a million visitors. Inspired by the gardens at Kew, it was founded in 1891 and is strongly research oriented with a magnificent library and numerous publications. It does advanced scientific work in fields that include fungi, mosses, algae, plant ecology, geography, plant nutrition, microbiology, physiology and pathology of fungi, and diseases and pests of ornamental plants. And, its Children's Adventure Garden is a national model.[32]

The Huntington Botanical Gardens in San Marino, California, was established in 1903, when Henry E. Huntington, the railroad magnate, acquired an estate there and decided to develop a library and art gallery with encircling gardens. The garden opened to the public in 1928. William Hertrich, an Austrian-trained botanist, was superintendent of the 207 acres. It contains camellias and wildflowers; gardens featuring sculpture, palms, roses, herbs, and Shakespearean and Japanese themes; and an unrivaled desert garden made by Hertrich on ten acres with twenty-five thousand plants.[33] The gardens blended Huntington's interest in adorning his home with a public commitment to horticulture. Twenty-first-century garden additions include the largest Chinese-style garden outside China and the Rose Hill Conservatory for Botanical Sciences that emphasizes programming for schoolchildren.

The Brooklyn Botanic Garden, founded in 1910, is a small oasis (fifty acres) in a busy city and is devoted to teaching botany, horticulture, and nature conservation. It is supported partially by a nonprofit society with enthusiastic dues-paying members and partially by the city of New York. It has three Japanese gardens; two gardens for roses; boulder, herb, local flora, and small model gardens; a Fragrance Garden for the blind, with Braille labels; and a superb collection of bonsai. The Botanic Garden started as an empty field but was cleverly planned by Frederick Law Olmsted and Calvert Vaux. Dr. C. Stuart Gager, its first director, was determined to bring plants and people together, and it is in the educational area that the garden has excelled. A special garden for children opened in 1914 and was refurbished in 1990. The vision has been public participation—to learn by growing.[34]

Longwood Gardens at Kennett Square, Pennsylvania, contains plants chosen for beauty and display and thus does not constitute a true botanical garden. The garden covers a thousand acres and includes an arboretum established about 1800 by Joshua and Samuel Peirce. In 1906 Pierre S. du Pont, prominent industrialist of the Du Pont Company and General Motors, bought the tract to save the arboretum from destruction. In 1921 he established the gardens as a permanent public institution. He conceived of Longwood as a cultural center devoted primarily to horticulture but also to architecture, music, and drama. Thus Longwood has gardens, conservatories, perhaps the most spectacular fountains in the United States, a singing-chimes tower, a pipe organ, and an open-air theater.

The outdoor gardens include the old arboretum, varied wildflowers, and more formal sections that focus on rock, topiary, rose, and water lily plantings. Especially evident is the influence of the Italian Villa d'Este and Villa Gamberaia and the French Versailles and Fontainebleau. The conservatories cover about four acres and vary from desert to tropical rain forest. Longwood has supported many activities of value to American horticulture. It has cooperated with the U.S. Department of Agriculture in sending plant explorers to the far reaches of the world, and it has supported the American Horticultural Society's project to computerize all plant species in American botanical gardens.[35] Its graduate training program in public horticulture, offered in association with nearby University of Delaware, began in 1967. It specifically trains professionals to work in the nation's botanical gardens.

The Fairchild Tropical Garden on the outskirts of Miami, Florida, occupies eighty-three acres. It was founded in 1935 and opened to the public in 1938 by Col. Robert A. Montgomery, businessman and avid plant collector. It was established in Florida because of its climate and named to honor Dr. David Fairchild, who, as head of the Plant Introduction Bureau of the U.S. Department of Agriculture, had brought many tropical plants to the state. Fifty-eight acres of the garden are maintained by Dade County, and the remaining twenty-five acres are maintained by the Fairchild Tropical Garden Association, which has planted and maintains a palmetum with more than five hundred species. The garden also possesses outstanding collections of cycads, bromeliads, and philodendrons; conducts important scientific research; and has a varied educational program for adults and schoolchildren.[36]

Challenges of Botanical Gardens

Elitism

Botanical gardens in the past have been much like art museums; the beauty of their collections has attracted an audience sensitive to aesthetic appeals—in this case, color, texture, design, perfume, and natural growth. Professional botanists, nurserymen, and keen amateur gardeners have come to the gardens to study plants and ways to grow them. Women's garden clubs (often the most elite of organizations) have also patronized the gardens. These groups neglected the interests of the general public. Furthermore, changing urban demographics have sometimes left a botanical garden like a beached whale on a barren and unfriendly shore.

Beyond the Garden Visit

The challenges for all botanic gardens are to attact people and to use innovative education programs that engage the public and raise their awareness of the issues involving the maintenance of biological diversity and sustainable living and the cultural, conservation, and scientific purposes of plant collection. Since 1998, the World Conservation Union (IUCN) has published a "Red List," a searchable database that records threatened species. Of four hundred thousand species of plants identified worldwide, 60 percent are threatened with extinction within this century, and approximately thirty-four thousand are threatened today. What is the appropriate role for botanical gardens to play in protecting these threatened species and in alerting the public to these impending losses?[37]

Garden Budgets and Conservation Commitments

Two hundred botanic gardens have developed seed banks for the storage of seeds, mainly of wild species. Seed banks take up little space, but can be expensive to run, both because of the need to maintain low temperatures and the necessity for ongoing viability tests. Declining botanic garden budgets and lack of public awareness of the need for seed banks place this practice at risk.[38]

Go Where the Plants Are

Many threatened plant species are found in the world's tropical regions, but botanical gardens are concentrated in the northern-temperate zone where collections must be maintained in conservatories where they are exposed to greater risk. The challenge is to develop more botanical gardens in tropical zones; in other words, where the plants grow, not where the visitors are.[39]

From Menageries to Zoos

Humankind has always been interested in the other animals of the world as sources of food and clothing, as companions or pets, and as strange and curious phenomena. The domestication of animals goes back many millennia, perhaps fifty thousand years for the dog. Queen Hatshepsut of Egypt in the 15th century BC had an extensive palace menagerie that she stocked with monkeys, leopards, birds, wild cattle, and a giraffe; she sent an animal-collecting expedition through the Red Sea to what is today Somalia. By 1000 BC the Assyrians fancied leopards and lions. King Solomon maintained herds of cattle, sheep, deer, and horses, as well as flocks of fowl; he traded with King Hiram of Tyre to obtain apes and peacocks or parrots. About that time, Emperor Wen Wang established a zoological garden in China.

After 700 BC the Greeks were setting up menageries, and Aristotle describes three hundred separate species in his *History of Animals* (4th century BC). The Mouseion at Alexandria possessed animals, and the Romans had aviaries and menageries, some of the latter with bulls, elephants, rhinoceroses, hippopotamuses, lions, bears, leopards, tigers, and crocodiles to be used in gladiatorial combats. Charlemagne had three small zoos in the 8th century. In 1230 Henry III had a menagerie in the Tower of London; Marco Polo saw Kublai Khan's great animal collection in the 14th century; and Cortez visited Montezuma's zoo at Mexico in 1519. Scholars suggest that from their beginnings, zoos required two basic elements: "wealth and leisure. There had to be enough money (to pay for food and housing and keepers) so that keeping animals in parks and cages did not interfere with the other luxuries of the owners of the zoos and parks. There also had to be sufficient leisure for enjoying the exhibits."[40]

Holy Roman Emperor Francis I established the first great modern zoo at Schonbrunn in Vienna in 1752, with a rococo pavilion where his wife Maria Theresa could breakfast while watching the animals. He sent collectors to America, and his son opened the zoo to the public in 1765. Other zoos were started at Madrid and at the Jardin des Plantes in Paris during the 18th century; the latter received animals from the Menagerie du Parc founded by Louis XIV at Versailles.

Sir Thomas Stamford Raffles, an English administrator who founded Singapore, was an animal lover and an admirer of the Jardin des Plantes zoo. He began the Zoological Society of London in 1826. Its royal charter called for the "advancement of zoology and animal physiology, and the introduction of new and curious subjects of the animal kingdom." The zoo, situated at one end of Regent's Park, opened first to society members in 1828 and to the public in 1846 with two llamas, a leopard, kangaroos, a Russian bear, emus, cranes, and other birds in suitable dens, aviaries, and paddocks. This zoo, with 650 species, has continued to be one of the world's greatest with excellent research as well as good showmanship. In 1931 it opened a five-hundred-acre branch thirty miles from London at Whipsnade, in Dunstable, Bedfordshire, the first wild-animal park in the world, that displays and breeds large groups of animals. Though the zoo faced financial challenges in the 1980s with declining attendance and high maintenance costs for the aging physical plant, more recently wealthy donors have come to the zoo's aid. Other outstanding European zoos are found in Antwerp, Amsterdam, Berlin, Munich, Frankfurt, Cologne, and Zurich.[41]

A revolution in zoo construction took place between 1902 and 1907, when Carl Hagenbeck, an animal dealer, set up his own zoo in Stellingen, a suburb of Hamburg. Beginning with a flat plain, Hagenbeck built an artificial, mountainous-like terrain with carefully constructed moats to contain the animals and with none of the customary cages and iron bars. This open-enclosure zoo was the prototype of the present spacious wild-animal parks that leading zoos in the world are beginning to acquire to supplement their city-restricted locations. In addition to revolutionizing zoo exhibitions, Hagenbeck's collecting practices added breeding of threatened species to zoo functions. Not only was Hagenbeck an innovator in zoo practices, but he also loved the animals he collected and developed techniques for training them with gentle methods using simple rewards of food tidbits instead of torture with whips and red-hot irons. Outside Hamburg, visitors can enjoy Hagenbeck's zoo today.[42]

The definitions of "menagerie" and "zoo" have changed over time. To review the evolution of menageries and zoos is to detect a changing purpose for these gardens or parks. In the 18th century, Europe's menageries made taxonomic collections (not unlike natural history collections) with specimens arranged in cages by "type." In addition to studying the differences among the specimens, the princely collectors of these menageries often sought the exotic to dazzle their guests. Zoological gardens emerged as more "sophisticated" menageries with an emphasis on natural settings for the specimens. Their purposes were education, research, and conservation (or protection of species). With the global threats to flora and fauna, conservation parks (or bioparks) emerged with immersion exhibits that allowed visitors to be "among the animals" and emphasized natural habitats and conservation. Today's zoological parks encompass conservation parks, aviaries, herpetariums, safari parks, insectariums, butterfly parks, and even endangered species rehabilitation centers. National parks and wildlife reserves are extending even further the boundaries of zoos.[43]

Some Leading American Zoos

The Philadelphia Zoological Garden (1854) is the oldest chartered zoo in the United States, though the tiny Central Park Menagerie in New York was the first actually to exhibit animals. Other prominent mainstream zoos are found in Chicago's Lincoln Park (1868), the National in Washington (1889), Milwaukee County (1892), New York's Bronx (1895), Saint Louis (1913), San Diego (1916), Fort Worth (1923), Detroit (1928), and Brookfield near Chicago (1934). The Arizona-Sonora Desert Museum at Tucson (1952) specializes in animals of the American desert despite its name. The public's attitudes toward U.S. zoos can be categorized in this way: zoos as jails (1865–1900), zoos as art galleries (1900–1950), and most recently, zoos as conservation facilities, with an emphasis on public education.[44]

Following the designs of the London Zoo, the Philadelphia Zoological Garden in Fairmount Park opened its exhibits to the public in 1874 in anticipation of the Centennial Exhibition planned for 1876. Many other zoos resulted from similar international expositions around the world. The Philadelphia Zoo included in its offerings the first children's zoo in the United States, a phenomenon quickly adopted by other zoological parks. Today the Philadelphia Zoo welcomes nearly a million family visitors each year. In addition to its animal collections, the carefully preserved Victorian era buildings and forty-three acres of gardens attract and charm its visitors.

The New York Zoological Society, formed in 1895 and opened to the public in 1899, adopted a plan radical for its day. Instead of showing native and foreign animals in cramped pens and paddocks, it tried to place them in free range in large enclosures and natural surroundings. William Temple Hornaday, the first director, was a strong and energetic leader who served for more than thirty years until his retirement at age seventy-two in 1926. He chose a new site for the zoo in the southern Bronx covering 252 acres. New York City purchased the land, constructed roads and buildings, and provided maintenance and keepers, while the society paid for animals and the curatorial and educational staff. The society also took over the Aquarium at Castle Clinton on the Battery in 1902 and operated it there until 1941; it reopened on Coney Island in 1957. Hornaday refused to employ the Hagenbeck system of moats, because he did not want to keep the public sixty or seventy feet away from the animals. He thought a zoo existed "to collect and exhibit fine and rare animals" and to enable "the greatest possible number of people to see them with comfort and satisfaction."

Hornaday, in addition to serving as the first director of the "Bronx Zoo," chaired the American Bison Society and led its effort to protect these vanishing North American animals. Of the 50 million bison once in the United States, only one thousand remained and Hornaday set about making sure that the zoo bred and protected them. In fact, at the start of the 20th century the Bronx Zoo shipped fifteen bison to Oklahoma, helping to return them to their original homes. Today many bison can trace their parentage back to the Bronx Zoo program. In addition to bison, the zoo also protected snow leopards, first exhibiting them in 1903. Under the leadership of the New York Zoological Society, later the Wildlife Conservation Society, the Bronx Zoo helped to form the Species Survival Program (SSP) that coordinates zoo breeding efforts for endangered species worldwide. What started with American bison extended to many other species.

Dr. W. Reid Blair succeeded Hornaday in 1926 and at once began experimenting with barless, moated parks; built a separate Ape House; and improved the educational program. This early effort at working with schools grew into a program that now serves 1.7 million schoolchildren each year. A real change of direction came in 1940 when Fairfield Osborn, son of Henry Fairfield Osborn, became president of the board. He believed that a zoo's chief function was protection of animals as part of the whole environment—forests, soils, waters, and wildlife. With these changes of purpose came many experiments in better exhibition techniques—an *African Plains*, *Lion Island*, Children's Zoo, Farm-in-the-Zoo, Conservation Exhibit, *World of Darkness* (nocturnal animals), *World of Birds*, Man and Animal in Tropical Asia, and the Skyfari aerial tramway. The recent *Congo Gorilla Forest* exhibit immerses visitors in the atmosphere of the forest, placing them nose-to-nose, through glass of course, with gorillas. Today the zoo houses four thousand animals and yearly attendance exceeds 2.5 million. The SSP program assists many zoos in breeding programs worldwide, and it has been called the "animal dating service." Today the zoo's mission is "to advance the study of zoology, protect wildlife, and educate the public."[45]

The National Zoological Park in Washington, D.C., established by Congress in 1889 and joined to the Smithsonian Institution a year later, was formed with the purpose of "the advancement of science and the instruction and recreation of the people." The zoo emerged in Rock Creek Park in the city's center thanks to the efforts of Hornaday, Smithsonian secretary Samuel Langley, and landscape architect, Frederick Law Olmsted. The founders sought not only to display exotic animals but also to provide a refuge for those species that were vanishing from the American landscape (especially bison and beaver). In 1975 the zoo opened the thirty-two-hundred-acre Conservation and Research Center in Front Royal, Virginia, to serve as a refuge for vanishing wildlife. This facility allows the zoo to pursue its dual functions of scientific research and conservation and public exhibition of animals. Like Kew Gardens in England, the National Zoo is a leader in training zoo professionals from around the world through its zoological medicine residency training and professional conservation programs. The zoo's formal mission statement reflects its commitment to the public and to professional training: "We are the nation's zoo, providing leadership in conservation science. We connect people with wildlife through exceptional animal exhibits, explore solutions through science-based programs, build partnerships worldwide, and share our discoveries."[46]

The Zoological Society of San Diego, founded in 1916, has become in a short time one of the leading mainstream zoos of the world. It began when a physician, Dr. Harry M. Wedgeforth, an enthusiastic animal lover, was outraged at the poor quality of the small menagerie shown at the Panama-California International Exposition at San Diego. He was determined to build the miscellaneous collection of monkeys, coyotes, and bears abandoned by the exposition into a first-class zoo. Assisted by dynamic Mrs. Belle J. Benchley, at times virtually the zoo director, "Dr. Harry" wheedled, pushed, and promoted to secure private and ultimately city tax support for the project.

The zoo occupies one hundred acres, with a series of canyons and almost perfect weather that have allowed it to develop an ideal moated system. It also has a superb collection of beautiful flowers, shrubs, and trees that makes it a veritable Garden of Eden. As early as 1926, the zoo developed a guided bus tour that permits visitors to see the animals roaming free in their moat-protected areas. The bus drivers are trained zoologists who point out the different animals and interpret them knowledgeably and with good humor.

The zoo's Department of Conservation and Research for Endangered Species (CRES) addresses issues of protecting biodiversity on a worldwide scale. The zoo's membership totals nearly a half million people, 130,000 of whom are children. The zoo features moving sidewalks over canyons; a superb walk-through aviary in one canyon; the Wedgeforth Bowl that seats three thousand spectators for a sea-lion show; a properly scaled-down Children's Zoo where youngsters may encounter turtles, antelopes, baby leopards, and elephants; a Skyfari ride; a man-made waterfall in Cascade Canyon; and koala bears feeding on their favorite eucalyptus trees.

Zoo officials had discussed developing a natural wild animal park or preserve, where animals would be free to live according to natural behavior patterns, to reproduce, and to be little disturbed by human intrusion on their territory. In 1972 at San Pasqual, thirty miles north of the downtown zoo, the Zoological Society of San Diego opened the San Diego Wild Animal Park. A bus links the two sections of the park, and a five-mile-long monorail, silent and unpolluting, winds through seven major preserve areas of the park perimeter, to allow zoo-goers to observe some of the fifteen hundred animals and birds as they eat, sleep, fight, and mate. The buildings and landscape of the Wild Animal Park reproduce the African environment. A one-and-a-half-acre lagoon filled with flamingoes, pelicans, and exotic fowl has a Congo River fishing village nearby astride a waterfall. The park also conserves endangered species of African plants in the garden and forest environment. A conservation/ ecology orientation center enlists visitor support for the underlying purposes of the park. The zoo has an exemplary breeding record and offers new vistas for zoological research. It is San Diego's answer to the commercial drive-through zoo.[47] Today the zoo in the city (one hundred acres) and its park in San Pasqual (eighteen hundred acres) contain more than seven thousand animals (twelve hundred species).

The Arizona-Sonora Desert Museum is an unusual zoo, starting with its name. Perhaps it is more like the European "ecomuseum" except that its focus is on animals, plants, and geology, rather than culture. (See chapter 5 for a discussion of the ecomuseum.) Founded in 1952 outside Tucson to protect the Sonora desert that spans from southern Arizona to Mexico, the museum developed within the desert landscape exhibition areas that combine plants, animals, and natural history into a compelling story for visitors. The museum encompasses ninety-eight acres of landscape with a few structures to service visitors, including an art institute. It reports 2,744 animals of 300 species; 1,217 plant types accessioned (of 72,000 plants); and 14,482 rocks and minerals, including 2,068 fossils. The museum acknowledges its unusual purpose, in this way: "Not a 'museum' in the usual sense, it is an unparalleled composite of plant, animal, and geologic collections with the goal of making the Sonora Desert accessible, understandable, and treasured." Nor is it a zoo, but it seems to fulfill the purposes of other organizations that define themselves as such.[48]

The Safari Zoo

The safari zoo is a commercial enterprise that allows visitors in their own automobiles to drive through an area in which wild animals and birds are roaming free. The car may encounter a lion "eyeball to eyeball," or a herd of curious camels may sniff it. The idea began in 1966, when Lord Bath invited the English public to gaze at the lions of Longleat from inside their cars on his Longleat estate in Wiltshire. South African and British developers sought to bring the safari experience to the United States, and a year later, Lion Country Safari opened near West Palm Beach, Florida, on 640 acres enclosed by moats and steel fencing. Prides of lions, herds of zebras, giraffes, ostriches, and other animals apparently grazed freely, and visitors could drive among them in their own cars (with windows closed) or in air-conditioned buses or rented cars. Outside the fenced area were a snake pit, children's zoo (with lion nursery), chimpanzee islands, exotic shorebirds, pygmy hippopotamuses, and sea lions. The project stressed recreation, conservation, education, and zoological research (through outside universities). It asserted that animals were as free there as wild populations, except that the predator-prey interactions were missing.

These privately owned wild animal parks proved popular in the 1970s, especially as features of amusement parks, and even Disney and Warner Brothers sponsored them. They offered a more natural way of viewing exotic animals. The animals, while appearing free, however are still confined by fences or moats, and the long lines of cars with their exhaust fumes are far from a natural environment; in essence, the observers have been caged as the animals formerly were. Today there remain only a few of this type of zoo that maintain the standards of professional zoos. The failure of the safari experience may result from the high costs of caring for the animals, maintaining such large areas with potentially dangerous animals, and the lack of commerical success for the sponsors.[49]

Challenges of Zoos

Changing Purpose

Museum News reports: "Visitor research confirms that there are many reasons people say they visit zoos. Seeing and learning about animals, spending time with family, and relaxing are chief among them." When outlining a zoo's function, zoo professionals (and advocates) include building public conservation awareness. The challenge is how to extend a family outing into an event that inspires individual action to save the planet's future. Bridging this significant gap is not easy. Conservation-centered exhibitions on zoo grounds do not necessarily result in citizen awareness or action. William Conway of the Bronx Zoo argues: "Our intent is to inspire interest and concern, for only then are people receptive to education and modifying the way they live. . . . But the real problem is telling them how."[50]

Challenges to the Biosphere

Increasing human populations with agricultural and industrial needs have cut into wild animal preserves, and hunters and poachers have relentlessly killed animals for fashion or trophies. In 1963, eighty countries joined together to create an international system for protecting endangered species. The meeting resulted in the creation of CITES, the Convention on International Trade in Endangered Species of Wild Fauna and Flora. Since then, CITES has been endorsed by 169 counties. CITES recognizes that commercial traffic in animal (and plant) products threatens the future of biodiversity, and international cooperation is fundamental to protecting both plants and animals from exploitation and extinction. International wildlife trade is diverse, ranging from ivory to exotic leather goods and even plant and animal materials for medicines. The convention assesses plants and animals and "ranks" them based on how endangered they are. Like the IUCN Red List for plants, this international convention seeks to protect the planet's biodiversity. These two international mechanisms along with the zoo community's Species Protection Program serve to protect the future of animal diversity.[51]

Conservation Action

Zoos in the 19th century sought to showcase exotic animals for visitors unable to travel to their natural climes. In some instances, like the

Bronx Zoo, they assumed leadership roles in protecting vanishing animals such as the American bison. In an odd twist, today's zoos find themselves in similar positions. Human encroachment on habitats continues at an alarming pace, and for some species, the zoo's inhabitants are all that remain. How should zoos protect threatened breeds? Is captivity the best course of action? What should be the role of zoos and international conservation organizations in protecting the world's biodiversity? What role should zoos play in raising political awareness to these threats to the planet's diversity?[52]

All Zoos Are "Local"

Many zoos in large cities find themselves as part of the city's bureaucracy, often a part of the Parks Department. Volunteer boards frequently oversee zoos in the United States and judge their successes and failures by local standards. Bringing in exotic, iconic animals to add to the city's luster is often the emphasis of these boards; the economic benefit to tourism prevails. With this emphasis on local concerns, how does a zoo play a role in worldwide conservation of endangered species? How does that zoo justify the costs for preservation of species perhaps continents away and never to be seen by weekend visitors?[53]

Notes

1. Mary Soderstrom, *Recreating Eden: A Natural History of Botanical Gardens*, Canada: Vehicule Press, 2001, p. 65.
2. H. Bruce Rinker, "The Weight of a Petal: The Value of Botanical Gardens," 2002, www.actionbioscience.org.
3. Nigel Rothfels, *Savages and Beasts: The Birth of the Modern Zoo*, Baltimore, MD: Johns Hopkins University Press, 2002, p. 199.
4. Vicki Croke, *The Modern Ark: The Story of Zoos Past, Present and Future*, New York: Scribner, 1997, p. 254.
5. www.bgci.org.
6. Marilyn Hicks Fitzgerald, *Museum Accreditation: Professional Standards*, Washington, DC: American Association of Museums, 1973, p. 8; A. W. Hill, "The History and Functions of Botanic Gardens," *Annals Missouri Botanical Gardens* 2 (1915): 185–240; Edward S. Hyams and William MacQuitty, *Great Botanical Gardens of the World*, New York: Macmillan, 1969, pp. 12–13; Edward S. Hyams, *A History of Gardens and Gardening*, New York: Praeger, 1971, pp. 9–125; George H. M. Lawrence, "The Historical Role of the Botanic Garden,"

Longwood Program Seminars 1 (1968–1969): 43–44; Howard S. Irwin, "Botanical Gardens in the Decades Ahead," *Curator* 16 (1973): 45–55; Ulysses Prentice Hedrick, *A History of Horticulture in America to 1860*, New York, 1950, pp. 3–4; Donald Wyman, "The Arboretums and Botanical Gardens of North America," *Chronica Botanica* 10 (Summer 1947): 405–408.

7. Hyams and MacQuitty, *Great Gardens*, pp. 18–22; Hill, "History and Functions," pp. 191–192, 194, 225; Lawrence, "Historical Role," pp. 34–35; Andrew Cunningham, "The Culture of Gardens," in *Cultures of Natural History*, eds. N. Jardine, J. A. Secord, and E. C. Spray, Cambridge University Press, 1996, pp. 38–56.

8. Hyams and MacQuitty, *Great Gardens*, p. 23; Hyams, *Gardens and Gardening*, pp. 126–128; Hill, "History and Functions," pp. 192–195, 226; Lawrence, "Historical Role," p. 34; J. D. Hunt, *Garden and Grove: The Italian Renaissance Garden in the English Imagination 1600–1750*, Princeton, NJ: Princeton University Press, 1996.

9. Hyams and MacQuitty, *Great Gardens*, pp. 34–43; Hyams, *Gardens and Gardening*, pp. 128–130; Lawrence, "Historical Role," pp. 34–35; Candice A. Shoemaker, ed., *Encyclopedia of Gardens: History and Design*, Chicago Botanic Garden, vol. 2, Chicago, IL: Fitzroy Dearborn, 2001; www.nationaalherbaium.nl.

10. Hyams and MacQuitty, *Great Gardens*, pp. 23, 82–85, 102–103; Hill, "History and Functions," pp. 192, 194, 197–201, 233; Lawrence, "Historical Role," p. 34; William C. Steere, "Research as a Function of a Botanical Garden," *Longwood Program Seminars* 1 (1968–1969): 43–47.

11. Hyams and MacQuitty, *Great Gardens*, pp. 107–108; Hill, "History and Functions," pp. 197, 203–206; Lawrence, "Historical Role," p. 35; Steere, "Research as a Function," p. 44. On the Wardian case, see Kenneth Lemmoy, *The Golden Age of Plant Explorers*, London, 1968, pp. 54, 183–184, 217; Shoemaker, *Encyclopedia of Gardens*, vol. 3, p. 1417.

12. Rinker, *Weight of a Petal*.

13. W. B. Turrill, *The Royal Botanic Gardens, Kew: Past and Present*, London: Herbert Jenkins, 1959, pp. 18–34; Mea Allan, *The Hookers of Kew, 1785–1911*, London, 1967, pp. 36, 151; Ray Desmonds, *Kew: The History of the Royal Botanic Gardens*, Harvill Press and Royal Botanic Gardens, Kew, 1998; Hyams and MacQuitty, *Great Gardens*, pp. 104–105, 108–109; Hyams, *Gardens and Gardening*, pp. 250–251; Hill, "History and Functions," pp. 206–207, 235.

14. Turrill, *The Royal Botanic Gardens, Kew*, pp. 20–32, 86–89; Allan, *Hookers*, pp. 36, 77–79, 88–89, 105–106, 109–110, 138–141, 146–152, 178–179, 200–201, 205–206; Hyams and MacQuitty, *Great Gardens*, pp. 108–110; Lawrence, "Historical Role," pp. 35–36; Hill, "History and Functions," pp. 207–209.

15. Turrill, *The Royal Botanic Gardens, Kew*, pp. 30–37, 47–55, 59–61, 65–66, 237–239; Allan, *Hookers*, pp. 211–237; Hyams and MacQuitty, *Great Gardens*, pp. 110–121; Steere, "Research as a Function," pp. 44–45; Lanning Roper on Wakehurst, *London Times*, July 27, 1975; www.kew.org.

16. Harold Roy Fletcher and William H. Brown, *The Royal Botanic Garden, Edinburgh, 1670–1970*, Edinburgh, 1970; Hyams and MacQuitty, *Great Gardens*, pp.

44–53; Hyams, *Gardens and Gardening*, p. 287; Hill, "History and Functions," pp. 201–203.

17. Hyams and MacQuitty, *Great Gardens*, pp. 82–85; Shoemaker, *Encyclopedia of Gardens*, vol. 1.

18. Hyams and MacQuitty, *Great Gardens*, pp. 76–81, 92–101; Hill, "History and Functions," p. 209; Shoemaker, *Encyclopedia of Gardens*, vol. 1, p. 133. www.bgbm.fu-berlin.de.

19. Hyams and MacQuitty, *Great Gardens*, pp. 122–125.

20. Hyams and MacQuitty, *Great Gardens*, pp. 174–177; Hyams, *Gardens and Gardening*, p. 281; Stanwin G. Shetler, *The Komarov Botanical Institute: 250 Years of Russian Research*, Washington, DC, 1967, pp. 127–128, 180–183; Shoemaker, *Encyclopedia of Gardens*, vol. 2, p. 728.

21. Hyams and MacQuitty, *Great Gardens*, p. 211; Hill, "History and Functions," pp. 210–212.

22. Shoemaker, *Encyclopedia of Gardens*, vol. 2, p. 227.

23. Hyams and MacQuitty, *Great Gardens*, pp. 220–227; Hill, "History and Functions," pp. 212–213.

24. Hyams and MacQuitty, *Great Gardens*, pp. 200–210; Hyams, *Gardens and Gardening*, p. 258; Hill, "History and Functions," p. 214.

25. Hyams and MacQuitty, *Great Gardens*, pp. 194–199, 211–219, 244–253; Hill, "History and Functions," pp. 210–211, 213–215.

26. Hyams and MacQuitty, *Great Gardens*, pp. 254–265; Hill, "History and Functions," p. 215; Shoemaker, *Encyclopedia of Gardens*, vol. 2, p. 711.

27. Hyams and MacQuitty, *Great Gardens*, pp. 232–238; Shoemaker, *Encyclopedia of Gardens*, vol. 3, p. 1122.

28. Hedrick, *History of Horticulture*, pp. 71–72, 85–92, 207–209, 423–424; Joseph Ewan, ed., *A Short History of Botany in the United States*, New York, 1969, pp. 2–5, 33–34, 38–39, 132–133; Christine Chapman Robbins and David Hosack, *Citizen of New York*, Philadelphia, PA, 1964, pp. 26, 4–99, 195–197; Hyams, *Gardens and Gardening*, p. 209.

29. Hyams and MacQuitty, *Great Gardens*, pp. 148–152; Carroll C. Calkins, ed., *Great Gardens in America*, New York, 1969, pp. 242–251; Ewan, *A Short History*, pp. 43–44; Wyman, "The American Arboretums and Botanical Gardens," pp. 437–438.

30. Soderstrom, *Recreating Eden*.

31. Hyams and MacQuitty, *Great Gardens*, pp. 132–136; Stephane Barry Sutton, *Charles Sprague Sargent and the Arnold Arboretum*, Cambridge, MA, 1970; Wyman, "The American Arboretums and Botanical Gardens," pp. 430–433; Edward P. Alexander, "Charles Sprague Sargent," in *The Museum in America: Innovators and Pioneers*, Walnut Creek, CA: AltaMira Press, 1997, pp. 173–188.

32. Hyams and MacQuitty, *Great Gardens*, p. 137; Irwin, "Botanical Gardens in the Decades Ahead," pp. 45–55; Wyman, "The American Arboretums and Botanical Gardens," pp. 442–444.

33. Hyams and MacQuitty, *Great Gardens*, pp. 156–163; Calkins, *Great American Gardens*, pp. 272–281; Wyman, "The American Arboretums and Botanical

Gardens," pp. 422–423; William Hertrich, *The Huntington Botanical Gardens, 1905–1949*, San Marino, CA, 1949.

34. Hyams and MacQuitty, *Great Gardens*, pp. 137–141; Charles Stuart Gager, "The Educational Work of Botanic Gardens," *Brooklyn Botanic Gardens, Contributions* 1 (1911): 73–85; Frances M. Miner, "The Botanic Garden—from the Educator's Viewpoint," *Longwood Program Seminars* 4 (1972): 14–19; Wyman, "The American Arboretums and Botanical Gardens," pp. 429–431; Shoemaker, *Encyclopedia of Gardens*, vol. 1, p. 194.

35. Hyams and MacQuitty, *Great Gardens*, pp. 142–147; Hyams, *Gardens and Gardening*, p. 312; Calkins, *Great American Gardens*, pp. 168–175; Wyman, "The American Arboretums and Botanical Gardens," pp. 447–448; *Longwood Gardens, A Visit to Longwood Gardens*, 8th ed., Kennett Square, PA, 1970; *Longwood Gardens, Fountains of Longwood Gardens* Kennett Square, PA, 1960; Lanning Roper, "Longwood Gardens: A Twentieth Century American Pleasure Ground," *Royal Horticultural Society, Journal* 82 (May 1957): 1–9.

36. Hyams and MacQuitty, *Great Gardens*, pp. 164–169; Wyman, "The American Arboretums and Botanical Gardens," pp. 425–426.

37. Rinker, *Weight of a Petal*; *International Agenda for Botanic Gardens in Conservation*, Botanic Gardens Conservation International, 2000, p. 32.

38. *International Agenda for Botanic Gardens in Conservation*, p. 46.

39. Gerald T. Donnelly, "The Climate Is Right," *Museum News* 68, no. 5 (September–October 1989): 45–48.

40. Harry Gersh, *The Animals Next Door: A Guide to Zoos and Aquariums of the Americas*, New York: Fleet Academic Editions, 1971, pp. 1–14; R. J. Hoage, Anne Roskell, and Jane Mansour, "Menageries and Zoos to 1900," in *New Worlds, New Animals: From Menagerie to Zoological Park in the Nineteenth Century*, eds. Robert J. Hoage and William A. Deiss, Baltimore, MD: Johns Hopkins University Press, 1996, pp. 8–15; John C. Coe, "The Evolution of Zoo Animal Exhibits," in *The Ark Evolving: Zoos and Aquariums in Transition*, ed. Christen M. Wemmer, Washington, DC: Smithsonian Institution, 1995, pp. 96–102.

41. James Fisher, *Zoos of the World: The Story of Animals in Captivity*, Garden City, NY: Natural History Press, 1967, pp. 21–57; Bernard Livingston, *Zoo: Animals, People, Places*, New York, 1974, pp. 15–35, 71, 233; Gersh, *The Animals Next Door*, pp. 1–14; *International Zoo Yearbook* 14 (1974): 257–327; Wilfrid Blunt, *The Ark in the Park: The Zoo in the Nineteenth Century*, London: Hamish Hamilton, 1976, pp. 10, 16–31; Bob Mullan and Gary Marvin, *Zoo Culture*, Urbana: University of Illinois Press, 1999; Michael Osborne, "Zoos in the Family: The Geoffroy Saint-Hilaire Clan and Three Zoos in Paris," in *New Worlds, New Animals*, pp. 34–36; Harriet Ritvo, "The Order of Nature: Constructing the Collections of Victorian Zoos," in *New Worlds, New Animals*, pp. 43–50.

42. Edward Alexander, "Carl Hagenbeck and His Stellingen Tierpark," in *Museum Masters*, pp. 311–339; Rothfels, *Savages and Beasts*, p. 199; John C. Coe, "The Evolution of Zoo Animal Exhibits"; Wemmer, *The Ark Evolving*, pp. 105–109; Fisher, *Zoos of the World*, pp. 138, 164–169; Livingston, *Zoo*, pp. 137–152; Gersh, *Animals Next Door*, pp. 14–15; Herman Reichenbach, "A Tale of

Two Zoos: The Hamburg Zoological Garden and Carl Hagenbeck's Tierpark,"
in *New Worlds, New Animals*, pp. 51–62; www.hagenbeck.de.

43. Vernon N. Kisling Jr., ed., *Zoo and Aquarium History: Ancient Animal Collections to Zoological Gardens*, Boca Raton, FL: CRC Press, 2001; Heini Hediger, *Man and Animal in the Zoo: Zoo Biology*, trans. Gwynne and Winwood Reade, London: Routledge, 1969.

44. *International Zoo Yearbook* 14 (1974): 257–327; Livingston, *Zoo*, pp. 236, 239–240, 280–282; Gersh, *Animals Next Door*, pp. 15–16, 70, 78, 85, 95–96, 111, 115, 120–121, 135, 141, 148–149; Andrew Rowan and Robert Hoage, "Public Attitudes Towards Wildlife," in *The Ark Evolving*, pp. 32–60; John C. Coe, "The Evolution of Zoo Animal Exhibits," in *The Ark Evolving*, pp. 102–105; Vernon N. Kisling Jr., "The Origin and Development of American Zoological Parks to 1899," in *New Worlds, New Animals*, pp. 109–126; Clark DeLeon, *America's First Zoostory: 125 Years at the Philadelphia Zoo*, Virginia Beach, VA: Donning, 1999; Elizabeth Hardouin-Fugier, *Zoo: A History of Zoological Gardens in the West*, London: Reaktion, 2002; www.PhiladelphiaZoo.org.

45. Alexander, "William Temple Hornaday," in *The Museum in America*, pp. 189–204; William Bridges, *Gathering of the Animals: An Unconventional History of the New York Zoological Society*. New York: Harper & Row, 1974, pp. 16–17, 20–38, 57–60, 99–122, 223–230, 387–388, 412, 414, 440–486, 505; Livingston, *Zoo*, pp. 263–279; American Association of Zoological Parks and Aquariums, *Zoos and Aquariums in the Americas*,Wheeling, WV, 1974, p. 97; "Elephant and Tiger and Rhinoceros Roaming the Bronx? Preposterous!" *New York Times*, August 17, 1977; Coe, "The Evolution," p. 109; John Fraser, "Museums and Civility," *Curator* 47, no. 3 (July 2004): 252–255; Jeff Hayward and Marilyn Rothenberg, "Measuring Success in the 'Congo Gorilla Forest' Conservation Exhibition," *Curator* 47, no. 3 (July 2004): 261–282.

46. www.nationalzoo.si.edu; Helen Lefkowitz Horowitz, "The National Zoological Park: 'City of Refuge' or Zoo?" in *New Worlds, New Animals*, pp. 126–135; Heather Ewing, "The Architecture of the National Zoological Park," in *New Worlds, New Animals*, pp. 151–164.

47. Belle J. Benchley, *My Life in a Man Made Jungle*, New York: Little, Brown, 1942; *International Zoo Yearbook* 14 (1974): 273, 308; Livingston, *Zoo*, pp. 93–120; American Association of Zoological Parks and Aquariums, *Zoos and Aquariums in the Americas*, p. 23; William Mortison, "Afroamericanus: A New Species of Zoo," *Museum News* 51 (November 1972): 28–33.

48. www.desertmuseum.org.

49. Randall L. Eaton, William York, and William Dredge, "The Lion Country Safari and Its Role in Conservation, Education and Research," *International Zoo Yearbook* 10 (1970): 171–172; Livingston, *Zoo*, pp. 121–136.

50. Tracey Linton Craig, "Changing the Way People Think," *Museum News* 67, no. 1 (September–October 1988): 52; George B. Rabb, "The Evolution of Zoos from Menageries to Centers of Conservation and Caring," *Curator* 47 no. 3, pp. 237–244; Jeffrey Hyson, "Education, Entertainment, and Institutional Identity at the Zoo," *Curator* 47, no. 3, pp. 247–251; Terry L Maple and Suma

Mallavarapu, "Values, Advocacy, and Science: Toward an Empirical Philosophy for Zoo and Aquarium Leadership," in *Museum Philosophy for the 21st Century*, ed. Hugh H. Genoways, Lanham, MD: AltaMira Press, 2006, pp. 177–200.

51. www.cites.org; www.redlist.org.

52. Michael Hutchins, "Zoo and Aquarium Animal Management and Conservation: Current Trends and Future Challenges," *International Zoo Yearbook* (London Zoological Society) 38 (2003): 14–28; William G. Conway, "Zoos in the 21st Century," *International Zoo Yearbook* 38 (2003): 7–13; Michael D. DeLapa, "Interpreting Hope, Selling Conservation: Zoos, Aquariums and Environmental Education," *Museum News* 73, no. 3 (May–June 1994): 48–49.

53. Michael Hutchins and William G. Conway, "Beyond Noah's Ark: The Evolving Role of Modern Zoological Parks and Aquariums in Field Conservation," *International Zoo Yearbook* 34 (1995): 117–130.

7

Children's Museums

It is important . . . how the [children's] museum will be laid out so that no visitor can get lost . . . where the live animals will be, where to find the young man who can identify the other half of the worm my little brother ate . . . where is the leader of the art class, the person who can tell me about my sick turtle? Where are the souvenirs, the supplies, the dinosaur exhibit, the drinking fountain, and can I still see my mother when I go in there to roam or explore by myself?

—Albert Heine, 1979[1]

Indianapolis Children's Museum second graders responses to "What's a museum?"
"A big thing that is a place to learn about hundreds of things."
"A museum is a building to learn in."
"It is a place where we can learn and have fun at the same time."
"Where you learn about neat stuff."

—quoted by Judy Otto, 1979[2]

To inspire children with this love for and pride in the institution, they must feel that it was created for them, and that in all of its plans, it puts the child first.

—Anna Billings Gallup, 1908[3]

Children's museums are a distinctive American institution. The Brooklyn Children's Museum (1899) was the first one in the world; today they are found worldwide and number about five hundred, with most in the

United States. Michael Spock, former director of the Boston Children's Museum, explains that children's museums fundamentally differ from other museums in that their very name specifies the audience, not the subject of their collections.[4] Young people between the ages of ten and fourteen were most often found in the early children's museums. Today, the age range is younger, with some museums focusing on preschool-age children. The preteen audience has become a less frequent user, forcing some museums to create special programs to attract them.[5]

The permanent collection of a children's museum may range from the rare and valuable to multiple examples of everyday objects and may include live animals. A children's museum collects objects, not for their rarity, but for their usefulness in interpretation or education. Their exhibitions may include objects, but their intent is to engage, intrigue, and inform their visitors. Their programs and workshops may include science puzzles and demonstrations, neighborhood nature walks, puppet shows, hands-on demonstrations, musical instruments and performance spaces, dance, costumes for "dress up" or playacting, painting and drawing, crafts demonstrations, planetariums, and nature centers. To adults, children's museums' activities appear fun, noisy, and at times even chaotic, but at best they are serious in their intent and educational value.[6]

Origins

Nineteenth-century educators identified and defined the qualities of "childhood" as a distinctive stage in human development. American educator John Dewey was especially influential in outlining the educational needs of children. His "model" school plan included a museum for students within its walls.[7] Some American museums created museum-schools where docents lectured to students and supervised them in conducting experiments in laboratory-like spaces, and local school systems assigned teachers to work in the museum. The overarching principle was that "play" is a child's "work."

Children's museums' roots lie in "children's galleries" found in such notable museums as the Victoria and Albert Museum in London, the Metropolitan Museum in New York, and the Smithsonian Institution. Samuel Pierpont Langley, Smithsonian secretary from 1887 to 1906, though an aeronautical engineer, created the first gallery for children at the Smithsonian. With the notion that "Knowledge Begins with Wonder," he oversaw the installation of exhibits with cases designed at a lower height for children and without the usual scientific labels. The guiding principle for the room's exhibitions was, in his words, "to attract, amuse and only incidentally, to instruct."[8] Langley's focus on the room's development was so strong that he referred to himself as its "honorary curator," in addition to being secretary of the institution. Langley dismissed suggestions that the room imitated the new Brooklyn Children's Museum, explaining that the Brooklyn model was a pedagogic institution rather than one designed to engage children's imaginations. The children's room opened in the south tower of the castle in 1901 and remained in place with few changes until 1939 when the space was filled by an exhibition to orient the public to all the Smithsonian's programs.[9]

American Models

In 1939 American Association of Museums director Laurence Vail Coleman classified children's museums in this way: (1) school museums, controlled by individual schools; (2) school system museums, controlled by boards of education; (3) children's museums, controlled by boards of directors; and (4) children's museums that are affiliated with subject-matter museums.[10] Regardless of the origins or affiliations, children's museums intend to serve the needs and interests of young people. Brooklyn Children's Museum curator Anna Billings Gallup explains the children's museum concept: "A [children's] museum can do the greatest good and furnish the most effective help to the boys and girls who love it as an institution . . . they must feel that it is created, and now exists for them, and that in all of its plans it puts the child first. The child must feel that the whole plant is for him, that the best is offered to him because of faith in his power to use it, that he has access to all departments, and that he is always a welcome visitor, never an intruder."[11] This principle helps to explain why a few galleries within museums were deemed insufficient. Children's museums emerged, not simply as extensions of museums, but as their own institutions.

Brooklyn Children's Museum

The Brooklyn Institute of Arts and Science opened the first building designed to serve children in December 1899. Curator William Henry

Goodyear proposed the idea as a means to use museum collections currently in storage. In 1900 a Brooklyn Children's Museum flyer addressed "To Our Young Friends" invited children in: "The management wishes you to use these collections to your own profit and pleasure, at all times. . . . Boys and girls, like yourselves, often find odd and curious animals, or plants, or minerals, about which they would love to learn something. Come to the Museum and bring them with you; someone will be found here who can tell you about them. . . . When you visit the Museum do not fail to ask the attendants to show or to explain to you any objects that may attract you. The attendants are here for that purpose: they are glad to have you ask questions." The flyer closed with an invitation to seek out the librarian, Miss Draper, with questions.[12]

In 1902 a young woman trained as a teacher and interested in sharing with children her love of biology and nature joined the museum staff. Assistant curator and subsequently curator in chief (or director), Anna Billings Gallup brought to this new type of museum her love of learning and of children and her commitment to making the museum serve children's interests and needs. She often followed young visitors around the museum exhibits to see what caught their fancy. She sought to create "an attractive resort for children."[13] Under her leadership the museum thrived, expanding its program offerings and reaching out to the community as John Cotton Dana did at the Newark Museum, only Gallup's audience was young people. When the Institute was expanding its building in the 1920s, the director invited Gallup to "bring the children back" into the museum. She declined this request based on her belief that, to be effective, the museum must put children first.[14]

Brooklyn seems to have done it all: worked with teachers, science clubs, Boy and Girl Scouts, the Americanization School (designed to teach immigrants English following World War I), and engaged children as both teachers (for the younger ones) and learners. Their collections served the children; they rejected the rare and fragile, collecting instead objects and specimens that children could use, handle, and experiment with. Gallup was renowned for simply opening exhibit cases to allow visitors to look closely and to handle objects. In 1968, long after Gallup retired, with the Victorian buildings needing repair and, ideally, expansion, the Brooklyn Children's Museum moved into an abandoned warehouse nearby the older building, reaching out to young people without experience in the former location. Known as MUSE, the warehouse's open spaces allowed for more active programming, especially in the areas of science and theater. In 1977 the Children's Museum returned to Bower Park into a new building and the MUSE facility closed. The new building, built underground and designed around a "stream" that flowed through it, offered better spaces for larger exhibitions and performances.

Today the Brooklyn Children's Museum is again undergoing physical expansion reflecting its continuing popularity. The new facility is scheduled to open in 2008. The museum has created formal alliances with community organizations to extend its reach to the area's children. These alliances tie the museum to the community even while the new building project is underway. The soon-to-be-opened building will bring the children's museum above ground, reasserting its prominence for Brooklyn's children. The interior spaces will be doubled and the building itself, like that of the 1977 construction, is innovative in design and in its commitment to being environmentally neutral, or "green."[15]

As noted earlier, as U.S. children's museums developed in the 20th century, they served younger visitors. However, in Brooklyn in the 1980s, the museum staff noticed that teens and preteens were dropping by after school. In just a few years these drop-ins numbered nearly seventy every day, and the museum determined to provide them with programming. The KidsCrew program was established, serving fifty students ranging from age seven to fourteen. The program offered homework help, a snack at "home place," and changing programs. To control the number of participants, the kids signed in daily and museum staff structured the late afternoon to blend schoolwork and museum activities. The popularity of the program forced its expansion to the "Museum Team" to serve the needs of older high school students. As the Association of Science Technology Center's (ASTC) Youth ALIVE! program began across the United States, Brooklyn joined the network. See chapter 11 for a discussion of Youth ALIVE![16]

In addition to serving as an exemplar for future children's museums, an important contribution of the Brooklyn Children's Museum was the personal leadership of Anna Billings Gallup. In addition to becoming a charter member of the new American Association of Museums (AAM) as it formed in 1906, she created the association's "Children's Division" in 1938 to extend its services to these emerging museums. She welcomed visitors to the museum and gave speeches about the museum to professional groups and civic organizations, especially reaching out to women's groups and individuals with interest in replicating the Brooklyn Museum in their own communities. One is tempted to describe her as the "Pied Piper" of American children's museums. For example,

Gallup may take direct credit for the children's museum that opened in Indianapolis in 1925.

Children's Museum, Boston

Whereas the Brooklyn Children's Museum emerged from an established museum, Boston's origins lie in a group of science teachers who had shared teaching collections among their classrooms. In 1913 the teachers exhibited them to the public in a city park building. Though at the start the museum was an adjunct to the Science Teacher's Bureau, within a year it had organized into its own entity focusing on exhibitions and programs to engage and educate children. It is really a blend of Coleman's classifications, mentioned earlier. Serving teachers and children emerged as coequal goals for the new museum. The museum has remained true to these origins not only by serving teachers, but also by promoting exchange among teachers and fellow museum professionals to educate children, whether in the museum or classroom. Charles J. Douglas, president of the Children's Museum described the museum at a 1920s AAM meeting: "It is a teaching organization which uses museum exhibits and apparatus as tools. It is not on account of these exhibits, mainly, that thousands of children come to us with enthusiasm and delight. No . . . They are drawn to us because here a meaning is put into these things, and natural phenomenon [are] made understandable."[17]

From 1962 to 1985 Michael Spock played a role in Boston similar to that of Brooklyn's Anna Billings Gallup. Like Gallup, Spock led Boston's museum with a firm commitment to children along with a democratic view of how the organization should operate to serve both audience and staff. It is intriguing to note that the museum had no separate "Education Department," rather its staff was organized to serve (educate) its young visitors. Of special importance in Boston was the exhibition development process that relied on visitors' participation to create the final product. Elements of exhibits would be created with materials that could be modified or even disposed of if they were found to be ineffective. In 1981, exhibit center director Elaine Heumann Gurian reported: "We think we are 65% right in the first installation of any exhibition, which means we are about 35% wrong. . . . We go through a process of observation, tryout, more observation, revision. . . . Modification of techniques is constant."[18] In the spirit of Brooklyn's

Gallup, Boston's children gained an important sense of ownership of the museum.

The sharing of materials for classroom use begun by the Science Teachers Bureau before the museum was even opened continued with the museum's 1960s MATCHBOX program. With funds from the U.S. Department of Education, the museum created multimedia "kits" and instructional materials, called "Materials and Activities for Teachers and Children" (MATCH), to be sent to elementary teachers for classroom use. For a modest fee, teachers could use these materials for a few weeks and return them to the museum for others to use. MATCH brought materials right to the classroom, linking teachers to the museum. Onsite at the museum, teachers could find additional resources in the library that became the "resource center."

The Children's Museum staff embraced novel and sensitive exhibition topics. Their respect for the interests and concerns of children are reflected in two important exhibitions: *What's Inside?* focused on explaining how objects work, complete with a toilet cut in half to expose its inner workings and *What If I Couldn't?* focused on the impact of disabilities on everyday activities. Each of these exhibitions addressed the human condition from the perspective of a child. They addressed in the most sensitive ways those questions that young people sometimes are discouraged from asking.[19]

Two collections held by the museum warrant attention. An exhibition of a Japanese teahouse has been part of the museum from its early days. Children remove their shoes to enter the space, decorated in traditional fashion with tatami mats on the floor and moveable wall screens. The intent is to help children appreciate cultural differences in a personal way through experience with the original objects. A sizeable Native American collection allows the museum to mount exhibitions on topics relating to Massachusetts' earliest residents. The collection has tightly linked the museum to the Native American community allowing for both cultural exchange and understanding. The very process of caring for these collections allows the museum to help their young visitors appreciate the value of original, sometimes fragile, objects.

As the 1970s began, the museum assessed its role within its community and found that it primarily served families and children of the middle and upper classes, neglecting large segments of Boston's children. After careful study, the museum sought to bring its resources to a more central location. In 1979, with the Museum of Transportation, the Boston Children's Museum moved from its site in a much-expanded mansion in Jamaica Plain in a historic neighborhood to a large industrial space, "The Wharf," in central Boston. The museum abuts four neighborhoods, is convenient to public transportation, and has large spaces to accommodate exhibitions and its resource center. No longer would location limit access.

In 2006 the museum closed for six months to complete a renovation of the wharf building, adding twenty thousand square feet to the one-hundred-thousand-square-foot space. In addition to easing public entry into the building, the redesign addresses interior and exterior spaces, taking better advantage of the waterfront location. Interior exhibitions were upgraded, while outside an outdoor learning center beside the water opened. While the museum was closed, the Internet allowed access to resources. The website welcomed "Kids," "Grown-ups," and "Teachers" with appropriate activities to do at home or in the classroom and provided updates on the construction. The museum's commitment to visitor programs, teacher resources, and early childhood education remained active during the expansion and freshening up.[20]

Boston's influence, like that of Brooklyn before it, has extended beyond children's museums to the broader museum profession. The museum's exhibition development process contributed to the growing use of exhibit teams, as discussed in chapter 10. The MATCHBOX project reinforced for all museums the importance of directly connecting with classroom teachers. Further, the kits inspired many museum "discovery rooms" that frequently offered boxes of materials on a particular subject for children and their families to explore together. Michael Spock and his staff, like Gallup before them, actively participated in AAM activities and reached out to museum professionals. The museum's staff helped to establish the American Association of Youth Museums in 1964, today the Association of Children's Museums (ACM).

Detroit Children's Museum

In 1917 the Detroit Museum of Art and the city's board of education created "a museum within a museum" to meet the needs of the area's children. Like the Brooklyn Children's Museum, the Detroit Children's Museum created exhibitions and offered classroom space for instruction using the museum's nonart collections that had been languishing in storage. However, these activities took place within the museum, not in separate quarters like Brooklyn. The museum hired, as part-time curator, a well-trained experienced teacher with a love for natural history, Gertrude A. Gillmore. In addition to creating museum programs to attract and appeal to children, she carefully linked the museum's activities to those of the classroom.[21]

The cooperation between museum and school system to serve children lasted until 1925 when the Detroit Museum of Art became the Detroit Art Institute and moved to a new location and the children's museum moved into its own building. At that time, the board of education assumed sole leadership and expanded the new museum's scope beyond art to science, history, and world cultures. Gillmore acquired appropriate objects to reflect that expansion. Former director Beatrice Parson wrote: "The Children's Museum in the truest sense of the word, was not established until December of 1925, when it moved into its present home under the exclusive control of the Board of Education. . . . It is organized on a basis of children's diversified interests, and is not an attempt to simplify for children the more elaborate art or natural history museums."[22] The value of separate quarters for children's museums prevailed.

As an extension of the board of education and very much in Boston's tradition, the Detroit museum worked closely with teachers. Individual school classes visited the museum's changing exhibitions. The museum loaned teachers objects from the collection to complement their classroom lessons. The museum also supplied appropriately certified museum-teachers as classroom instructors. These services continue today. With the help of the Children's Museum Friends, founded in 1971 to supplement the board of education's financial resources, the museum continues to mount changing exhibitions, provide performance space for music and dance, lend materials to classroom teachers on topics ranging from geography to careers, and participate in Detroit's annual Multicultural Children's Day. The museum also serves non-Detroit school students and families with weekend programming and has added preschool programs to its offerings. Today, the museum is "devoted to stimulating the intellectual curiosity and *natural* love of learning among metropolitan Detroit youth, families and adults."[23]

Indianapolis Children's Museum

In 1925, after a trip to the Brooklyn Children's Museum to meet Miss Gallup, Mary Stewart Carey returned to Indianapolis determined to create for her city an institution to meet the needs of the city's children.

While Brooklyn had its collection and Boston enjoyed the tradition of teachers sharing materials, the new museum in Indianapolis took a different path. Civic activist Carey created "Museum Week" in December 1925. For one week she personally solicited objects from the public for a new museum. Not only did she write to teachers and other adults, but she sent individual letters to children, seeking gifts to place in the museum that would be meaningful to Indianapolis' citizens. Her requests were taken so seriously that the new museum had to move twice in its first year to accommodate its growing collections. Through the process the museum collected stuffed fish, Italian tiles, artworks, and souvenirs from abroad.[24]

Today, the museum is the largest children's museum in the United States, with visitation exceeding a million each year. Its collections total more that 110,000 objects representing three broad domains: nature, culture, and the American experience. Through a cooperative program with the public library system, one can peruse selected collections online. Between 1925 and 1976, the museum occupied a series of large houses in Indianapolis, including founder Carey's; each time moving to ever-larger quarters to meet growing demands for its programs.

The museum's current facilities are an expansion of the 1976 building and provide four levels of exhibitions, theaters, research laboratories, and computer stations as well as a shop and restaurant. The building's third floor includes *Playscape*, where very young visitors can explore and climb in a safe environment. On that same level *Story Avenue* provides comfortable venues, including a traditional dining room table with chairs, to promote storytelling and intergenerational conversations. The museum's expansion has allowed for increased programming for adolescents, who demand more independence for their explorations than a younger audience does. In addition to providing programs for this audience, the museum also taps them to staff programs for younger visitors.[25]

Children's Museums Come and Go

These earliest children's museums suggest different models for creating a museum within a community. In 1939 a group of elementary school teachers joined together and in 1941 opened a children's museum in Fort Worth, Texas. The Fort Worth Children's Museum contained one hundred thousand square feet of exhibition space, complete with an observatory and a four-hundred-acre nature center to serve the community's children. Like other children's museums its collections were intended to "introduce the world to children."[26] In 1968, after nearly thirty years of service to the community, the museum changed its name to the Fort Worth Museum of Science and History for the express purpose of "welcoming all visitors regardless of age." As the museum's website reports: "During its first 40 years, the Museum was a quiet place where one could dream of the past or contemplate the future in relative solitude. All that changed in the 1990s. Collaborations with other museums and science centers allow the Museum to offer large, world-class traveling exhibits, and the old-fashioned static displays have been replaced by interactive, hands-on exhibits. Although its name, location, size, and scope have changed dramatically since 1941, the Museum still serves a similar purpose: to provide a learning environment to all who pass through its doors."[27]

The Texas example suggests that the museum sought to reach out beyond its audience of children to all residents and visitors to Fort Worth, in part, by changing its name. In Rochester, New York, the opposite happened at the Margaret Woodbury Strong Museum. In 1982 the Strong Museum opened to the public. Strong died in 1969 and left half a million objects, along with a substantial endowment, to found a museum. She had collected everyday household objects, including many dolls and toys. For nearly ten years the small museum staff, operating out of the Strong residence, studied what form of museum would best honor her collections. Consultants from history museums around the United States offered their advice, recommending a traditional history museum that focused on the region's industrial development. The museum moved from the Strong estate to an imposing, some said forbidding, new building in downtown Rochester. The ground floor featured carefully researched, thematic exhibitions, while open storage shelves filled the second floor.

Despite the museum's prominent downtown location, attendance was poor and the staff began to reassess the museum's focus. Just as the first staff had studied the gift collections, the process began again, but this time with a closer look at Strong herself. The research uncovered a charter she had obtained for a "museum of fascinations." Where the early museum consultants had emphasized how her collections revealed the history of the region, the new assessment considered how the objects revealed her own fascination with "play" from gardening to dolls and toys. As well as reviewing the collection and Strong's personal interests, the museum staff assessed the museum's actual and potential audience from a marketing perspective. The collections and audience suggested a reinterpretation of the museum, moving away from history exhibitions to exhibits that would engage the public in activities that are appropriately described as play, regardless of the visitor's age.

The Strong Museum that began as a traditional history museum has emerged as a variant of a children's museum with a special focus on "play." The museum's new mission is "to explore play in order to encourage learning, creativity and discovery." As director Rollie Adams suggests: "At last the museum had a mission close to the heart of its founder, rooted in its core collections . . . and of utmost social and educational importance." The reconfigured building that opened in July 2006 with a new facade that looks like a giant stack of children's blocks contains interactive exhibitions and play spaces, a butterfly garden, and space set aside for a preschool with a play-based curriculum. The museum's tradition of scholarship remains, but the emphasis has shifted from history to play in all its complexities. Even the name has changed; today the Margaret Woodbury Strong Museum is Strong—The National Museum of Play. Adams prefers to describe the museum as a "family-oriented history museum" rather than a children's museum. He emphasizes the museum's commitment to collecting in the tradition of the museum's founder.[28]

Children's Museums' Impact

One must not discount the personal influence of many children's museums' staff members. As committed educators, they focus their attention (and talents) not only on the children in their own museums, but also on their fellow museum professionals, and by extension, on visitors to any museum. Curious, and in many instances, gregarious too, they asked questions, tried out different approaches to all elements of interpretation, and shared both their successes and slipups. When Boston Children's Museum tapped staff regardless of title to serve as "developers" to lead exhibition planning, other museums watched and began to imitate the practice. The developers provided different skills and were from any level of the museum's hierarchy. At the same time, funding from the National Endowment for the Humanities required that scholars be involved in planning exhibitions, and this provided further impetus for exhibit development teams.

Boston's willingness to try out and revise exhibit elements with the help of visitors supported formative evaluation in other museums. In

Indianapolis, the children's museum formalized its commitment to evaluation with the help of Indiana University researchers. In addition to adding to exhibition development costs, this commitment added time to the process. Peter Sterling, a former director of Indianapolis Children's Museum, argued that in children's museums it's the programs, objects, and space that attract visitors, not the staff scholarship; however, when it came to exhibitions, the museum carefully studied its practices to improve its product. While seemingly less spontaneous and free-form than Boston, the commitment to the quality of a child's experience was the same.[29]

Discovery Rooms, *Explore Galleries*, and *Hands-on Spaces* in museums of all disciplines find their origins in the work and success of children's museums. They have been defined as "a separate area, within the context of a larger institution, containing a collection of objects that can be touched and examined. It offers self-paced, self-directed educational activities."[30] Museums set aside spaces where children and their families slow down their museum visit to touch objects, read labels especially written for them, or perhaps complete a puzzle designed to help them understand a specimen from the museum's collection. In addition to these separate spaces within museums, some exhibitions have adapted the concept and created exhibit "carts" or "stations" where objects—a beaver pelt or a wooden shoe—can be handled within the exhibit.

At the end of the 20th century, museum evaluators focused on museum visits as a social process involving a museum's messages and the complex relationships among the museum's visitors. John Falk and Lynn Dierking write eloquently about the gestalt of the museum experience in their book, *The Museum Experience*.[31] Jeff Patchen, director of the Indianapolis Children's Museum writes: "[M]any parents who come to places like museums are equally coming for themselves. It is really about child *and* adult learning. Museum educators across all disciplines began to direct programs to family groups rather than segmenting adults and children. These efforts mirrored and extended the intergenerational learning so common in children's museums."[32]

If you conjure an image of a "museum," it will most likely be an imposing building in the center of an urban area. To enter, you might have to climb a flight of stairs. It might resemble a classical temple or a bank building of a bygone era. Contrast this image with the children's museums that have sprung up in the last twenty years. You will find them in decommissioned schools, large houses on shady streets, or abandoned warehouses. Mix in to these different edifices a different notion of museum practice where the museum's community is present both at its creation and as partner in its development and evolution. Each of the examples of children's museums cited here reveals a different way to relate to the community, but in each instance that community is at the core of the museum's success.

Challenges

What's in a Name?

Elaine Heumann Gurian, once Boston Children's Museum exhibit center director, writes: "I do not like *museum* because we are more than a museum, and I do not like *children's* because we are not a museum for children only."[33] Gurian is not alone in this attitude and as new children's museums have developed they have adopted names designed to attract visitors, not to turn away some as "too old." Their variety is impressive: Eureka! (Halifax, UK), Magic House (St. Louis, Missouri), Port Discovery (Baltimore, Maryland), Young at Art (Davie, Florida), and Please Touch (Philadelphia, Pennsylvania).

Children's Museums and Isolation

Isolating visitors by age can be detrimental to intergenerational learning and people without children are unlikely to visit. Peter Marzio at the Smithsonian's 1979 Conference on Children in Museums said: "I concluded that when a children's museum seemed to be really working, it was also a great museum for adults; and if that were true, why couldn't a great adult museum be also very great for children . . . the thing I detested about the idea of children's zones and children's museums is that they could become simply another block being added to the elements that tend to split families apart rather than being a place where families could be kept together."[34]

Sustainability

Like many small community-based organizations, children's museums may emerge from groups that are both inexperienced and unprepared to provide institutional structure to ensure the museum's future. Educational administrator Gordon Ambach writes:

Entrepreneurs who started the children's museums boot-strapped them into existence, but like business entrepreneurs, they often lack the organizational capacity to grow them to the next level. . . . Let's get some venture capital hot-shots and incubate and grow children's museums.[35]

Technology and Children's Museums

The tradition of hands-on, interactive exhibitions and engaging experiences has prevailed in children's museums around the world. Today they are faced with how to add technology to the process, and how to afford the costs. With audiences that have experience with surround sound, high-definition visuals, and the fast pace of computer games, what's the appropriate role for the museum? How should children's museums incorporate technology that often allows for passive observation into the museum's atmosphere?[36]

Research

Former Indianapolis Children's Museum director Peter Sterling has argued persuasively that children's museum staff are not hired for their scholarly or academic experience or even inclination. A result of this reality is that little research into children's museums has taken place. The 1991 book *Bridges to Understanding* states the case: "Unfortunately for the advancement of research, many children's museums have unpublished research studies and evaluation reports lying in desk drawers or at the back of files that are not looked at after a problem has been solved. In fact, most of the published works from children's museums are *not* theoretically based research studies but informational or descriptive articles."[37]

Are Children's Museums Museums?

Peter Marzio, after visiting children's museums in the early 1970s, noted: "I also concluded, frankly, that children's museums, in the way that I had defined museums, weren't really museums; rather, at their best they were these marvelously large, expensive, exciting teaching machines which were sometimes very effective, from my point of view."[38] As children's museums have proliferated, one is left with the question of how to assess their place in the definition of museumness. If they are museums, should they be focused on interpreting objects and specimens for their visitors over creating engaging activities for young people? Are these options mutually exclusive?

Notes

1. Albert Heine, "Making Glad the Heart of Childhood," *Museum News* 58, no. 2 (November–December 1979): 24.

2. Judy Otto, "Learning about 'Neat Stuff': One Approach to Evaluation," *Museum News* 58, no. 2 (November–December 1979): 38.

3. Anna Billings Gallup, quoted in Suzanne LeBlanc, "The Slender Golden Thread, 100 Years Strong," *Museum News* 78, no. 6 (November–December 1999): 49.

4. LeBlanc, "The Slender Golden Thread," p. 49; Stephen E. Weil, "The Ongoing Transformation of the American Museum," *Daedalus*, Summer 1999, p. 247.

5. Elaine Heumann Gurian, *Civilizing the Museum*, London: Routledge, 2006, p. 22.

6. Gabrielle V. Pohle, "The Children's Museum as Collector," *Museum News* 58, no. 2 (November–December 1979): 32–37.

7. George E. Hein, "John Dewey and Museum Education," *Curator* 47, no. 4 (2004): 413–427.

8. Smithsonian Archives, RU 55, file 17.

9. Smithsonian Archives, RU 55, file 17; LeBlanc, "The Slender Golden Thread."

10. Eleanor M. Moore, *Youth in Museums*, Philadelphia: University of Pennsylvania Press, 1941, p. 1.

11. Edward P. Alexander, *The Museum in America: Innovators and Pioneers*, Walnut Creek, CA: AltaMira Press, 1997, p. 140.

12. Brooklyn Institute of Arts and Sciences flyer, 1900, Smithsonian Archives, RU 55, file 17.

13. Cassandra Zervos, *Children's Museums: A Case Study of the Foundations of Model Institutions in the United States*, thesis, Pennsylvania State University, 1990, p. 36.

14. Alexander, *The Museum in America*, p. 140.

15. www.brooklynkids.org.

16. Brenda Cowan and Stacey Shelnut, *Schools Out . . . Kids In*, Brooklyn Children's Museum, Robert Browne Foundation, 1997.

17. Adelaide B. Sayles, *The Story of the Children's Museum of Boston*, Boston, MA: George H. Ellis Press, 1937, p. 27.

18. Elaine Heumann Gurian, "Adult Learning at Children's Museum of Boston," in *Museums, Adults and the Humanities*, ed. Zipporah Collins, Washington, DC: American Association of Museums, 1981, p. 194.

19. Gurian, "Adult Learning," pp. 289–291.

20. www.bostonchildrensmuseum.org.

21. Zervos, *Children's Museums*, p. 74.

22. Zervos, *Children's Museums*, p. 76.

23. www.detroitchildrensmuseum.org.

24. Zervos, *Children's Museums*, pp. 94–95.

25. www.childrensmuseum.org.

26. Helmuth Naumer, "The Great Incorporation: The Youth Museum and Education," in *Museums and Education*, ed. Eric Larrabee, Washington, DC: Smithsonian Institution, 1969, p. 130.

27. www.fwmuseum.org.

28. G. Rollie Adams, manuscript, with permission; personal correspondence, 2007.

29. Cynthia Robinson and Warren Leon, "A Priority on Process," in *Ideas and Images: Developing Interpretive Exhibits*, eds. Kenneth L. Ames, Barbara Franco, and L. Thomas Frye, Nashville, TN: American Association for State and Local History, 1992, p. 212.

30. Judith White, *Snakes, Snails and History Tails, Building Discovery Rooms and Learning Labs at the Smithsonian Institution*, Washington, DC: Smithsonian Institution, 1991, p. 11.

31. John H. Falk and Lynn D. Dierking, *The Museum Experience*, Washington, DC: Whalesback Books, 1992.

32. Quoted in John H. Falk and Beverly K. Sheppard, *Thriving in the Knowledge Age: New Business Models for Museums and Other Cultural Institutions*, Lanham, MD: AltaMira Press, 2006, p. 99.

33. Gurian, "Adult Learning," p. 275.

34. *Proceedings of the Children in Museums International Symposium*, Washington, DC: Office of Museum Programs, Smithsonian Institution, 1979, p. 168.

35. Nina Freedlander Gibans, *Bridges to Understanding Children's Museums*, Cleveland, OH: Case Western Reserve University Press, 1999, p.149.

36. Gurian, *Civilizing the Museum*, p. 28.

37. Gibans, *Bridges*, p. 143.

38. *Proceedings of the Children in Museums International Symposium*, p. 168.

II

FUNCTIONS

8

To Collect

The presence of an object in a museum is always evidence of some previous moment of travel and collection, or a prior displacement that creates the visual availability to which the museum owes its identity and purpose. . . . To be a museum object, the collectible must have a connection to an originary [*sic*] context and be extractable. When moved, all such objects lose something of their original value, and in exchange gain display value in the new context of the collection.

—Mark Sandberg, 2003[1]

Museums exist to preserve objects of cultural and scientific importance. This function makes them unique. It permeates virtually every aspect of their operations, from collecting to conservation to scholarship and exhibition.

—Steven H. Miller, 1996[2]

Collections are the foundation of everything that takes place in museums, libraries and archives. They are vitally important, in part because objects take on unanticipated and surprising meanings over time. For instance, a botanical specimen we know little about today may yield clues to the cure of a disease tomorrow.

—Mary Chute, 2005[3]

Collecting is an instinctive drive for most human beings, as well as for various beasts, birds, and insects; dogs bury bones, ants store grain, and bees honey, and some birds collect bright objects in their nests. Physical security for long has been an underlying purpose of collectors, and Lewis Mumford has perceptively observed that "granary, bin, and cellar are village prototypes of library, archive, museum, and vault."[4] Collections still offer some physical security today; art objects, for example, often provide a hedge against inflation and, in time of war, may be portable and command a ready market. Collections also usually give their possessors social distinction—power, prestige, and status. Such distinction may ripen into a kind of immortality if the collector leaves his life's work to a museum, thus assuring "the survival on earth of the collector's name inscribed over a museum door."[5] The collector also may take joy in the chase, in running down clues and bargaining with owners or dealers. Collecting in a few instances has become a neurotic obsession, "a kind of gambling passion" that has driven its practitioners even to cheating and theft.

Collectors may perform great services for museums and indeed for society as a whole. They preserve objects of artistic, historical, and scientific importance for the enlightenment and enjoyment of present and future generations. Collectors, too, may become knowledgeable about the stream of objects that passes through their hands, and their research may make them leading authorities in their field of collection. They may even, through their research and personal interests, expand the scope of a museum's collection. American collector and founder of the National Gallery, Andrew Mellon preferred the advice of the dealer Joseph Duveen to that of museum directors or curators.[6]

Why Museums Collect

Most museums collect because of the belief that objects are important and evocative survivals of human civilization worthy of careful study and with powerful educational impact. Whether aesthetic, documentary, or scientific, objects tell much about the universe, nature, the human heritage, and the human condition. Museums thus carefully study and preserve their holdings so as to transmit important information to the present generation and posterity.

The first function of museums to appear historically was that of collection, and collection remains the predominant reason for many a museum's existence. In 1970, British museum scholar Alma S. Wittlin defined six purposes for both ancient and modern museum collections that suggest the changing nature of museums over time. Her purposes, or categories, are these:

Collections as economic hoards
Collections that convey social prestige
Collections that reveal "magic"
Collections that express group loyalty
Collections to stimulate curiousity and inquiry
Collections as a means of emotional experience

Wittlin's categories reveal the complex nature of museum collections as reflections of human and social institutions and further attest to the power of objects within societies.[7]

These basic generalizations hold true for all museums, but each type has special characteristics. Art museums may concentrate on beauty, and their mission is often defined as the direct transmission of the artist's aesthetic understanding to the beholder through the picture or object. Some art museum directors are so devoted to the idea of direct aesthetic communication that they begrudge any interpretation of the object beyond the simplest identification label placed as inconspicuously as possible, and they bar other interpretation devices from their galleries. Other directors are more interested in works of art as documents, whose creators had insight into, and gave a clear view of, the social conditions of their day; thus the object transmits historical information and understanding. Some art museums combine the two points of view by keeping their main galleries aesthetically pure with a minimum of interpretation and providing interpretation elsewhere in the museum.[8]

The history museum treats artifacts or objects as social documents—often as important for the historian, argue the museum curators, as the library's printed books or manuscripts. Historian Thomas Schlereth provides this overview for the study of objects: "*Material culture* properly connotes the physical manifestations of culture and therefore embraces those segments of human learning and behavior which provide a person with plans, methods, and reasons for producing and using things that can be seen and touched. . . . To put it still another way, material culture entails cultural statements that can take the form of plowshares, hallstands, political campaign buttons, service stations, funerary art, electric washing machines, short gowns or dog-trot houses."[9] Material culture becomes especially vivid and impressive when displayed in period rooms, historic houses, or historical villages.

The history museum collects the surviving objects of an age or ages and is especially interested in ethnography and social history. The science museum may be similar to the history museum if it collects industrial paraphernalia of the past but more like the art center if its exhibits focus on explaining the processes of science or technology. And then there are ethnographic museums like the Musee du Quai Branly that display their collections like art.

The natural history/science museum does a different kind of collecting in that it gathers specimens of geology, paleontology, and biology, and identifies and classifies them. This taxonomic kind of collecting has led to great advances of knowledge and is still important in the study of natural history/science. Botanical gardens and zoos are special museums in the natural history field with collections of living, rather than inanimate, specimens. Often their collections are taxonomic like that of natural history/science museums and increasingly they focus on those species deemed to be at risk of extinction. Efforts to identify threatened collections (species), such as the Red List of Threatened Species, the international Convention on International Trade in Endangered Species of Wild Fauna and Flora (CITES) program, and zoos' Species Protection Program (SPP), all expand the purpose of collecting to protecting the earth's biodiversity.

An innovation in many museums is the use of collections as educational tools rather than as a protected repository for objects. These types of museums range from memorials of events or individuals to museums with missions relating to a single subject or institutions with primarily educational functions as well as the ever-expanding children's (or youth) museums and art or science centers. The American Association of Museums (AAM) Accreditation Committee modified its definition of museums in 1978 to encompass those institutions that "own or use" objects. While technically noncollecting institutions, most of them use (and acquire) objects as aids to serve their educational purposes.

How Museums Collect

Gifts and bequests are the most common way museums acquire collections. Many, probably most, private collectors cannot bear to see dispersed the objects on which they have lavished so much attention and thought; thus they donate them to appropriate museums. Their generosity is often heightened by the desire to preserve their names as important donors and by the tax laws that make it worth their while. In Great Britain, heavy inheritance taxes often cause the executors of an estate to give paintings or objects to the nation in partial payment. In the United States, such materials may have greatly appreciated in value since a donor obtained them, and in certain circumstances, and subject to limitations and conditions, the fair market value may be deducted from tax obligations.[10] Dealers are sometimes important in this process, because they may have helped the private collector secure his objects and may counsel him on giving them where they will be best preserved and used. Many smaller museums, rarely able to purchase objects, are almost totally dependent upon gifts and bequests.

Larger or wealthier museums also acquire objects by purchase from private sources, dealers, or at auction. Internet auction sites such as eBay have revolutionized access to objects, allowing museum curators to literally "shop online" for desired objects, whether for accessioning or as props for exhibitions. Collections may be built steadily over a period of time by knowledgeable curators whose studies enable them shrewdly to judge and even anticipate values. Here again dealers may be useful in discovering objects and calling them to the attention of museums or museum patrons. A recent Metropolitan Museum of Art purchase is instructive. After learning of the availability of Duccio di Buoninsegna's *Madonna and Child* (c. 1300), the museum worked with the owners, the auction house, and private donors to raise between forty-five and fifty million dollars to purchase the painting. Though technically bought at auction, the purchase process was far more complex.[11]

Museums also obtain collections by field work and expeditions. Natural history museums send curators to gather scientific specimens in many parts of the world. Some anthropological museums obtain the bulk of their collections by means of archaeological expeditions, and art museums also collect archaeological and ethnographic materials in this manner. Historic preservation projects depend on archaeological digs to help provide historical authenticity for their architecture, furnishings, landscapes, and interpretive activities; this historical archaeology results in collections of materials to be used for both research and interpretation.

Still another way that museums acquire collections is by exchange or loan. Enlightened museum professionals like to see objects used well and fittingly. Sometimes, exchanges will mutually benefit and improve several collections. In 1980 the Boston Athenaeum sold two portraits by

Gilbert Stuart of George Washington and his wife Martha Dandridge Custis to the Museum of Fine Arts, Boston, and the Smithsonian Insititution's National Portrait Gallery. The pair now hang in either venue on an agreed-to rotating schedule.

Collections Planning

"The decision establishing the scope of the museum's collections is probably the most important one that the governing board can make," wrote Carl E. Guthe in 1959, in discussing small history museums, but the statement applies equally well to today and to all types and sizes of institutions.[12] The relevance of a museum's holdings distinguishes it from a household attic filled with obsolete and often broken and useless discards. In making a plan, the museum should first consider its mission or purpose and define it succinctly but clearly. What is it to collect? How to preserve, authenticate, and research its collections? How to exhibit and interpret them? How does the present collection fit into this plan? Should objects that do not fit within the collection be deaccessioned? What are the resources (fiscal, human, and physical) necessary to meet this plan? Wise answers to these basic questions can provide the framework that results in a first-class, high-quality museum.

In today's museums the curator oversees the institution's approaches to most of the questions above. The words "curate" and "curator" are from the Latin "to care." Curate means to care for souls, and a curator is a person responsible for objects and books in museums and libraries. He or she is responsible for the museum objects from acquisition to disposal; others may address issues of conservation needs, storage conditions, and public exhibition alongside the curator. From the 19th century on, museum curators generally emerged from scholarly, academic training with a deep understanding of the background and context of museum objects, whether butterflies or lithographs. As the 21st century opens, curators find themselves members of museum staff teams with broader responsiblities for objects and their public interpretation. As Barbara Franco notes: "Curatorial roles now demand technical knowledge of electronic collection management systems, sophisticated historical interpretive skills, and the ability to manage and produce complex exhibition projects."[13]

Art museums must decide what period to cover, what geographic area to encompass, and what kinds of materials to gather. A small American regional museum, for example, may confine its collections to paintings and sculpture produced in its area during the era since European settlement. Yet pressures may arise to lengthen the chronological period, to expand the geographic scope, or to even widen the art forms represented. Local collectors might urge the museum to accept and enlarge their collections, no matter how inappropriate for the museum's mission. The museum can sometimes expand the scope of its collection by means of temporary exhibits obtained on loan from private collectors, other museums, or traveling exhibitions. Museums may also decide to devote themselves to a special field such as modern art, American art, decorative art, furniture, textiles, glass, or ceramics or to the works of a single artist.

The history museum can define its field of collection more readily; its period may extend from prehistory to the present or may cover some portion of that era, and its area may be determined chiefly by its location and geographic field—municipality, region, or nation. Difficulties begin, however, if inhabitants of the area belonged to various jurisdictions from locality to nation and had connections with, and imported materials from, other areas. Typically, a museum will outline in considerable detail the history of the chosen period and area and then subject potential additions to the collection to careful and rigorous analysis. A midwestern state history museum, for example, might confine its collection of American Indian materials to cultures that once inhabited the area, except for a few objects from outside cultures to be used for comparison. For example, it will accept a few decorative art objects brought back by a state resident who once served as minister to Spain but will not take an extensive collection of Spanish barber bowls amassed by the same diplomat. In some history museums, the plan may be very specialized—devoted to a specific topic, time period, or even an individual.[14]

Certain guidelines help determine whether objects have historical value. In general, relics ("something left behind after decay, disintegration, or disappearance") are not suitable; a piece of the Charter Oak, a lock of Washington's hair, or a shell fragment picked up at Gettysburg tell us almost nothing of historical significance. On the other hand, objects with complete documentary records frequently have great value; a labeled piece of colonial furniture can transmit much social history, and even one with a well-defined family tradition can be helpful. Association pieces also have worthwhile emotional overtones; the portable writing desk on which Jefferson composed the Declaration of Independence or the "star-spangled banner" that Francis Scott Key saw flying at Fort McHenry are precious treasures of the National Museum of American History. The rise in social history has added to the value of everyday objects used by ordinary men and women as they offer evidence of the daily lives of citizens, not just those of the rich, famous, or perhaps infamous.[15]

All museums share a challenging collection problem in deciding what to gather from the contemporary scene. Art museums must establish a policy toward the works of living artists. Typical objects of everyday life—even from twenty-five years ago—are exceedingly difficult to find; beautiful and unusual artifacts tend to survive, but not the commonplace ones. Thus, century-old wedding dresses, ball gowns, and officer's uniforms are comparatively plentiful, but not everyday housedresses or men's work clothes. The interpretive value of everyday objects is difficult to determine, and has been generally neglected by traditional, academic historians. As we enter the 21st century, the academy's growing interest in the vernacular may help with the preservation of those objects (at least for the future). Gaps in the future museum collections can be avoided if museums adopt an outline of the history they wish to follow and a rational system of collecting designated contemporary objects. A systematic review of these materials will help to maintain control of this type of collection. For example, where collecting is not possible, photographs may be retained rather than the objects themselves.[16]

Science museums must also define their scope. The small natural history museum may limit itself to telling a broad scientific story with the flora and fauna of its locality or region; sometimes it can take advantage of the living specimens of the botanical gardens and zoos of the area. Science and natural history museums may find themselves in situations where they must take a public stand with their collecting practices as they reflect issues of conservation and protection of the planet. The technical museum or science center must decide how many historical objects to gather or whether to devote itself solely to explaining natural and physical phenomena and technological equipment and processes.[17]

These decisions by a museum governing board will apply to all future collection policies. The question remains, however, of what a museum should do with materials acquired in the past that do not conform to the new policy. The best advice here is that the board review its mission and proceed cautiously, adhering scrupulously to the conditions under which such objects were acquired until legal remedies can be found. Obviously, whatever plan a museum adopts should ideally be written down as completely and clearly as possible. It should be understood by both governing board and staff and be revised periodically to incorporate decisions made in day-to-day policy determination and implementation.

In developing such a program, the experience of the National Park Service may prove helpful, especially for history and natural science museums. The Park Service has worked out very specific procedures to guide managing collections.[18] The central elements are:

Written Scope of Collections statement to define the purpose, extent, and use of museum objects; a Collection Management Plan to guide management and care of collections; and an Emergency or Disaster Plan to protect objects on exhibit or in storage.

Accession objects upon receipt, recording registration data, establishing item or series number, inventory controls and legal proof of ownership; inventory items periodically.

Exhibit and store objects according to their specific environmental needs and vulnerabilities.

Use housekeeping procedures and preventive conservation to protect objects from degradation; examine objects periodically to assure protection.

Use conservation treatments only to ensure protection.

Deaccession objects outside the scope of collections according to written NPS policies and Procedures.[19]

The AAM Accreditation Commission reports that lack of collections planning is a major impediment to a museum's successful accreditation. A 2002 joint project assessing the status of effective collections planning by AAM and the Smithsonian's National Museum of American History revealed six important elements to effective collections planning (they conclude that planning should be ongoing, not a single plan to be filed and forgotten).

1. Identify the museum's audience(s) and how their needs will be served by collections.
2. Review the strengths and weaknesses of the existing collections.

3. Include a "gap analysis" contrasting the real and ideal collection.
4. Set priorities for acquisition and deaccessioning based on the needs assessment and gap analysis.
5. Identify "complementary collections" held by other museums or organizations that may affect the museum's collections choices.
6. Take into account existing or needed resources (funds, space and staff).[20]

The Ideal of Unrestricted Ownership

Negotiations between a prospective donor and a museum that wishes to acquire his or her collection may often result in complex and delicate bargaining. Should the collection be kept intact, not intermixed with objects from other collections? Should the collection remain always on exhibit? Should it have its own wing or gallery with the name of the donor prominently displayed? Should the collection be accepted as an extended or long-term loan in the hope that it may eventually ripen into a gift or bequest? The museum may be tempted to agree to such conditions in order to obtain possession of important articles or collections.

Any of these restrictions, however, offers possible future trouble for the museum. Whether the collection be old master paintings, the uniform and equipment of a prominent Revolutionary general, or South American butterflies, what happens if in the future, the museum obtains a larger and better collection in the same field? From a logical and psychological viewpoint, it would be far better to combine the old and new materials (and place some items in storage) in order to obtain a more effective exhibit. Also intensive study of museum objects may result in new attributions of artists or makers and even expose out-and-out fakes. Is the dead hand of the donor to prevent needed revisions and adjustments?

From the museum's point of view, it is usually best not to accept gifts with conditions attached. Museums, of course, should have proof of ownership of each article in their holdings, and they are well advised to have a standard gift agreement form that makes clear that articles are given outright and unconditionally. Occasionally, a governing board may decide that a collection (or a single object) is so important that it will be accepted with conditions. In such instances, a formal agreement should make clear the terms.

Extended loans from individuals are even more likely to give a museum difficulties. Sometimes lenders use the loan device as a means of receiving free and safe storage for their possessions and have even been known to leave them in their wills to museums other than the one storing them. Loans may be terminated at inconvenient times, and disputes may develop over the treatment the museum gives the objects. In general, a museum is wise to avoid taking extended loans from individuals, but if it decides to do so, it should devise a legal agreement that clearly makes provision for security, insurance, inspection, exhibition, and termination of the loan.

Two kinds of loans, however, are most useful and should be encouraged. The first is the loan for temporary exhibits that are so common today and desirable when they add to knowledge by showing objects in new and significant relationships. Here again, the museum must cover the whole loan process carefully with mutually agreed upon provisions for packing, transportation, care, and insurance. Extended loans from one museum to another are also entirely legitimate. Sometimes a museum lends articles outside its field of collection to a museum that will exhibit and use them appropriately; the conditions under which the lending museum originally received the objects may make it difficult to relinquish ownership, but an extended or permanent loan allows the materials to be put to desirable use. Sometimes, too, a large museum will lend materials from storage to a smaller museum that will exhibit them well; in this situation, the lending museum may check on the loan and renew it periodically. Again, in both instances, careful records agreed to by both parties should be kept.[21]

The Place of the Dealer

In Roman days, there were dealers in art objects, good ones and untrustworthy ones. During the Middle Ages, secondhand dealers and jewelers bought and sold art. Until the 17th century, the dealer was usually an agent, often a courtier, rather than a shopkeeper. Some of the great artists also served as dealers; the most successful of all, perhaps, was Rubens. Art objects have been auctioned from early times, and there is the story of the Roman collector who fell asleep during a sale and whose nodding head was taken to mean that he was approving bids. He awoke to find he had bought unwanted items worth 1,800,000 sesterces. Paintings and art objects were sold at trade fairs in the Middle Ages and even later; but by the 16th century, artists had organized exhibitions of art for sale, and cities began to regulate auctions. For a time, Amsterdam was the chief art sales center, to be followed by Paris, which, after the French Revolution, was joined by London. Two great auction houses were founded there—Sotheby's by Samuel Baker in 1744, and Christie's by James Christie in 1766.[22]

During the 19th century, many changes took place in the developing profession of the art dealer. He found, authenticated, promoted, and sold art, often becoming a connoisseur and critical authority in the process. Some dealers, such as Paul Duran-Ruel in Paris, the friend of the impressionists, began to manage a group of artists, discovering new talents, buying paintings on speculation, exhibiting and promoting, and serving as bankers and confidants.

Dealers, both European and American, became important in the United States after the Civil War in persuading wealthy collectors to acquire old master paintings and other art objects. They sought outstanding works of art, enlisted art history experts such as Bernard Berenson, Wilhelm von Bode, and W. R. Valentiner to validate them, and took advantage of rivalries among the collectors to demand high prices from which they reaped great profits. Sir Joseph (later Lord) Duveen of London was one of the most enterprising, enthusiastic, and entertaining of all the dealers; his adventures in uncovering masterpieces and playing upon the sensitivities of his wealthy clients make dramatic and diverting reading.[23] Robert C. Vose, Michel Knoedler, and Jacques Seligman and his son, Germain, are other examples of those who helped make New York City a great international art mart, while William MacBeth and Robert Macintyre served collectors of American art well. Parke Bernet, established in 1937, became the leading American auction firm and in 1964 was purchased by Sotheby's of London. In 2003, Sotheby's had more than one hundred offices worldwide, and its auction sales produced a turnover of just under 2 billion dollars. In 2000 Sotheby's conducted the first international auction via the Internet.[24]

At the same time that dealers serve the interests of museums as collectors, they also provide an element of competition, especially for those objects considered of great public value. At the close of the 20th century, private collecting—often with the aid of dealers—inflated value, especially of art objects, and precluded public museums with limited budgets from acquisitions. In history museums, collectors of objects ranging from motorcycle gang paraphernalia to Gustav Stickley furniture have increased the value of objects, therefore limiting many museums' ability to add to their collections. The popularity of Public Television's *Antiques Roadshow* has caused even casual collectors to inflate the potential value of their objects and restrict a museum's interest in acquiring them. Alma Wittlin's "collections that convey social prestige" have evolved into potential monetary resources for the collector and in some instances meant the objects have remained in private hands.[25]

Determining Authenticity

In deciding to add items to their collections, museums must be on guard against forgeries and fakes. Forgeries are copies of paintings or objects made for fraudulent, usually profitable purposes. Fakes are genuine artworks of little worth that are altered, or added to, so as to enhance their value. Forgers are occasionally driven by psychological obsession—a desire to commit a perfect fraud that will fool the greatest authorities. Han van Meegeren, for example, thought that the world failed to recognize his great talent and vowed to take in the experts by creating paintings in Vermeer's exact style. D. G. van Beuningen, the great Dutch collector whose motto was "rely on your own taste and never ask advice," paid 1,600,000 florins for van Meegeren's spurious *Last Supper*, and the prestigious Boymans Museum of Rotterdam bought his *Christ and the Disciples at Emmaus* for 520,000 florins.[26] In 1990 a British Museum exhibition included objects from all ages that are held by museums around the globe. Its catalog declared: "Not a single object has been included here merely because it deceived an untutored layman. Most have been validated thrice over, an initial purchase by an experienced collector, or publication by a leading scholar and an acquisition by a great museum."[27]

There are three chief ways of authenticating objects—by scientific, historical, or stylistic analysis—and a museum should use all three of them in considering accessions. Scientific evaluations provide data that can help to define the physical nature, composition, and structure of an object. Visual and microscopic examinations are used to reveal the surface condition of an object as well as information about artistic techniques. An object's internal structure, including past restorations and repairs, can be detected using radiography and other examination methods that do not require the removal of samples. As a group, all of the preceding methods are considered to be "nondestructive," because none require taking samples. Methods of analysis that do require small samples sometimes are called "destructive techniques," although only minute samples are needed for most types of materials analysis or identification. Many different methods are available to provide information about the composition of an object, but the specific test must be selected on the basis of the information needed. In some instances, the age or authencity of the object can be supported or disproved with the assistance of scientific studies.[28]

Historical analysis tries to establish the provenance (history of ownership) of an object by tracing its history through surviving records or oral testimony. Many times this may be difficult because of missing records, but a museum should always try to gather as much of the object's history as possible. Historical analysis also examines the authenticity of the details shown in the painting or object; the forger or faker may make mistakes about costumes, decorative arts, or inscriptions for the period he or she is trying to represent. Stylistic analysis compares the object with known productions of the same maker or in the same cultural era; a knowing connoisseur or art historian may be able to see differences in style that reveal an object's fraudulent nature.

The unresolved controversy over Goya's Black Paintings illustrates the complexities of establishing authenticity. Spanish scholar Juan Jose Junquera, commissioned to write a book on the paintings, turned to historical records to establish the placement of the paintings' original venue, Goya's country house, in La Quinta, outside Madrid. He studied an early 19th-century inventory of the household, and a purportedly contemporary article about Goya's paintings at La Quinta. Through this careful analysis of the historical records, he cast doubt on the existence of the second floor of La Quinta where the paintings were supposedly painted on the wall along the staircase before their removal and sale. In a nifty bit of detective work, he even questioned the date of the inventory itself based on linguistic analysis of the inventory's term for "desk." In his *New York Times Magazine* article describing questions on the authenticity of the Black Paintings, Arthur Lubow suggests that art historians "determine the attribution of a painting in two ways: historical documentation or physical examination . . . each art historian tends to tilt toward the archive or the canvas." He cites British scholar Juliet Wilson-Bareau's own questioning of the attribution of the Black Paintings to Goya from her perspective of thirty years of stylistic analysis of Goya's works.[29]

Importance of Records

Museum collections lose much of their value if they are not properly recorded. *Museum Registration Methods* states it this way: "Whenever any work of art, or scientific specimen, or historical object enters a museum, it must be identified immediately by some clear and ready means and its entry and subsequent disposition must be accurately and permanently recorded."[30] The important thing is that every object has its own individual number painted on or attached to it and that this number be entered in the museum's records.

Museums should keep three types of information: Collections management information, beginning with acquisition information; physical descriptive information; and artistic, historical, and/or scientific contextual information, including significance to the museum's collections. The initial acquisition record shows object name, source, how the object was acquired (gift, purchase, exchange), date of receipt, brief physical description, and what is known regarding the object's context. At the time of acqustion, museums assign an acquisition number to each transaction and a catalog number to each object in the transaction. These numbers provide the links between the objects and the information maintained by the museums. Most museums today use a three part numbering system. For example, say, 2001.38.15 indicates the fifteenth item in the thirty-eighth acquisition in the year 2001.

More in-depth cataloging information is added to the initial acquisition information as museum staff conduct their research. This information may include artist or maker, history and importance of use, period of design and manufacture, and biographical information relating to people connected to the object. More precise physical descriptive information also is added, such as exact measurements, marks, materials, colors, and condition. Ongoing collections management information is added as an object is used by the museum; this details exhibit, location, and loan histories. Museums today usually organize this data by acquisition and object number.

Museums keep all correspondence, legal documents, newspaper clippings, and other miscellaneous records concerning the object in file folders. These files are managed according to archival standards as they form the permanent records of the museum. These files also are organized by acquisition and object number. Museums create indices as needed and may use such information as donor, maker, location, subject, or special research topics.

At a minimum, initial acquisition information should be maintained by all museums. There also should be similar records covering incoming and outgoing loans. A museum should keep duplicate collections records in a separate location safe from fire, theft, or other hazards. Additionally, the most conscientious museums have developed formal disaster plans to guide the staff as they protect museum objects from natural and man-made disasters.[31]

Computerization has greatly affected the form and uses of collections records. Internal controls for collections, especially at museums with vast holdings, have been greatly strenghtened. "Using computers, museums can track object locations, prepare exhibition lists, general forms (receipts, insurance forms, deeds of gift), manage images, and organize conservation, publication, and exhibition histories. Exhibitions on all subjects benefit from this amazing resource for the conceptualizers, curators, and designers, too. Interconnectivity of computer systems has not been easy, nor moved in a straight line. Establishing agreement among museums, especially internationally, about the most basic museum vocabulary has been complex. Cultural sensitivity along with differing national standards have hampered both basic communication and potential cooperation."[32]

Ethics of Acquisition

Museums are becoming more and more concerned about illicit trade in foreign art and archaeological objects. Stolen objects smuggled into the United States have turned up in the art market, and have found their way into museums by purchase or through gifts and bequests by private collectors. Museums with anthropological collections urge all museums to take great care in investigating the provenance of objects so as to guarantee that acquisitons have complied with laws protecting the national patrimony of the country of origin. Art museums take reasonable precautions against acquiring objects illicitly exported from foreign lands, but they argue that the primary responsibility for enforcing these laws rested with the countries of origin. They point out that a museum acquiring objects by field collection or excavation could be much surer of their provenance than a museum purchasing objects in the art market or receiving them by gift or bequest.[33]

The United Nations Educational, Scientific and Cultural Organization (UNESCO) in 1970 adopted a Convention on the Means of Prohibiting and Preventing the Illicit Export, Import and Transfer of Ownership of Cultural Property. Under it, each ratifying state would establish an export certificate for important cultural property and no state would import such property without a certificate. Provision was also made for the return of stolen property to the state of origin. The

United States ratified the convention in 1983 and by 2003 a total of one hundred countries were signatories.[34]

Two examples from the early 1970s reveal the complex relationships between museums, dealers, and undocumented property. In 1972, the Metropolitan Museum of Art announced that it had purchased for about 1 million dollars a previously unknown Greek calyx krater of the 6th century BC made by the potter Euxitheos and the painter Euphronios. The Italian police asserted that the krater had been looted from an Etruscan tomb in 1971. Before its purchase, the museum had inquired about its origin from the dealer, who reported that he had secured it from an Armenian dealer, whose father had acquired the vase in fragments in London in 1920. The situation changed dramatically in February 2006 when the Metropolitan Museum (Met) and the Italian government agreed to terms regarding the museum's Italian holdings. Met director Phillippe de Montebello in a recent interview explains the Met's plans to return the *Euphronios krater* to Italy this way: "The world is changing, and you have to play by the rules. It now appears that the piece [krater] came to us in a completely improper way—through machinations, lies, clandestine night digging. As the representative of an honorable institution, I have to say no, that is not right."[35]

The J. Paul Getty Museum entered the antiquities market in the 1970s continuing the aggressive collecting style of the museum's founder and bringing to bear its vast financial resources. When the Getty's Malibu villa reopened in 2006, the museum's curator of antiquities had resigned and was under indictment by Italian authorities for buying looted goods. The complicated details of the case suggest destruction of ancient sites, faked ownership records, rigged auctions to inflate values, and perhaps most shocking the breaking up of ancient artifacts and selling of the fragments at ever-increasing prices. Though this case's outcome is unknown, its details and those of the Met reveal the darkest side of museum collecting.[36] To protect its antiquities, the Italian government has initiated discussions with major museums to create a long-term loan program. The program would allow museums to display such objects, but the Italian government would retain ownership. It is an imaginative approach to the long-standing tensions.

A special category of stolen artifacts are those items once owned by victims of the Nazi regime (1933–1945). This Nazi "loot" was taken from victims of the Holocaust, public and private museums and galleries, and religious and educational institutions. The Association of Art Museum Directors estimates that about one thousand items held by American museums require further study regarding their provenance during the Nazi era.[37] Marie Malaro includes an instructive example in *A Legal Primer on Managing Museum Collections*:

> In *Menzel v. List*, the Menzels purchased a painting by Marc Chagall in 1932 for about $150 at an auction in Brussels, Belgium. In 1941, when the Germans invaded Belgium, the Menzels were forced to flee the country, and the painting was left behind in their apartment. On their return six years later, the painting was gone, having been taken by the Germans. In 1955, Klaus Perls and his wife, proprietors of a New York art gallery bought the painting from a Parisian art gallery for $2,800. The Perls knew nothing about the history of the painting and did not question the Paris gallery. Klaus Perls testified that it would have been an "insult" to question a reputable dealer as to the title. Several months later the Perls sold the painting to Albert List for $4,000. In 1962, Mrs. Menzel noticed a reproduction of the painting in a book, which gave List's name as the owner. She requested the return of the painting, but List refused to surrender it. Mrs. Menzel then instituted an action for replevin [return of misappropriated property] against List, and he in turn brought the Perls into the suit, alleging that they were liable to him for breach of an implied warranty of title . . . After much litigation, Mrs. Menzel was awarded her painting, and the Perls were ordered to pay List the value of the painting as of the date the painting was surrendered to Mrs. Menzel.[38]

International groups of museum organizations and the U.S. Department of State are working to establish policies to balance the rights of owners with the interests of museums in exhibiting objects lacking fully documented provenance, especially for the years 1933 to 1945.[39]

In addition to purloined objects, federal legislation passed in 1990 protects Native American cultural items—human remains, funerary objects, sacred objects, or objects of cultural patrimony—under the Native American Graves Protection and Repatriation Act (NAGPRA). This legislation mandates the return to lineal descendants, culturally affiliated Indian tribes, and Native Hawaiian organizations of objects held by public and private museums that have received federal funding. As of 2003, NAGPRA recorded repatriated museum holdings totaling 27,777 human remains; 558,799 associated funerary objects; 1,185 sacred objects; and 644 objects that are both sacred and patrimonial.[40]

The question of acquisitions involving the patrimony of other nations remains a thorny one. As long as the countries of origin are unable to enforce protective laws, smuggling and illicit sales are sure to take place. The decision of museums not to acquire objects of doubtful provenance will not cause the market for such materials to dry up, and in some cases may result in collections of value being kept from public knowledge and even destroyed. Still, responsible museum professionals, museum governing boards, and their professional affiliates cannot condone the acquisition of stolen and looted objects. Individual museums and museum professional organizations are adopting statements of policy that acknowledge the importance of establishing the provenance of objects to be acquired and exhibited in museums. As attorney Paul Bator writes: "Western collectors and museum officials sometimes assert that, over all, the practice of exporting antiquities has materially aided the preservation of the artistic patrimony of mankind. And it is demonstrable that in many countries rich in antiquities and archaeological treasures, the record of preservation has been miserable, sometimes on account of extrinsic factors like war and poverty, but also on account of indifference, corruption, and inefficiency."[41]

Ethics of Dispersal

Just as a museum has a right (and indeed a duty) to define its field of acquisition and adopt clear policies relating to accessions, so also it ought to establish principles of disposing of materials that are outside its scope or that it cannot use for exhibition, study, or loan. Collection management certainly includes out-go, as well as in-flow. The difficulty here, however, is that a museum is a public trust and that deaccession and disposal of objects can lead to public criticism and affect future collections donations. Even the boards of museums that accept no public funds occupy a trusteeship relationship that is subject to some state supervision.

Deaccessioning is the term used by museums to describe "out-go." You will not find the term in the dictionary. Author Marie Malaro defines it as "the process used to remove permanently an object from a museum's collection. The definition presupposes that the object in question once was 'accessioned,' that it was formally accepted and recorded as an object worthy of collection status."[42] Generally agreed reasons for this practice are (a) an item does not fit within the museum's "scope of collections," (b) the museum cannot provide proper care for the object, (c) the item is in poor condition, and (d) the museum owns an abundance of like objects. In addition to these reasons for deaccessioning museum objects, museums have used other, less agreed-upon justifications, including lack of storage space, changing curatorial interests, and potential income from an item's sale, sometimes creating a public outcry over these actions.[43]

Many museum objects offer little difficulty if they are deaccessioned. Some museums (especially those dealing with history and science) may even accept objects with the understanding that they may not be accessioned but will be sold or otherwise disposed of for the benefit of the museum. Other objects may have been received years earlier and lie outside a museum's agreed-upon field (for example, stuffed birds or seashells in a small art museum); if such objects cannot be returned to the donors, no one can reasonably oppose their disposal. Items damaged beyond reasonable repair or actual duplicates also arouse little controversy. Similarly, objects more useful in other collections (for example, Egyptian scarabs in a local history museum) can be placed on long-term loan, given, or even sold to another, more appropriate, museum.

Major problems are encountered, however, when items are sold for financial reasons or traded or sold to upgrade the quality of a collection. Art museums often experience special difficulties because of varying opinions of the importance and monetary value of art objects. Museums follow three general practices in this area. Some museums sell or exchange nothing. A second policy permits sales or exchanges only with other museums or similar nonprofit institutions. The third practice is for the museum freely to sell or exchange works of art to which the museum has unrestricted title in order to refine and enhance its collections. Museum professional organizations have established within their codes of ethics standards for the use of funds gained from deaccessioning. The American Association of Art Museum Directors (1992) states: "Proceeds should be restricted to acquisitions of new works of art." The AAM Code of Ethics (1993) requires that disposals be solely for "advancement of the museum's mission. . . . Proceeds . . . in no event shall they be used for anything other than acquisition or direct care of collections." The American Association for State and Local History (AASLH, 1992) argues forthrightly that "collections shall not be deaccessioned or disposed of in order to provide financial support for institutional operations, facilities maintenance, or any reason other than the preservation or acquisition of collections." The International Council of Museums policy (2004) is that the proceeds "should be used solely for the benefit of the collection and usually for acquisitions to that collection."[44]

The Metropolitan Museum of Art stirred considerable controversy in deaccessioning some of its holdings in 1970. The museum bought at auction in London the superb portrait by Velazquez of *Juan de Pareja* for 5 million dollars. Though part of the purchase price was contributed by the trustees, some of it was raised by deaccessioning and selling paintings from the Adelaide Milton de Groot Collection. Miss de Groot stated in her will that "without limiting in any way the absolute nature of this bequest," requested the museum not to sell any of the works of art but to keep what it wished and give the remainder to one or more important museums that it should select. The Metropolitan trustees interpreted the de Groot bequest as precatory, requesting that they not be sold, but not prohibiting the museum from selling paintings from her bequest.

When the de Groot sales were discovered, acrimonious arguments filled the newspapers and art journals and the attorney general of New York State investigated. The Metropolitan issued a white paper that gave a detailed history of all disposals from 1971 to 1973, and adopted, with the participation of the attorney general's office, new procedures for deaccessioning and disposal of works of art. The process included (1) promptly informing the attorney general whenever the museum deaccessioned any work of art worth more than five thousand dollars; (2) requiring that any sale, except to another museum, of a deaccessioned work of art worth more than five thousand dollars be at public auction; (3) giving adequate public notice prior to sale of a deaccessioned work of art worth twenty-five thousand dollars on exhibition within the past ten years; (4) stipulation that the museum would deviate from a nonbinding restriction of a donor only with the consent of the donor or his heirs and on notice to the attorney general; and (5) binding restrictions could be removed only with court authority and appropriate notice to the attorney general. Thus, the Metropolitan's deaccessioning process underwent considerable change as a result of the New York attorney general's intervention. Not all museums agreed with the revision. The Museum of Modern Art, which had forty years of experience with frequent disposal of paintings and sculpture, argued that professionals and specialists in the field of modern art—its own staff, outside art historians, and professionals on its board—were better qualified to make judgments about dispositions than the attorney general's office.[45] This example provides a sense of the complexity

of the issues around deaccessioning. The press often highlights deaccessioning controversies, but in fact the process generally occurs with
little fanfare.

Ideally, museums should design their own disposal procedures
based on the highest professional ethics, both in deciding upon
the deaccessioning and carrying out the sales or exchanges. The
AAM and AASLH current codes of ethics, adopted in 1993 and 2002
respectively, outline specific guidelines for deaccessioning collections and the acceptable uses for funds gained from the sale of collections.

Challenges

Research

As the 21st century opens, the very nature of research has changed.
The Internet and sophisticated communciation systems allow researchers to pursue their interests from their own desks. The place of
museum collections (regardless of type) in the conduct of research has
diminished. Twenty years ago an anthropologist reported that academic training for anthropologists no longer relied on museum collections. She bemoaned the fact that recent graduate anthropologists had
never entered a museum to use its collections. With this changing academic emphasis and expanding information access, how should museums make their collections available? How should they balance caring
for collections—physically and intellectually—with collections-based
public exhibitions? In addition to questioning the role of museums as
scholarly centers, the challenge revolves around the fundamental question of a museum's audience.[46]

Storage

Ask any museum director how much of the collection is on view and
often you will learn that only a tiny portion of the museum's objects are
accessible to the public. This fact adds not only to the museum's financial obligation to care for its objects but also to its burden in providing
appropriate, protected environments for items that perhaps will never
be on view. Heritage Preservation's *A Public Trust at Risk* on the status
of U.S. museum preservation issued in 2006 reveals that more than 59
percent of the three thousand reporting museums suggest that the stor-

age facilities for collections are too small and inadequate to protect the objects.[47]

Computerization of Collections Information

National computer systems for collections information have enjoyed mixed success. The Canadian Heritage Information Network (CHIN), the Getty Art and Architecture Thesaurus, and the U.S. MARC archives initiative all have their proponents and detractors. As global computer communication evolves, the systematic recording of collections information will further develop. And with that process comes the fundamental issue of institutional control and public access.[48]

Ownership Rights and Responsibilities

Repatriation, or issues of ownership of collections acquired through imperialism and international conflict, remains grist for museum policy makers. Questions surrounding ownership of objects from the Nazi era (1933–1945) especially complicate the issue. Canadian anthropologist Miriam Clavir writes: "The word 'collected,' which usually has a positive value in Western society, has often been replaced . . . with words such as 'taken' and 'stolen.'"[49]

Contemporary Collecting

Collecting objects from the recent past results in, at least, two challenges: the first is the care of objects that may be designed to be disposable, and the second involves questions of "authority" when it comes to interpreting their meaning or value. This is a special challenge for history museums.[50]

Permanent Collections

As museums compete for audiences—especially for "return" visitors—how do they care for and display their permanent collections? With temporary exhibitions created to offer visitors new museum experiences, where do the museum's basic, long-term collections fit? "What is the future of collecting and the future of museums, and of the permanent collection?" Philip Conisbee, senior curator, National Gallery of Art, Washington, D.C., wonders. In an age of special exhibitions, will anyone stand up for museums as places that acquire, tend, and study our greatest art, and then simply put some of it out on view for quiet contemplation. "This is an important issue that perhaps needs to be thought about more, and addressed more, by all museums."[51]

Protecting Collections in Wartime

Should protecting collections in wartime be a role for international museum organizations? Neil Brodie, director of the Illicit Antiquities Research Centre at Cambridge (UK) writes: "Why has no concerted international action been taken to block the trade and sale of materials looted from archaeological sites and cultural institutions during wartime? There are three ways in which wars threaten cultural materials: the most obvious is damage from military attack, but another threat is removal of materials (booty) for profit, to fund the war or for propaganda purposes, with the final means perhaps the most disburbing, that of destroying cultural materials to erase ethnic or religious symbols within a society (cultural cleansing). In Afghanistan in 1996, 70 percent of the National Museum's collections were missing, some reportedly for purposes of paying soldiers." See Matthew Bogdanos, "Casualties of War: The Looting of the Iraq Museum," *Museum News* 85, no. 2 (March–April 2006) for a discussion of the impact of the U.S. invasion on Baghdad.[52]

Notes

1. Mark Sandberg, *Living Pictures, Missing Persons: Mannequins, Museums and Modernity*, Princeton, NJ: Princeton University Press, 2003, p. 182.
2. Steven H. Miller, "Guilt Free Deaccessioning," *Museum News* 75, no. 5 (November–December 1996).
3. Mary Chute, acting director Institute of Museum and Library Services, Heritage Preservation press release, December 8, 2005.
4. Quoted in Douglas and Elizabeth Rigby, *Lock, Stock and Barrel: The Story of Collecting*, Philadelphia, PA: Lippincott, 1944, p. 6.
5. Maurice Rheims, *The Strange Life of Objects: 35 Centuries of Art Collecting and Collectors*, New York, 1961, p. 43.
6. Rigby, *Lock, Stock and Barrel*, pp. 3–82; Rheims, *Strange Life of Objects*, pp. 17–49; Pierre Cabane, *The Great Collectors*, New York, 1963, pp. xii–xviii; Alma S. Wittlin, *Museums: In Search of a Usable Future*, Cambridge, MA: MIT Press, 1970, pp. 3–60; W. G. Constable, *Art Collecting in the United States of America: An Out-*

line and History, London, 1964, pp. 97–99; Aline B. Saarinen, *The Proud Possessors: The Lives, Times and Tastes of Some Adventurous American Art Collectors*, New York, 1958; Russell Lynes, *The Tastemakers*, New York, 1954; Neil Harris, "Collectors, Collections, and Scholarly Culture," American Council of Learned Societies, Occasional Paper No. 48, 2000; Neil Harris, *Cultural Excursions: Marketing Appetites and Cultural Tastes in Modern America*, Chicago, IL: Chicago University Press, 1990; Meryle Secrest, *Duveen: A Life in Art*, New York: Knopf, 2005; Kevin F. McCarthy, Elizabeth H. Ondaatje, Arthur Brooks, and Andras Szanto, *A Portrait of the Visual Arts, RAND Research in the Arts*, Santa Monica, CA, 2005, pp. 13–29.

7. Wittlin, *Museums: In Search*, pp. 13–60; McCarthy et al., *A Portrait of the Visual Arts*, see chap. 3 for discussion of current art collecting patterns; Suzanne Keene, *Fragments of the World: Uses of Museum Collections*, Oxford, UK: Butterworth, Heinemann, 2005.

8. James Cuno, ed., *Whose Muse? Art Museums and Public Trust*, Princeton University Press and Harvard University Press, 2004.

9. Thomas Schlereth, *Material Culture Studies in America*, Nashville, TN: American Association of State and Local History 1982; Keene, *Fragments of the World*; Simon Knell, ed., *Care of Collections*, Leicester, UK: Routledge, 1994; Simon Knell, *Museums and the Future of Collecting*, UK: Ashgate, 2004.

10. IRS Publication 526 (December 2005).

11. Calvin Tomkins, "The Missing Madonna," *New Yorker*, July 11 and 18, 2005; McCarthy et al., *A Portrait of the Visual Arts*, pp. 72–74.

12. Carl E. Guthe, *The Management of Small History Museums*, Nashville, TN: American Association of State and Local History, 1959, p. 16; Marie Malaro, *A Legal Primer on Managing Museum Collections*, Washington, DC: Smithsonian Institution Press, 1998; Anne Fahy, ed., *Collections Management*, London: Routledge, 1995 (essays that cover most subjects relating to current collections management with an international perspective).

13. Barbara Franco, "The History Museum Curator of the 21st Century," *History News*, Summer 1996, pp. 6–10; Nancy Villa Bryk, "Reports of Our Death Have Been Greatly Exaggerated: Reconsidering the Curator," *Museum News* 80, no. 2 (March–April 2001).

14. Franco, "The History Museum Curator"; Bryk, "Reports of Our Death."

15. Guthe, *The Management of*, pp. 13–23; Eugene F. Kramer, "Collecting Historical Artifacts: An Aid for Small Museums," *History News* 25 (August 1970): technical leaflet no. 6; Arthur C. Parker, *A Manual for History Museums*, New York: Columbia University Press, 1935, pp. 9–29; Laurence Vail Coleman, *The Museum in America: A Critical Study*, 3 vols., Washington: 1939, 1:118–121; Thomas J. Schlereth, "History Museums and Material Culture," in *History Museums in the United States: A Critical Assessment*, eds. Warren Leon and Roy Rosenzweig, Urbana: University of Illinois Press, 1989, pp. 294–320; L. Thomas Frye, "Museum Collecting for the 21st Century," Common Agenda for History Museums Proceedings, February 1987, pp. 32–38.

16. G. Ellis Burcaw, "Active Collecting in History Museums," *Museum News* 45, no. 3 (March 1967): 21–22 and *Museum Work*, pp. 61–62; Coleman, *Museum*

in America, 2:244–245; Bengt Nystrom and Gunilla Cedrenius, "Spread the Responsibility for Museum Documentation—A Programme for Contemporary Documentation at Swedish Museums of Cultural History," Stockholm: SAMDOK Council, 1982; Thomas J. Schlereth, "Defining Collecting Missions: National and Regional Models," Common Agenda for History Museums Proceedings, February 1987; Frye, "Museum Collecting"; Thomas J. Schlereth, "Collecting Today for Tomorrow," *History News* (March–April 1982): 29–37; Candace Floyd, "Chinatown," *History News* (June 1984): 7–11; Edith P. Mayo, "Contemporary Collecting" *History News* (October 1982): 8–11.

 17. Coleman, *Museum in America*, 1:120–121.

 18. "NPS Servicewide Standards for Managing Museum Objects," in *Museum Handbook*, Part I, National Park Service, revised 1990.

 19. In 1999 the NPS deaccessioned 749 objects to agencies outside the federal government. This is a tiny number in a collection that numbered 80 million items. Kathleen T. Byrne, "Deaccessioning Museum Collections," *CRM* no. 5 (2000).

 20. James B. Gardner and Elizabeth Merritt, "Collections Planning: Pinning Down a Strategy," *Museum News* 81, no. 4 (July–August 2002); John Simmons, "Managing Things: Crafting a Collections Policy," *Museum News* 83, no. 1 (January–February 2004).

 21. Coleman, *Museum in America*, 2:236–241; Guthe, *The Management of*, pp. 25, 27; Burcaw, *Museum Work*, pp. 50–51; Malaro, *A Legal Primer*; Fahy, *Collections Management*.

 22. Germain Bazin, *The Museum Age*, New York: Universe, 1967, pp. 16–17, 84–86, 107–114; Rheims, *Strange Life of Objects*, pp. 98–101, 105–110, 173–202; Constable, *Art Collecting*, pp. 56, 42–43, 99–104, 145; Secrest, *Duveen*; Samuel N. Behrman, *Duveen*, New York, 1952; Rene Gimpel, *Diary of an Art Dealer*, New York, 1966; Germain Seligman, *Merchants of Art: 1880–1960: Eighty Years of Professional Collecting*, New York, 1961; www.sothebys.com; www.christies.com.

 23. Secrest, *Duveen*.

 24. www.christies.com; www.sothebys.com.

 25. McCarthy et al., *A Portrait of the Visual Arts*, pp. 72–74.

 26. Otto Kurz, *Fakes: A Handbook for Collectors and Students*, 2nd ed., New York, 1967, pp. 329–334; George Savage, *Forgeries, Fakes, and Reproductions: A Handbook for the Art Dealer and Collector*, New York, 1963, pp. 206–209, 221–222, 227, 231–232; Cabane, *The Great Collectors*, pp. 153–157; Lawrence Jeppson, *The Fabulous Frauds: Fascinating Tales of Great Art Forgeries*, New York, 1970, pp. 149–195.

 27. Mark Jones, ed., *Fake? The Art of Deception*, London: British Museum Trustees, 1990, p. 11.

 28. Paul Coremans, "The Museum Laboratory," in *The Organization of Museums: Practical Advice*, Paris: United Nations Educational, Scientific and Cultural Organization, 1967, pp. 94–96; Richard Buck, "On Conservation," *Museum News* 52 (March 1974): 16–19; Savage, *Forgeries, Fakes, and Reproductions*, pp. 34, 227, 231; Kurz, *Fakes*, pp. 22–31; Thomas B. Brill and George J. Reilly, "Chemistry in

the Museum," *Chemistry* 45 (May 1972): 6–9; Clements L. Robertson, "The Visual and Optical Examination of Works of Art," *Museum News* 46 (December 1967): 47–52: technical supp. no. 20; Brian Ramer, personal correspondence.

29. Arthur Lubow, "The Secret of the Black Paintings," *New York Times Magazine*, July 27, 2003; Robert Hughes, *Goya*, New York: Knopf, 2003.

30. Dorothy H. Dudley et al., *Museum Registration Methods*, 3rd ed., Washington, DC: American Association of Museums, 1979, p. 3; Malaro, "Accessioning Is the Formal Process Used to Accept and Record an Item as a Collection Object" and "Collections Management Policies,"in *A Legal Primer*, pp. 43–51; Timothy Ambrose and Crispin Paine, *Museum Basics*, London: Routledge (with International Council of Museums), 1993; Rebecca A. Buck and Jean Allman Gilmore, *Museum Registration Methods*, Washington, DC: American Association of Museums, 1998; Valerie Dorge and Sharon L. Jones, *Building an Emergency Plan: A Guide for Museums and Other Cultural Organizations*, Los Angeles, CA: Getty Conservation Institute, 1999, (based on workshops with step-by-step guidance); "Recovering from Disaster," special issue, *History News* 61, no. 2 (Spring 2006), includes technical leaflet #234, which provides extensive bibliographic information on disaster planning.

31. Robert G. Chenall, James Blackaby, and Patricia Greeno, *Nomenclature for Museum Cataloguing*, Nashville, TN: American Association of State and Local History, 1988; *The New Museum Registration Methods*, Washington, DC: American Association of Museums, 1998, p. 17.

32. Katherine Speiss, personal correspondence.

33. Ann Zelle, "Acquisitions: Saving Whose Heritage?" *Museum News* 49 (April 1971): 19–26; The International Foundation for Art Research (IFAR) Reports maintains a database for stolen art that encompasses these categories: fine arts, decorative arts, antiquities, ethnographic objects, Asian art, and miscellaneous objects; Russell Chamberlin, *Loot! The Heritage of Plunder*, New York: Facts On File, 1983.

34. UNESCO agreements (1983, U.S. signatory); Stephen E. Weil, *Making Museums Matter*, Washington, DC: Smithsonian Press, 2002.

35. *Metropolitan Museum of Art, Report on Art Transactions*, New York: Metropolitan Museum of Art, June 20, 1973, pp. 23–24; Karl E. Meyer, *Plundered Past*, New York: Atheneum, 1973, pp. 86–100; Bonnie Burnham, *The Art Crisis*, London: Collins, 1975, p. 137; John L. Hess, *The Grand Acquisitors*, Boston: Houghton Mifflin, 1974, pp. 141–151; Metropolitan Museum of Art, *The Euphronios Krater: A Report to the Members of the Corporation*, March 7, 1974; Thomas Hoving, *The Chase, the Capture: Collecting at the Metropolitan*, New York, 1975, pp. 40–56; Deborah Solomon, "Stolen Art," *New York Times Magazine*, February 19, 2006; Peter Watson and Cecilia Todeschini, *The Medici Conspiracy*, New York: Public Affairs, 2006, pp. 327–328.

36. "An Odyssey of Antiquities Ends in Questions at the Getty," *New York Times*, October 15, 2005; "Italy Goes on the Offensive with Antiquities," December 26, 2005; "Murky World of Antiquities Trade," *Los Angeles Times*, December 28, 2005; Watson and Todeschini, *The Medici Conspiracy*.

37. *Art Museums and the Identification and Restitution of Works Stolen by the Nazis*, American Association of Art Museum Directors Report, 2001.

38. Malaro, *A Legal Primer*, p. 75.

39. *AAM Guidelines Concerning the Unlawful Appropriation of Objects during the Nazi Era*, 1999, amended 2001; Lynn H. Nicholas, *The Rape of Europa: The Fate of Europe's Treasures in the Third Reich and the Second World War*, New York: Vintage, 1994; Stephen E. Weil, "The American Legal Response to the Problem of Holocaust Art," *Art, Antiquity and Law* 4, no. 4 (December 1999): 285–300.

40. www.cr.nps.gov, NAGRPA FAQ 10/28/2003; Forum, "NAGPRA at 10," *Museum News* 79, no. 5, pp. 42–49.

41. Paul M. Bator, *The International Trade in Art*, Chicago, IL: University of Chicago Press, 1981, p. 21; Klaus Muller, "The Culture of Globalization," *Museum News* 82, no. 3 (May–June 2003).

42. Malaro, *A Legal Primer*, p. 138; Evan Roth, "Deaccession Debate," *Museum News* 69, no. 2 (March–April 1990).

43. Miller, "Guilt Free Deaccessioning"; S. Weil, "Deaccession Practices in American Museums," *Museum News*, February 1987, a comprehensive review of museum deaccessioning practices with detailed references to good practices; Iain Robertson, "Infamous Deaccessions," *Museums Journal* (March 1990): 32–34.

44. "Codes of Ethics," www.aam-us.org; www.icom.org; www.aaslh.org.

45. Franklin Feldman and Stephen Weil, editors, *Art Works: Law, Policy, Practice*, New York: Practising Law Institute, 1974, pp. 1115–1134; John Jacob, "The Sale or Disposal of Museum Objects," *Museums Journal* 71 (December 1971): 112–116; *Metropolitan Museum, Report on Art Transactions*; Metropolitan Museum of Art, *Metropolitan Museum of Art, Procedures for Deaccessioning and Disposal of Works of Art*, New York: Metropolitan Museum of Art, June 20, 1973; "White Paper Published—Guidelines Emerge," *Museum News* 52 (September 1973): 6; Russell Lynes, *Good Old Modern: An Intimate Portrait of the Museum of Modern Art*, New York, 1975, pp. 295–297; Malaro, *A Legal Primer*, p. 140; Nancy Einreinhofer, *The American Art Museum: Elitism and Democracy*, New York: Leicester University Press, 1997.

46. Michael Ames, *Cannibal Tours and Glass Boxes: The Anthropology of Museums*, Vancouver, Canada: University of British Columbia Press, 1992, p. 41.

47. *A Public Trust at Risk*, Washington, DC: Heritage Preservation, 2006, p. 2.

48. "Getty Trust's Gallery Systems," www.gallerysystems.com; Keene, *Fragments of the World*.

49. Steven Kern, "Peter Paul Rubens's 'Allegory of Eternity': A Provenance Research Case Study," *Museum News* 85, no. 2 (March–April 2006); Nancy Yeide, Konstantin Akinsha, and Amy Walsh, *AAM Guide to Provenance Research*, Washington, DC: American Association of Museums, 2001; David Montgomery, "Peru Tries to Recover Gold from Yale's Ivory Tower," *Washington Post*, March 9, 2006; Miriam Clavir, *Preserving What Is Valued: Museums, Conservation and First Nations*, Vancouver: University of British Columbia Press, 2002.

50. Edmund Barry Gaither, "Hey That's Mine," in *Museums and Communities: The Politics of Public Culture*, eds. Ivan Karp, Christine Mullen Kreamer, and

Steven D. Lavine, Washington, DC: Smithsonian Institution, 1992; Frye, "Museum Collecting"; Candace Floyd, "Chinatown," *History News*, June 1984, pp. 7–11.

51. Blake Gopnik, "Doing Their Own Thing: Museums Give Permanent Collections Special—and Overdue—Attention," *Washington Post*, November 27, 2005.

52. Neil Brodie, "Stolen History: Looting and Illicit Trade," *Museum International* 55, nos. 3–4 (2003).

9

To Conserve

Anything, absolutely anything—from a flint arrowhead to a space-craft, from a dugout canoe to the *Queen Mary*—may end up in a museum, and the museum must know how to care for it.

—Philip R. Ward, 1991[1]

There's a silent thief stealing away with millions of dollars of artwork each year. The thief's name? Poor conservation.

—David Hugh Smith, 1982[2]

Collections have suddenly become something of a burden to museums. Most museum directors now feel like directors of geriatric hospitals whose budgets are devastated by patients whose survival for another day depends on expensive, high technology support systems. Conservators in museums are like a host of relatives who guard the wall plug of the life support systems.

—Miriam Clavir, 2002[3]

Not until the 20th century did museums clearly realize that one of their chief functions as well as an all-important duty was to pass on their collections in pristine condition to succeeding generations. Science had advanced far enough to point out that, just as all human beings must die, so all objects must deteriorate. At the same time, scientists learned to slow the degradation of museum materials, and a new profession of scientifically knowledgeable "conservators" began to replace the artists

217

and craftsmen commonly known as "restorers." Conservators know how to preserve materials, that is, to prevent, stop, or retard deterioration, and also how to restore objects that had undergone decay or alteration. In France today, the preferred term for these professionals is *conservator-restorer*, acknowledging the duality of the role in caring for collections.[4]

A 2005 *Heritage Preservation Heritage Health Index* outlines the status of U.S. museums' collection care practices this way:

> Eighty percent have no paid staff responsible for collections care.
> Seventy percent have not assessed collections conditions or needs.
> Eighty percent do not have adequate environmental controls in place.
> Sixty-five percent of collections suffer from improper storage conditions.
> Eighty percent do not have a plan to protect collections in case of emergency.

A Public Trust at Risk: The Heritage Health Index Report on the State of America's Collections published by Heritage Preservation with funding from the Institute of Museum and Library Services (IMLS) is based on a project involving more than three thousand museum professionals from institutions large and small across the United States. The survey sample includes collecting museums, historical societies, collecting libraries, and archives.[5]

And, on a more local level, consider this exchange from the Small Museum Association summer workshop in Hagerstown, Maryland, in 1998. The first speaker was a staff member of a local historical society. The society had been given a collection of assorted buttons from a local collector, including political campaign buttons. The staff had no experience caring for a collection like this, so the speaker went to the Internet for advice and found the websites of button collectors who described how to clean and care for buttons. She went on to describe in detail what products she used and how she went about cleaning each button. After her talk, she moved to the back of the room. Next on the program was a professional conservator, who walked up to the podium, hesitated, shuffled her papers, and seemed uncomfortable. Eventually, she took a deep breath and said, "Please disregard everything the first speaker just said." The audience gasped. It was a pretty dramatic moment because the Internet advice from hobbyist collectors was absolutely contrary to what a professional conservator would have done.

This chapter outlines desirable museum principles and practices to care for objects, concluding with more generalized discussions of professional conservation concerns. Where there are references to conservators, it should be understood that this position does not exist in most museums and therefore these activities are carried out by a wide variety of staff from the director to volunteers. Nonetheless, all museums and museum professionals should strive to meet the basic standards described here. The goal is to protect the objects, a mainstay of museums' missions. The footnotes provide more in-depth reading.

The Nature of Museum Objects

The conservator is interested in the materials of which museum objects are made—not primarily their aesthetic form, but their molecular/atomic composition and structure. These objects range from the everyday, used detritus of life to those made from the finest materials to adorn their owner or for public display. The conservator wants to know about their condition—how much they have deteriorated and how they can be stabilized for a long future. In doing this work, he or she is dealing with four chief classes of substances: organic materials, metals and their alloys, siliceous and equivalent materials, and easel and mural paintings. Harold J. Plenderleith, former keeper of the British Museum research laboratory, authored *The Conservation of Antiquities and Works of Art: Treatment, Repair, Restoration* (1962), the classic reference for scientific museum conservation. In the revised second edition (1971), A. E. A. Werner, then the keeper of the laboratory, collaborated with Mr. Plenderleith. These volumes remain valuable basic reference tools.[6]

Organic materials include hides, leather, parchment, paper, bone, ivory, textiles, and wood. They are of animal or vegetable origin, carbon based, and with cellular structure. They are susceptible to deterioration by light, variations in humidity and temperature, dryness or brittleness, and excessive humidity (dampness) that produces molds, mildew, and other biological reactions.

Gold, silver, lead, tin, copper (and its alloys), iron, and steel are the chief metals. They are inorganic, much more stable than organic materials, and little affected by light, temperature variations, or biological reaction. They differ in their resistance to deterioration from variations in humidity and from impurities in the air or the ground. Gold is the only metal that remains virtually intact under all conditions. The others suffer from corrosion that may produce a pleasing patina or heavy incrustation that ultimately transforms the metal into the mineral ore from which it was extracted. Silver exposed to air tarnishes and, if underground for a long period, may take on a patina. Copper and iron are easily oxidized in air and especially in the ground. Copper and bronze show brown, blue, or green patinas, and iron can be completely transformed into rust.

Siliceous and equivalent materials consist of natural stone, bricks, pottery and other ceramics, and glass. Natural stone varies in its resistance to deterioration. Granite and basalt are relatively impervious, but limestone and sandstone are vulnerable to industrial sulfur fumes, automobile emissions, temperature and humidity variations, saline efflorescences, and cryptomatic vegetation (molds and mosses). Bricks and pottery, both of clay, are similar to natural stone in their resistance. If baked at higher temperatures, they are equivalent to stone of average resistance; if baked at low heat or air-dried, they correspond to soft natural stone. Ceramics fired at high temperatures have great resistance to deterioration, but water with salt in solution can produce efflorescences in them. High humidity can dull the transparency of normally stable glass and lead to crizzling with a multitude of small cracks.

Easel and mural paintings are complex chemical compounds that contain in their various layers both organic and inorganic materials. The outer layer of varnish is completely organic; the paint layers and ground or coating are usually a combination of organic and inorganic; the support, if wood or canvas, is organic, or if metal or a wall substance, inorganic. Adhesives used between the layers are organic. Varnish, which normally lasts only twenty to fifty years before losing its elasticity, also turns yellow. Mediums or vehicles of oil or distemper in the paint layers become brittle and subject to dampness, while the ground or foundation is susceptible to high humidity. Soft wood and canvas supports of easel paintings attract insects and are distorted by dampness; saline efflorescences and mold attack murals. Decay also weakens the adhesives between layers and results in unsticking and blisters.

These categories of objects may, of course, be combined in ways that make their care more complicated. These descriptions neglect the collections of botanical gardens and zoos that have their own special concerns regarding the professional standards of care for living collections. Botanical garden herbariums carefully preserve dried plants and seeds, allowing gardens to exchange species. Today these simple practices are complemented with international seed banks protecting species' DNA, sometimes in cooperation with botanical gardens or even international governmental initiatives. Norway's effort to freeze DNA samples on the island of Svalbard reflects heightened international concerns. The zoos' Species Survival Plans (SSPs) are a cooperative approach to maintaining biodiversity, a special form of conservation. The SSPs form an international matrix for "matchmaking" to ensure the maximum biodiversity within zoos. The fundamental elements include good animal care in terms of nutrition, social systems, mating systems, reproductive and parental influences, environmental factors, medical health, and reproductive biology and genetics. With the vanishing of wild animals of so many types, zoo populations form the future for many species. In the basic sense, they are the ultimate conservators.[7]

Basic Conservation Practices

The environment has a powerful influence on objects, which tend to establish equilibrium with their surroundings. Whenever the environment changes, the objects are likely to suffer. Thus, when archaeologists open a tomb, objects apparently in perfect condition may shrink or warp and sometimes even turn to dust. The changes in the relative humidity and temperature of the atmosphere cause such deterioration.

Museums therefore need to provide a stable environment with constant relative humidity and temperature for the varied objects in their collections. The two qualities are closely related; in fact, relative humidity is defined as the ratio of the amount of water vapor present in the air to the greatest amount possible at the same temperature. As those familiar with central heating so well know, increasing the temperature of a building in winter reduces the humidity markedly and may result in too dry an atmosphere, while lowering the temperature may raise the humidity so much that it reaches the dew point and water condenses on walls and objects. A temperature of sixty to seventy-five degrees Fahrenheit or about twenty degrees centigrade is comfortable for museum visitors year round. At that temperature the relative humidity should not fall below 50 percent or organic materials such as paper, parchment, and leather will become brittle; canvas will go slack; and textiles and the adhesives used in making furniture will dry out and deteriorate. Similarly, if the relative humidity exceeds 65 percent, mold and mildew will grow on glue, leather, and paper; wood will swell and canvases tighten; and oxidation of metals will increase. The ideal relative humidity for most museum objects at temperatures of about seventy degrees Fahrenheit is 50 to 65 percent. But, keep in mind that it's the very variation of a stable environment that can be most damaging.

Air-conditioning systems can provide the constant relative humidity and temperature desirable for the museum environment and mitigate atmospheric pollution. Obviously, every museum should strive to obtain such climate control for its entire buildings, but especially for its exhibition and storage spaces. Contaminated air may blacken lead pigments, tarnish metals, or bleach out or stain materials. And, Nathan Stolow warns that merely crowded galleries can produce high levels of carbon dioxide and ammonia that are damaging to paintings.[8] Though it may be difficult to raise money for such a purpose (the saying goes that nobody ever gave a museum a ton of coal in memory of his mother), air-conditioning in the long run is more important for the museum than the acquisition of million-dollar objects. In instances where controlling the conditions of large spaces becomes impossible, museums can create "microclimates" for objects. These can be individual areas within a room or actual cases that allow for closer control of the conditions for the objects. They can be as simple as covering the glass of an exhibit case with fabric that the visitor removes to see the object and replaces afterward, or as complicated as individual controls for the case's internal atmosphere.

Another important part of the museum environment is lighting. Strong light or ultraviolet rays damage watercolors, paintings, paper, textiles, and other materials, usually by fading or embrittlement. Although enjoying a return to favor in art museums out of aesthetic considerations, natural light is especially destructive because of ultraviolet radiation and should be controlled by blinds, curtains, or special glass. Incandescent bulbs give off heat, which must be lessened in museum cases. The ultraviolet emissions of fluorescent tubes can be reduced to safe levels by plastic sleeves. Too much light intensity from spotlights or too high a general illumination should also be avoided.

The *Heritage Health Index Report* suggests that museums begin their conservation efforts with the most basic environmental conditions for their objects. Even with the most limited resources museums can establish conditions so that they "do no harm" to artifacts. A critical element to maintain this most basic standard is that storage areas, while out of the public view, are central to the ongoing conservation/preservation needs of collections. Clean, dry, temperature-controlled spaces are fundamental to caring for objects. Although complex, expensive conservation practices may be out of the reach of many museums, careful storage practices are not.[9]

Negligence results in exposure of objects to excessive light, heat, or humidity, infestations of pests, or actual accidents that result in physical destruction of the object. Stolow recounts an arresting incident that happened in a Canadian art gallery. "A cleaner was operating an electric floor polisher when he moved too far ahead, unplugging the machine. Forgetting to 'turn off' the polisher he then walked over to plug in the cord. Since the electric polisher was still 'on,' it proceeded to dance along the floor on its own before he could rush to stop it. As it careened over the floor and swerved to the wall the metal handle scraped and scuffed a number of paintings before it could be turned off."[10]

Common sense precautions include:

Ensuring the relative humidity and temperature in storage and display areas are kept stable and at appropriate levels for items;

Ensuring the light levels are at an appropriate level for objects on display;

Keeping storage areas unlit when access is not required;

Checking that materials used in storage and display—wood, fabrics, paints, adhesives, plastics, and rubber—are not harmful to items;

Keeping storage areas clean, tidy, and uncluttered;

Providing sufficient space in storage containers to avoid crushing or abrasion of items;

Not storing items on top of or inside one another;

Raising stored items/storage containers off the floor in case of flooding;

Cleaning items only following expert advice;

Storing items in secure areas;

Checking collections on a regular basis against pest infestation;

Avoiding handling whatever possible, and then only using cotton gloves;

Not smoking, eating, or drinking in the vicinity of collections;

Ensuring all staff (and volunteers) understand the principles and practice of preventive conservation.[11]

These descriptions of the care of objects reflect current museum practice and tradition, but it is important to understand that as the very nature of museums is expanding, so too are the demands on conservation. For example, interactive exhibitions change the nature of the gallery space that impacts on the environment and security of the objects regardless of their origin. One example will reveal the demands of changing museum practices. What should a technology museum do with an automobile? Should their resources be put into keeping the car in "running order," or into maintaining it as a static artifact? If the former path is chosen, as time goes by mechanical elements of the car will need to be replaced, and some would argue that compromises its integrity as an object, while meeting its needs as an operating machine. One compromise seems to be establishing "archival" machines that are not kept in running order, but rather maintained as a record of the car as artifact of a time period, complete with original engine parts, upholstery, and even paint finishes.[12]

Exhibition Concerns

Special exhibitions are increasingly used by museums to attract visitors, promote scholarly research, and increase public enlightenment. They usually involve borrowing materials from several museums, and a curator ought to have a leading role in deciding when objects in his or her care should be lent. The curator may approve highly of the purposes of a temporary or traveling exhibit and also know that the museum may wish to borrow materials from other museums from time to time. The curator, however, should carefully consider the dangers to which such exhibits expose objects. Can they stand the jolting and jarring of travel and the changes in humidity and temperature they are sure to encounter? Can they be properly packed for transport? Will the borrower provide careful handling, dependable environmental control, and protection against fire, vandalism, and theft? These practical questions will help the curator decide whether the proposed exhibit is important enough to justify the risks to the objects in his or her care.[13]

In order to respond rationally to requests for loans, the wise curator may well decide, with advice from conservators, to classify objects as to their ability to travel safely. Some objects will be too delicate and fragile to stand any shipping. Others may be allowed to travel only occasionally to exhibits of exceptional importance with strictly specified conditions of packing, handling, and protection during transit and on exhibition. In another category will be placed objects sound, stable, and structurally strong enough to be included in traveling exhibitions. Once the decision has been made to lend objects, arrangements must be made for their packing, transport, exhibition, repacking, and return travel. The whole transaction must be covered by written agreements and by insurance. A new role, that of exhibition conservator, who joins a team that may include security, registrar, designer, and architect, assumes the following duties: evaluation of conditions, establishment of environmental controls for each object, assessment of safety (in transport, especially), monitoring storage and gallery conditions, and coordination with designers and architects to ensure safety and special conditions for each object on view.[14] Once again, many museums will assign such a role to a staff member, regardless of his or her title and normal responsibilities.

The packing can be as elaborate as the situation requires. If the distances involved are short, the objects may be taken by car or van with abundant padding and careful separation but without special cases. Caroline Keck's *Safeguarding Your Collection in Travel* shows the small museum how to instruct a carpenter to build a solid, watertight, shock-absorbing case in which objects can be "floated" with inner cushioning provided by some of the new plastic foam materials. A reliable commercial packing firm may be used, though its work should be carefully supervised. A larger museum will have its own trained packing staff. In instances of important international exhibitions of extremely rare objects, as Nathan Stolow points out, conservators know how to build ideal containers with preconditioned packing materials or silica gel panels that will maintain about the same humidity and temperature that the objects enjoy in their "home" museum. Trained packers should do the packing, unpacking, and repacking of loans, because at these points the most damage to objects is likely. Packing material should be stored in the same atmospheric conditions as the exhibition spaces. Those who did the unpacking should do the repacking, and the same materials should be used.[15]

Transport should be carefully planned. If a carefully checked and reliable moving company is used, the lending and receiving museum staffs should supervise the loading and unloading. The transportation should be direct, without layovers or transshipments. For extremely rare objects, a museum staff member should accompany the shipment, going and coming. Upon arrival, the objects still within their packing cases should be allowed to "rest" reaching equilibrium in their new setting. Ideally that atmosphere is the same whether in a storage area or gallery. Even the conditions of the packing materials, if they are to be reused, should be kept in near-constant conditions. The installation of borrowed materials is the responsibility of the curator of the borrowing museum; he should see that they have the same protection as those of his own museum. All of the arrangements should be clearly written down and agreed to by both parties. The lending museum will photograph the objects before they leave and describe any weaknesses or defects, and the borrowing museum will do likewise before returning them. In addition to physical security, overall protection, including insurance, should be provided with written agreements between lender and borrower.[16]

Conservation Tasks

At the start of the 20th century, international purchases of artworks flourished. The traffic flowed from Europe west to the United States. Art dealers in European capitals sought artworks and offered them to American industrialists intent on adding luster to their surroundings and prestige. Dealers promoted restoration practices to attract buyers and make a sale. Restorers worked to make the object more attractive; their interests lay in sales and not in the integrity of the work. From these beginnings emerged in the mid–20th century professional conservation practices overseen by museums with responsibilities for protecting cultural artifacts for the public good rather than profit. As the 21st century begins, the role of conservation has become even more complex with museums recognizing that objects document the past and that their modification or restoration should be rare and guided by the "intent" of their maker, or in some cases their owner.[17]

The conservator that we know today has developed since the mid–20th century. Previously, the restorer took an empirical approach to conservation. He knew certain practical treatments to use on deteriorating art and historical objects and with skilled hands applied them; he would frequently describe himself as an artist. Charles Willson Peale, for example, made himself sick using arsenic to preserve his specimens.[18] The conservator uses knowledge of science (especially chemistry and physics) to examine objects/artifacts, to determine appropriate treatment to maintain them in stable condition, or to restore them to a previous condition. Within the museum, he or she is responsible for establishing and maintaining environmental conditions to protect the object, whether in storage, on display, or in transit.

The conservator has two classes of duties. As adviser on preventive conservation, he or she helps the curator work out operating procedures and practices, and as a skillful scientist and craftsman diagnoses and treats deteriorated or altered objects. The first role may be the most important as the conservator can establish institutional practices that protect objects, and thereby avoid the necessity for restoration. Today, this is called preventative conservation. Some of the more practical elements of a conservator's advice have been described. A second role begins with inspection of a museum's holdings in cooperation with the curator and assignment of priorities for objects that need treatment; which often becomes a continuing responsibility with periodic inspections of which written records are kept.

In this treatment work, the conservator observes several guiding principles. One of these is to examine the objects to be worked on, using the latest scientific methods, in order to understand as thoroughly as possible the nature and prognosis of the deterioration and any alterations. A second principle requires the conservator to make as few changes as possible and to keep any changes reversible in the future. For example, fifty years ago a restorer might have decided that a polychrome wood sculpture was so worm eaten that he would replace a considerable portion with new wood, shaped and painted as nearly like the original as he could make it. A more conservative kind of restoration—say, fumigation of the statue to stop worm damage and minimum repainting with soluble paint—would have preserved it for the better treatment that could be given now. The treatment options change with scientific research. A detailed account of everything discovered about the object, good or bad, and every step taken in repairing or restoring it should become part of the museum record of the object. If further work is needed in the future, judgments can be made based on the record.

Another of the conservator's rules is not to use conjecture in restoration or reconstruction of objects. If he or she cannot find out by research what their actual appearance was, restoration should not proceed. This area is a very dangerous one, for conservators sometimes know so much about objects and their normal appearance in a historical period that they are tempted to go ahead intuitively, even when they lack authentic evidence. Another pitfall here is to use today's taste in restoring an object. For example, the H. F. du Pont Winterthur Museum acquired an early-19th-century wooden sculpted man's bust with several bad cracks; it had been cleaned down to the wood. In restoring it, the question arose whether to paint it a stone color or to use a natural finish that would show off the wood grain. Modern taste would have dictated the latter course, but research into the early-19th-century practice and faint traces of paint led to painting it stone color. Conservation must be guided by careful research beyond science into the fundamental cultural context of the object, Miriam Clavir argues that: "Conservation is more than a set of physical preservation techniques, it is also an interpretive activity which involves a complex of artistic, scientific and historical ideas which influence the approach to treatment whether they are acknowledged or not."[19]

Two roles have expanded for conservators. The first is involved with protecting the museum's environment from insects and other pests that can harm the objects. "Integrated pest management" (IPM) seeks to protect the collection, and even the museum environment, by using natural approaches and compounds that will get rid of the pests, but not harm the environment, either inside or outside the museum. Some large museums actually have integrated pest managers on staff who keep up with the latest "natural" solutions to protecting collections areas. Nathan Stolow argues: "Traveling exhibitions and exchanges are increasing in frequency, involving movement of possible infected objects between tropical and more temperate countries . . . measures for control of insect and fungus deterioration is of global concern; ethnographic, natural history and archival materials are especially vulnerable."[20]

Secondly, conservators also are often involved in the creation of institutional emergency plans with detailed instructions on how to protect the collections in time of fire, flood, or other disaster. Conservators not only assist in creating the plans, but also in carrying out special "triage" activities as a museum staff responds to disasters. Often conservators assemble disaster "carts" that hold items for use in protecting or stabilizing collections in case of emergencies. In the 1980s there was a national emphasis on creating operative disaster plans for museums across the country. The Getty Institute's *Building an Emergency Plan* identifies thirty recent disasters affecting cultural institutions around the world ranging from fires, floods, earthquakes, hurricanes, and volcanic eruptions to wars and terrorist bombings from 1981 to 1997.[21] The recent experiences of New Orleans' museums during Hurricane Katrina are extreme cases, while broken water pipes and invading squirrels are much more common.

At the close of the 20th century, object conservation has stepped out of the office and lab spaces of museums and entered the galleries. In

1996 the Walters Art Gallery in Baltimore, Maryland, dedicated major gallery space to revealing to visitors the tasks performed by the museum's conservators. The objects on view reflected the care and attention of the conservator to the object and its context. Some of the exhibition cases included scientific instruments and explained their use by conservators. The purpose of the exhibition was to alert visitors to the role of conservation, the importance of the decisions made by the conservator, and on another level the investment of the museum as a public institution in caring for objects for public benefit. As the 21st century opened, when the original Star Spangled Banner required conservation, the National Museum of American History placed the work-in-progress on view as an exhibition. Visitors could watch the conservators as they worked and from surrounding label texts understand the decision-making process for restoring and conserving the object to protect it for future generations. Another brilliant example is the Lunder Conservation Center at the Smithsonian American Art Museum that opened in 2006. On the museum's top floor, visitors can watch conservators at work through glass walls. Conservation practices have become a permanent exhibition. No longer is conservation seen as a supporting function carried out in labs and offices out of public view.[22]

As an example of a comprehensive approach to conservation policies, in the Netherlands there is a project underway to address the needs of that nation's collections. It may hold important lessons (or guidance) to future museum conservation practices. There are some nine hundred museums in the Netherlands, and about twenty are funded and operated by the central government. In 1989 the government sought to measure the needs of the collections in all the nation's museums. The Delta Plan for Preservation of the Cultural Heritage began by identifying the "backlogs for registration and conservation," thereby quantifying the need and following on by creating a strategy to improve museum collections protections. The first steps involved simply identifying the number of collections, creating a national typology, and from there establishing priorities for conservation needs. "The Plan has resulted in . . . a far more professional approach with regard to collection management and conservation. Norms, guidelines, and standards of quality with regard to collections have been developed." The Delta Plan ended in 1999 and the Cultural Heritage Authorities (Erfgoed Inspectie), who are responsible for the inspections of all national museums to ensure proper preservation of collections, warned in their evaluation of the plan (2000) that it is crucial that the government not forget about museums after this investment. Such massive support has really helped by increasing awareness of collection preservation/ conservation needs, providing air-conditioning in storage facilities, and improving conditions. This important attention should not lapse because of diminished financial support.[23]

Challenges

Technical and Cultural Aspects of Conservation

As science has allowed for greater understanding of the physical nature of objects, the cultural interpretation of the artifact may be misunderstood. As museum donors and audiences expand, the importance of understanding both the cultural and physical aspects of objects becomes more complex, and perhaps more important. Canadian conservator Miriam Clavir summarizes the issues this way: "[T]he conservation professional bases much of his or her decisions on scientific examination, knowledge of materials, and scientific reasoning, he/she also recognizes the importance of cultural knowledge. For example, the artist's intent and the object's social history are important foundations for making decisions regarding the object. Conservation work often adds to the information regarding both these phenomena. However, the conservator is expected to unearth this new information on the basis of expert observations of the physical object rather than on the basis of the traditional curatorial specializations of art and history. It is important to recognize that cultural information informs both the conservation decision-making process and conservation objectives."[24] These complexities especially impact the training process for museum conservators.

Caring for New Materials

These changes in the very nature of museum collections affect museum storage and display techniques along with the training required for the museum conservation staff. Canadian conservator R. J. Barclay describes the challenges this way, suggesting that the very nature of museums is undergoing important changes when it comes to collections. "Conservators are anything but conservative. Even so, the greatest challenge is yet to come: the twentieth century can be characterized by the widespread use of synthetic materials in the creation of artefacts and works of art coupled with an abandonment, or at least a subjugation, of traditional techniques. These two facts together will oblige the discipline of museum conservation to face wider and more diverse demands in the next century—provided, of course, that the artefacts of our material culture continue to occupy centre stage in our museums."[25]

New Museum Models and Conservation

What should be the role for conservation as museums change their emphases from collecting and scholarship to public service? Adding conservation practices to exhibition cases is one way that museums engage the public with their preservation functions. American anthropologist Carolyn Rose opines: "While the last decade has been challenging for museum conservation, even more challenges lie ahead. What really constitutes a museum today? Certainly it is not what we thought of at the beginning of the century, or even 30 years ago. As museums struggle with evolving and often mandated roles as businesses rather than institutions of higher education or research, and as entertainment centers rather than collections repositories, many traditional conservation approaches are outdated. To be effective, conservation strategies must consider the museum's changing objectives."[26]

Conservation and Historic Preservation

What of the impact of the changing nature of the museum "envelope" from a stand-alone building to a site, or perhaps even a town? American anthropologist Carolyn Rose writes: "[P]roblems . . . arise when whole groups of objects or entire historic city centers fall into disuse. One no longer wonders only how to conserve paintings, art, and archaeological objects in the great traditional museums, but also how to prevent the destruction of those monuments, urban contexts, craft items and ethnographic objects in danger of being either destroyed or dispersed by the tide of modernization . . . one must negotiate a very narrow path with destruction on one side and mummification on the other."[27]

Protection and Public Access

Alessandra Malucco Vaccaro argues: "Striking a balance between the demands of conservation and the rights of the public is one of the most difficult challenges, but it is also the most urgent to undertake in order to secure the future of the past."[28] The caves at Lascaux in southwestern France are a perfect example of these conflicting demands. Four teenagers discovered the fifteen-thousand-year-old paintings 250 meters below ground in late 1940. With the end of World War II, the entry was expanded and visitors began to arrive at the rate of more than one thousand a day. After little more than twenty years of such visitation, the paintings began to show damage from the elevated levels of carbon dioxide. In the spring of 1963 the caves were permanently closed to the public and the atmosphere was returned to its earlier levels. In 1980 the Dordogne Tourism Department created a replica of the cave, duplicating both its contours and ancient images. This replica opened to public viewing in 1983. Thus, today the public is excluded from viewing these ancient images to ensure their very existence.

Notes

1. Philip R. Ward, "Conservation: Keeping the Past Alive," *Museum International* 43, no. 1 (1991): 7.

2. David Hugh Smith quoted in *Museums for a New Century*, Washington, DC, American Association of Museums, 1984, p. 40.

3. Miriam Clavir, *Preserving What Is Valued: Museums, Conservation and First Nations*, Vancouver, Canada: University of British Columbia Press, 2002, p. 28.

4. H. J. Plenderleith and A. E. A. Werner, *The Conservation of Antiquities and Works of Art: Treatment, Repair, Restoration*, London: Oxford University Press, 1971; Patrick Boylan, "The Conservator-Restorer," *Museum International* 39, no. 4, 1987; Nicholas Stanley Price, M. Kirby Talley Jr., and Alessandra Malucco Vaccaro, eds., *Historical and Philosophical Issues in the Conservation of Cultural Heritage*, Los Angeles: Getty Conservation Institute, 1996; Marcia Lord, "Editorial" and Gael de Guichen, "Preventive Conservation: A Mere Fad or Far-reaching Change?" and Eleonore Kissel, "The Restorer: Key Player in Preventative Conservation," *Museum International* 51, no. 1 (1999); Giorgio Torraca, "The Scientist in Conservation," *Getty Conservation Institute Newsletter* 14, no. 3 (1999); Graeme Gardiner, "Prevention Rather Than Cure: Preservation versus Conservation," *Museum International* 46, no. 3 (1994): 54–56; R. J. Barclay, "The Conservator: Versatility and Flexibility," *Museum International* 45, no. 4 (1993); "Conservation and Preservation Issue," *Museum News* 68, no. 1 (January–February 1989); Calvin Tomkins, "A Picasso Face-lift," *New Yorker*, May 24, 2004; Gregory J. Landrey et al., *The Winterthur Guide to Caring for Your Collections*, Winterthur, DE: Henry Francis Du Pont Winterthur Museum, 2000.

5. *A Public Trust at Risk: The Heritage Health Index Report on the State of America's Collections*, Washington, DC: Heritage Preservation, 2005. The full report can be accessed at www.heritagehealthindex.org.

6. Plenderleith and Werner, *The Conservation of Antiquities and Works of Art*; The Getty Conservation Institute offers up-to-date information on conservation approaches on their website www.getty.edu/conservation.

7. Melissa Fay Greene, "Breeding Zoo Stock," *Museum News* 68, no. 1 (January–February 1989): 58–59; Nigel Rothfels, *Savages and Beasts: The Birth of the Modern Zoo*, Baltimore, MD: Johns Hopkins University Press, 2002, p. 199.

8. Nathan Stolow, *Conservation and Exhibitions: Packing, Transport, Storage and Environmental Consideration*, London: Butterworth, 1987, p. 173; Karen Motylewski, "A Matter of Control," *Museum News* 69, no. 2 (March–April 1990).

9. *A Public Trust at Risk*; The following websites are very helpful in answering basic conservation inquiries: the Canadian Conservation Institute, www.cci-icc.gc.ca; the Getty Institute, www.getty.edu/conservation/institute; and the American Institute of Conservators, www.aic.stanford.edu.

10. Stolow, *Conservation and Exhibitions*, p. 214.

11. Timothy Ambrose and Crispin Paine, *Museum Basics*, London: Routledge with the International Council of Museums, 1993, p. 163; *Caring for Collections*, Washington, DC: American Association of Museums, 1984.

12. Peter Mann in *Care of Collections*, ed. Simon Knell, Routledge, Leicester University, 1994, pp. 36–37; Suzanne Keene, *Fragments of the World: Use of Museum Collections*, Oxford, UK: Butterworth, Heinemann, 2005, p. 164.

13. Rebecca A. Buck and Jean Allman Gilmore, *The New Museum Registration Methods*, Washington, DC: American Association of Museums, 1998.

14. Stolow, *Conservation and Exhibitions*, p. 2.

15. Caroline K. Keck, *Safeguarding Your Collection in Travel*, Nashville, TN: American Association for State and Local History, 1970; Stolow, *Conservation and Exhibitions*.

16. Marie Malaro, *A Legal Primer on Managing Museum Collections*, Washington, DC: Smithsonian Institution, 1985, pp. 156–183, 276–290.

17. Clavir, *Preserving What Is Valued*; Meryle Secrest, *Duveen: A Life in Art*, New York: Knopf, 2005, pp. 219, 252, 376–377; Jonathan Ashley-Smith, "The Ethics of Conservation," in *Care of Collections*, Simon Knell, ed.

18. Edward P. Alexander, "Charles Willson Peale," in *Museum Masters: Their Museums and Their Influence*, Nashville, TN: American Association of State and Local History, 1983, p. 60.

19. Clavir, *Preserving What Is Valued*, p. 41; Sherman E. Lee, *Past, Present, East and West*, New York: George Braziller, 1983, p. 37; James Cuno, ed., *Whose Muse? Art Museums and Public Trust*, Princeton University Press and Harvard University Press, 2004, pp. 32–35; Tony Bennett "Out of Which Past?" *The Birth of the Museum: History, Theory and Politics*, New York: Routledge, 1995.

20. Stolow, *Conservation and Exhibitions*, p. 23; David Pinniger, *Pest Management in Museums, Archives and Historical Houses*, London: Archetype Publications,

2001; David Pinniger and Peter Winsor, *Integrated Pest Management: Practical, Safe and Cost-effective Advice on the Prevention and Control of Pests in Museums*, London: Museums and Galleries Commission, 1998; Lynda, Zycherman, ed., *A Guide to Museum Pest Control*, Washington, DC: Association of Systematics Collections, 1988; Mary-Lou Florian, *Heritage Eaters*, London: James and James, 1997.

21. *Building an Emergency Plan: A Guide for Museums and Other Cultural Institutions*, Los Angeles, CA: Getty Conservation Institute, 1999; K. Sharon Bennett, ed., *SEMC Disaster Response Handbook*, Charleston, SC: South East Museums Conference, 1999; *Field Guide to Emergency Response*, Washington, DC: Heritage Preservation, 2006; "Recovering from Disaster," *History News* 61, no. 2 (Spring 2006), this is a special issue with a comprehensive resource list, including Internet aid.

22. Joyce Hill Stoner, "Conservation Center Stage," *Museum News* 76, no. 3 (May–June 1997).

23. M. Kirby Talley Jr., "The Delta Plan: A Nationwide Rescue Operation," *Museum International* 51, no. 1 (1999): 11–15; Clara von Waldthausen, restorer of photographs, personal correspondence.

24. Clavir, *Preserving What Is Valued*, p. 42; Karen Zukowski, "The Importance of Context," in *Conservation in Context: Finding the Balance for the Historic House Museum Conference Proceedings*, National Trust of Historic Preservation and Andrew. W. Mellon Foundation, 1994.

25. R. J. Barclay, "The Conservator: Versatility and Flexibility," *Museum International* 45, no. 4 (1993).

26. Carolyn L. Rose, "Conservation of Museum Collections," *GCI Newsletter* 14, no. 3 (1999): 17.

27. Malucco Vaccaro, "Introduction, Section III," in *Historical and Philosophical Issues*, p. 205.

28. Malucco Vaccaro, "The Emergence of Modern Conservation Theory," in *Historical and Philosophical Issues*, p. 206.

10

To Exhibit

You begin with a group of objects and then you build a room like a glove around them.

—Gaillard E. Ravenel, 1985[1]

Some museum professionals lose sight of the fact that exhibition is by its very nature an interpretive act. The process of selecting and arranging objects is at bottom a fabrication and, as such, a statement about what the fabricators suppose an object to say.

—Lisa C. Roberts, 1991[2]

By shaping the exhibition-as-a-world separate and apart from the external reality of society beyond its walls, each museum contributes to casting the world-as-an-exhibition in its renderings of culture, history, nature or technology.

—Timothy Luke, 2002[3]

Collecting is a very human activity. Showing (or showing off to) others your precious objects of any type follows. Alma Wittlin has categorized the reasons behind collecting urges (see chapter 8). But, how to organize the objects for viewing? As early as the 17th century, "rules" for organizing natural history collections were set down and exchanged among collectors.[4] The Italian *studiolo* with its cosmos in miniature emerged as an expected setting for fine and decorative objects. Collectors knew what to expect when traveling to see other collectors' objects.

Emerging from these displays for the cognoscenti were arrangements of objects seeking to advance understanding. Displays evolved into exhibits: the purpose became public education and the audience expanded.

Several forces contributed to the changed attitudes toward exhibitions. Perhaps strongest has been the steady democratization of Western society, which transformed museums into cultural and educational institutions serving the general public. Also important was the influence of world's fairs that demanded less cluttered exhibits, often with large objects that could be easily seen and walked around, as well as dramatic displays to attract and hold popular attention. In the 20th century, U.S. theme parks built on these traditions, further pressuring museum diplays to modify traditional visual storage showcases and seek more popular appeal. Additionally, the rise of department stores with compelling, sales-producing arrangements of goods influenced museum exhibition design.[5] Museums have added multimedia elements, brought "explainers" and first-person actors into galleries, and, as the 21st century opens, museum websites offer another dimension to exhibitions.

This chapter and the two that follow ("To Interpret" and "To Serve") discuss elements of museum interpretation—how museums convey their messages to visitors. Together, these three chapters provide a full picture of a museum's interpretive options.

Kinds of Exhibits

An exhibit may be defined as a showing or display of materials for the purpose of communication with an audience. Museums may display objects against stark backgrounds, alone, or sometimes with unobtrusive written labels offering the visitor the most basic information (artist, maker, date of production, and museum catalog number). The objects on display may be organized in many ways: by type, by chronology, or with a didactic message for visitors. The artwork, the artifact, or the object dominates. Such a process seems simple, but why and how does a museum place the objects or artwork within the exhibit? One 19th-century example in Berlin reveals the complexity of these decisions and how an institution's interpretive messages change. In the mid-19th-century, academically trained art historians—a first in museum history—designed Berlin's Old Masters Painting Gallery exhibitions balancing three competing principles: aesthetics, historical perspectives, and systematic organization. The overall guiding principle for the galleries' design was the public's appreciation for paintings. The museum placed its most important works in the main galleries with lesser works along the periphery. The exhibition's interpretive function guided not only the artwork placement, but also the basic design of the building housing them. Interestingly, within fifty years, another principle dominated, that of placing the objects within their historical settings, not actual period rooms, but spaces that evoked the artistic ambience of the assembled artworks. So the interpretation and the exhibitions changed. Victoria Newhouse in her recent volume *Art and the Power of Placement* quotes museum director Walter Hopps, who in discussing the impact of exhibition installations, states: "the values change in a room when one picture is moved: it's like the way a dinner party changes according to the guests."[6]

Museums have two chief classes of exhibits—permanent and temporary. Many of their collections, including their masterpieces and landmark objects, are on display at all times, unless being studied, repaired, or on loan to another museum. Temporary exhibits on special themes may feature objects from the museum's collection brought from storage or their usual display places, perhaps supplemented by loans from other museums and collectors. Other special exhibits may consist chiefly of loans from museums or of prepackaged displays obtained from a traveling exhibition service. Temporary exhibits offer museums an opportunity to attract visitors to return, or to bring in visitors with interests relating to the exhibit theme. Historic houses, with static installations of their collections, when space allows, use temporary exhibits to lure visitors to return. These exhibits allow museums to modify and expand their interpretive messages, perhaps as a result of new scholarship or in an effort to attract new audiences.

One form of temporary exhibition, the "blockbuster," has gained prominence in the United States since the 1970s. The Metropolitan Museum's 1974 *Treasures of Tutankhamen*, shortened to King Tut, traveled to six venues, with crowds totaling 8 million. *Van Gogh's Van Goghs: Masterpieces from the Van Gogh Museum*, an exhibition at the Los Angeles County Museum of Art in 1999, is documented as the largest, attracting eight hundred thousand visitors (most blockbusters attract about three hundred thousand) but reports from museums across the United States show these numbers rising with each new exhibition.[7] These exhibitions are intended to gain maximum public impact, often assembling artworks or objects of international fame. They frequently draw on new scholarship and international teams of curators, and they take over the public's image of an institution for the duration of the show. Federal indemnity of insurance costs has allowed U.S. museums to participate in such international exchanges of major artworks or collections. To complement the exhibit itself, the museum creates special interpretive programming. The exhibition becomes an opportunity for the museum to attract the public to the show and to the museum and community. Even the museum shop and restaurant follow the exhibit theme with items for sale and special menus. In 1996 the Philadelphia Museum of Art hosted an international retrospective exhibition of Paul Cezanne's works, called *Cezanne*. The three-month long exhibit attracted more than a half million people to the museum. The city's convention and visitor's bureau created "package tours" that included exhibition tickets, discounts at local eateries and hotels, and in some cases, airline tickets. The city reported that the exhibition contributed 86.5 million dollars to its economy.[8]

Museums have begun providing visitors with "experiences" within their galleries designed to help them understand the object and its context. Kenneth L. Ames describes the exhibition experience this way: "Exhibitions are primarily nonverbal, sensory expriences. People may read the words we write, but they are more likely to get caught up in the multisensory experience we try to provide."[9] The 19th-century diorama—whether in a natural history or history museum—sought to place objects within their "natural" settings, thereby increasing visitors' understanding of their context or meaning. In technology museums and science centers visitors push buttons to make machines or models "work." Other types of museums adapted these "hands-on" experiences to their exhibits. In some museums, visitors even encounter representations of individuals from the past, come to "tell a story" to those in the gallery. For example, at the Chicago Historical Society's exhibition *We the People: Creating a New Nation*, visitors might have met a Frederick Douglass reenactor and listened to his commanding oratory, while in another gallery a "bootblack" appeared to shine an imaginary gentleman's shoes to earn the twenty-five cents to gain admission to the world's fair.[10] At the National Gallery of Art's 1974 *African Art in Motion* exhibition, masks decoratively hung on the walls could be seen on videos within the gallery in use as elements of traditional dance rituals. In a sense, the exhibition "case" has been shattered and the messages of museum exhibitions expanded.

This deconstructing of the museum exhibit case is the result of a variety of influences, some intentional and others inadvertent.[11] Children's museums, since their inception in the 19th century, have sought to engage the observer with items to touch, technological processes to try, and even clothing to try on. The 1970s efforts to create children's rooms (galleries) within museums brought these techniques into mainstream museum exhibitions. The National Museum of Natural History's Discovery Room not only involved visitors in activities, but from the start sought their involvement as the room developed its displays.[12] International expositions continue to expose visitors to technological advances often in ways that may be adapted by museums. U.S. theme parks from Anheuser Busch's Busch Gardens with its European themes to Universal Studios' joint venture with Disney in Florida provide families with not only museum-like exhibits, but also experiences that range from hair-raising roller coaster rides to musical performances. Though both these latter forms of exhibition seek to entertain and amaze, they have influenced museum developers and designers and affected visitors' expectations of exhibitions.

Creating the Exhibition

The chief components of a museum's exhibition's development are (a) a concept (message) or story line, (b) objects to be displayed, (c) the setting that may include custom-built elements and layout within a museum building and (d) "front end" evaluation studies or audience research. Depending on a museum's staff size, the concept or story line may emerge from an individual curator's, researcher's or even collector's investigations or may reflect a small museum's lunch table discussion of how to attract more visitors. Today's exhibitions frequently result from a team effort. Whether ideas or objects are the exhibition's starting point, the clarity of the concept profoundly affects the final product. Though this discussion of exhibition elements begins with "the idea," another element—the objects—can just as readily be the starting point for a museum exhibition. Regardless of which comes first, it is the melding of the objects with the ideas that forms the basis for an interpretive exhibition and makes it more than simply a display of items from a museum's storage rooms. Effective exhibitions factor into the concept and design process the museum's spaces and how they can be used to engage visitors and further the exhibitions' intent. Not all museum spaces are equal and the exhibit design process should acknowledge early on the impact of the exhibition environment. At the

U.S. Holocaust Memorial Museum in Washington, D.C., even the elevators that take visitors to the exhibit entry contribute to the interpretive message by evoking a sense of confinement and "transport." Careful attention to identifying an exhibition's potential audience, especially through direct research, guides exhibition developers' decisions from central themes and messages to object placement and design.

Ken Ames in *Ideas and Images: Developing Interpretive History Exhibits* provides eleven guidelines for excellent museum exhibitions. Though written for history museums, they apply to museum exhibitions in any discipline.[13]

1. Excellence in museum exhibitions extends from an institution's mission statement that reflects a commitment to public interpretation. "Interpretation does not just inform us but pushes us to a deeper and more subtle understanding of some aspect of the world around us. Really interpreting is a difficult and challenging business."

2. The best exhibitions emanate from a clear sense of purpose, or focus. As exhibit teams develop the exhibition—from selecting objects to writing interpretive labels—they must be guided by that focus.

3. First class exhibitions benefit from what Ames calls "the chaos" of brainstorming among their developers.

4. An excellent exhibition evolves from a dynamic creative process that recognizes and seizes on serendipity.

5. Museum resources must be committed to exhibitions to achieve excellence, and not the least of these resources is time to develop the exhibit.

6. The best museum exhibitions reflect the strengths of the museum, whether collections, location, or intellectual rigor.

7. Excellent exhibitions acknowledge the "medium" and present the public with nonverbal, sensory experiences. As Ames states it, "The challenge is to help visitors *feel* the interpretation."

8. Quality exhibitions require talented people, whether museum staff, academic scholars, consultants, or a combination of all. And, as stated above, museum resources must support these qualities.

9. The best exhibitions show that the museum knows their audiences. Ames asks: "Does the exhibition talk to the audience? Lecture? Preach?"

10. Award-winning exhibitions recognize the processes outlined above and use them to achieve excellence.
11. Evaluation of the process and the product are fundamental to the success of the final exhibition and to the vitality of the museum as an interpretive institution.

Before addressing exhibition development steps, a word about exhibition teams is necessary. The typical team includes a curator, a designer, an educator, a subject specialist such as an historian or scientist, and in some instances the museum's development officer.[14] In the United States, exhibition development teams emerged in the late 1970s as the result of several influences. The National Endowment for the Humanities' (NEH) growing support for interpretive exhibitions nationwide required museums to include scholars or specialists in the humanities. Museums often drew on university scholars to supplement their staff and meet NEH standards. At the same time, the childrens' museums exhibit process involving teams, led by the Boston Children's Museum's active professional outreach, raised professional awareness of the value of teams in exhibit development. By the 1980s, the Kellogg Foundation supported a nationwide project to support museums creating exhibits with teams and assessing their value at the end of the process.[15] Both the financial support and professional attention to teams increased their use by museums of all sizes and disciplines. The days of the single curator conceiving and installing an exhibition are past. In response to questions about the team process, staff of the Museum of Florida History report: "We know two things for sure. It is much easier to produce exhibits without the team process. The product, however, is much better with the team process."[16]

Preparing the Exhibit Script

The exhibit starts with a concept, an idea, or a point of view that is developed in one of two ways. First, it may be stated as a theme and through careful study and research analyzed and divided into subthemes. Then objects can be sought and arranged in exhibit units to elucidate the story. A second approach begins with a collection of objects and from them develops a theme and subthemes. Often both approaches are used simultaneously, and a kind of storyboard arrangement results, with themes listed in one column and appropriate objects in another; exhibition devices may be added later in a third column.[17]

Developing a clear exhibition concept with subthemes and exhibit units obviously requires intensive research. The researcher must be able to write an authoritative essay on the subject of the exhibition. To do this, the normal methods of historical and scientific research are employed with careful examination of primary sources. Then exhibit units are devised to make the story abundantly clear—preferably with actual objects enhanced by effective exhibition techniques. In a small museum, the curator or even the director may do the whole job—research, exhibition design, and installation. In a larger institution, a research assistant may assemble the literary materials, a curator the objects, and a designer the presentation plan. The audience for the exhibit should be defined and preferably sampled; members of the team should identify and contact prospective audience(s) to find what they want to know about the subject and how they respond to some emerging exhibit concepts and designs.[18]

Selecting the Objects

George Brown Goode, of the Smithsonian Institution describes exhibitions this way: "An efficient educational museum may be described as a collection of instructive labels, each illustrated by a well-selected specimen."[19] As the exhibit team crafts the exhibition's purpose and themes, they must also turn their attention to the objects that will help visitors understand their messages. Frequently, the narrative script has a parallel document, the object list that identifies specific objects to be used. Careful object-based research should guide the process. Objects may need to be borrowed from other institutions to complement the museum's collection. In preparing the object list, the collections manager, curator, or registrar will locate a potential object to review its condition and appropriateness for display. In addition to selecting appropriate artifacts, the team must address the needs of the objects to be displayed. As the exhibit develops, curators and conservators may discover that an object needs conservation or it may require special conditions for display.

With today's understanding of the need to care for museum objects, whether watercolors or ethnographic materials composed of ancient grasses, exhibit elements may be designed to protect the items on display. For example, a delicate object may require special conditions or a "microclimate." This may be as sophisticated as a sealed case with special temperature and humidity controls or as simple as a black cloth that visitors pick up when viewing the object and return to cover it when they step away. As the exhibit team works, it must address these needs. This process becomes even more demanding if the objects will be on view for a long time or if they are to travel to other museums.

Creating the Layout

As the exhibit script is developing, the designer joins the team to consider space requirements. First and foremost, the museum building itself, whether historic house or art museum with expansive gallery spaces, will affect basic design considerations. In addition to the concept of the exhibition and the needs of its objects, the designer must address the visitors' needs as they move both into and within the exhibition spaces. In the United States with the passage of the Americans with Disabilities Act in 1990, public museums must provide access to all visitors, including those with limited mobility or developmental or emotional limitations. This law has caused exhibit designers to ensure that their designs adequately accommodate all visitors within exhibit spaces.

As the exhibit team begins to map out the placement of objects, supporting materials, and exhibit "furniture" in the museum, they must address a series of questions. How do you introduce or orient visitors to the exhibit's concepts? Does the exhibit design, and perhaps its messages, suggest a single pathway through its spaces? Or, if the exhibition has "subthemes" how are they differentiated from the main theme? How do you accommodate visitors with different levels of interest or knowledge? Does the exhibit need spaces within it to accommodate groups of visitors (especially school groups)? How and where do you place audiovisual elements—computer touch screens, video or audio elements, even small theater spaces—to give visitors a break in their progress through the exhibition spaces? How do groups of visitors comfortably use interactive elements? How do the exhibit elements "lure" visitors through the exhibit spaces. Former National Gallery of Art designer Gaillard Ravenel was a master at placing objects within exhibit spaces to literally draw you into the next gallery. In *The Splendors of Dresden* exhibition to open the National Gallery's east building in 1978, he cut away walls between the galleries to allow visitors to get a peek at an object so that they would want to move through the gallery to see it from a better vantage point. How do you engage visitors to respond to the exhibition's messages? Simple comment notebooks, talk-back boards, and even computer monitors where visitors can register their reactions are becoming more and more common near an exhibit exit.[20]

Choosing the Design Techniques

For many years museums presented their exhibits in rectangular or square rooms, utilizing the four walls and floor for pictures and cases. This arrangement could become monotonous and dull and has sometimes been called "the tyranny of the rectangular room"; modern designers prefer curved, angled, or screen walls; movable panels; varied divisions; angles; and platforms "to reduce the sheer acreage of floors." Such devices add appeal and change of pace, thus diminishing museum fatigue and boredom. Victoria Newhouse identifies and discusses five core decisions for displaying art as "the length, texture, and color of walls, the choice of frames for paintings and pedestals for sculptures, how labeling is best handled, the space's scale, the quality of light, and how the works are placed in relation to each other."[21]

Traditionally, museums protected most exhibited objects in cases—wall or table types, usually rectangular or square, and freestanding. New materials, better ways of mounting glass and plexiglas, and contained lighting have improved these cases and made them less bulky and more attractive, though they often pick up confusing reflections. It is better wherever possible to show objects without cases, protecting them by suspending them out of reach or by placing them so that a platform or pebbled surface keeps back the visitor. If a case must be used, its shape can be individually tailored so as to give an object the space most appropriate for its nature. Old-fashioned wall or table cases often acquired from stores can be remodeled with light boxes above and sloping front glass to reduce reflection, and they and modern standard cases can be placed in a continuous gallery wall that also contains panel displays. Science centers and children's museums added demonstration spaces and visitor-based activities into museum exhibitions.

Another display technique is the diorama. It began as a life-sized exhibit with three-dimensional specimens or objects in the foreground amid realistic surroundings, often with a curved, painted background. The habitat groups of natural history museums—for example, one portraying an African watering hole—showed animals in a proper setting. American taxidermists and designers William Temple Hornaday and Carl Akeley set the standard for dioramas at the end of the 19th century (see chapter 3). Full-scale groups are expensive and take up much exhibition space. Karen Wonders writes: "It was the scenic attraction of dioramas which led the American Museum of Natural History (AMNH) to devote such a large percentage of the museum budget toward the creation of monumental diorama halls. As a result, during its diorama heyday, the AMNH had a larger exhibition staff than that of the Metropolitan Museum of Art, its sister institution across Central Park. In justifying this expenditure, the director of the American Museum of Natural History in 1937 is reported to have declared: 'They buy their art; we must *make* ours.'"[22]

Lighting is one of the chief tools of the exhibit designer. Art museums long have considered natural daylight, preferably from above, the ideal light for viewing paintings. Today's modern systems for controlling natural light, supplemented by artificial light, have made such lighting possible even as museums seek to protect their collections from ultraviolet damage.[23] However, most museums rely on either incandescent or fluorescent lighting, as they remain uniform, cool, and controllable. Lighting may give the object on display a proper setting, for example, recreating the very light under which it was created. For the general exhibit designer, lighting is, as James Gardner asserts, "the most flexible and forceful display technique available." No longer is viewing to be left to chance; lighting will emphasize roundness, solidity, or surface qualities. An artful mixture of general and spotlighting adapted to individual objects brings out qualities that would be missed under bland, overall illumination. Lighting also need not embrittle or fade artworks on paper or textiles, so long as the intensity is controlled.[24] New lighting technology featuring halogen spots and nearly invisible lighting fixtures have revolutionized exhibition lighting. And, when museums either build new exhibition halls or redesign existing galleries, sources of natural light are being included in the basic building structures.

Multimedia options provide great opportunities for museums to assist visitors in placing the exhibition and its objects in a broader context. Computer monitors in the corners of galleries may offer visitors options on a touch screen. At San Francisco's Asian Art Museum, monitors within the galleries allow one to learn more about an artist, the technique, an object's history, or even the original setting for an object on display. In this instance, the visitor takes control of his or her own interpretation threads. Video introductions to an exhibition allow the museum to set the stage for the exhibition and orient visitors to what they will experience in the galleries, or at historic sites around the property. Audio commentaries that a visitor can carry along while viewing the exhibition are becoming both more common and more flexible. The taped acoustaguide format has exploded recently with museums experimenting with technology from iPods to messages broadcast to personal cell phones. These audio components, like the gallery computer monitors, can provide all manner of ancillary information for the museum visitor.

Some museums are beginning to create a complement to the onsite museum exhibition on the Internet. Visitors (and nonvisitors) can "enter" these virtual exhibitions from their computer screens. The National Museum of American History's *Within These Walls* is an example of how the Internet allows visitors to get "inside" museum objects to better understand their construction and historical context. Access this exhibit at www.americanhistory.si.edu/house. Just how these opportunities will be used by the public is developing. Questioning of museum visitors, at least those who walk through the doors, reveals that they have used the Internet to better orient themselves to the museum and to organize their visit. Designer Tom Hennes recently outlined in the journal *Curator* how natural history museums are taking advantage of the Internet to better communicate with visitors and to give them links to nonmuseum resources related to current natural history exhibitions and larger ecological issues.[25] These cyberdimensions for museum-to-visitor communication are contributing to the deconstruction (or destruction) of the traditional exhibition cases and designs.

Knowing Your Visitors

In the 1970s, Michael Spock and the Boston Children's Museum staff knew a lot about their visitors. Yet when they added new exhibitions to their spaces, they proceeded with caution and purpose. Their teams wrote labels and constructed exhibit elements in inexpensive materials and put them "on the floor" for the kids and then stood back to watch and judge how their efforts were working. Because their efforts were "defined" as temporary, making changes in response to the audience was simplified. This deliberateness of exhibit design influenced contemporary museum practice in an incredibly short time frame. Paying attention to its visitors allows a museum to create exhibitions that communicate comprehensible and compelling messages. The process begins with knowing who the visitors are, and involves three stages: front-end evaluation, formative evaluation, and summative evaluation. Front-end evaluation studies visitors and potential audiences before the exhibit process begins. It identifies visitors' expectations and knowledge of the exhibit topic. Formative evaluation occurs during the exhibition development process as elements are tested and then revised, affecting label tone and language, object selection and placement, exhibit furniture, and even the exhibit's traffic flow. Summative evaluation once an exhibition is open to the public allows museum staff to assess the exhibition's impact and effectiveness; at best it allows for refinements of exhibition elements based on direct audience feedback.[26]

Labels

Labels are a basic means by which a museum transforms a collection of objects into a storytelling exhibition that communicates effectively with its chosen audience. They must attract the viewer's attention; convey information about the objects on display in a concise, yet understandable way; and, by successfully provoking curiosity, motivate the visitor to look at the whole exhibition. The viewer who must stand while reading quickly experiences museum fatigue and will skip long labels entirely so they should be kept incisive.

There are several types of labels. The main label, often called a text panel because of its size and prominence, briefly and clearly introduces the themes of the exhibit. This label will be prominently placed and may consist of artwork and text; it is similar to the title page of a book. A secondary topic label (sometimes a case label) will be used for the exhibition's subthemes; though not so prominent as the text panel, its headline will have large letters and its subhead, while brief, will be long enough to give the gist of the subtheme. These labels are essential to understanding the exhibition and will carry its overall message to viewers who do no more than read them and look at the objects.

Other explanatory labels, longer and of smaller type size, give facts, figures, and explanations for interested viewers and specialists but can be ignored by less-interested visitors. Caption labels also are usually supplied for most individual objects; they briefly give the chief facts, such as name of the object, maker, date, and place of origin. If a donor's name must be included, it should come last and in smaller type.

George Brown Goode was right when he wrote in 1895 that "the preparation of labels is one of the most difficult tasks of the museum man."[27] It involves two distinct processes—literary composition and visual appearance. On the literary side, the problem is to translate the detailed knowledge and often the jargon of the curator into a short explanation using language readily understood by the layman. This approach calls for a straightforward literary style and clarity of content so as to obtain maximum readability. The second requirement of a label is typographic legibility. Lettering must be large enough to be readable at the distance from which it is observed (ordinary typewritten labels cannot be read from more than fifteen inches away). Easily recognized typefaces should be used consistently, short paragraphs with proper indentation, no excessively long width of line, and the colors of letters contrasting with the background color. The exhibit designer plays a part in producing high-grade labels. He or she wants them to fit into the general design tastefully and be legible and close enough to the objects they describe that their relationship is readily apparent. The labels must be well lighted, the essential ones placed high enough not to be obscured by crowds, and the others kept at an easy-to-read height.

Goode considered "the art of label writing in its infancy," and one sometimes wonders how much museums have learned about it since that day. Still, labels remain the basic means of enabling viewers to understand exhibitions. Guidebooks and catalogs help, and audio and visual elements are useful adjuncts, but thus far no one has found a satisfactory substitute for a well written, visually attractive label.[28] Beverly Serrell offers rules for creating quality labels based on research and recommendations from researchers and colleagues: careful visitor orientation (both spacially and in terms of content) keeps visitors' attention; more visitors read shorter labels than longer ones; labels next to an object will be read more than labels with numerical keys to a group of objects; labels with concrete, visual references will cause visitors to read-look-read-look; visitors will read interesting labels aloud, increasing social interactions and engaging chilidren too.[29]

Challenges

Authority

For decades U.S. museum professionals have dicussed "the curatorial voice (or tone)" of exhibitions. Understood within these conversations was a sense that an exhibition was to reflect a single authoritative perspective in its labels (and in the selection and placement of objects). In some sense, the exhibit was to make concrete scholarly conclusions. With the democratization of museums and culture, that single authortative voice has been challenged. Twenty-first-century exhibitions seek to give voice to differing perspectives, often providing contradictory interpretations to visitors. As Steven Dubin suggests: "Displays of power have always been what museums do. But exhibitions today commonly reflect the interests of groups that are ideologically different from those previously in control—groups that are only recently flexing their muscle, having just elbowed their way into the cultural spotlight. To be sure, new viewpoints are being expressed in established institutions, channelled along disparate racial, ethnic, and doctrinal lines. But old voices are just as frequently being raised to fight back their challenge." Spencer Crew and Lonnie Bunch, then staff members at the National Museum of American History, introduced visitors to the idea of multiple voices in their introductory label for the exhibition *Between a Rock and a Hard Place* (see chapter 5). The professional discussions now reflect "authorship" of exhibitions with museum staff and outside experts credited for their roles in creating the final product on the exhibit's very walls. But as Jan Ramirez of the Museum of the City of New York suggests: "If you're going to structure exhibitions so that people of a variety of backgrounds can come and find themselves, you are going to have to jostle people. Because you know, in creating room for one group to come and find themselves, you're eclipsing the tradtional story that you were telling for another. And they may be your benefactors."[30]

Controversy

Museum exhibitions are interpretations—from concept to display techniques and wall texts. The Royal Ontario Museum's *Into the Heart of Africa*; the National Air and Space Museum's *The Last Act: The Atomic Bomb and the End of World War II*, better known as Enola Gay after the aircraft the carried the bomb; the National Museum of American Art's (today Smithsonian American Art Museum) *The West as America: Images of the Frontier, 1820–1920*; the Museum of the City of New York's *Gaelic Gotham: A History of the Irish in New York City*; the Brooklyn Museum of Art's *Sensation;* Ontario Science Centre's *A Question of Truth* are exhibitions that resulted in public controversy over content, interpretation, and the sources of funding. In the early 1990s in the United States the potential for controversy had a chilling effect on both exhibition topics and interpretive messages. Exhibition teams are aware that their decision-making processes may be subject to public scrutiny. Has public interest in museum topics and approaches had a negative or positive impact on museum exhibitions? Some would argue a negative impact, while others would suggest that involving the public in the interpretive process engages them more fully with the museum as a public institution. Canadian curator Hooley McLaughlin states it this way: "An awareness of this role as mediator between public interest groups and the public in general greatly affected my thinking during the development of the exhibition, *A Question of Truth*. This balancing act of viewpoints cemented for me the understanding that scientific knowledge, or any aspect of cultural knowledge for that matter, placed into a museum setting, exhibits a dynamic changing interface with the public, our visitors."[31]

Blockbusters and Museum Interpretation

The mere popularity of museum exhibitions impacts the capacity of staff to remain effective interpreters of any discipline. Long lines and crowded galleries mean that interpretive messages can be lost or at best limited in their effectiveness. Interpreters or docents can be especially vulnerable to crowded situations where guided tour presentations devolve into stale recitations. A RAND report concludes: "[M]useums have attempted to broaden their outreach and marketing efforts with special exhibitions, blockbusters, and attempts to make museums the center of social activity and general entertainment. However, is an outreach strategy based on blockbuster exhibits feasible, considering that the costs of putting on these exhibits may place them beyond the reach of all but the largest museums? Moreover, attempts to make museums an entertainment attraction have led some to question what the longer-term effects of such efforts will be on museums' ability to fulfill their traditional missions."[32]

Research

In the description of the process for developing exhibitions, the role of research appeared in many guises: (a) selecting the concept(s); (b) choosing the objects that reflect both the exhibition message and serve as authentic "exemplars"; and (c) understanding the expectations of the exhibition visitors. In each instance the research process is time-consuming with the results of the processes unknown and sometimes altering the entire development of the exhibit from its theme(s) to actual layout. As museums seek to keep costs under control and oversight boards happy with management, the vicissitudes of these research processes can raise tensions. This can be especially difficult if some of the efforts are contracted out to nonmuseum staff. An additional element affecting museum research may be the interests of the museum sponsors, especially if they have corporate images to maintain.

Authenticity

The National Museum of American History exhibitions have evolved from case after case of items sytematically displayed with only basic identifying labels to full-scale settings of objects, both authentic and reproductions, ranging from a barracks in a World War II War Relocation Authority Camp to an elevated car recreating the trip from Chicago's Loop to the suburbs. How do these exhibition techniques affect the museum's resources for caring for collections? And, what of the public's interest is seeing "the real thing" in a museum? How do these techniques, so frequently associated with theme parks and other entertainment forms, alter the public's expectations for museums and their support for the costly practices of caring for artifacts? As the Internet increases access to information and images from museum collections and exhibitions, what is the most effective role for the in-place museum exhibition especially as it seeks to help "visitors" understand collections?[33]

Design Wins

With international communication and travel—both in real time and through the media and cyberspace—increasing, how do museums compete for the public's interests when high-quality design is available in shopping malls, themed restaurants, and even airport terminals? The shrinking of the world puts great pressure on museum exhibitions to compete for the public attention. This is especially complicated by the museum's commitment to care for collections that can be expensive, often unappreciated by the public. Twenty-first-century museums must find the balance between caring for their collections and creating exhibitions that lure the public through their doors. The process is made more complex by new competitors, not just the traditional cultural activities.

Measuring Success

When an exhibition closes and the staff, board, and public review it, how do they measure its success? Michael Kimmelman in the *New York Times* suggests: "The question should not be how many people visit museums, but how valuable are their visits?"[34] But what is the measuring device if it is not attendance? Museum board members may review an exhibit's costs and its impact on attendance and related shop sales to assess its success. First-time visitors to a museum may base a decision to return on their experience with the exhibition. Museum funders may consider future support for the museum on the exhibition publicity (positive or negative). Exhibit corporate sponsors may have their own criteria. Museum website managers may report that the museum's website elements relating to the exhibit reveal increased public interest in the exhibition topic. Professional evaluators may report that the exhibition's messages have been misinterpreted by the public or that the exhibit has brought in a new group of visitors. Michael Belcher writes: "If but one visitor leaves an exhibition with a new sense of wonder, understanding or useful purpose, that exhibition can be said to have succeeded."[35]

Notes

1. Gaillard E. Ravenel, "Designer, National Gallery of Art (US)," *New York Times*, September 10, 1985.

2. Lisa C. Roberts, quoted in James W. Volkert, "Monologue to Dialogue," *Museum News* 70, no. 2 (March–April 1991): 46.

3. Timothy Luke, *Museum Politics: Power Plays at the Exhibition*, Minneapolis: University of Minnesota Press, 2002, p. 224.

4. Giuseppe Olmi, "Science Honour-Metaphor: Italian Cabinets of the 16th and 17th Centuries," in *Grasping the World: The Idea of the Museum*, eds. Donald Preziosi and Claire Farago, Hants, UK: Ashgate, 2004, pp. 129–156; Paula Findlen, *Possessing Nature: Museums, Collecting and Scientific Culture in Early Modern Italy*, Berkeley: University of California Press, 1994.

5, Neil Harris, "Cultural Excursions: Marketing Appetites and Cultural Tastes in Modern America," *Museum News* 69, no. 5 (September–October 1990).

6. Rudiger Klessmann, *The Berlin Museum*, New York: Abrams, 1971, p. 58. "Wilhelm von Bode invented a 'Berlin Style' of his own in the Kaiser Friedrich Museum exhibitions rooms. His Italian interiors in particular, with their delicate blending of color and material and their harmonious arrangement of pictures and sculptures, frames and chests, have been widely admired and frequently imitated"; Victoria Newhouse, *Art and the Power of Placement*, New York: Monacelli Press, 2005, p. 10.

7. Kevin F. McCarthy, Elizabeth H. Ondaatje, Arthur Brooks, and Andras Czanto, *A Portrait of the Visual Arts: Meeting the Challenges of a New Era*, Santa Monica, CA: RAND, 2005, p 32. The origin of the blockbuster phenomenon is much older. The City of Manchester, England, hosted Art Treasures of the United Kingdom in 1883 that attracted more than a million visitors in four months. In addition to building temporary exhibition space, the city added a special train station to its railroad lines to move visitors to the exhibit hall; Randolph Starn, "A Historian's Brief Guide to New Museum Studies," *American Historical Review* 110, no. 1 (February 2005): 94; Newhouse, *Art and the Power*, p. 25.

8. Philadelphia Museum of Art, press release, September 18, 1996.

9. Kenneth L. Ames, Barbara Franco, and L. Thomas Frye, eds., *Ideas and Images: Developing Interpretive History Exhibits*, Nashville, TN: American Association for State and Local History, 1992, p. 319; Jane Bedno and Ed Bedno, "Museum Exhibitions: Past Imperfect, Future Tense," *Museum News* 78, no. 5, pp. 38–43; Elaine Heumann Gurian, "Noodling Around with Exhibition Opportunities," in *Civilizing the Museum*, New York: Routledge, 2006, pp. 150–161.

10. Catherine M. Lewis, *The Changing Face of Public History at the Chicago Historical Society and the Transformation of an American Museum*, DeKalb: Northern Illinois University Press, 2005.

11. Harris, "Cultural Excursions"; Neil Harris, "Exhibiting Controversy," *Museum News* 74, no. 5 (September–October 1995); Pere Alberch, "The Identity Crisis of Natural History Museums at the End of the Twentieth Century," in *Towards the Museum of the Future: New European Perspectives*, eds. Roger Miles and Lauro Zavala, London: Routledge, 1994; Charles Saumarez Smith, "Museums, Artefacts and Meaning," and Philip Wright, "The Quality of Visitors' Experiences in Art Museums," in *The New Museology*, ed. Peter Vergo, London: Reaktion Books, 1989; Ivan Karp and Steven D. Lavine, eds., *Exhibiting Cultures: The Poetics and Politics of Museum Display*, Washington, DC: Smithsonian Institution Press, 1991; Luke, *Museum Politics*.

12. Judith White, *Snakes, Snails and History Tails: Building Discovery Rooms and Learning Labs at the Smithsonian Institution*, Washington, DC: Smithsonian Institution, 1991.

13. Ames, Franco, and Frye, *Ideas and Images*, pp. 213–224.

14. David Dean, *Museum Exhibition: Theory and Practice*, London: Routledge, 1994, p. 157.

15. Mary Ellen Munley, "Education Excellence in American Museums," *Museum News* 65, no. 2 (December 1986): 51–57.

16. Ames, Franco, and Frye, *Ideas and Images*, p. 190, see Cindy Robinson and Warren Leon in *Ideas and Images* for discussion of exhibit team challenges, pp. 211–232; *Museum News* 70, no. 2 (March–April 1991), this issue is on museum exhibition techniques; Steven Lubar, "The Making of 'America on the Move' at the National Museum of American History," *Curator* 47, no. 1 (January 2004): 19–51; Lisa C. Roberts, *From Knowledge to Narrative: Educators and the Changing Museum*, Washington, DC: Smithsonian Institution, 1997, pp. 86–88; Elaine Heumann Gurian, "Let's Empower All Those Who Have a Stake in Exhibitions," in *Civilizing the Museum*, New York: Routledge, 2006, pp. 162–166.

17. Roberts, *From Knowledge to Narrative*; Ames, Franco, and Frye, *Ideas and Images*; Arminta Neal, *Help! for the Small Museum: A Handbook of Exhibit Ideas and Methods*, Boulder, CO:, 1969, pp. 21–27.

18. Joseph Wetzel, "Three Steps to Exhibits Success," *Museum News* 50 (February 1972): 20; Lothar P. Witteborg, "The Temporary Exhibit in Science Museums," in *Temporary and Travelling Exhibits*, United Nations Educational, Scientific and Cultural Organization, pp. 15–29.

19. George Brown Goode, *Annual Report of the Board of Regents of the Smithsonian Institution for the Year Ending June 30, 1889*; Neil Harris, "Museums, Merchandising, and Popular Taste: The Struggle for Influence," in *Material Culture and the Study of American Life*, (Winterthur Conference Report), 1975; Edward P. Alexander, "George Brown Goode," *Museum Masters: Their Museums and Their Influence*, Nashville, TN: American Association of State and Local History, 1983, pp. 277–310.

20. John Beetlestone, Colin H. Johnson, Melanie Quin, and Harry White, "The Science Center Movement: Contexts, Practice, Next Challenges," *Public Understanding of Science* 7, no. 1 (January 1998): 5–26; Mary Alexander, "Do Visitors Get It? A Sweatshop Exhibit and Visitors' Comments," *Public Historian* 22, no. 3 (Summer 2000): 85–94; Stephen T. Asma, *Stuffed Animals and Pickled Heads: The Culture and Evolution of Natural History Museums*, Oxford University Press, 2001, p. 234; Sharon Macdonald, "Accessing Audiences: Visiting Visitor Books," *Museum and Society* 3, no. 3 (November 2005): 119–136.

21. Newhouse, *Art and the Power*, p. 214; Ned J. Burns, *National Park Service Field Manual for Museums*, pp. 72–78, 85–86; Asma, *Stuffed Animals and Pickled Heads*, pp. 234–236.

22. Karen Wonders, *Habitat Dioramas: Illusions of Wilderness in Museums of Natural History*, Uppsala, Sweden: Acta Universitatis Upsaliensis, 1993, p. 76; Edward P. Alexander, "Carl Ethan Akeley" and "William Temple Hornaday,"

in *The Museum in America: Innovators and Pioneers*, Walnut Grove, CA: AltaMira Press, 1997.

23. Newhouse, *Art and the Power*, p. 250.

24. Russell Lynes, *Good Old Modern: An Intimate Portrait of the Museum of Modern Art*, New York, 1975, pp. 268–269; Bayer, "Aspects of Design," pp. 257–258; James Gardner and Caroline Heller, *Exhibition and Display*, London, 1960, pp. 59–103, 112–123; James H. Carmel, *Exhibition Techniques, Traveling and Temporary*, New York, 1962, pp. 115–116; Newhouse, *Art and the Power*, pp. 250–253; Penny Ritchie Calder, "Lighting the Way," *Museum Practice*, Winter 2006, pp. 36–40.

25. Tom Hennes, "Hyperconnection: Natural History Museums, Knowledge and the Evolving Ecology of Community," *Curator* 50, no. 1 (January 2007): 87–108.

26. Beverly Serrell, *Exhibit Labels: An Interpretive Approach*, Walnut Creek, CA: AltaMira Press, 1996, p. 33; John Beetlestone et al., "The Science Center Movement," pp. 8–10; Joaneath Spicer, "The Exhibition: Lecture or Conversation?" *Curator* 37, no. 3 (1994): 185–197; S. Bicknell and G. Farmelo, *Museum Visitor Studies in the '90s*, London: Science Museum, 1993; Judy Diamond, *Practical Evaluation Guide: Tools for Museums and Other Informal Educational Settings*, Walnut Creek, CA: AltaMira Press, 1999.

27. George Brown Goode, *Smithsonian Annual Report*, 1895.

28. Goode, *Smithsonian Annual Report*, 1895.

29. Serrell, *Exhibit Labels*, pp. 234–235; Diane F. Cohen, "Words to Live By," *Museum News* 69, no. 3 (May–June 1990); Nancy Tieken, "Take a Long Look," *Museum News* 70, no. 3, pp. 70–72; George Weiner, "Why Johnny Can't Read Labels," *Curator* 6 (1963): 143–156; Don W. Wilson and Dennis Medina, "Exhibit Labels: A Consideration of Content," *History News* 27 (April 1972): technical leaflet no. 60; Ralph H. Lewis, *Manual for Museums*, National Park Service, U.S. Department of Interior, U.S. Government Printing Office, 1976, pp. 26–27, 121–123, 312–314; William Hayett, *Display and Exhibit Handbook*, New York, 1967, pp. 45–58; P. R. Adams, "The Exhibition," in *The Organization of Museums*, United Nations Educational, Scientific and Cultural Organization, pp. 129–130; James H. Carmel, *Exhibition Techniques, Traveling and Temporary*, pp. 101–109; Jean Gabus, "Aesthetic Principles of Educational Exhibitions," *Museum* 18 (1965): 16–23; Gardner and Heller, *Exhibition and Display*, pp. 104–111; Neal, *Help!*

30. Jan Ramirez quoted in Steven C. Dubin, *Displays of Power: Memory and Amnesia in the American Museum*, New York: New York University Press, 1999, pp. 9, 227; Lubar, "The Making of 'America on the Move.'"

31. Hooley McLaughlin, "A Question of Truth," in *A Manual for Museum Exhibitions*, eds. Barry Lord and Gail Dexter Lord, Walnut Creek, CA: AltaMira Press, 2002, p. 478; Danielle Rice, "Modern Art: Making People Mad," *Museum News* 76, no. 3 (May–June 1997); Michael Ames, *Cannibal Tours and Glass Boxes*, Vancouver: University of British Columbia Press, 1992, pp. 158–160; Edward Linenthal, *History Wars: The Enola Gay and Other Battles for the American Past*,

New York: Metropolitan Books, 1996; Mike Wallace, "The Battle of the Enola Gay," *Museum News* 74, no. 4 (July–August 1995); Lonnie G. Bunch, "Fighting the Good Fights," *Museum News* 74, no. 2 (March–April 1995); Steven Lubar, "Exhibiting Memories," *Museum News* 75, no. 4 (July–August 1996); Robert C. Post, "A Narrative for Our Time: The *Enola Gay* 'and after that, period,'" *Technology and Culture* 45, no. 2 (2004): 373–395; Pamela Walker Laird, "The Public's Historian," *Technology and Culture* 39, no. 3 (1998): 474–482; *The Journal of American History*, December 1995 includes articles on *Enola Gay* from a variety of perspectives; Roberts, *From Knowledge to Narrative*; Michael Ames, "The Politics of Public Taste: Pornography and Blasphemy," in *Cannibal Tours and Glass Boxes*, p. 162.

32. McCarthy, Ondaatje, Brooks, and Czanto, *A Portrait of the Visual Arts*, p. 41.

33. David Ruth, "Podcast Tour Opens Doors to Richmond National Battlefield Park," *Legacy* 17, no. 5 (September–October 2006).

34. Michael Kimmelman, "Museums in a Quandary: What Are the Ideals?" *New York Times*, August 26, 2001.

35. Michael Belcher, *Exhibitions in Museums*, London: Leicester University Press, 1991, p. 213; James Cuno, ed., *Whose Muse? Art Museum and Public Trust*, Princeton University Press and Harvard University Press, 2004, p. 185.

11

To Interpret

The pleasantest form of introduction to objects of art is undoubtedly the companionship of someone who knows them and who leads us to them and instills into us by words and behaviour his familiarity and love for them. Visits to museums in company with such people are engraved on our memories and affect the whole future of our aesthetic experience.

—Bejamin Ives Gilman, 1905[1]

A good museum attracts, entertains, arouses curiousity, leads to questionings—and thus promotes learning.

—John Cotton Dana, 1926[2]

Now, the task of education is about not just interpreting objects but also deciphering interpretations—in other words, anticipating and negotiating between the meanings constructed by visitors and the meanings constructed by museums.

—Lisa C. Roberts, 1997[3]

In 1986 Gordon Ambach, then New York State's commissioner of education, wrote that all museum activities were "interpretive." He argued that merely by collecting or choosing to place an object on view, museum staffs were interpreting the object, attributing importance to it within the museum's subject matter, and anticipating the expectations of visitors viewing the artifact or artwork.[4] Through collecting, conserving, or exhibiting objects, museums make judgments, and in

257

the words of postmodernists, ascribe meaning (and power) to the objects and the very institutions that contain them. In a sense, museum interpretation (or education) is the multilayered process of museums issuing messages—intended and inadvertent—to the public.

This chapter and chapters 10 ("To Exhibit") and 12 ("To Serve") discuss elements of museum interpretation—how museums convey their messages to visitors. Together, these three chapters provide a full picture of a museum's interpretive options.

Interpretation Defined

For the purposes of this discussion museum interpretation/education encompasses how museums communicate their message(s) to the public. It ranges from exhibitions discussed in chapter 10 to tours (how visitors travel through museum spaces) and programs (museum activities designed to engage audiences, including "virtual" tours and other experiences). This chapter ends with discussions of museum initiatives designed for young people as casual visitors or members of a class trip.

Historian Freeman Tilden defined interpretation for the National Park Service in *Interpreting Our Heritage*, a work that has become a major reference for history museum staffs. His six principles provide important guidance for museum practice.

1. Any interpretation that does not somehow relate what is being displayed or described to something within the personality or experience of the visitor will be sterile.
2. Information, as such, is not interpretation. Interpretation is revelation based upon information. But they are entirely different things. However, all interpretation includes information.
3. Interpretation is an art, which combines many arts, whether the materials presented are scientific, historical, or architectural.
4. The chief aim of Interpretation is not instruction, but provocation.
5. Interpretation should aim to present a whole rather than a part, and must address itself to the whole person rather than any phase.
6. Interpretation addressed to children should not be a dilution of the presentation to adults, but should follow a fundamentally different approach.[5]

Twenty years later, Edward Alexander expanded this definition somewhat and posited that good interpretation contains these five basic elements:

1. It seeks to teach certain truths, to reveal meanings, to impart understanding. Thus, it has serious educational purpose.
2. It is based on objects, whether animate or inanimate; natural or man-made; aesthetic, historical, or scientific.
3. It is supported by sound scientific or historical research that examines each museum object, undergirds every program, analyzes the museum's audience, and evaluates its methods of presentation so as to secure more effective communication.
4. It makes use, wherever possible, of sensory perception—sight, hearing, smell, taste, touch, and the kinetic muscle sense. The sensory approach, with its emotional overtones, should supplement but not replace the customary rational avenue to understanding provided by words and verbalization; together they constitute a powerful learning process.
5. It is informal education without the trappings of the classroom, is voluntary and dependent only on the interest of the viewer. It may furnish one with strong motivation to read further, to visit other places, and to seek other ways of satisfying one's newly aroused curiosities.[6]

The *Belmont Report* commissioned by President Lyndon Johnson and issued in 1969 defined the role of U.S. museums as fundamental educational institutions, complementing libraries and, most significantly, public schools.[7] This formal governmental recognition of museums as educational institutions became a catalyst for innovation in museum interpretation and educational programming, supported by federal education funding and funding from the National Endowments for Arts and Humanities.[8] Twenty years after the Belmont report, the American Association of Museums (AAM) convened a task force on museum education, which could be considered a synonym for interpretation, and issued a report calling attention to the need for museums to address interpretation in forthright ways to meet the needs of their diverse audiences. Two elements of that report, *Excellence and Equity: Education and the Public Dimension of Museums* (1992), warrant inclusion here, but the volume itself is an important touchstone for museum interpretation in the 21st century.

Just as Tilden and Alexander codified interpretive principles, the AAM Task Force listed six recommendations relating to what they defined as "Learning." These recommendations offer a more institutional framework, reflecting the changing emphasis of U.S. museums from storehouses to educational centers:

1. Develop and expand audience research methods that will test and document how people learn in the museum environment. Apply the findings to exhibitions and program development.
2. Develop educational experiences for schoolchildren, families, and adults that reflect a knowledge of the different learning styles visitors bring to museums.
3. Experiment with exhibition and program strategies and innovative technologies to enhance the capacity of museums to reach a wider audience through exhibitions and programs.
4. Assess the effectiveness of exhibitions and programs in an ongoing evaluation process that encourages revision and experimentation to improve the visitor's experience of learning from objects and exhibits.
5. Utilize the growing potential for extending the educational role of museums beyond their walls through electronic media, and conduct systematic studies to assess the effectiveness of these resources.
6. Establish "learning laboratories" in selected museums for research, experimentation, and dissemination of information about exhibitions and program development, implementation, and evaluation as well as about the special nature of museum learning and museum audiences.[9]

In addition to these specific recommendations for excellence in museum practice, the report broadens museum responsibilities to the public, using the very terms of the museum definition adopted by the International Council of Museums (ICOM) in 1995. "*Excellence and Equity* is based on the expanded notion of *public service* and education as a museum-wide endeavor that involves trustee, staff, and volunteer values and attitudes; exhibitions; public and school programs; publications; public relations efforts; research; decisions about the physical environment of the museum; and choices about collecting and preserving. These elements are among the many that shape the educational messages museums convey to the public."[10] Just as Ambach suggested, all museum activities convey interpretive decisions and emphases.

Visiting the Museum

Orientation

Visitors to museums benefit from an overview of the institution before they start their visits whether the museum is a large public building or a simple domestic row house. If they understand the nature of the collections, their arrangement, and the setting, they may make choices about what they wish to see and know how to find their way. More and more visitors are using the Internet to organize their visit. Museum websites offer the prospective visitor information on exhibitions and programming along with the important details of travel directions, parking, fees, and museum services. Onsite visitor orientation can be achieved in many ways. A lecture or some other kind of media presentation, a selective exhibition arranged to illustrate general themes and gallery or building locations—any of these approaches, when imaginatively and tastefully conceived, provide a useful introduction to a museum. The chief components of successful orientation materials and programs are: (1) details of exhibits and museum spaces that will help visitors decide what to see, and serve as recognizable guideposts during a visit; (2) representation of overall themes that add meaning to the museum exhibits, spaces, and experiences.

Many museums offer information orientation to their buildings with prominent desks at entry points, complete with friendly staff eager to assist visitors in enjoying their museum visits; there may even be computer terminals for visitors to use to plan their visit. Small museums may provide colorful maps or brochures that highlight museum elements—whether individual objects, gallery spaces, or even pathways—designed to introduce the visitor to the collections as they amble. Regardless of the format, its purpose is to assure that visitors are comfortable within the museum and thereby more able to enjoy its collections, spaces, and programs. Michael Belcher suggests that there are four basic elements to visitor orientation. They are geographical (orientation desks and building maps), intellectual (videos and publications), conceptual (orientation areas and publications), and psychological (general museum brochures and promotional materials). Attending to each of these visitors' needs improves the quality of the visit.[11]

The Tour

Museum tours may be divided into two chief classes—self-guided and personally conducted. In the first, visitors make their way about the museum at their own pace. The visit may be so rambling that it even defies the term "tour." Printed materials may aid visitors: a guidebook or a handout that details the museum layout and describes elements of the collections, including their creators or context. In the United States in the 1970s, cassette tapes with commentary on the exhibitions or museum objects added to the information available to visitors. With the development of computer microchips, handheld devices or "wands" that visitors carry replaced tape machines and headphones. By pushing a button on the wand, visitors can select information of interest to them. The visitor is no longer confined to the order of the taped commentary. In fact, wands may offer multiple levels of interpretive information: basic object identification; details of the object's origins or historical, artistic, or scientific context; and period music to add another sensory element to the visit. Today, museums are experimenting with broadcasting both audio and video interpretive messages to visitor's cell phones, iPods, and MP3 players.[12]

Personally conducted tours, though more expensive for museums to offer, add a valuable human dimension to interpretation and can extend the length of a museum visit.[13] Paid staff members or volunteers, often known as docents, may provide such tours to visitors. Each type requires careful oversight by museum staff, ongoing training in both content and technique, maintaining uniform standards of preparation and presentation that includes both evaluation and coaching, and day-to-day scheduling. Perceptive teacher-guides—well prepared, wise, flexible, friendly, and unrehearsed in their presentation styles—can make museum tours a pleasant, even memorable, learning experience. Excellent guides possess sensitivity, curiosity (about both the museum's subjects and people in general), and friendliness. Volunteer docents may make many smaller museums economically possible, and they also serve as important ambassadors of the museum to the community at large.

Beyond Static Exhibitions

Multimedia elements within museum exhibitions add to the opportunity for visitors to enjoy a rich learning experience. Visitors may encounter presentations in the museum galleries that add both information and context to the exhibitions. Early in the 20th century, the Deutsches Museum in Munich demonstrated various scientific phenomena in the museum's halls, often attracting large crowds.

Sounds, smells, historical vignettes offered by actors, and opportunities to touch reproduction objects and ask questions may engage the visitor in valuable ways to enhance his or her experience. Tours may include stops to "try your hand" at some historical, scientific, or artistic practice broadening the visitors' experiences and increasing the opportunities for learning.

Museum interpretation can be enhanced by human actors demonstrating industrial practices, providing first-person historical "testimony," or guiding visitors through the creative process for an artwork. For example, the manufacture of cloth with its carding, spinning, and weaving done by hand or by early machines can be far more enlightening and exciting than a label with illustrations of the process. In the botanical garden, cultivating, harvesting, potting, pruning, and plant-propagating techniques arouse great interest in visitors. At the Palais de Découverte in Paris, visitors may encounter scientific researchers available in the museum galleries to describe their current work and its public implications.[14]

All these activities involve a high degree of visitor participation, either psychological or actual. They better explain processes; they combine sensory perception with rational analysis; and they dramatize collections of objects. A basic underlying challenge is that of authenticity. Even if the equipment, processes, and costumes are thoroughly researched, is the demonstrated craft over-romanticized? What of the tedium of such work? Are the early industrial demonstrations too neat and clean? Is the tyranny of the machine understood and what of the social evils of the labor of women and children? What of the biospheres without insects? And, each of these demonstrations or presentations only approaches true authenticity.

Another process of interpretation especially popular in outdoor history museums is that of role-playing (or "living history") by museum staff. Here the interpreter tries to learn everything possible about the historical period and to conduct him or herself as if living then; the interpretation is normally given in the first person. Often the guide performs everyday tasks of the period; the "housewife" may kill a chicken, scald it, pluck the feathers, cut it up, and fry it. The "farmer" may fell a tree with an ax, cut it to size by chopping and wedging, and carry seasoned wood to the fireplace. Meanwhile, each one talks with visitors about daily life and chores. This interpretation sometimes involves the visitors and may extend to "live-in" situations where students don period costumes, occupy a historic house or shop, and participate in activities, such as cooking or crafts.

First-person interpretation has an immediacy that makes it appealing to museum visitors. Each of these "dramatic" forms can engage the
visitor in very personal ways, placing the historical issues of the day in
a personal setting. The major challenges of these forms lie in the
preparatory research and the necessity to "limit" the dramatic license
of the actors. Plimoth Plantation (Massachusetts) has re-created the
17th-century village and inhabited it with staff representing historical
figures. As visitors encounter these "residents" going about their daily
chores, they can ask questions of their lives and aspirations and learn
something of the 17th-century worldview. If, on the other hand, the visitor asks about Sturbridge Village (an 1850s re-created village not far
away), the staff member will feign ignorance of such a place and wonder what the visitor is asking. The constriction of the staff to 1627
makes for some unusual and potentially frustrating conversations
about the plantation. Colonial Williamsburg's experiments with first-
person interpretation involve careful introductions for visitors. For example, you may be invited to sit on a jury at the Court House and hear
the presentation of an 18th-century case and participate in the judg-
ment, or you may follow "The Other Half Tour" that focuses on the
Colonial city's slave and free black populations and their perceptions
of the town and its inhabitants.[15]

These interpretive experiences reflect a shift in museum emphasis
from collections to audiences. In the 1980s, U.S. museum evaluators began to study the museum "experience" as a whole, rather than simply
focusing on elements of the museum's interpretive offerings, especially
specific exhibitions. These evaluations ranged from questionnaires for
visitors to complete at the end of their visit to postvisit, face-to-face in-
terviews. Just as with exhibitions, evaluators studied visitors both before and after their museum visits, sometimes using the marketing
technique of "focus groups" to gauge visitors' expectations. In 1992
museum evaluators John Falk and Lynn Dierking proposed a way to
consider museum experiences from the visitor's perspective rather
than that of the museum. They suggested an "interactive experience
model" overlapping three elements of a visitor's museum experience:
the visitor's personal interests, the social dynamic of the visit, and the
museum's physical setting. Building on Alma Wittlin's notion that the
best museum exhibitions create dialogues with visitors rather than offering the curator's monologue, Falk and Dierking reflected on how
museum visits are by their very nature complex events. They concluded:

1. Each visitor learns in a different way, and interprets information through the lens of previous knowledge, experience, and beliefs.
2. All visitors personalize the museum's message to conform to their own understanding and experience.
3. Every visitor arrives with an agenda and a set of expectations for what the museum visit will hold.
4. Most visitors come to the museum as part of a social group, and what visitors see, do, and remember is mediated by that group.
5. The visitor's experience within the museum includes docents, guards, concessionaires, and other visitors.
6. Visitors are drawn to museums because they contain objects outside their normal experience. Visitors come to "look" in a variety of ways.
7. Visitors are strongly influenced by the physical aspects of museums, including the architecture, ambience, smell, sounds and "feel" of the place.
8. Visitors encounter an array of experiences from which they select a small number.
9. The visitor's attention is strongly influenced by the location of exhibits and by the museum's orientation.[16]

Writing for the journal *Curator*, Jan Packer emphasizes the impact of visitors' interests on the museum experience, further suggesting that visitors come to museums interested in "learning for fun," for the very pleasure of the process rather than to learn or understand some specific fact or idea.[17] The ascendance of museum audiences over museum collections is affecting 21st-century museum interpretation.

Public Programs

A more traditional form of museum interpretation is the lecture and its variations, slide or film showings, field trips, campfire talks, or study tours. The storyteller has exercised a popular human role from the earliest times; a skilled, personable speaker can communicate effectively and distinctively with his audience. Thus, a museum will do well to organize general or specialized lecture series to develop understandings of its fields of interest and of its collections. They also provide outlets for staff research. Such lectures and programs also may be taken outside the museum walls to other venues or through the Internet to widen the audiences.

Operating any kind of public program demands careful planning and attention to details. The selection of pertinent subjects; the preparation of the talks, discussions, or programs with excellent visual materials, or actual objects; the setting for the program; and the identification of the prospective audiences must be considered. A museum will do well to develop a series of conferences, forums, workshops, and seminars that present aspects of its program in considerable depth and appeal to specialized audiences. Such activities may encourage visitors to return and can build a core of enthusiastic and loyal supporters of the museum, whether they are members, an organized Friends of the Museum group, or regular attendants at a special event. They give back to the museum in a variety of ways from contributions, donations to collections and, most importantly, raising the museum's public profile.

The special event has strong promotional overtones and gives much opportunity for publicity. Such a program of specialized interpretation may take many forms. A smaller museum may organize an occasional event of this kind, perhaps taking advantage of an anniversary or the fact that some current moment gives its collection or field of interest special relevance. In smaller communities, collaborative programs among cultural institutions extend the potential audiences and broaden the museum's appeal. Larger museums will do well to offer regular programs that interpret their various fields of interest.

To put it simply, the secrets of success of public programs—demonstrations, conferences, workshops, film series, artistic performances, musical events, and the like—are (1) imaginative and thorough planning; (2) careful assessment of the audience's interests and needs; (3) efficient execution, with attention to detail; and (4) friendly hospitality shown by all members of the museum staff. When these events succeed, the museum acquires a large group of backers who understand its objectives and program in considerable depth. They constitute the kind of preferred support that every museum seeks and needs. If poorly planned, however, they may negatively affect the museum's reputation and impact its public support.[18]

Publications

The interpretation described thus far has taken place in the museum, and there can be no real substitute for the museum visit to show objects in all their vivid three-dimensional reality. But there are ways to take the museum story beyond its walls and to reach even larger audiences than onsite visitors. These discussions begin with print publications and conclude with those museum materials in a wide variety of formats.

Publications are a special form of communication with the public, extending the museum's interpretation. Books, periodicals, and pamphlets can tell the museum story in a carefully considered, thoughtful manner. They often act as long-term ambassadors for the museum on the shelves of public and even personal libraries. The museum should control all printed pieces that it issues and should give careful attention to securing factual accuracy and high quality in their design and production.

It is important for museum publications to serve the museum's interpretive focus and to present the public a unified design image for the institution. To succeed with these publications, the museum must commit staff time and resources to the details of ensuring accuracy and visual appeal. Publications with too narrow an audience may drain museum resources. A successful publication of any type balances the museum's interpretive emphasis with profit.

Guidebooks

These often-inexpensive publications are useful to visitors while visiting the museum, and allow them to take away something from the museum for future reference. While providing guidance for visitors in the museum, these booklets can reinforce a museum's themes and provide bibliographic references to extend the opportunity for learning.

Exhibition Catalogs

Often glossy attractive publications, catalogs further the museum's opportunity to interpret the collections and to provide context and additional detail to exhibition themes and object labels. They provide staff an outlet to publish their research thereby adding to scholarly discourse for the museum. More than souvenirs of the exhibit, they too are rich ambassadors of the museum to collectors and specialists, as well as the general public. They also create for the museum an official record of the exhibition's objects and its messages.

Newsletters

Newsletters can be issued on a regular basis and offered to museum members as a benefit of membership. They provide a good outlet for staff-written articles. Some museums offer online newsletters to their members to avoid printing expenses and to allow for more timely communication.

Annual Reports

Annual reports, sent to members and contributors, combine an opportunity for extending interpretive themes while promoting the museum's programs, both past and future. Often their pages acknowledge donors' contributions to the museum. Further, they serve as an informal record of museum activities.

Occasional Publications

A museum should consider publishing specialized books that may include scholarly studies or research reports; commemorative booklets, popular treatments of a museum's theme; or items for discrete audiences, ranging from collectors to younger readers.

School Kits

Since the 19th century, American museums have offered materials for use by school classes. These kits have grown to be varied in both emphasis and form—written lessons for classrooms, illustrated texts, stories written to engage young readers, trunks of reproductions, and varied audiovisual materials, including enhancements for school and home-based computer programs. The best of these materials are curriculum based, linking the museum to the classroom.

Nonprint Media

Another way to reach the public outside the museum walls is through audiovisual and electronic mediums. Films, television productions, videos, DVDs, compact discs, and Internet websites can be effective because the viewer may concentrate attention upon images so realistic and true to life that he or she identifies with the situations and feelings being portrayed there.

Orientation Material

Many major museums now sell audiovisual materials that highlight their collections so that visitors can "previsit" the museum from home. More and more visitors are using museums' websites to organize their onsite visits. Websites are helping to both orient visitors and market special museum programs.[19]

Content-based Materials

After Ken Burns's television documentary *The Civil War* appeared on Public Television, attendance at related historic sites dramatically increased. A more informed public arrived at these sites to see for themselves what was represented in Burns's films. The message is clear that television can further the interpretation of museum exhibitions. And, the advances in communication on the Internet are just being fully realized by museums. Specific museum-centered media complement exhibits and even public programs, extending their reach and expanding the limitations of object labels. The Smithsonian's Museum of American History has begun to put its exhibitions on the web (www.Americanhistory.si.edu) for use by teachers, visitors planning their Washington trip, and researchers with all manner of interests.

Curriculum-based Materials

Virtual tours for far away students, interactive classroom materials on the web, and living history programs that involve students in their classrooms in problem solving across time and space are just a few of the innovative ways that nonprint media is being used to extend the interpretive reach of museums. Colonial Williamsburg's curriculum-based materials include all of the above. They are designed for a school-age audience, involving teachers (the customers, after all) in their creation. Their website, www.history.org, reflects very creative approaches to school audiences.

As with all museums interpretive programs, publications—whether print or another media—require careful planning, including a cost-benefit analysis of the effort. Issues of accuracy (including control of content), staff commitment and scheduling, potential audience(s), and matching the media to the museum's message are critical to success.

Youth Activities

Young people, remarked a European museum director, "lack the background knowledge possessed by adults but nevertheless prove such excellent spontaneous observers that nine-to-twelve-year-old children may be considered the brightest and most inspiring of all museum guests."[20] Freeman Tilden warned that interpretation addressed to children should follow a fundamentally different approach or, at best, a separate program. Thus, museums can offer great experiences for young people when their programs are carefully tailored to the interests of this specialized audience. An Institute of Museum and Library Services' study in 2002 revealed that fifteen thousand U.S. museums spent 1 billion dollars and expended 18 million hours of staff time on kindergarten through twelfth grade education programming.[21]

A museum should provide special opportunities for individual youthful visitors of different ages. At Colonial Williamsburg, for example, young people (ages seven to twelve) on the Tricorn Hat Tour bowl on the green, try on wigs at the peruke makers, get lost in the holly maze, put themselves in the pillory and stocks at the gaol, drink lemonade in a tavern, and eat gingerbread at the bakery. At San Francisco's Exploratorium, young people take the role of "explainers" to answer visitors' questions. In some museums, there are spaces designed specifically to engage the curiosity of young people. Even in the 19th century, museum spaces designed for young people were common in museums ranging from the Victoria and Albert Museum in London to the Smithsonian castle building on Washington's mall. Today under the rubric of "discovery rooms," these spaces offer young visitors the opportunity for hands-on experiences with materials relating to the museum's content and collections. Carefully trained staff help to make the experience memorable, often engaging the whole family in the child's exploration.

Usually, however, the most common way to reach the young audience is through the schools. The traditional method is the teacher-organized field trip. Advance planning and close cooperation between museum and school are required if this approach is to be effective. School visits that are warmed-over or diluted versions of adult tours led by condescending staff or docents can destroy students' interest and diminish their potential as future adult visitors. Yet the combining of words, objects, and experience in classroom and museum offer opportunities for rich learning experiences.

The school system and classroom teacher should be partners in developing the museum visit (both actual and virtual). The first step is to adapt museum interpretation to the school curriculum. The museum education staff should take the lead and invite teachers and curriculum advisers to participate in planning. The museum activities should relate to classroom experiences and curriculum requirements. When themes and programs are agreed upon, the museum might send pre-visit materials to the school, including model lessons, exhibits, classroom kits of reproductions, publications, multimedia materials, and even staff. The museum also should build a guide force with the flexibility and skill to engage young people. Post-tour activities might require students to prepare reports on their experiences in a variety of media that involve writing, drawing, and public-speaking skills. Both museum staff and teachers should carefully evaluate projects and make suggestions for improvements.

Another way in which museums and schools can work together is through a museum club, a voluntary activity that takes place after school, on weekends, or during holidays. A science club may prepare individual projects in the museum for a science fair, and students may rely on museum resources to prepare for National History Day competitions. The most interested young people may serve as junior curators of the museum.

Today in the city of Baltimore, Maryland, young people visit the city's museums in school-organized groups, they participate in after-school programs that are often organized for them by some sort of "service" organization, and they may even spend the night or the weekend on the USS *Constellation* participating in educational activities as well as programs that build self-reliance and are just for fun. At the city's National Great Blacks in Wax Museum in a disadvantaged neighborhood, young people have become even more involved with the museum's programs and its staff seeking not only guidance on schoolwork, but advice on personal challenges. These students have been as young as eight and many have volunteered at the museum through their teenage years and become, in effect, staff members and mentors for other younger children.

In 1992 the Association of Science-Technology Centers (ASTC) initiated a national program that acknowledged this expanding role of museums. Youth ALIVE! began as a national network offering museums assistance serving the needs of adolescents. Its goal was to create sustainable youth programs in U.S. science centers and museums. The network attracted seventy-two museums and science centers, and today has expanded into five regional offices that serve the interests of museums seeking to connect with young people in the community. It's a partnership that brings together the needs of the museums and science centers and those of young people seeking employment and life skills that are developed through science programming of all sorts. Researchers have found that the program has had a life-changing impact on some teens, and institutionally opened the participating museums to better serving adolescents' needs and interests.[22]

In recent years, museums have joined the charter-school movement in the United States. These schools seek to offer alternative approaches to learning for students. Museums with their collections and staff with educational training are natural partners. In 1997 the Henry Ford Museum opened its own charter school, the Ford Academy, on the museum grounds. It's a partnership among the museum, the Ford Motor Company, and the Wayne County schools. The academy boasts hands-on learning, training in technology, and global connections through the Ford Company network. Building on the success of the academy, the Henry Ford Learning Institute advises others in Michigan on how to create charter schools. As of 2005, there were 216 charter schools across the state serving more than eighty thousand students. In New York City, four museums joined forces to create the New York City Charter School in the Manhattan neighborhood of Chelsea. The museum members include: the American Museum of Natural History, the Brooklyn Museum of Art, the Jewish Museum, and the Children's Museum of Manhattan. Opened since 1994, the school has served students in grades seven through twelve. Like the Ford Academy, the New York school is part of the metropolitan school system, but relations between the museums and the school system have not been smooth.[23]

Understanding Learning in Museums

In the United States, as early as the 1920s, museums were seeking to understand both the potential and impact of museums on visitors or learners.[24] The AAM's work with Arthur Melton and Edward Robinson in the 1930s elevated the importance of understanding the experiences of visitors in museum galleries.[25] The open education movement of the 1960s attracted museums as educational players. Harvard educator Howard Gardner's catalog of ways of learning, published in 1983, inspired museum educators and provided intellectual support for their efforts to advance the role of learning in the museum setting.[26] Add to this rich intellectual climate in the United States the attention and potential funding from the National Endowments for the Arts and Humanities and federal educational agencies and educational initiatives within museums were nearly irresistible.[27] Both the rationale and the resources merged.

In the early 1970s in the United States, museums were extending their educational offerings especially for school-age children. Museums offered to supplement classroom education, partnering with the school systems to fully integrate the classroom and museum experiences.[28] Teachers joined the growing ranks of educational staff in museums to create dynamic programs for students. For example, Old Sturbridge Village built an educational facility next to the historic area with spaces for student activities ranging from hearthside cooking to splitting wood shingles. Teachers joined the village staff during summer months to write curriculum materials that tied the village experience directly to the classroom.[29] Within U.S. public education, social studies reforms that emphasized "inquiry" learning and national science curricula that engaged students in hands-on experiments further stimulated museum programs. A national research project into U.S. art museums' educational offerings during the 1973–1974 academic year resulted in a telephone directory–sized report describing and analyzing more than one hundred projects.[30] Regardless of a museum's subject matter, educational offerings had become expected and *The Art Museum as Educator* chronicled their impressive variety.

Within this rich milieu of educational programs for school students, U.S. museums also pursued innovative adult programs as well. Educator Malcolm Knowles coined the phrase "andragogy," which means "the art and science of helping people learn," to complement "pedagogy" applied to teaching children.[31] Knowles outlined those elements essential to adult learning experiences and museums quickly adapted them to their programming for both their docents and adult visitors. He argued that successful adult education follows these principles: (a) adults need to know why they need to learn something, (b) they learn best through experiences, (c) they approach learning as "problem solving," and (d) adults learn best when the topic is of immediate value. The AAM's *Museums, Adults, and the Humanities: A Guide to Educational Programming*, published in 1981, describes the theory and practice of adult education in both classrooms and museums.[32]

Museums across the disciplines offer hands-on activities, lessons based on historical documents and objects, art translated into dance in the galleries, and experiments in basic scientific laws. Museum learning is no longer limited to didactic exhibitions with complementary lectures and demonstrations. Educational thinkers have stimulated a greater variety in learning opportunities within (and beyond) the museum. Museum educators read and adapted the ideas and philosophies of writers Benjamin Bloom, Jerome Bruner, Howard Gardner, Jean Piaget, Mihalyi Csikszentimihalyi, and Lev Vytgosky to museum programs. Today, museum education programs run the gamut from structured docent-led tours to flexible museum spaces where students of all ages pursue their own interests with museum staff (or peer) guidance. In *Learning in the Museum*, George Hein summarizes what researchers know about learning in museums. He concludes:

1. People "learn" in museums . . . absorbing specific messages contained in exhibits . . . responding to the experience of the museum visit. People have enriching, stimulating, rewarding, or restorative experiences . . . learn[ing] about themselves, the world . . . they have aesthetic, spiritual and "flow" experiences.
2. [T]o maximize their potential to be educative, museums need first to attend to visitors' practical needs . . . includ[ing] orientation, amenities, making the museum's agenda clear.
3. People do attend to exhibits . . . incorporat[ing] the content of museums into the agendas they bring with them.
4. People make unique, startling connections in museums.
5. Museums are not efficient places for traditional "school" education.
6. Staff should never underestimate the value of wonder, exploration, expanding of the mind, providing new cognitively dissonant and aesthetic experiences.
7. [T]he museum must allow [visitors] to connect what they see, do and feel with that they already know, understand, and acknowledge.[33]

Museums have absorbed and modified the tradition of displaying objects in a rational order—sometimes with explanatory labels and sometimes without—to extend the idea of a museum as an educational venue where visitors become engaged with settings, objects, ideas, performances, conversations, and as a whole, with experiences.

Challenges

Declining Docent Corps

U.S. museums of all disciplines are struggling with a diminishing pool of volunteers to serve as docents, especially for weekday programs. The tradition of women seeking volunteer work in museums is fading, although some sites are effectively attracting the newly retired of both sexes to special project work. In addition to expanding the pool of potential volunteers, museums are using new approaches to guiding visitors without relying on staff or volunteers. The flexibility of audio/visual and web-based devices can ease the shift from guided to self-guided experiences.[34]

National School Curriculum Reform and Museums

U.S. national curriculum reform is especially challenging as standardized testing of students is forcing school systems to focus classroom instruction on "the test." Time away from school for field trips is becoming more and more difficult to arrange. School trips to museums are declining. Museums are seeking ways to bring interpretive messages to students in innovative ways that complement the demands of testing. Distance-learning techniques are being developed to allow museums to come to schools—sometimes with complete historical re-enactments and follow-up student discussions.

Marketing

Blockbuster exhibits and special events—concerts, charity benefits, political rallies, membership galas—each place the museum before the public, establishing its "brand." The Swedish Tourist Board has estimated that every year the salvaged 17th-century battleship *Vasa* attracts several hundred million dollars into the Swedish economy. Museums may be cornerstones for a community's economic vitality. How do museums balance their roles as interpreters of culture, art, and science with their commercial interests and needs?[35]

Research

Early 20th-century research studies of museums and their visitors focused on how visitors viewed exhibitions, establishing basic understandings of such things as traffic patterns (visitors turn right when entering a gallery) and label word limits (twenty-five words). As the variety of activities taking place within a museum's galleries (or on its website) has multiplied, how should museums assess their value? Museum researchers have applied a growing number of assessment tools from time-and-motion studies to focus groups. Each of these techniques answers important questions, but the overall impact of a museum on its visitors remains elusive. In the world of competition for leisure time, it's important for museums to be able to argue for their continued value (and public support) based on hard evidence.[36]

Interpretive Authority?

As the social history movement has contributed more to academic history programs and as university public history programs have emerged, history museums struggle with how to represent multiple perspectives in their interpretation and avoid stereotyping. They face questions of both the nature of evidence and "interpretive" authority, which is especially complicated when special interest groups are aroused.[37]

Museums as Emotional, Sensual Settings

In more and more museums, visitors encounter people (staff or volunteers) who are in the galleries and museum classrooms specifically to interact with visitors. Some are straightforward teachers; others may be in the guise of theatrical dress or mode, representing an alternate reality. Their role is to draw visitors in to the museum's subject, to engage him or her in an experience beyond passively viewing exhibitions. In discussing natural history museums, Stephen Asma argues: "Museums . . . must continue to address our emotional faculties. They must continue to be sensual places. Museums would do well, however, to think about which emotions they should cultivate in their patrons . . . [to] create the sense of wonder and edification that leads to the pursuit of understanding."[38]

Museums as Restorative

Why include restorative in a list of interpretive challenges rather than within the text of discussions of museum's educational roles? It appears as a challenge based on its perceived lack of value within both programming options and financial support. Whoever went before a museum funder to seek support to open quiet, sparsely inhabited galleries where visitors might wander and wonder? Here's just one description of a visitor's "restorative" experience in a museum: "The museum does give free time—freedom to loiter and tarry, to indulge the long double-take, the retracing of steps, the dreamy pause, the regress and ingress of reverie. . . . it is a tempo of consciousness disarming to the modern audience . . . [and] the commercial media implants the belief that a well-adjusted mind is an excited mind."[39]

The "Constructivist" Museum

George Hein argues that "visitors make meaning in the museum, they learn by constructing their own understandings. The issue for museums is to determine what meanings visitors make from their experiences, and then to shape the experience to the extent possible by the manipulation of the environment. Every museum building will send a message (or multiple messages); every exhibition will evoke feelings, memories, and images; every encounter with an object brings about a reflection (even if it is only incomprehension and frustration); every social interaction reinforces connections, stimulates new ones, or triggers personal anxieties."[40] What are the steps museums should take to address this multilayered approach to their audiences? Where are the museum experiments in constructivism as an educational approach? What are their lessons? The Ontario Science Centre and England's Eden Project seem to be the most likely to provide visitors with opportunities to control and perhaps construct their learning. Chapter 12 includes descriptions of both institutions.

Notes

1. M. S. Prichard with notes by Bejamin Ives Gilman, "Guides in the Museum," Gilman Archives, Boston Museum of Fine Arts, June 15, 1905.

2. J. C. Dana, quoted in *The New Museum, Selected Writings of John Cotton Dana*, American Association of Museums and the Newark Museum, 1999, p. 9.

3. Lisa C. Roberts, *From Knowledge to Narrative: Education and the Changing Museum*, Washington, DC: Smithsonian Institution Press, 1997, p. 3.

4. Gordon Ambach, "Museums as Places of Learning," *Museum News* 65, no. 2 (December 1986): 37; see discussion of museums as interpretive institutions in Peter Vergo, ed., *The New Museology*, London: Reaktion Books, 1989.

5. Freeman Tilden, *Interpreting Our Heritage*, Chapel Hill, NC: University of North Carolina Press, 1957, p. 8.

6. Edward P. Alexander, "What Is Interpretation?" *Longwood Program Seminars* 9 (1977): 2–7; *The Interpretation Program of Colonial Williamsburg*, pp. 11–12.

7. *America's Museums: The Belmont Report*, Washington, DC: American Association of Museums, 1969.

8. George E. Hein, *Learning in the Museum*, London: Routledge, 1998, pp. 54–55.

9. *Excellence and Equity: Education and the Public Dimension of Museums*, Washington, DC: American Association of Museums, 1992, p. 17.

10. *Excellence and Equity*, p. 6.

11. Michael Belcher, *Exhibitions in Museums*, London: Leicester University Press, 1991, p. 101; Robert L. Wolf, "The Missing Link: The Role of Orientation in Enriching the Museum Experience" in *Patterns in Practice*, Washington, DC: Museum Education Roundtable, 1992, pp. 134–142; Hein, *Learning in the Museum*, p. 117.

12. Julia Beizer, "The Pods Have Landed," *Museum News* 84, no. 3, (September–October 2005): pp. 15–17; David Ruth, "Podcast Opens Doors to Richmond National Battlefield Park, *Legacy* 17, no. 5 (September–October 2006): 32–33; Catherine McCarthy, "Cool Technology in a Ranger-led Tour, *Legacy* 17, no. 5 (September–October 2006): 34–37; Peter Samis and Stephanie Pau, "'Artcasting' at SFMOMA: First-Year Lessons, Future Challenges for Museum Podcasters Broad Audience of Use," San Francisco Museum of Art, March 2006, www.sfmoma.org; Peter Meng, *Podcasting and Vodcasting*, IAT Services, University of Missouri, March 2005.

13. Hein, *Learning in the Museum*, p. 137.

14. Daniel Beysens, "1 Researcher, 1 Exhibit," *ECSITE newsletter*, no. 65 (Winter 2006): 6–7.

15. Jay Anderson, ed., *Living History Reader, Volume I: Museums*, Nashville, TN: American Association for State and Local History, 1991; Warren Leon and Margaret Piatt, "Living History Museums," in *History Museums in the United States: A Critical Assessment*, eds. Warren Leon and Roy Rosenzweig, University of Illinois Press, 1989, pp. 64–97; Christy Coleman Matthews, "A Colonial Williamsburg Revolution," *History News* 54, no. 2 (Spring 1999): 6–11; Candace Tagorra Matelic, "Through the Historical Looking Glass," *Museum News* 58, no. 4 (March–April 1980): 35–45.

16. John H. Falk and Lynn D. Dierking, *The Museum Experience*, Washington, DC: Whalesback Books, 1992, pp. 136–150; Elaine Heumann Gurian, "Answers to the Ten Questions I'm Most Often Asked," *Civilizing the Museum*, New York: Routledge, 2006, pp. 137–149.

17. Jan Packer, "Learning for Fun: The Unique Contribution of Educational Leisure Experiences," *Curator* 49, no. 3 (July 2006): 329–342.

18. Alexander, "What Is Interpretation?" pp. 30–33; Ned J. Burns, *Field Manual for Museums*, National Park Service, pp. 275–279, 297–302; Hal Golden and Kitty Hanson, *How to Plan, Produce and Publicize Special Events*, Dobbs Ferry, NY, 1966; Tilden, *Interpreting Our Heritage*, pp. 3–10, 26–31; Susan K. Nichols, ed., *Museum Education Anthology*, Washington, DC: Museum Education Roundtable, 1984; Susan K. Nichols, ed., *Patterns of Practice*, Washington, DC: Museum Education Roundtable, 1992. Each of these volumes provides a wide array of museum education discussions, both practical and theoretical.

19. Jay S. Miller and Kelly Farrell, "Interpretation on the Web," *Legacy* 17, no. 5 (September–October 2006): 26–31.

20. Peter Michelsen, "The Outdoor Museum and Its Educational Program," in *Seminar on Preservation and Restoration*, Williamsburg, VA, 1963 pp. 201–217.

21. *True Needs, True Partners: Museums and Schools Transforming Education*, Washington, DC: Institute of Museum Services, 1996; Ann Bay, *Museum Programs for Young People*, Washington, DC: Smithsonian Institution, 1973; Bonnie Pittman-Gelles, *Museums, Magic and Children Youth Education in Museum*, Washington, DC: Association of Science Technology Centers, 1982; Barbara Y. Newsom and Adele Z. Silver, eds., *The Art Museum as Educator*, Berkeley: University of California Press, 1978.

22. Suzanne LeBlanc, "Lost Youth: Museums, Teens and the Youth ALIVE! Project," *Museum News* 72, no. 6, pp. 44–46; For current information on Youth ALIVE! see www.astc.org/profdev/youth; L. Baum, G. E. Hein, and M. Solvay, "In Their Own Words: Voices of Teens in Museums," *Journal of Museum Education* 25, no. 3, pp. 9–13.

23. Wendy Pittman and William S. Pretzer, "Museums and the Charter School Movement" and "The Most Public of Public Schools," *Museum News* 77, no. 3 (September–October 1998): 40–51; Robert Forloney, NYC situation, personal correspondence, February 2007.

24. Henry C. Atyeo, *The Excursion as a Teaching Technique*, New York: Teachers College Press, 1939; Marguerite Bloomberg, "An Experiment in Museum Instruction," New Series, no. 8, 40, Washington, DC: American Association of Museums, 1929; Stephen F. Borhegyi, ed., The Modern Museum and the Community, paper presented at the International Congress of Anthropological and Ethnological Sciences, 1956; Katherine Gibson, "An Experiment in Measuring Results of 5th Grade Class Visits to an Art Museum," *School and Society* 21, no. 5 (1925): 658–662; Benjamin Gilman, "Museum Fatigue," *Scientific Monthly* 12, (1916): 62–74; Grace Fisher Ramsey, *Educational Work in Museums in the United States*, New York: H.W. Wilson, 1938.

25. E. S. Robinson, "The Behavior of the Museum Visitor," New Series, no. 5, Washington, DC: American Association of Museums, 1928; A. W. Melton, "Problems of Installation in Museums of Art," New Series, 14, Washington, DC: American Association of Museums, 1935; Chandler Screvan, "What Is Formative Evaluation?" in *Introduction to Formative Evaluation*, Washington, DC: American Association of Museums, 1974, pp. 59–68.

26. Howard Gardner, *Frames of Mind: The Theory of Multiple Intelligences*, New York: Basic Books, 1985.

27. Hein, *Learning in the Museum*, pp. 54–55.

28. Susan Nichols Lehman and Kathryn Igoe, eds., *Museum School Partnerships: Plans and Programs, Sourcebook no. 4*, Washington, DC: American Association of Museums, 1981.

29. Peter S. O'Connell and Mary Alexander, "Reaching the High School Audience," *Museum News* 58, no. 2 (November–December 1979): 50–56.

30. Newsom and Silver, *The Art Museum as Educator*.

31. Malcom S. Knowles, "Andragogy," in *Museums, Adults, and the Humanities*, ed. Zipporah W. Collins, Washington, DC: American Association of Museums, 1991, pp. 49–60; http://tip.psychology.org/Knowles.

32. Collins, *Museums, Adults, and the Humanities*; Bonnie Sachatello-Sawyer, Robert Fellenz, Laura Gittings-Carlson, Janet Lewis-Mahony, and Walter Woodbaugh, *Adult Museum Programs: Designing Meaningful Experiences*, Walnut Creek, CA: AltaMira Press, 2002. Reflects 1996–1999 study of museums' adult programs.

33. Hein, *Learning in the Museum*, p. 153.

34. McCarthy, "Cool Technology in a Ranger-led Tour."

35. Michael Kimmelman, "Museums in a Quandary: Where Are the Ideals?" *New York Times*, August 26, 2001; Neil Harris, *Cultural Excursions, Marketing Appetites and Cultural Tastes in Modern America*, Chicago, IL: University of Chicago Press, 1990; Neil G. Koder and Philip Koder, *Museum Strategy and Marketing: Designing Mission, Building Audiences, Generating Revenue and Resources*, San Francisco, Jossey-Bass, 1998.

36. Neil Harris, "Cultural Excursions: Marketing Appetites and Cultural Tastes in Modern America," *Museum News* 69, no. 5 (September–October 1990).

37. Matthews, "A Colonial Williamsburg Revolution"; Eric Foner, "The Historian in the Museum," *Museum News* 85, no. 2 (March–April 2006): 45–49; Edward Linenthal, *History Wars: The Enola Gay and Other Battles for the American Past*, New York: Metropolitan Books, 1996.

38. Stephen T. Asma, *Stuffed Animals and Pickled Heads: The Culture and Evolution of Natural History Museums*, Oxford, UK: Oxford University Press, 2001, p. 35; Hein, *Learning in the Museum*, p. 179.

39. Hein, *Learning in the Museum*, p. 139; Didier Maleuvre, "A Plea for Silence: Putting Art Back in to the Art Museum," in *Museum Philosophy for the 21st Century*, ed. Hugh H. Genoways, Lanham, MD: AltaMira Press, 2006, p. 167; Glenn D. Lowry, "A Deontological Approach to Art Museums and the Public Trust," in *Whose Muse? Art Museums and the Public Trust*, ed. James Cuno, Princeton University Press and Harvard University Press, 2004, p. 140.

40. Hein, Learning in the Museum, p. 149.

12

To Serve

A backward glance at museum development shows that museums only fully develop their potential for action when they are actually involved in the major problems of contemporary society. Museums are institutions intended to serve society and only thus can they continue to exist and function.

—Jan Jelinek, 1975[1]

In twenty-five years, museums will no longer be recognizable as they are now known. Many will have incorporated attributes associated with organizations that now are quite distinct from museums . . . the process has been and will continue to seem gradual and inevitable . . . the emerging hybrids will be embraced by the museum community . . . there is the opportunity for the changed museum to make a more revelant contribution to our society.

—Elaine Heumann Gurian, 1995[2]

A very important feature of the majority of museums today, in contrast to what characterized them in the mid-1940s, is the extent to which they have become visitor-centered.

—Kenneth Hudson, 1998[3]

The typical 19th-century museum with its emphasis on objects and specimens was sometimes a static and even forbidding place for the general public. It was dead quiet and could be musty; visitors felt constrained to talk in hushed tones there. In the 20th century, the rise of varied education and interpretation programs changed all that. Museums attracted hordes of visitors, many of them young and lively. A large portion of the museum staff began to give attention to people as well as objects. Museums began to look outward to their visitors (audiences) rather than focusing on their internal resources, especially their collections that were often rooted in 19th-century scholarship and practice. Some museums became community cultural centers; even dropping the word *museum* and adopting art, science, history, or heritage *center*. As the 21st century begins, this opening of the museum—whether gradual or abrupt—continues apace in small and large communities across the world.

This chapter and chapters 10 ("To Exhibit") and 11 ("To Interpret") discuss elements of museum interpretation—how museums convey their messages to visitors. Together, these three chapters provide a full picture of a museum's interpretive options.

The Changing Concept of "Museum"

When Theodore L. Low wrote *The Museum as a Social Instrument* for AAM's Committee on Education in 1942, he advocated that museums make popular education their predominant goal, superior to, but including, acquisitions, preservation, and scholarly study. He opposed having museums confine their attention to the upper strata of society and urged that they vigorously seek to serve "an intellectual middle class." He argued in the same general terms that John Cotton Dana had used in conceiving the Newark Museum as a vehicle for community pride and betterment.[4] Low, of course, could not have conceived how the 1960s would change the meaning of "social instrument," nor could he have anticipated the impact of the civil rights, anti–Vietnam War, and women's movements on the "establishment" and on all cultural institutions, including museums. His arguments for opening museums to broader audiences ended up with powerful support from social forces across the United States.

The transformation of many museums in the United States into cultural centers has not been universal, nor has it extended to poorer and underprivileged classes. A 1972 Harris Poll asked museum directors to evaluate the two museum purposes most important to themselves, the public, and the trustees, and to identify those purposes most successfully carried out by their institutions. "Encouraging of positive social change" ranked at the bottom of six suggested purposes in the directors' opinions and was ranked as most important by only 6 percent of the directors, 2 percent of the public, and 3 percent of the trustees, and most revealing, this goal was reported as successfully accomplished by only 3 percent of the museums surveyed.[5] Despite this 1972 snapshot of museums, the effort to make museums institutions of popular education, as Low had conceived them, was largely achieved within the 20th century.

About the same time as the Harris Poll, Brooklyn Museum director Duncan Cameron published his notions of a museum in the journal *Curator* and in the United Nations Educational, Scientific and Cultural Organization's (UNESCO) *Journal of World History*; his thesis was that museums occupy two ends of a spectrum from "temple" to "forum." He described the temple as representing the "victor's" resting place for spoils, while the forum was the site for engaging in "battles" of ideas. His essay is worth a close reading as it laid out what has become (and remains) a challenge to museum practice. He asserted that "museums must concern themselves with the reform and development of museums *as museums*. They must meet society's needs for that unique institution which fulfills a timeless and universal function—the use of the structured sample reality, not just as a reference but as an objective model against which to compare individual perceptions. . . . In the absence of the forum, the museum as temple stands alone as an obstacle to change. . . . From the chaos and conflict of today's forum the museum must build the collections which will tell us tomorrow who we are and how we got here. After all, that's what museums are all about."[6] Even a cursory review of the subsequent years of museum practices suggests that the tensions between temple and forum remain today.

In 1995 the International Council of Museums (ICOM) revised its definition of museum to read: "a non-profit making, permanent institution *in the service of society and of its development*, and open to the public, which acquires, conserves, researches, communicates and exhibits for the purposes of study, education and enjoyment, material evidence of people and their environment."[7] This broad-based definition reflected the reality of museum practice and propelled museums even further toward public service. In contrast, the American Association of Museums's (AAM) definition endured but the association convened a national task force to address the roles of museums. Its 1992 report *Excellence and Equity* called for museums to attend to their audiences and communities (another term for "society") as part of their professional practice. The report concluded with this charge: "The community of museums in the United States shares the responsibility with other educational institutions to enrich learning oppportunities for all individuals and to nurture an enlightened, humane citizenry that appreciates the value of knowing about its past, is resourcefully and sensitively engaged in the present, and is determined to shape a future in which *many experiences and many points of view are given voice* [emphasis added]."[8] Cameron's forum emerges as the desirable posture for U.S. museums.

As the century changed, the American Academy of Arts and Sciences summer 1999 issue of *Daedalus* sought to both define and project current American museum practices. Bonnie Pittman opened the essays with this overarching statement: "Museums are more than the repositories of the past, with memories and objects both rare and beautiful. Museums are cultural, educational, and civic centers in our communities—centers for exhibitions, conservation, research, and interpretation; they are theaters and movie houses, job-training programs, schools and day-care centers, libraries and concert halls . . . forums for their communities."[9] These essays like Cameron's, suggest that service to audiences trumps the traditional demands of collections and cements the museum solidly within communities. Stephen Weil closes his essay, "The Ongoing Transformation of the American Museum" noting "that it [the museum] is so potentially open-textured as a destination, so adaptable to a variety of public uses should not—at least in the emerging and visitor-centered museum—be regarded as a defect. Rather, it should be understood as one of its greater glories."[10] In a sense their discussions extend the thoughts of George Brown Goode, Dana, Low, and Cameron calling for museums to broaden their educational commitment.

Expanding Museum Practices

Early in the 20th century, the American librarian and museum director John Cotton Dana outlined eleven basic museum activities for what he described as the "New Museum."

1. Entertain—and be ready to try to interest and instruct—such as may have time to visit casually.
2. Entertain and more definitely and generally instruct—in classes and conducted groups, by labels, leaflets, handbooks, talks, and illustrated lectures [through exhibits and museum visits].

3. Entertain, interest, and still more definitely instruct children [through exhibitions and museum visits and in coordination with schoolwork and recognizing learning styles].

4. Prepare and lend to schools objects and groups of objects with related instructional aids designed to assist teachers.

5. In coordination with school system authorities, create changing exhibitions with related instructional aids to be placed in schools to entertain and instruct both teachers and students.

6. Open museum spaces or branch institutions with exhibitions featuring museum collections complete with staff to instruct visitors.

7. Discover collectors and specialists and experts in the community and secure their cooperation in adding to the museum's collections, in helping to identify, describe and prepare labels and leaflets; in arousing the interest of young people in the museum's work. . . . This development of the collecting habit among the young, with its accompanying powers of observation, its training in handwork, its tendency to arouse interests . . . leading toward sound civic interest through doing for one's community. . . .

8. Lend to individuals, groups, and societies for any proper use and for any reasonable length of time . . . museum's objects . . . [to] be of more service to the community than when they are resting, relatively unseen and unused, in the museum's headquarters.

9. Prepare and display, at the headquarters, at branches, and in schools carefully selected objects which are products of the community's activities in field, factory, and workshop. . . . These may be planned to attract and interest the business man, or to draw to them the women, or to arouse in young people a healthful curiousity in the activities of their community. . . .

10. Keep the museum and its activities continually before the community in the daily press, and publish and distribute as many leaflets, posters, broadsides, and cards descriptive of the museum's acquisitions as conditions seem to warrant.

11. Connect the work the museum may do, its objects, and all the activities of the staff, with all the resources of the public library.[11]

Travel around the world and you will find museums of all types and sizes practicing just what Dana outlined. His "advices" remain revelant except for changes in the language of new technologies and the recognition of the shrinking of the world through enhanced communications.

Museums and the Performing Arts

An editorial in the American Association of Museum's *Museum Work* in 1920 looked back over the previous quarter-century and reported that museums in this country had adopted, in order, the following practices: exhibition of objects and specimens, publication of popular bulletins, loans of duplicate materials, docent service, storytelling, music, and loans of rare objects.[12] If the writer could have looked ahead, he would doubtless have been astonished to see museums conducting theater programs; showing documentary, classic, and avant-garde films; hosting dance recitals, costume balls, and galas; and offering festivals, fairs, and assorted happenings.

It was natural for museums, with their spacious galleries and entrance halls, to offer musical concerts from time to time. By 1919, the Pennsylvania Academy for the Fine Arts was staging such events at the head of its main staircase, and art museums across the country had similar programs. The AAM at its annual convention in 1919 endorsed including music among the activities of art and other museums as an appropriate addition to their educational programs.[13] Toward the end of the 20th century as many museums added wings to their buildings, they often encorporated auditoriums or theaters for use in a variety of public programs from traditional lectures to musical and dramatic performances. Obviously, the performing arts offered the museum an opportunity to enhance its influence as a community cultural center. Otto Wittman, director of the Toledo Museum of Art, summed it up this way:

> In our largest metropolitan centers, there are theaters, concert halls, specialized art and music schools, as well as museums. However, along the Main Streets of most American cities . . . the museum is often the community's only cultural center. They give added dimension and meaning to the lives of many of us. They enrich and broaden our children's education. They are on the front lines of America's cultural growth.[14]

As Wittman notes, in most U.S. cities the museum also is a natural center for social events. Openings of special exhibits furnish occasions for lectures, performances, and parties. Many museums have added restaurants to serve staff, visitors, and indeed the whole community and may be used for private events. Some museums even add to their interpretation by serving food that reflects an exhibition's subject matter.

From Neighborhood to Community Museum

In the 1960s another approach to broadening the museum audience was to establish neighborhood branches. While this term has fallen into disuse in the United States, one of the earliest and most successful neighborhood branches was the Anacostia Neighborhood Museum created as a bureau of the Smithsonian Institution in 1967 to serve a predominantly black neighborhood in Washington, D.C. The Smithsonian provided financing (supplemented by federal and foundation funds) and expert consultation (when asked) for the new institution situated in an old movie theater. The planning and administration were left to the community through an advisory committee of local residents, but with its meetings open to everyone. John R. Kinard, social worker, minister, and Anacostia resident, became director of the museum and provided inspiring leadership for more than twenty years.

The museum assembled exhibits about African heritage, local history of Anacostia, and current urban problems. *The Rat: Man's Invited Affliction* was perhaps its most spectacular exhibit that traveled to other cities and was the subject of a television show. Centerpiece of the display were rats prowling about a large case strewn with discarded junk and garbage, and coming up to portholes where they could be viewed eye-to-eye. The exhibit made clear the life cycle of the rat; its evil role as destroyer of food, disease carrier, and attacker of small children; and how it could be controlled by community action for cleanliness, proper food storage, and building construction.

The museum was, however, much more than exhibits. It served as a cultural arts center with workshops in arts and crafts, had a useful small library and its own bus to transport children and exhibits, and lots of musical, dance, and dramatic performances. It also provided a meeting place for community groups, an urban planning center that distributed educational materials throughout the community, and a training facility that taught skills relating to design and fabrication of museum exhibits. In short, "the museum's role is to enliven the community and enlighten the people it serves."[15] The Anacostia Community Museum that opened nearly twenty years later replaced the movie theater site with purpose-built spaces for exhibitions and community programming. Today the formal name of the museum is the Anacostia Museum and Center for African American History and Culture, and the facility in the neighborhood is still called the community museum.

When the Brooklyn Children's Museum's two Victorian mansions were condemned in 1967, it decided, while awaiting construction of its new building, to open a neighborhood museum in a two-story converted automobile warehouse in the Stuyvesant–Crown Heights section of Brooklyn. Appealingly named MUSE, the project was to test the feasibility of setting up small neighborhood museums in the metropolitan area. The director, Lloyd Hezekiah, considered a museum to be a theater, rather than a cathedral or temple, and thus MUSE offered a rich variety of programs—planetarium shows, live animals, hands-on exhibits, science and craft demonstrations, puppet shows, music, dance, theater presentations, and take-home collections. Workshops for children and adults treated anthropology, astronomy, anatomy, dance, photography, art, poetry, consumer education, sex education, drug abuse, aviation, creative writing, theater, public speaking, music, and other subjects. In addition there were school group visits; traveling cases for classroom use; innovative exhibits, including space science and liquid-light mixing; and street festivals. The museum stationed its staff members near all this activity so as to help children and adults make the most of it.[16]

These two examples reflect the trend for larger, more established organizations to sponsor neighborhood-based museums. In other communities, community organizations created their own museum-like organizations, often adopting provocative names like "The New Thing Art and Architecture Center" or "Studio Watts Workshop."[17] Since their beginnings in the 1960s, community museums have developed across the United States; the bicentennial celebrations stimulated a flurry of these institutions. As with the neighborhood museums, they encorporated traditional museum activites such as school tours and exhibitions with literacy programs and well-baby classes. Just as Dana had reached out to Newark's immigrant populations at the start of the century, museums with an ethnic focus targeted new audiences for museums. African Americans, Hispanics, and Native Americans have come together to create museums to serve the needs of their communities. These museums have expanded and blurred traditional museum activities.[18]

Museum Outreach

A parallel development with neighborhood and branch museums were the efforts of some museums to reach out to serve new museum audiences both within the museum or in the surrounding communities. The best programs combined the efforts of the museum with the needs and interests of the audiences to be served. An example from New York City reveals the variety and creativity of such programming. In 1971 the Museum of the City of New York, once a traditional historical museum, began to stage community-oriented exhibitions and programs that addressed social problems. An exhibition, *The Drug Scene in New York*, represented the impact of drug addiction on the community; through the text and programming former addicts warned viewers of its perils. The exhibition created a sensation that was followed by an exhibition on venereal disease. In the museum's galleries a seventy-second clock rang loudly to remind visitors that someone contracts syphillis or gonorrhea that frequently, and free blood tests were offered.[19]

In 1990 the Boston Children's Museum (BCM) sought to expand its audience from its usual young children and their families to adolescents, especially those "at risk" through the *Kid's Bridge* program. The museum staff, social service agency workers, and school system representatives along with teenagers themselves molded the program to meet the needs of the teenagers. At the museum, teenage visitors encountered a specially designed exhibition space and museum-based activities. Outside the museum neighborhood-based activities were designed to teach life skills to young adults. The museum trained older students to serve as role models or mentors to younger ones and program activities took place not simply in the museum but across Boston's neighborhoods. This initiative—like most of BCM's efforts—engaged the intended audience in both identifying the issues and creating appropriate programs to address them. While the museum had always worked closely with schools in the past, in this instance it broadened its outreach efforts even more. From Boston, the *Kid's Bridge* exhibition component moved to the Smithsonian Insitution as part of a three-year national tour. But, it is in Boston that the outreach and social activism of the *Kid's Bridge* exhibition and programs took form.[20]

These discussions have focused on outreach for ethnic and minority populations, but many museums have reached out to a wide range of new audiences, including the disabled, nursing home residents, and other populations unable to take full advantage of museum programming. Museum educators often have been the initiators of these efforts, building on their traditions of connecting with teachers and a sense of community service. Budgetary restraints, especially in the United

States, more recently have limited museum outreach as museums require accountability for their programs. A review of outreach efforts at the end of the 20th century reveals a decline in that practice, but museums continue to partner with other museums and community organizations with joint programs and to expand museum spaces to satellite facilities.

Twenty-first-century Museum Forms

In the first section of this volume appear references to changing museum practices and vivid examples of growing public service within museums of all types. The expanded notion of museum audiences and the elevation of public service functions seem to have been institutionalized. Though Cameron doubted that museums could successfully combine the "temple" and "forum" functions, museums seem to have accomplished it to a considerable degree. But, there are some institutions that may serve as predictors for the museums of the future. These institutions are consciously and publicly striving to serve the public, as Elaine Heumann Gurian suggests "blurring" the boundaries between museums and other public service agencies. In discussing tribal community museums, Native American museum professional Karen Coody Cooper states: "In fact, many tribal cultural institutions refuse to use the term 'museum,' reinforcing the message that for some Native people the word carries negative connotations and strong associations with the egregious treatment Native communities received."[21] Some museums have described themselves and their initiatives as "museum different," and "unmuseum" to reassure and attract audiences. Snapshots of new museum practices are offered here, but the reader will learn even more from each museum's website.

The Field Museum

On the occasion of its centennial celebrations in 1993, Chicago's Field Museum (www.fieldmuseum.org) turned its considerable worldwide research resources on Chicago itself. The museum acknowledged its very location as a source for both its collections (upper-Midwest and the Plains) and its daily visitors. Creating the Center for Cultural Understanding and Change (CCUC), the museum focused on the city's diverse neighborhoods pursuing research, informal education programming, and outreach. Its first newsletter reported that the museum was moving away from "temples for contemplation of civilization's progress . . . into more open and inclusive public spaces."[22] The CCUC formally linked the Field with more than twenty community organizations through the Cultural Diversity Alliance creating cooperative programs and exhibitions both at the Field and across the city. It engaged young interns (undergraduate and graduate students) to pursue urban anthropology research to better understand the impact of community and place on the city and to address the larger implications for what it means to be an "American." As a result of these initiatives, in 2005 the Field created a new division of Environment, Culture, and Conservation (ECCo) institutionalizing the museum's commitment to urban research and programming issues. While the Field Museum continues to welcome more than a million visitors each year to see its exhibitions and participate in its programs, its profile has greatly sharpened within its host city. It functions both as temple and forum, at times blending the two.

MassMOCA

In 1986 Thomas Krens, then director of the Williams College Museum of Art (Massachusetts), was looking for space to show large works of art that did not fit within the museum galleries. Rather than beginning the usual building project, Krens looked for alternative spaces and encountered the mayor of North Adams (just five miles east of Williamstown) who was worrying about the city's future as he watched its last factory close. As the discussions developed, the museum and the town joined forces to create a most unusual art museum space that became known as MassMOCA (Massachusetts Museum of Contemporary Art). Opening in 1999, the museum inhabits more than twenty-five buildings along the streets and industrial alleys of North Adams, transforming a dying industrial town into an innovative center for the arts. There is certainly no sense of a "temple" edifice there. MassMOCA advertises itself as "an open platform" rather than a traditional museum box. Visitors to the museum can expect not only to see displays of art, but also to encounter artists—visual, cinematic, audio, and performing—creating their works both with and for the public. Because of MassMOCA, North Adams has become an important cultural tourism destination, bringing economic benefit to the community. Additionally, MassMOCA is an employer of the town's citizens, adding to the community's economic health. As the MassMOCA website (www.massMOCA.org) announces: "The arts create and bestow community identity. Identity rallies hope, productivity, pride and economic vibrancy. These are base conditions for a healthy community." MassMOCA adds another dimension to Cameron's "forum," (the Roman venue where citizens exchanged both goods and ideas) as it serves as a setting for citizens and visitors to interact within the context of the artistic process thereby enriching the museum visit.

Lower East Side Tenement Museum

Beginning in 1988, New York's Lower East Side Tenement Museum (www.tenement.org) offered public tours of the apartments at 97 Orchard Street. These tours focused on the conditions of actual immigrant families that lived there at the turn of the 20th century. From the outset the focus was on collecting and interpreting the urban, immigrant experience, not on collecting and preserving their objects. The museum did furnish the apartments with appropriate historically acurate materials, but the emphasis was on the personal histories of the residents. Costumed interpreters led the tours, engaging visitors in the details of the life experiences of different families at Orchard Street. Stimulated by visitors' post-tour comments, the staff sought to bring the stories of the tenement up to present-day immigration issues with give-and-take discussions that became known as "kitchen conversations." When a group of student visitors, who happened to be immigrants, mentioned that they arrived in New York without any kind of welcome or orientation to the city, the museum with the *New York Times* created an immigrant guide to the city in English, Spanish, and Chinese. Both of these museum activities reflect the institutional mission: "To promote tolerance and historical perspective through the presentation and interpretation of the variety of immigrant and migrant experiences on Manhattan's Lower East Side, a gateway to America." In 2005 the museum began a campaign to get the neighborhood designated a historic landmark district, the first such district that commemorates the urban, immigrant, working-class, and economically deprived experience. In addition to seeking landmark status, the museum is also working with local banks to revitalize the neighborhood through low-interest loans to landlords who agree to rehabilitate their properties and maintain affordable rents.[23]

In December 1999 the International Coalition of Historic Site Museums of Conscience (www.sitesofconscience.org) was created under the sponsorship of three American philanthropic foundations. The coalition formed around a commitment to "the obligation of historic sites to assist the public in drawing connections between the history of our site and its contemporary implications. We view stimulating dialogue on pressing social issues and promoting humanitarian and democratic values as our primay function." In addition to the Lower East Side Tenement Museum, the founding members were the Gulag Museum at Perm 36 (Russia), District Six Museum (South Africa), Liberation War Museum (Bangladesh), Workhouse (England), Project to Remember (Argentina), Slave House (Senegal), Terezin Memorial (Czech Republic), and the U.S. National Park Service. By 2006 the group had grown to thirteen and established standards for accreditation that are as direct as they are simple; the coalition is open to any museum which:

Works to interpret history through sites.
Engages in programs that stimulate dialogue on pressing social issues and promote humanitarian and democratic values as a primary function.
Shares opportunities for public involvement in issues raised at their sites.

In his essay, Duncan Cameron charges that "by failing to provide meaningful interpretation of the collections museums are, by that omission, guilty of misrepresentation, distortion of fact and encouragement of attitudes towards cultures other than our own which are dangerous and destructive.[24] Cameron could have been a contented time-traveler to the founding sessions of the sites of conscience coalition.

Ontario Science Centre

Celebrating thirty years of attracting visitors to its interactive, hands-on spaces and galleries in 2006, the Ontario Science Centre (www.ontariosciencecentre.ca) launched an assessment of its practices and developed a new way of doing business, especially in terms of its visitors. As part of the centre's anniversary, staff created a programmatic template "Agents of Change" to revitalize its practices. The recognition that the world of science information sources had enlarged exponentially since 1969, drove the process. From visitor research, especially focused on teenagers, staff discussions, and outreach to partners in business and the academy, the centre's new mission emphasizes engaging visitors as "partners," developing problem solving skills and innovation, and reaching beyond the centre's walls to influence Canadian attitudes toward science. The goal is to "move from being an attraction-based place to visit, to being a leader in building relationships beyond the site, beyond the visit."[25]

The exhibition spaces are being redesigned to meet these new approaches. The centre seeks to answer these questions: "Is it possible to influence the attitudes, skills and behaviors of an individual through his or her engagement at the science centre? If we can, then how do we create a platform for 21st-century innovation? What are the physical and dynamic conditions necessary to enable this to occur?"[26] The centre's teams have created seven clusters of exhibits. The cluster that seems to seek to engage visitors/partners most is the *Hot Zone*, which features multimedia elements exploring current scientific research through real-time field diaries and Internet connections with research projects worldwide. They plan to involve students directly in discussions of "hot" science topics. *Challenge Zone* provides visitors with everyday materials to solve a scientific "challenge" within a specified time limit. The focus is on problem solving, sometimes requiring visitors to partner with other visitors, who may be strangers. *Citizen Zone* provides a place where you can join up as a researcher for an ongoing research project. Current opportunities have focused on environmental monitoring either onsite or through webcams. Each of these elements brings the visitor (partner) into the exhibit space and into the ideas surrounding that space. And, the visitor directly affects his or her own experience. These activities suggest the constructivist museum philosophy, where the visitor is involved in actively making sense of the ideas, not simply passively observing what the museum presents. See chapter 11 for a discussion of constructivist museums.

The Eden Project

Southwest England is the home of a project that combines the research and educational emphasis of a botanical garden with the visitor-centered activities of a theme park along with ecological messages about our planet's future. Opened in 2001 after five years of planning, the Eden Project (www.edenproject.com) is situated in an abandonded china clay quarry. Well funded by the UK government and the European Union, the project aligns support for culture with economic development. Two spherical structures, "biomes," tower over visitors and offer "environments" for viewing plants, engaging with staff members, watching performances, listening to music, hearing stories, and looking at art. One biome re-creates the humid tropics, while the other mimics the warm temperate zone. A dry tropics biome is planned. "The Eden team attempts to fashion an experiential understanding that is as emotional, visual, kinetic and spiritual as it is linguistic or intellectual . . . visitors sometimes use Eden as a means of retrieving their own memories, of telling their own life stories or narrating critical incidents from their personal life." This description reflects the constructivist idea of learning experiences.[27]

A visitor's experience at Eden is "more than a botanic garden or good day out. The Project's interpretative and educative practice emphasizes intentionality, shaping conduct, altering cultural values and ways of thinking. It adapts the narrative template stressing interrelationships between plants, and human cultures."[28] One of Eden's interpretive practices known as "kissing," involves guides interacting with visitors casually and seemingly spontaneously, rather than making formal presentations about particular plants or vistas.[29] The site has grown into a "must see" venue for Cornwall vacationers, drawing more than a million visitors a year, well beyond the expected 750,000. Staff report that they strive to offer visitors more than a "green theme park," basing their exhibits on sound science while also developing public programs that reflect current thinking on how people learn. To remain true to the core value of ecological responsibility, a new initiative includes retrofitting the site's mechanical systems with the most ecologically sensitive equipment, and discussions are underway about how to handle the volume of automobile traffic and requisite parking to mitigate impacting the site (and its environs). Though nontraditional in its approaches to visitors, the project maintains a commitment to scientific research and to education in spite of using practices often associated with entertainment.

An Imagined Museum

Professor Simon Knell in the *Museum and Society* article, "The Shape of Things to Come: Museums in the Technological Landscape," offers this profile of how a museum might evolve; his setting is Britain, but the idea seems applicable elsewhere:

> The museum, then, is unlikely to be replaced by a digital entity. . . . Technologies tend to sit side by side, each ideal for its own task. . . . Let me use

a traditional small town museum somewhere in the English midlands to explain what I mean. This museum is run by a small team, and occupies [an] old building with more space than it can maintain. The visitor experience consists of poorly interpreted objects of a kind seen in many local museums in Britain. . . . The staff are imaginative but there is clearly too little revenue. . . . on my last visit, there in the corner of one of the galleries, I noticed an old photograph of some ancient urns still in the ground. The picture was from the early twentieth century and showed a street not far away. . . . Next to the photograph was one of the pots. Here was an interpreted object, an object which speaks of the historical event of its discovery, and of the deep past it exposed. Suddenly this pot becomes real, concrete and powerful. . . . Perhaps a better future for this museum is to slim down the enterprise, to put the most important material into compact storage, reduce the size of the buildings and physical holdings, and make a major commitment to online interpretation—narratives and reference materials—and digital collecting. A temporary exhibition space or two could be created and used to cycle themed and well-interpreted displays, support school visits and act as a venue for community activities. If these complementary resources are sold to schools, and better commercial use is made of the photographic archive . . . a more sustainable and effective museum is created. The audience is extended, technologies and institutions are working in a complementary fashion, and the real, by this means, also gains a more secure future.[30]

Knell's scenario accentuates a museum's strengths, while using new technologies to extend its reach to audiences, both known and new.

Globalism

In the first decade of the 21st century, the world continues to shrink for museums and their visitors, too. At the close of the 20th century, Marcia Lord in the journal *Museum International* reminded us that regardless of a museum's size, through the World Wide Web museums could reach many more "visitors" than they would ever welcome through their doors. Size no longer seemed important.[31] In another way, museums are reaching around the globe through satellite museums that bring collections from one country to another without requiring any special partnerships (or loan forms). In the past the mention of the Guggenheim Museum evoked images of Frank Lloyd Wright's building on Fifth Avenue in New York; today it refers to another spectacular building in Spain, a collection in Venice, a gallery (with the Russian

State Hermitage) in Las Vegas, and gallery space in Deutsche Bank in central Berlin. From San Francisco, the Exploratorium has reached out through the Internet since 1993 to cybervisitors, others planning museum exhibitions, and teachers in their classrooms to encourage better teaching of scientific principles. Outside Paris, the Cite des Sciences et de l'Industrie at La Villette works beyond its exhibition spaces to link with other European Science Centers through an international organization, European Network of Science Centers and Museums (ECSITE) that shares information, exhibitions, and research into museum practices and science education.[32] The Internet makes these linkages simple, inexpensive, and valuable to both museum staff and their visitors (both actual and virtual). In a recent *Curator*, designer Tom Hennes describes the potential for these linkages for natural history museums: "Each museum inhabits an important and unique position in such a network, linking to a series of other networks—communities of visitors; educational systems; communities in areas under study, evaluation or protection; nongovernmental organizations; governments; and other museums. Moreover, the museum links them not only to *itself*, but to each other. This is important because those links allow new clusters of individuals and organizations within the aggregated network to interact and share their own knowledge across it. Agency is not driven solely to and from the museum; they can arise spontaneously as well and in many unpredictable, new directions."[33]

When the next edition of this volume is written, perhaps it won't even appear on paper, but rather be made accessible through new communications systems. And, updates to the text will be provided by virtual readers. As George Hein once warned: "write fast, Mary, the world as you know it is changing very fast."

Challenges

Post-colonial Museums

Art historian Carol Duncan writes about the universal museums that emerged in the 19th century to display objects acquired often through conquest. As the world shrinks, what's to become of such institutions? Several threads are emerging that may, in the long-term, become trends. In Washington, D.C., the Smithsonian's National Museum of the American Indian presents itself as a setting where Native Americans come together to exhibit their culture in their own ways and to serve their communities that were for so long represented by others. As the museum's first director liked to describe the museum as it was being developed, it is a "museum different."[34] Across the Atlantic in France and Sweden are two new museums representing the culture of domi- nated peoples in very different ways. In Paris, the Musee du Quai Branly recently opened at the foot of the Eiffel Tower, showcasing objects from Musee des Arts Africains and Oceaniens and the Musee de l'Homme's ethnographic collections. The MQB as it is being called by the locals, displays these objects as "jewels" within an elaborate presentation box for visitors to admire. However, in addition to those visiting to see the new museums, the MQB is attracting a new audience, unanticipated by planners. Young continental French with noncontinental parentage are flocking to the museum to see objects that could have been owned or used by their grandparents often from lands they have never seen. They are using the museum to understand their cutural identities.[35] To the north in Gothenburg, Sweden, the Museum of World Culture opened in December 2004 to provide Swedes and Scandinavians with a view of other cultures. The museum's mission is: "In dialogue with others, The Museum of World Culture is a forum for emotional and in- tellectual encounters that help people feel at home wherever they are, trust each other and accept joint responsibility for the planet's con- stantly changing future."[36] Its exhibitions and programs are being de- veloped collaboratively with a representative of the culture it seeks to describe and understand. Like the neighborhood museum movement in the United States in the 1960s, the museum has brought in its audi- ences to help provide both authenticity and hegemony. Each of these approaches suggests a sea change in how museums present the cul- tural patrimony of subjugated people. How will they influence other more traditional museums holding such collections?

Research

If the emphasis of museums is public service, what forms of research are necessary to support such activities? In Chicago, The Field Museum is using its youthful neighbors to study its own environs, while in Toronto, the Ontario Science Centre is not only researching the concept of innovation, but also studying how it can promote innovation within both its staff and visitors. With such a public mission, what role should museums assume in conducting basic research? Is this a task that should be done in partnership with others—the academy, business, or government? The answers to these questions not only affect the museum, but also the academic training of staff.

Authority

As museums become more audience centered, they assume a new important role in empowering their audiences. Brazilian ICOM chair Maria de Lourdes Horta describes the process: "A museum without walls and without objects, a true virtual museum, is being born in some of those communities, which look in wonder to their own process of self-discovery and recognition. . . . For the moment, in my country, [museums] are being used in a new way, as tools for self-expression, self-recognition, and representation; as spaces of power negotiation among social forces; and as strategies for empowering people so that they are more able to decided their own destiny."[37] This empowerment becomes complex as diverse audiences join museums as partners and decision makers. As curator Jan Ramirez noted elsewhere, when new voices join the discussions, those already represented can be threatened. See challenges in chapter 10.

Authenticity

Dialogue overheard between grandmother and granddaughter visiting Rome: "So, Grandma, is this real, or is it Disneyland?"[38] Recent public surveys reveal that the public "is hard pressed to tell the difference between museums, exhibits in department stores or airports, and historic districts or theme parks."[39] Simon Knell suggests that museums continue to do what museums do best, leaving others to complement the museum with technology and with what might be called "entertainment." This challenge seems especially important as museums reach out to attract and engage new audiences, perhaps for the first time. Research, authenticity, and protecting collections are museum activities that require skill and attention, in addition to time, all activities that may be foreign to new constituents.[40]

Collections

A 2005 Heritage Preservation Heritage Health Index and the Netherland's Delta Project testify to the current needs of museum collections. How does a museum balance those needs with its interests in serving the public? Of special impact is the addition of new collections to current holdings, adding even more pressure and expense to those museum activities. Adding storage space may be the easy part, and ensuring that the museum has the research and intellectual tools to understand the collections may be both more complex and costly.

Cultural Tourism

The caves of Lascaux in France have been closed to visitors for nearly fifty years to preserve the ancient wall art that was threatened by changes in atmospheric conditions caused by visitors. This is an extreme case, but worldwide communication and inexpensive travel bring more and more visitors to cultural venues from museums to ancient sites. Their very presence changes the nature of the experience for both the visitor and the site. Admission fees, reservations, and timed ticketing are becoming more and more common. These practices at best control crowding, but at worst limit public access.

Measures of Success

In the 1980s American museums created outreach programs to serve visitors who did not traditionally visit museums. In addition to creating programs in the museum for these groups, museums offered programming outside the museum to reach those populations unable to visit. While these programs were popular with the new constituents, their longevity was short-lived as museums struggled with measuring both their effectiveness and their value to the museum's mission. It's easy to measure the success of a museum's exhibition or program by counting visitors, but how does a museum evaluate its public service efforts? How does it judge where best to put its resources?

Notes

1. Jan Jelinek, *Museum* 25, nos. 1–2 (1975): 112.
2. Elaine Heumann Gurian, "A Blurring of Boundaries," *Curator* 38, no. 1 (1995): 31.
3. Kenneth Hudson, "The Museum Refuses to Stand Still," *Museum International* 50, no. 1 (1998): 46.
4. Theodore L. Low, *The Museum as a Social Instrument*, New York: American Association of Museums, 1942, pp. 20, 29–36; Theodore L. Low, *The Educational*

Philosophy and Practice of Art Museums in the United States, New York, 1946. For criticism of Low's thesis and his rebuttal, see Wilcomb E. Washburn, "The Museum's Responsibility in Adult Education," *Curator* 7 (1964): 33–38 and "Scholarship and the Museum," *Museum News* 40 (October 1961): 16–19; Theodore L. Low, "The Museum as a Social Instrument: 20 Years Later," *Museum News* 40 (January 1962): 28–30; Joel J. Orosz, epilogue to *Curators and Culture: The Museum Movement in America, 1740–1870*, Tuscaloosa: University of Alabama Press, 1990, pp. 248–256.

5. *Museums USA*, Washington, DC: National Endowment for the Arts, 1973, pp. 25–35.

6. Duncan Cameron, "The Museum, a Temple or the Forum," *Journal of World History* 14, no. 1, pp. 189–204; Gail Anderson, ed., *Reinventing the Museum: Historical and Contemporary Perspectives on the Paradigm Shift*, Walnut Creek, CA: AltaMira Press, 2004.

7. Kenneth Hudson, *Museums of Influence*, Cambridge, UK: Cambridge University Press, 1987, pp. 15–17.

8. *Excellence and Equity: Education and the Public Dimension of Museums*, Washington, DC: American Association of Museums, 1992, p. 25.

9. Bonnie Pittman, "Muses, Museums and Memory," *Daedalus*, Summer 1999, p. 1; Ellen Hirzy et al., *Mastering Civic Engagement: A Challenge to Museums*, Washington, DC: American Association of Museums, 2002.

10. Stephen E. Weil, "The Ongoing Transformation of the American Museum," *Daedalus*, Summer 1999, p. 254; Glenn D. Lowry, "A Deontological Approach," in *Whose Muse? Art Museum and Public Trust*, ed. James Cuno, Princeton University Press and Harvard University Press, 2004, p. 143.

11. The New Museum Series, no. 1, The Elm Tree Press, Woodstock, VT, 1917 [in *The New Museum*, Selected Writings of John Cotton Dana, American Association of Museums and the Newark Museum, 1999, pp. 27–28]; Richard Grove, "Pioneers in American Museums: John Cotton Dana," *Museum News* 57, no. 3 (May–June 1978).

12. *Museum Work* 2 (February 1920): 130.

13. *Museum Work* 2 (February 1920): 29–30, 145–160; *Museum Work* 7 (March–April 1925): 163–172; Winifred E. Howe, *A History of the Metropolitan Museum of Art*, 2 vols., New York, 1913, 1946, 2:144–149.

14. Otto Wittman, "Museums at the Crossroads," *Museum News* 44 (September 1965): 19.

15. *Museums: Their New Audience*, Washington, DC: American Association of Museums, 1972, pp. 32, 52–53; Caryl Marsh, "A Neighborhood Museum That Works," *Museum News* 47 (October 1968): 11–16; John R. Kinard and Esther Nighard, "The Anacostia Neighborhood Museum," *Museum* 24 (1972): 102–109; John Kinard, "To Meet the Needs of Today's Audience," *Museum News* 50 (May 1972): 15–16; Dillion Ripley, *The Sacred Grove*, New York: Simon & Schuster, 1969, pp. 104–111; Zora Martin-Felton and Gail S. Lowe, *A Different Drummer: John Kinard and the Anacostia Museum*, Washington, DC: Smithsonian Institution, 1992.

16. *Museums: Their New Audience*, Washington, DC: American Association of Museums, 1972, pp. 36, 73–76; Lloyd Hezekiah, "Reflections on MUSE," *Museum News* 50 (May 1972): 12–14.

17. *Museums: Their New Audience*.

18. Lonnie G. Bunch, "The Fire This Time: Race, Memory, and the Museum," *Museum News* 84, no. 6 (2005); Christy S. Coleman, "African American Museums in the 21st Century," in *Museum Philosophy for the 21st Century*, ed. Hugh H. Genoways, Lanham, MD: AltaMira 2006, pp. 151–160.

19. Joseph Veach Noble, "Drug Scene in New York," *Museum News* 50 (November 1971): 10–15; "The City Museum in a New Role Offers Multimedia V. D. Exhibit," *New York Times*, March 25, 1974; *Museums: Their New Audience*, pp. 31, 36–37, 50–51, 70–72.

20. *Annual Report*, Boston Children's Museum, 2003.

21. Karen Coody Cooper, *Living Homes for Cultural Expression*, Washington, DC: National Museum of the American Indian, Smithsonian Institution, 2005, p. 9.

22. Alaka Wali and Madeleine Tudor, "Introduction: Understanding Civic Activism and City Life," *Perspectives in Civic Activism and City Life* 1, (Summer 2000): ii.

23. Ruth J. Abram, president Lower East Side Tenement Museum, Preservation and the Restoration of Conscience Conference remarks, October 16, 2005; Maggie Russell-Ciardi, "Place-based Education in an Urban Environment," *Museum International* 58, no. 3 (2006): 71–77.

24. Cameron, "The Museum, a Temple or the Forum," p. 196.

25. Lesley Lewis and Jennifer L. Martin, "Science Centers: Creating a Platform for 21st Century Innovation," in *Museum Philosophy for the 21st Century*, pp. 107–116.

26. Lewis and Martin, "Science Centers," p. 112.

27. John Blewett, "The Eden Project—Making a Connection," *Museum and Society* 2, no. 3 (November 2004): 180.

28. Blewett, "The Eden Project," p. 178.

29. Blewett, "The Eden Project," p. 179.

30. Simon Knell, "The Shape of Things to Come: Museums in the Technological Landscape," *Museum and Society* 1, no. 3 (November 2003): 141, with permission; James Cuno, ed., *Whose Muse? Art Museum and Public Trust*, Princeton, NJ: Princeton University Press, 2004, p. 153.

31. Marcia Lord, "Editorial," *Museum International* 51, no. 4 (1999): 3.

32. www.ecsite.net.

33. Tom Hennes, "Hyperconnection: Natural History Museums, Knowledge, and the Evolving Ecology of Community," *Curator* 50, no. 1 (January 2007): 106.

34. W. Richard West, *Washington Post*, August 2, 2004.

35. Caroline Brothers, "For Some, a Museum Hits Close to the Heart," *International Herald Tribune*, August 18, 2006; Alan Riding, "Imperialist? Moi? Not

the Musee du Quai Branly," *New York Times*, June 22, 2006; Helen Rees Leahy, "A World Apart: Musee Quai Branly," *Museum Practice*, Winter 2006, pp. 12–17.

36. Cajsa Lagerkvist, "Empowerment and Anger: Learning How to Share Ownership of the Museum," *Museum and Society* 4, no. 2 (July 2006): 52–66; Helen Coxall, "Open Minds: Inclusive Practice," in *Museum Philosophy for the 21st Century*, pp. 139–149.

37. Maria de Lourdes Horta, *Museums for a New Millennium: A Symposium for the Museum Community*, Washington, DC: Smithsonian Institution and American Association of Museums, 1997, pp. 107–108 [quoted in Weil, *Daedalus*].

38. Leni Preston, personal communication, 2007.

39. Randolph Starn, "A Historian's Brief Guide to New Museum Studies," *American Historical Review* 110, no. 1 (February 2005): 91.

40. Knell, "The Shape of Things to Come," pp. 132–146.

13

The Museum Profession

[Museum directors] are well educated, but not primarily scholars . . .
not much given to writing books. They are essentially communica-
tors and organizers whose main interest lies in making their collections and exhibitions attractive and interesting to the general public.
. . . They are super-energetic, enterprising, sociable, friendly people,
with wide interests, who spend a lot of time on the shop floor with
their customers.

—Kenneth Hudson, 1998[1]

Ours is one of the few professions which is charged with being relevant both for today's people and for those who will come after us.
We stand as a link between the past and the future, and it is our duty
to be a strong link.

—Joseph Veach Noble, 1970[2]

Museum Directors, more than other people, ought to think hard and
often about what they are doing and why. Most don't.

—Nelson Goodman, 1983[3]

A museum employee in the United States who applies for a passport to
travel abroad is in a quandary when filling out the blank for "Occupa-
tion." To list *director, curator, registrar,* or *educator* obviously is not specific enough. To choose art historian, historian, or scientist may be a bit
pretentious; so one falls back on *museum director, museum scientist,* or

museum educator, and all appears fitting. Perhaps this very process suggests that a museum profession exists. Of course, Albert E. Parr was right when he argued that museums encompass "a plurality of professions."[4] They hire administrators, art historians, historians, scientists, educators, exhibit designers, editors, registrars, librarians, public relations directors, and many other specialists. But so do universities, industries, and businesses. In our complex culture, numerous workers follow more than one calling; thus a person trained in history may be at once a member of the historical, museum, university teaching, and historic preservation professions and an archivist, librarian, or other related specialist. Museum professionals do not keep their roles as separate as did Chekhov when he wrote: "Medicine is my lawful wife, literature my mistress. When I am tired of the one, I spend a night with the other."

What Is a Profession?

The fact that museum studies courses have multiplied and that frequent references are made to "the museum profession" does not mean, as Dr. Parr seemed to think, that someone is "attempting to homogenize our careers and force us all into the mold of a single profession."[5] Directors, curators, educators, designers, and other museum professionals will always have varied specialties, just as doctors and lawyers do. The paramount essence of the museum profession is a common cause and goals. Objects and their stories are important, whether artistic, historical, or scientific, and well-tested standards have been developed for their collection, conservation, and interpretation. A professional must, of course, possess specialized knowledge usually acquired after intensive academic or equivalent training. American museums have greatly increased their professionalism by improving their published literature, adopting standards for museum practice, proposing guidelines for museum training courses, and agreeing upon an internal code of ethics. These and many other endeavors have been encouraged chiefly through the American Association of Museums (AAM) and the United Nations Educational, Scientific and Cultural Organization's (UNESCO) International Council of Museums (ICOM) provides international leadership from its headquarters in Paris.[6]

Other professional organizations touch upon the museum field and enlist loyal followers with specific professional interests. The American

Association for State and Local History (AASLH) began as a committee of the more academic American Historians Association in the 1930s with activities such as annual meetings, publications, seminars, and panels of consultants to serve history museums, especially the small ones. Subgroups of museum workers joined together forming the American Association of Art Museum Directors (AAMD), the College Art Association, the National Trust for Historic Preservation, the Directors of Systematic Collections, the Association of Science Museum Directors, and more recently, the Museum Education Roundtable, the Association of Science-Technology Centers (ASTC), and the Association of Children's Museums (ACM).[7] In addition to regular publications, these organizations offer annual conferences, training workshops and seminars, internships, and other training opportunities, often with grants from national agencies and private foundations.

American Association of Museums

As it emerged, the museum profession has had two main objectives—internally to build a sense of unity in the institutions and individuals that comprise it, and externally to secure recognition and aid from the general public, philanthropic foundations, businesses, and federal, state, and municipal governments. The AAM, founded in 1906, organized with both institutional and individual members, strives to raise professional standards. In the United States museums are highly independent and individualistic, with diverse subject-matter fields and of varied size and financial strength. Museum workers of differing backgrounds are generalists in small museums but highly specialized experts in the larger ones—curators, educators, designers, conservators, and many others. To weld these divergent, sometimes clashing, institutions and their creative, often opinionated, individuals into a profession has not been easy.

From the first, the AAM held an annual meeting, established working committees, and issued publications. In 1923 it received a three-year challenge grant from the Laura Spellman Rockefeller Memorial and established a paid staff at headquarters at the Smithsonian Institution. For the next thirty-five years, the association, with the scholarly Laurence Vail Coleman as its director, gathered data on American museums, initiated programs such as those that established so-called trailside museums in national and state parks, and conducted research on audience responses to exhibits. Six "conferences" or satellite groups of the association formed representing regional interests: New England (1919); Midwest (1928); Western (1942); Northeast, now Mid-Atlantic (1947); Southeast (1951); and Mountain Plains (1954). Until 1951, foundations (chiefly the Laura Spellman Rockefeller Memorial and Carnegie Corporation of New York) paid about one-half the association's operating budget and took care of the research and publishing costs of its books. At the close of its fiftieth year, the association had 620 institutional and 1,625 individual members paying dues totaling twenty-seven thousand dollars.[8]

Joseph Allen Patterson, director from 1958 to 1967, brought to the association his promotional experience from the Museum of Modern Art and made the organization "far more vigorous than one would have dreamed from its relatively quiet existence . . . for many, many years."[9] Patterson transformed *Museum News* into a first-rate magazine; he established a useful *Museums Directory* for North America. He energized the regional conferences, visiting their sessions regularly; set up museum training seminars; hosted foreign museum professionals; arranged annual meetings of museum trustees; sponsored group trips to Europe, and opened discussions to create a program to accredit museums. Most promising of all, he appeared before congressional committees that secured the National Museum Act and included museums in the legislation leading to the establishment of the National Endowments for the Arts and Humanities.[10] Patterson's initiatives have been pursued by able leadership in AAM's central offices in Washington, D.C. Funds for museum projects have been secured through the National Science Foundation, the National Museum Act, the National Endowments for the Arts and Humanities, and other federal agencies. In 1975 the association helped secure authorization of an Institute of Museum Services in the Department of Health, Education, and Welfare to fund museum operating expenses.[11] In 1997 the Institute of Museum Services (IMS) joined with the nation's libraries to become the Institute of Museum and Library Services (IMLS). In 1977 association membership totaled 5,583 with 1,194 institutions; 3,512 individuals; 315 libraries; 422 trustees; and 140 foreign members, and dues collected for the previous year exceeded 352,000 dollars.[12]

With solid, reliable federal funding that is often complemented with support from state agencies, museums across the United States have flourished. AAM's leadership has addressed professional issues such as a code of ethics, encouraged professionalization through both its accreditation and assessment programs, and continued to publish *Mu-*

seum News and other topical texts from time to time. At the end of the 20th century, the association turned its attention to reviewing and refining its purposes through a national commission on Museums for a New Century. Inviting the public to join conversations about museum practices, the commission's report, issued in 1984, reflected public expectations that museums should continue to protect their collections for the "public good"; provide learning experiences for visitors of all ages, not simply children on school trips; and that as public institutions they should strive to diversify their staff to reflect the nation's changing demographic profile.[13] The commission's work was followed by a national task force to address issues of the growing diversity of U.S. communities and how museums should position themselves to address their changing audience(s). The task force issued its report *Excellence and Equity* in 1992.[14] See chapter 11 for a full discussion of the report's recommendations. As AAM celebrated its centennial in 2006, its membership totaled 2,762 institutional members and 13, 998 individual members with an annual budget of over 9 million dollars.[15]

Code of Ethics

Most professions pride themselves on possessing a system of principles and rules, self-enforced and peculiar to their calling. What is usually referred to as a code of ethics takes its place somewhere between the dictates of ordinary morality and the actual laws of the land. One can also argue that a great portion of an ethical code is unwritten in that it must be applied to situations that arise spontaneously and are not covered clearly by statements previously set down.

The AAM adopted a code of ethics unanimously at its twentieth annual meeting in 1925, but for many years it was largely forgotten. It set forth principles to be followed by the museum and its personnel. Some of its injunctions—for example, museum workers must not accept commissions or gifts from businesses, museums should refuse to acquire objects obtained through vandalism, and trustees must be discreet in discussing administrative and executive matters with staff members—are still relevant today.[16]

About fifty years later, the association appointed a committee to examine ethical questions relating to museums and museum personnel. The committee report was adopted, again unanimously, at the association's 1978 annual meeting. That code of ethics first considered the collection—the need for its physical care and conservation, the avoidance of acquiring objects illegally excavated or stolen and smuggled from their country of origin, and the proper disposal of objects in museum collections. Appraisals, commercial use, availability of collections, truth in presentation, and the use of human remains and sacred objects were also examined. Each museum was urged to develop and make public a statement of policy for each of these areas.[17] Following adoption of this profession-wide code, interest groups within AAM created their own codes that focused on those issues of particular importance to their professional practices; for example, the museum educator's code stressed the responsibility to present accurate interpretation, respecting the perspectives of a museum's diverse audiences.

In 1990 AAM again addressed ethical issues, creating a new code of ethics to complement those of earlier years. While other codes had been unanimously agreed upon by both the association's leadership and members, this version opened a fierce debate around the use of funds gained from the sale of collections. The tradition had been that collections funds were to be restricted to the purchase of collections; leaders of the history museum community vehemently opposed this section of the code as too restrictive. They argued that history museums often responsibly deaccession objects that no longer meet the museum's mission and that funds from the sale of collections therefore should be restricted to collections care, not simply to future purchase of additional collections. After nearly a year of debate at both national and regional professional meetings, the language was modified to broaden the potential use of funds from the sale of collections. AAM's new code went into effect in 1993; along with the code, the association created a formal permanent Committee on Ethics and within the accreditation process required individual museums to have a code of ethics to guide both board and staff.[18]

A code of ethics is highly desirable, both for its educational effect on trustees, director, and staff and for its reassurance to the public. It is far better for the profession to consider, agree upon, and enforce ethical principles and rules rather than letting a state attorney general, acting in his or her capacity as supervisor of charitable trusts, seek legislative regulation. The increasingly public nature and accountability of museums have made the code both desirable and necessary.

Accreditation

A most important step in strengthening the museum profession was the decision of the American Association of Museums to create a program to accredit museums that met accepted standards. A panel of leading museum officials worked with the Federal Council on the Arts and Humanities to produce *America's Museums: The Belmont Report* in 1968 for President Lyndon Johnson. It called for limited federal support for museums and urged "that the American Association of Museums and its member institutions develop and agree upon acceptable criteria and methods of accrediting museums." U.S. Representative John Brademas of Indiana, in an address to the association's annual meeting in 1969, said: "The museum community should develop standards of accreditation against which the excellence of individual museums can be measured. Federal support should not be provided to museums which do not reach a level of quality accepted in the museum field."[19]

The AAM appointed a committee to study accreditation, and its plan was adopted in 1970 and a semi-independent accreditation commission was created. The accreditation process begins with an individual museum conducting a rigorous self-examination of its administration, curatorship, exhibitions, interpretive program, and organizational planning. It answers a long and searching questionnaire devised by the commission composed of experienced museum leaders appointed by the association. If the answers to the questionnaire are satisfactory, the commission sends an onsite evaluation committee of two or more museum professionals to verify the facts by talking with museum board and staff members and examining the plant and procedures. After reviewing the questionnaire and visiting committee report, the commission would then grant accreditation; table it for a maximum of one year, while specific weaknesses were corrected; or refuse it entirely.

For the purposes of accreditation, a museum is defined as "an organized and permanent nonprofit institution, essentially educational or aesthetic in purpose, with professional staff, which owns and utilizes tangible objects, cares for them, and exhibits them to the public on some regular schedule."[20] Accreditation means that a museum meets this definition and the accepted standards of the profession, without presuming to distinguish among various grades of achievement or excellence beyond the established minimums. The commission's original definition of a museum as one "which owns and utilizes tangible objects" offended planetariums, art and science and technology centers, and children's museums. The definition was broadened to include "owns or utilizes" in 1988 and since then they have begun to be accredited. As of 2005 the basic criteria is "institutions that use and interpret objects and/or sites for public presentation of regularly scheduled programs and exhibits."[21] The accreditation commission steadily has refined and improved its materials and procedures, giving special attention to training visiting committee members so as to secure more uniform results. Reaccreditation has been instituted for museums, requiring an update every ten years with a simpler process than used for the original accreditation.

As of 2006, 771 museums have been accredited. For the year 2005—as a snapshot of the process—103 museums sought accreditation and of those, 58 received accreditation, 5 were rejected, 22 were tabled for further review and 18 were not judged based on an incomplete review or other circumstance.[22] When these figures are compared with the total of more than sixteen thousand museums reported by the American Association of Museums, it is clear that while considerable progress is being made, the program has not met the needs of the majority of U.S. museums. The accreditation process has done much to establish generally accepted standards for museums, to increase public respect for them, and to create a sense of pride in the museum profession. The greatest problem facing the program remains greater museum participation.[23]

To complement accreditation, with the support of IMS, in 1981 AAM began to offer a series of "assessments" for individual museums not yet ready to apply for accreditation, known as the museum assessment program or MAP. The MAP assessment begins with a self-study not unlike accreditation, followed by senior museum professionals visiting the museum to review and discuss its practices. Following the visit, the review team writes a report with suggestions for improvements. While the accreditation process is like a "final exam," the MAP process provides museums with peer guidance on how to capitalize on institutional strengths and address weaknesses. Today there are four assessments available: Institution (IMAP), Collections Management (CMAP), Public Dimension (PDA), and Governance (GMAP). As of 2006, the association had conducted fifty-five hundred assessments; they are especially valued by museums with modest budgets. The assessments not only prepare museums for future accreditation, but also nurture professional attitudes among staff, the all-important volunteers, and boards of trustees.[24]

International Council of Museums

The movement of American museum workers toward professionalism has been assisted by international developments. In 1946 UNESCO was constituted, and it promptly set up a Museums Division, and partially subsidized the nongovernmental International Council of Museums (ICOM), also organized in 1946. ICOM established national committees that have grown to number 111 around the world, and 30 international committees devoted to subjects such as archaeology and history, education, outdoor museums, costume, regional museums, and security.[25]

Museums were seen as an especially valuable avenue for international communication in a world of hundreds of languages and dialects, as well as widespread illiteracy. Georges Salles of France, president of ICOM, put it well in 1956:

> UNESCO's aim is to bring people together through cultures and the exchange of their spiritual heritage. And museums are most advantageously placed to help in the good work. They are the only place in the world where, with the object as interpreter, a language is spoken that everyone can understand.[26]

Dr. Grace L. McCann Morley, on leave as director of the San Francisco Museum of Art, in 1946 was counselor for the UNESCO Preparatory Commission and then for two years was in charge of the Museums Division. Chauncey L. Hamlin, president of the Buffalo Museum of Science and a past president of the American Association of Museums, was ICOM's first president. Georges-Henri Riviere of the Musee de l'Homme in Paris was director, from 1947 to 1965, and then became its permanent adviser.

UNESCO in 1948 began to publish *Museum*, today *Museum International*, in French and English. Its purpose is "to serve as a medium for the exchange of professional opinion and technical advice, to provide a stimulus to museums and museum workers in the development of their services to society; it would strive to reach a worldwide audience beyond the confines of continental Europe; and it would support UNESCO's aims by enlisting museum professionals in the common task of spreading knowledge and promoting international understanding as a positive contribution to peace."[27]

UNESCO and ICOM created a documentation center in Paris that attempted to gather all important museum publications. The International Centre for the Study of Preservation and Restoration of Cultural Property (known as the Rome Centre) was opened in 1977. The triennial conferences begun in 1948 enabled museum leaders from around the world to know each other and to inspect firsthand the museums of the regions where the meetings were held. The international committees have hosted meetings and training seminars around the world, enhancing the training opportunities of the triennial conference. International exchanges have brought both exhibits and museum personnel together.

UNESCO (always with the help of ICOM) formulated and sought universal adoption of international agreements such as the Hague Convention for the Protection of Cultural Property in the Event of Armed Conflict (1954) and the Convention on the Means of Protecting and Preventing the Illicit Export, Import and Transfer of Ownership of Cultural Property (1970). UNESCO is also interested in historic preservation and in 1949 enlarged its Museums Division into the Division of Museums and Monuments. The International Council of Monuments and Sites (ICOMOS) appeared in 1965 as a kind of sister organization to ICOM but with its own headquarters in Paris.[28]

Museum Publications

The AAM is an important source of publications. From 1918 to 1926, it issued the bimonthly *Museum Work*, with articles and the proceedings of its annual meetings. In 1923 it started *Museum News*, a semimonthly bulletin of four to twelve pages that included short articles and sometimes papers read at the annual meeting. In 1959 *Museum News* became a much larger, well-illustrated magazine with longer articles and special departments. A monthly *Bulletin* with a "Washington Report," placement listings, and classified ads began in 1968 when *Museum News* began to appear only six times yearly. The *Bulletin* was enlarged and renamed *AVISO* in 1975. In 2007 continuing to provide information on governmental practices, training opportunities, and a job bank, *AVISO* became a completely online publication.

Reading *Museum News* and *AVISO* regularly keeps museum professionals informed about current issues, but there are other useful periodicals. *Curator*, formerly a quarterly published by the American Museum of Natural History and now published by AltaMira Press, offers peer-reviewed articles on a range of museum issues. *History News* has been the regular publication of the American Association for State and Local History since 1940, and today it appears every other month and includes occasional "Technical Leaflets," with practical advice. The National Trust for Historic Preservation's quarterly *Historic Preservation*, established in 1949 and issued today as *Preservation*, features articles on museums. The Museum Education Roundtable's quarterly *Journal of Museum Education* that began as *Roundtable Reports* in 1971 provides in-depth articles on museum education issues. Founded in 1973, the Association of Science-Technology Centers (ASTC) represents centers as institutions without individual memberships. Its newsletter, *ASTC Dimensions* and that of the European Network of Science Centres and Museums, *ECSITE Newsletter* offer center staffs vehicles to address common problems. The U.S. Association of Children's Museums (ACM) publishes both a quarterly journal, *Hand-to-Hand* and a quarterly newsletter, *ACM Forum*. With the rising costs of publications, more and more professional organizations are opting for online publications.

An international quarterly of great importance is *Museum* (1948), today *Museum International*, published by UNESCO in Paris with the assistance of ICOM. *ICOM News* (1948) is a quarterly bulletin featuring short articles and announcements. The International Institute for Conservation of Historic and Artistic Works (IIC) publishes *Studies in Conservation* (1954) quarterly and *Reviews in Conservation* annually, along with *Bulletin*, a bimonthly newsletter. The Museums Association of Great Britain's *Museums Journal* (1901) is of exceptional value, with stimulating articles and discerning reviews of exhibitions and books; known today as *Museum and Society* it appears directly on the Internet, greatly enhancing accessibility and professional exchange. *Museum Practice*, also a Museums Association publication, published in hard copy, addresses practical museum challenges with sound advice and guidance.[29]

In addition to its professional journal and newsletter, AAM's publications have ranged from technical volumes relating to subjects such as museum registration to occasional works on special topics, the 1981 *Museums, Adults and the Humanities* is one example. The 1984 *Museums for a New Century* and 1992 *Excellence and Equity* reports have become important documents reflecting and affecting museum practices and standards. Recently, the association has supported republishing important works; for example, in 1999, with the Newark Museum, it compiled and reissued the writings of John Cotton Dana as *The New Museum, Selected Writings of John Cotton Dana*. As part of their centennial activities, the association just published an attractive and informative history of America's museums *Riches, Rivals and Radicals: 100 Years of Museums in America*. The association's publications catalog lists more than one hundred publications; it can be accessed at www.aam-us.org. At the annual conference, the bookstore enjoys a lively business.

Museum Studies

Previous generations of American museum workers received their training in traditional academic subjects, usually at the graduate level, in art or art history for art museums, history for history museums, and biology, chemistry, or anthropology for science museums. They learned the nuts-and-bolts side of museum operations on their first job. Since American museums were numerous and intensely individualistic, with the majority privately controlled, many staff members had unorthodox backgrounds, sometimes with no degrees at all. An agreeable pastime at meetings of museum professional organizations was discussing how those present had entered the profession.

This system was uncertain, haphazard, and wasteful for both individuals and institutions. Yet only a few American museums were willing to devise training courses. Sarah Yorke Stevenson, a wealthy Philadelphian, Egyptologist, and assistant curator at the Philadelphia Museum (later the Philadelphia Museum of Art) designed a program to train art curators and welcomed her first students in 1908. At first the training required only one year, but quickly expanded to two, offering students classes in both the history and functions of museums and including visits to the city's many museums. Mrs. Stevenson developed the curriculum, taught the classes, and lobbied AAM to develop standards for museum practice in administration, economics, and training. The course ended with Mrs. Stevenson's death in 1921.[30] In 1923 at Harvard and the Fogg Art Museum, Paul J. Sachs taught a graduate course in museum work and problems for a quarter-century. A collector and connoisseur himself, Sachs insisted that his students be solidly grounded in art history and thoroughly familiar with art objects. He brought in museum directors and curators to speak to his classes; took his students to visit museums, private galleries, and auction halls; and introduced them to leading collectors and dealers. Students participated in organizing exhibits at the Fogg and served as interns there and elsewhere under close professional supervision. The focus was art history scholarship and connoisseurship.[31] At about the same time as the Sachs class was developing, John Cotton Dana began the Newark Museum's apprenticeship program. Where the Harvard emphasis was scholarship and art, in Newark the study focused on both libraries and museums and offered students hands-on instruction with an emphasis on practical skills. Interestingly, all of Dana's students between 1925 and 1942 were women.[32]

In recent years, dozens of museum studies programs for both undergraduate and graduate students have been organized to prepare students for careers in all kinds of museums. Though AAM created a Museum Studies Committee (1983–1985) to study these programs and consider creating some kind of "certification" program for them, the committee's work has languished. Despite this lack of centralized control, more and more colleges and universities offer museum studies courses, certificates, and even degrees.

What should one say about the value of museum studies and their future? There can be little doubt of their usefulness for students who seek museum careers. Quality courses combine essential subject matter knowledge, museum theory and bibliography, and actual practice of accepted techniques. Graduates understand the common history, philosophy, and purposes of museums, what their chosen personal role involves, and how specialists with varied interests constitute a team that can produce an excellent, effective organization. Museums themselves gain much from the programs because their staff members come to them with an understanding of both the ideal and the real museum worlds, ready to devote themselves to the opportunities of their positions without taking time and energy to find out what museums are all about. As more and more museums create their exhibitions and public programs using staff teams, this understanding of the complexities of museums is even more valuable. A strong sense of common purpose and staff interdependence may be the most valuable contribution of a sound program in developing a true profession. It also goes without saying that the networking possibilities among program participants and faculty provide entrée to the profession.[33]

Challenges

Research/Scholarship

In the main, museum professionals are actively engaged in their day-to-day work and only a few take time to reflect and to report on their experiences to stimulate debate and raise the quality of museum practices. In the many small, busy museums there is little pressure to do so. Professor Genoways says it this way in his introduction to *Museum Philosophy for the 21st Century*: "It is my belief that museologists have not engaged in enough of these [philosophical] discussions. . . . We take little time to ask and discuss the "why," "who," "where," "what," and "why again" questions. I believe that, if museums are going to meet the challenges of the 21st century, museum workers must become more scholarly and engage in discussing and writing about these issues."[34]

As museums compete with appealing leisure time opportunities from movies to themed restaurants and theme parks, the importance of a museum's authenticity and accuracy rises, and it is best maintained through professional discourse, often through publication. Duncan Cameron suggests: "The public generally accepted the idea that if it was in a museum, it was not only real, but represented a standard of excellence."[35] More recent public surveys reveal that Americans "trust" museums and with this trust comes a responsibility to accuracy, authenticity, and professionalism.[36]

What Is the Universe of American Museums?

How many museums are there in the United States? Even the national museum association hesitates to identify a number. Nor can they report reliable visitation totals. Perhaps most frustrating is that there has been little analysis of the impact of museums on city, state, or regional economies. Although such reports exist for blockbuster exhibits, totals usually provided by the local tourism office, there is scant reliable information on how museums contribute to our national economic health.

Federal Support for Museums

AASLH is leading a national effort to study the potential for converting IMLS federal support from a grant program to state block grants such as those available to libraries. This effort has roots in IMLS's previous "general operating support" program that ran afoul of the Congress and has been replaced by project grants. Museum directors long for the days when IMLS funds could be used to pay for museum operating expenses, costs so difficult to raise from private sources. The outcome of this effort will depend on the museum community's ability to unite behind the idea and then apply its political muscle.[37]

Museum Boards Can Rule with Impunity

It seems every few years or so the press reports that a museum director has lost his or her job based on a conflict with the museum's governing board of directors. The nature of the conflict is often shrouded in secrecy. With the growing professionalism of museum staff do volunteer boards of directors provide the best oversight for "the public good" for museums?

Are Museums without Collections "Museums"?

In chapter 1 Stephen Williams suggests rather forcefully that museums without collections are not museums. In contrast, Stephen Weil viewed the very openness of the term *museum* as strength. What's the appropriate role for our professional organizations on this issue? Today, AAM's accreditation process includes noncollecting institutions; should it?

Notes

1. Kenneth Hudson, "The Museum Refuses to Stand Still," *Museum International* 5, no. 1 (1998): 50.
2. Joseph Veach Noble, "Museum Manifesto," *Museum News* 48, no. 8 (April 1970): 19.
3. Nelson Goodman, Foreword, and Sherman Lee, *Past, Present, East and West*, New York: George Braziller, 1983, p.1.
4. Albert E. Parr, "A Plurality of Professions," *Curator* 7 (1964): 287–295; "Policies and Salaries for Museum Faculties," *Curator* 1 (1958): 13–17, and "Is There a Museum Profession?" *Curator* 3 (1960): 101–106.
5. Parr, "A Plurality," p. 294.
6. Wilbur H. Glover, "Toward a Profession," *Museum News* 42 (January 1964): 11–14; Wilcomb E. Washburn, "Professionalizing the Museums," *Museum News* 64, no. 2 (December 1985); Hugh H. Genoways, "To Members of the Museum Profession," in *Museum Philosophy for the 21st Century*, ed. Hugh H. Genoways, Lanham, MD: AltaMira Press, 2006, pp. 221–234; Stephen E. Weil, "In Pursuit of a Profession: The Status of Museum Work in America," in *Rethinking the Museum and Other Meditations*, Washington, DC: Smithsonian Institution, 1990, pp. 73–89; Andrew Decker, "The State of Museums: Cautious Optimism Prevails," *Museum News* 67, no. 2 (March–April 1988): 31–32.
7. www.aam-us.org; www.astc.org; www.aamd.org; www.childrensmuseums .org; www.collegeart.org.

8. American Association of Museums, *Museum Work*, 8 vols., Washington, DC: American Association of Museums, 1918–1926; American Association of Museums, *Annual Reports*, 34 vols., Washington, DC: American Association of Museums; Ellen C. Hicks, "The AAM after 72 Years," *Museum News* 56 (May–June 1978): 44–48.

9. Charles Parkhurst, *Museum News* 45 (April 1967): 4.

10. Patterson's career is best traced through *Museum News*, volumes 38 (March 1959) to 45 (April 1967), see "Points of View."

11. Director Kyran McGrath's administration can be followed in *Museum News*, volumes 46 (1968) to 53 (May 75), see "From the Director."

12. Ernst and Ernst, *AAM Audited Financial Statement*, April 30, 1977.

13. *Museums for a New Century*, Washington, DC: American Association of Museums, 1984.

14. *Excellence and Equity: Education and the Public Dimension of Museums*, Washington, DC: American Association of Museums, 1992.

15. American Association of Museums staff, personal communication.

16. *Code of Ethics for Museum Workers*, New York: American Association of Museums, 1925; reprinted in *Museum News* 52 (June 1974): 26–29.

17. "Museum Ethics: A Report," *Museum News* 56 (March–April 1978): 21–30; Mary Francell, "Ethics Codes: Past, Present and Future," *Museum News* 67, no. 4 (1988): 35; "Roundtable Discussion," *Museum News* 67, no. 4 (1988): 38–41.

18. www.aam-us.org. See "Code of Ethics."

19. Marilyn Hicks Fitzgerald, *Museum Accreditation Professional Standards*, Washington, DC: American Association of Museums, 1973, p. 3.

20. Fitzgerald, *Museum Accreditation*, pp. 7–9.

21. "Looking at Accreditation," *Museum News* 55 (November–December 1976): 15–41; www.aam-us.org, see "Accreditation."

22. American Association of Museums staff, personal communication.

23. Weil, "In Pursuit of a Profession," pp. 84–87.

24. American Association of Museums staff, personal communication.

25. Grace Morley, "Museums and UNESCO," *Museum* 2 (1949): 11–12; Stephen Thomas, "ICOM and AAM," *Museum News* 48 (October 1969): 27–29; *ICOM News* 29, no. 3 (1976): 67–68; www.icom.museum.

26. "UNESCO's Tenth Anniversary," *Museum* 9 (1956): 133–134.

27. Federico Mayor, director-general UNESCO, editorial, *Museum International* 50, no. 1 (1998): 4.

28. Robert R. Garvey, "International Council of Monuments and Sites—ICOMOS," *ICOM News* (Autumn 1972): 5; "UNESCO's Tenth Anniversary," pp. 133–143; *Museum* 12 (1959): 64; *ICOM News* 25 (December 1972): 223–226; 26 (Spring 1973).

29. www.icom.museum; www.iiconservation.org; www.museumsassociation .org (United Kingdom).

30. Karen Cushman, "Museum Studies: The Beginnings: 1900–1926," *Museum Studies Journal* 1, no. 3 (Spring 1984): 8–18.

31. Edward P. Alexander, "A Handhold on the Curatorial Ladder," *Museum News* 52 (May 1974): 3–25; Kathryn Brush, *Vastly More Than Brick and Mortar: Reinventing the Fogg Art Museum in the 1920s*, Harvard University Press and Yale University Press, 2003; Edward P. Alexander, "Paul Joseph Sachs," in *The Museum in America: Innovators and Pioneers*, Walnut Creek, CA: AltaMira Press, pp. 203–218; Sally Ann Duncan, "Harvard's Museum Course," *American Art Journal* 42, nos. 1–2 (2002): 2–16.

32. Cushman, "Museum Studies: The Beginnings," p. 14.

33. Weil, "In Pursuit of a Profession," pp. 73–89; Roundtable Discussion: "Risk and Opportunity: The Museum as Career Choice," and Commentaries from Museum Studies Directors: "Into the Real World," *Museum News* 77, no. 4 (July–August 1998); Genoways, "To Members of the Museum Profession," pp. 221–234.

34. Genoways, *Museum Philosophy for the 21st Century*, p. x.

35. Duncan Cameron, "The Museum, a Temple or the Forum," *Journal of World History* 14, no. 1, p. 195.

36. Roy Rosenzweig and David Thelen, *The Presence of the Past: Popular Uses of History in American Life*, New York: Columbia University Press, 1998, pp. 89–114.

37. www.AALSH.org.

Readings

Many of these texts may be classified in multiple categories, although each is listed only once. Chapter notes may be used to guide further reading.

General Texts

Alderson, William T., ed. *Mermaids, Mummies, and Mastodons: The Emergence of the American Museum*. Washington, DC: American Association of Museums, 1992.

Alexander, Edward P. *The Museum in America: Innovators and Pioneers*. Walnut Creek, CA: AltaMira Press, 1997.

———. *Museum Masters: Their Museums and Their Influence*. Nashville, TN: American Association for State and Local History, 1983.

Ambrose, Timothy, and Crispin Paine. *Museum Basics*. London: International Council of Museums with Routledge, 1993.

Anderson, Gail, ed. *Reinventing the Museum: Historical and Contemporary Perspectives on the Paradigm Shift*. Walnut Creek, CA: AltaMira Press, 2004.

Bator, Paul M. *The International Trade in Art*. Chicago: University of Chicago Press, 1983.

Bazin, Germain. *The Museum Age*. Translated by Jane van Nuis Cahill. New York: Universe, 1967.

Carbonell, Bettina, ed. *Museum Studies: An Anthology of Contexts*. Blackwell, 2004.

Cato, Paisley S., Julia Golden, and Suzanne B. McLaren, eds. *MuseumWise: Workplace Words Defined*. Society of the Preservation of Natural History Collections, 2003.

Conn, Steven. *Museums and American Intellectual Life, 1876–1926.* Chicago: University of Chicago Press, 1998.

Harris, Neil. *Cultural Excursions: Marketing Appetites and Cultural Tastes in Modern America.* Chicago: University of Chicago Press, 1990.

Hein, Hilde. *The Museum in Transition: A Philosophical Perspective.* Washington, DC: Smithsonian Institution Press, 2000.

Hellman, Geoffrey T. *The Smithsonian: Octopus on the Mall.* Philadelphia: Lippincott, 1967.

Hudson, Kenneth. *Museums of Influence.* Cambridge: Cambridge University Press, 1987.

———. *A Social History of Museums: What the Visitors Thought.* Atlantic Highlands, NJ: Humanities Press, 1975.

Karp, Ivan, Christine Mullen Kreamer, and Steven D. Lavine. *Museums and Communities: The Politics of Public Culture.* Washington, DC: Smithsonian Institution Press, 1992.

Luke, Timothy W. *Museum Politics: Power Plays at the Exhibition.* Minneapolis, MN: University of Minnesota Press, 2002.

Menand, Louis. *The Metaphysical Club: A Story of Ideas in America.* New York: Farrar, Straus & Giroux, 2001.

Miles, Roger, and Lauro Zavala. *Towards the Museum of the Future: New European Perspectives.* London: Routledge, 1994.

Newhouse, Victoria. *Towards a New Museum.* New York: Monacelli Press, 1998.

Orosz, Joel J. *Curators and Culture: The Museum Movement in America, 1740–1870.* Tuscaloosa, AL: University of Alabama Press, 1990.

Phelan, Marilyn E. *Museum Law: A Guide for Officers, Directors, and Counsel.* Evanston, IL: Kalos Kapp Press, 1994.

Preziosi, Donald, and Claire Farago, eds. *Grasping the World: The Idea of the Museum.* Hants, UK: Ashgate, 2004.

Ripley, S. Dillon. *The Sacred Grove: Essays on Museums.* New York: Simon & Schuster, 1969.

Sherman, Daniel J., and Irit Rogoff. *Museum Culture: Histories, Discourse, Spectacles.* Minneapolis, MN: University of Minnesota Press, 1994.

Vergo, Peter, ed. *The New Museology.* London: Reaktion Books, 1989.

Weil, Stephen E. *Beauty and the Beasts.* Washington, DC: Smithsonian Institution Press, 1983.

———. *Making Museums Matter.* Washington, DC: Smithsonian Institution Press, 2002.

———. *Rethinking the Museum and Other Meditations.* Washington, DC: Smithsonian Institution Press, 1990.

Witcomb, Andrea. *Re-imagining the Museum: Beyond the Mausoleum.* New York: Routledge, 2003.

Wittlin, Alma. *Museums: In Search of a Usable Future.* Cambridge, MA: MIT Press, 1970.

Art Museums

Bourdieu, Pierre, Alain Darbel, and Dominique Schnapper. *The Love of Art: European Art Museums and Their Public*. Palo Alto, CA: Stanford University Press, 1990.

Brush, Kathryn. *Vastly More Than Bricks and Mortar: Reinventing the Fogg Art Museum in the 1920s*. Harvard University Press and Yale University Press, 2004.

Burt, Nathaniel. *Palaces for the People: A Social History of the American Art Museum*. Boston: Little, Brown, 1977.

Cuno, James, ed. *Whose Muse? Art Museums and the Public Trust*. Princeton University Press and Harvard University Press, 2004.

Duncan, Carol. *Civilizing Rituals: Inside Public Art Museums*. London: Routledge, 1995.

Einreinhofer, Nancy. *The American Art Museum Elitism and Democracy*. Leicester University Press, 1997.

Elkins, James. *Pictures and Tears: A History of People Who Have Cried in Front of Paintings*. New York: Routledge, 2001.

Finley, David. *A Standard of Excellence: Andrew W. Mellon Founds the National Gallery of Art at Washington*. Washington, DC: Smithsonian Institution Press, 1973.

Klessmann, Rudiger. *The Berlin Museum Painting in the Picture Gallery*. Translated by D. J. S. Thomson. New York: Abrams, 1971.

Kopper, Philip. *America's National Gallery of Art*. New York: Abrams, 1991.

Newhouse, Victoria. *Art and the Power of Placement*. New York: Monacelli Press, 2005.

Nicholas, Lynn H. *The Rape of Europa*. New York: Vantage Books, 1994.

Norman, Geraldine. *The Hermitage: A Biography of a Great Museum*. New York: Forum International, 1997.

Tompkins, Calvin. *Merchants and Masterpieces: The Story of the Metropolitan Museum of Art*. New York: Dutton, 1970.

Natural History Museums

Ames, Michael. *Cannibal Tours and Glass Boxes*. Vancouver: University of British Columbia Press, 1992.

Asma, Stephen. *Stuffed Animals and Pickled Heads: The Culture and Evolution of Natural History Museums*. Oxford, UK: Oxford University Press, 2001.

Clifford, James. *In the Museum of Man*. Cambridge, MA: Harvard University Press, 1988.

———. *The Predicament of Culture: 20th Century Ethnography, Literature and Art*. Cambridge, MA: Harvard University Press, 1988.

———. *Routes, Travel and Translation in the Late 20th Century*. Cambridge, MA: Harvard University Press, 1997.

Davis, Peter. *Museums and the Natural Environment: The Role of Natural History Museums in Biological Conservation*. New York: Leicester University Press, 1996.

Findlen, Paula. *Possessing Nature: Museums, Collecting and Scientific Culture in Early Modern Italy*. Berkeley: University of California Press, 1994.

Foucault, Michel. *Order of Things: An Archaeology of the Human Sciences*. New York: Vintage Press, 1973.

Fowler, Don D., and David R. Wilcox, eds. *Philadelphia and the Development of Americanist Archaeology*. Tuscaloosa: University of Alabama Press, 2003.

Godwin, Joscelyn. *Athanasius Kircher: A Renaissance Man and Quest for Lost Knowledge*. London: Thames and Hudson, 1979.

Haraway, Donna. *Primate Visions: Gender, Race and Nature in the World of Modern Science*. London: Routledge, 1989.

Harris, Neil. *Humbug: The Art of P. T. Barnum*. Boston: Little, Brown, 1973.

Nash, Stephen, and Gary Feinman, eds. *Curators, Collections and Context, Anthropology at the Field Museum*. Chicago: The Field Museum, 2003.

Sandberg, Mark. *Living Pictures, Missing Persons: Mannequins, Museums and Modernity*. Princeton, NJ: Princeton University Press, 2003.

Preston, Douglas J. *Dinosaurs in the Attic: An Excursion to the American Museum of Natural History*. New York: St. Martin's, 1986.

Rea, Tom. *Bone Wars: The Excavation and Celebrity of Andrew Carnegie's Dinosaur*. Pittsburgh, PA: University of Pittsburgh Press, 2001.

Sheets-Pyenson, S. *Cathedrals of Science*. Kingston: McGill-Queen's University Press, 1988.

Stearn, William T. *The Natural History Museum at South Kensington*. London: Heinemann, 1981.

Wonders, Karen. *Habitat Dioramas: Illusions of Wilderness in Museums of Natural History*. Uppsala, Sweden: Acta Universitatis Upsaliensis, 1993.

Yanni, Carla. *Nature's Museums: Victorian Science and the Architecture of Display*. Baltimore, MD: Johns Hopkins University Press, 1999.

Science Museums

Cossons, Neil, ed. *Making of the Modern World: Milestones of Science and Technology*. London: Science Museum and John Murray Publishers, 1992.

Danilov, Victor J. *America's Science Museums*. Westport, CT: Greenwood Press, 1990.

Farmelo, Graham, and Janet Carding. *Here and Now: Contemporary Science and Technology in Museums and Science Centers*. London: Science Museum, 1996.

Grinell, Sheila. *A New Place for Learning Science: Starting Science Centers and Keeping Them Running.* Washington, DC: Association of Science Technology Centers, 1992.
Hindle, Brooke. *Technology in Early America: Needs and Opportunities.* Chapel Hill: University of North Carolina Press, 1966.
Pearce, Susan M., ed. *Exploring Science in America.* London: Athlone, 1996.

History Museums

Guthrie, Kevin M. *The New-York Historical Society: Lessons from One Nonprofit's Long Struggle for Survival.* New York: Andrew Mellon Foundation and Jossey-Bass, 1996.
Handler, Richard, and Eric Gable. *The New History in an Old Museum: Creating the Past at Colonial Williamsburg.* Durham, NC: Duke University Press, 1997.
Hosmer, Charles B. *Presence of the Past: A History of the Preservation Movement in the United States before Williamsburg.* New York: Putnam, 1965.
Lowenthal, David. *The Heritage Crusade and the Spoils of History.* Cambridge University Press, 1997.
———. *The Past as a Foreign Country.* Cambridge University Press, 1985.
Parker, Arthur C. *A Manual for History Museums.* New York: Columbia University Press, 1935.
Rosenzweig, Roy, and Warren Leon, eds. *History Museums in the United States: A Critical Assessment.* Urbana: University of Illinois Press, 1989.
Rosenzweig, Roy, and David Thelen. *The Presence of the Past: Popular Uses of History in American Life.* New York: Columbia University Press, 1998.
Wallace, Michael. *Mickey Mouse History and Other Essays on American Memory.* Philadelphia, PA: Temple University Press, 1996.
West, Patricia. *Domesticating History: The Political Origins of America's House Museums.* Washington, DC: Smithsonian Institution Press, 1999.
Whitehill, Walter Muir. *Independent Historical Societies.* Cambridge, MA: Harvard University Press, 1962.

Botanical Gardens and Zoos

Blunt, Wilfrid. *The Ark the Park: The Zoo in the Nineteenth Century.* London: Hamish Hamilton, 1976.
Bridges, William. *Gathering of the Animals: An Unconventional History of the New York Zoological Society.* New York: Harper & Row, 1974.
Croke, Vicki. *The Modern Ark: The Story of Zoos, Past, Present and Future.* New York: Scribner, 1977.

DeLeon, Clark. *America's First Zoostory: 125 Years at the Philadelphia Zoo*. Virginia Beach, VA: Donning, 1999.

Fisher, James. *Zoos of the World: The Story of Animals in Captivity*. Garden City, NY: Natural History Press, 1967.

Gersh, Harry. *The Animals Next Door: A Guide to Zoos and Aquariums of the Americas*. New York: Fleet Academic Editions, 1971.

Guillery, Peter. *The Building of the London Zoo*. Royal Commission on the Historical Monuments of England, 1993.

Hardouin-Fugier, Elizabeth. *Zoo: A History of Zoological Gardens in the West*. London: Reaktion, 2002.

Hoage, Robert J., and William A. Deiss, eds. *New Worlds, New Animals: From Menagerie to Zoological Park in the Nineteenth Century*. Baltimore, MD: Johns Hopkins University Press, 1996.

Hunt, J. D. *Garden and Grove: The Italian Renaissance Garden in the English Imagination 1600–1750*. Princeton, NJ: Princeton University Press, 1996.

Hyams, Edward. *A History of Gardens and Gardening*. New York: Praeger, 1971.

Hyams, Edward, and William MacQuitty. *Great Botanical Gardens of the World*. New York: Macmillan, 1969.

Jardine, N. J., A. Secord, and E. C. Spray, eds. *Cultures of Natural History*. Cambridge University Press, 1996.

Kisling Jr., Vernon N., ed. *Zoo and Aquarium History: Ancient Animal Collections to Zoological Gardens*. Boca Raton, FL: CRC Press, 2001.

Rothfels, Nigel. *Savages and Beasts: The Birth of the Modern Zoo*. Baltimore, MD: Johns Hopkins University Press, 2002.

Shoemaker, Candice A., ed. *Encyclopedia of Gardens: History and Design*. Chicago and London: Chicago Botanic Garden and Fitzroy Dearborn, 2001.

Soderstrom, Mary. *Recreating Eden: A Natural History of Botanical Gardens*. Canada: Vehicule Press, 2001.

Children's Museums

Bay, Ann. *Museum Programs for Young People*. Washington, DC: Smithsonian Institution Press, 1973.

Cleaver, Joanne. *Doing Children's Museums*. Charlotte, VT: Williamson, 1988.

Curzon, Rebecca E. *Children of the Castle*. Washington, DC: Smithsonian Institution Press, Office of Museum Programs, 1979.

Fuller Jr., Melville W. *The Development and Status of Science Centers and Museums for Children in the United States*. Chapel Hill, NC: University of North Carolina Press, 1970.

Gibans, Nina Freedlander. *Bridges to Understanding Children's Museums*. Cleveland, OH: Case Western Reserve University Press, 1999.

Kriplen, Nancy. *Keep an Eye on the Mummy: History of the Children's Museum of Indianapolis*. Indianapolis: Children's Museum of Indianapolis, 1982.

Maher, Mary, ed. *Collective Vision: Starting and Sustaining a Children's Museum.* Washington, DC: Association of Youth Museums, 1997.
Moore, Eleanor M. *Youth in Museums.* Philadelphia: University of Pennsylvania Press, 1941.
Office of Museum Programs. *Proceedings of the Children in Museums International Symposium.* Washington, DC: Smithsonian Institution Press, 1982.
Pittman-Gelles, Bonnie. *Museums, Magic and Children: Youth Education in Museums.* Washington, DC: Association of Science-Technology Centers, 1981.
Sayles, Adelaide B. *The Story of the Children's Museum of Boston.* Boston, MA: George H. Ellis Press, 1937.
Seuert, Patricia A., Aylette Jenness, and Joanne Jones-Rizzi. *Opening the Museum: History and Strategies Toward a More Inclusive Institution.* Boston, MA: The Children's Museum, 1993.
Zervos, Cassandra. *Children's Museums: A Case Study of the Foundations of Model Institutions in the United States.* Thesis, Pennsylvania State University, 1990.
Zucker, Barbara Fleisher. *Children's Museums, Zoos and Discovery Rooms: An International Reference Guide.* New York: Greenwood Press, 1987.

Collections

Buck, Rebecca, and Jean Allman Gilmore. *The New Museum Registration Methods.* Washington, DC: American Association of Museums, 1998.
Chamberlin, Russell. *Loot! The Heritage of Plunder.* New York: Facts On File, 1983.
Chenhall, Robert G., James R. Blackaby, and Patricia Greeno. *Nomenclature for Museum Cataloging.* Nashville, TN: American Association of State and Local History, 1988.
Fahy, Anne, ed. *Collections Management.* London: Routledge, 1995.
Keck, Caroline K. *A Handbook on the Care of Paintings*, rev. ed. Nashville, TN: American Association for State and Local History, 1967.
Keene, Suzanne. *Fragments of the World: Uses of Museum Collections.* Oxford, UK: Butterworth Heinemann, 2005.
Knell, Simon, ed. *Care of Collections.* UK: Routledge, 1994.
———. *Museums and the Future of Collecting.* UK: Ashgate, 2004.
Malaro, Marie. *Legal Primer on Managing Museum Collections*, 2nd ed. Washington, DC: Smithsonian Institution Press, 1998.
Pearce, Susan. *On Collecting: An Investigation into Collecting the European Tradition.* London: Routledge, 1995.
Reibel, Daniel B. *Registration Methods for the Small Museum.* Nashville, TN: American Association of State and Local History, 1978.
Schelereth, Thomas. *Material Culture Studies in the U.S.* Nashville, TN: American Association of State and Local History, 1982.

Conservation

Clavir, Miriam. *Preserving What Is Valued: Museums, Conservation and First Nations*. Vancouver: University of British Columbia Press, 2002.

Keck, Caroline K. *Safeguarding Your Collection in Travel*. Nashville, TN: American Association for State and Local History, 1970.

Plenderleith, H. J., and A. E. A. Werner. *The Conservation of Antiquities and Works of Art: Treatment, Repair and Restoration*. Oxford University Press, 1971.

Price, Nicholas Stanley, M. Kirby Talley Jr., and Alessandra Melucco Vaccaro, eds. *Historical and Philosophical Issues in Conservation of Cultural Heritage, Readings in Conservation*. Los Angeles: Getty Conservation Institute, 1996.

Stolow, Nathan. *Conservation and Exhibitions: Packing, Transport, Storage and Environmental Considerations*. London: Butterworth, 1987.

Interpretation

Alderson, William T., and Shirley Payne Low. *Interpretation of Historic Sites*. Nashville, TN: American Association for State and Local History, 1976.

Ames, Kenneth L., Barbara Franco, and L. Thomas Frye, eds. *Ideas and Images: Developing Interpretive History Exhibits*. Nashville, TN: American Association for State and Local History, 1992.

Collins, Zipporah W., ed. *Museums, Adults, and the Humanities*. Washington, DC: American Association of Museums, 1981.

Dean, David. *Museum Exhibition: Theory and Practice*. London: Routledge, 1994.

Dubin, Steven C. *Displays of Power, Memory and Amnesia in the American Museum*. New York: NYU Press, 1999.

Falk, John H., and Lynn D. Dierking. *Learning from Museums: Visitor Experiences and the Making of Meaning*. Walnut Creek, CA: AltaMira Press, 2000.

———. *The Museum Experience*. Washington, DC: Whalesback Books, 1992.

Greenberg, Reesa, Bruce W. Ferguson, and Sandy Nairne. *Thinking about Exhibitions*. London: Routledge, 1996.

Harwit, Martin. *An Exhibit Denied: Lobbying the History of* Enola Gay. New York: Copernicus, 1996.

Hein, George E. *Learning in the Museum*. London: Routledge, 1998.

Hein, George E., and Mary Alexander. *Museums: Places of Learning*. Washington, DC: American Association of Museums, 1998.

Karp, Ivan, and Steven D. Lavine, eds. *Exhibiting Culture: The Poetics and Politics of Museum Display*. Washington, DC: Smithsonian Institution Press, 1991.

Larrabee, Eric, ed. *Museums and Education*. Washington, DC: Smithsonian Institution Press, 1968.

Lord, Barry, and Gail Dexter Lord, eds. *The Manual for Museum Exhibitions*. Walnut Creek, CA: AltaMira Press, 2002.

Luckhurst, Kenneth W. *The Story of Exhibitions*. London: Studio Publications, 1951.

Newsom, Barbara Y., and Adele Silver, eds. *The Art Museum as Educator*. Berkeley, CA: University of California Press, 1978.

Nichols, Susan, and Kim Igoe, eds. *Museum-School Partnerships: Plans and Programs (Sourcebook #4)*. Washington, DC: Center for Museum Education, George Washington University, 1981.

Nichols, Susan K. *Patterns in Practice: Selections from the Journal of Museum Education*. Washington, DC: Museum Education Roundtable, 1992.

Nichols, Susan K., Mary Alexander, and Ken Yellis, eds. *Museum Education Anthology*. Washington, DC: Museum Education Roundtable, 1984.

Munley, Mary Ellen. *Catalyst for Change: The Kellogg Project in Museum Education*. Washington, DC: American Association of Museums, 1986.

Roberts, Lisa C. *From Knowledge to Narrative, Educators and the Changing Museums*. Washington, DC: Smithsonian Institution Press, 1997.

Sachatello-Sawyer, Bonnie, Robert Fellenz, Laura Gittings-Carlson, Janet Lewis-Mahony, and Walter Woodbaugh. *Adult Museum Programs: Designing Meaningful Experiences*. Walnut Creek, CA: AltaMira Press, 2002.

Tilden, Freeman. *Interpreting Our Heritage*. Chapel Hill, NC: University of North Carolina Press, 1957.

Wittlin, Alma. *The Museum: Its History and Tasks in Education*. London: Routledge and Paul Keagan, 1949.

Museum Profession

American Association of Museums. *Excellence and Equity: Education and the Public Dimension of Museums*. Washington, DC: American Association of Museums, 1992.

American Association of Museums. *Museums for a New Century: A Report on the Commission on Museums for a New Century*. Washington, DC: American Association of Museums, 1984.

Burcaw, G. Ellis. *Introduction to Museum Work*, 3rd ed. Walnut Creek, CA: AltaMira Press, 1997.

Falk, John H., and Beverly K. Sheppard. *Thriving in the Knowledge Age: New Business Models for Museums and Other Cultural Institutions*. Lanham, MD: AltaMira Press, 2006.

Gurian, Elaine Heumann. *Civilizing the Museum*. London: Routledge, 2006.

Schwarzer, Marjorie. *Riches, Rivals and Radicals: 100 Years of Museums in America*. Washington, DC: American Association of Museums, 2006.

Suchy, S. *Leading with Passion, Change Management in the 21st Century Museum*. Lanham MD: AltaMira Press, 2004.

Index

Aal, Hans, 122
Abraham Lincoln Presidential
  Library and Museum, 129
Abreu, Luiz de, 148
Academy of Natural Sciences
  (Philadelphia, PA), 63
accreditation, museum, 308, 310. *See
  also* museum profession
acquisition methods: dealers in art
  objects, 197; ethics and illicit
  trade, 202, 205; of museums, 44,
  196; records, 201
Adams, Rollie, 178
Adolphus, Gustavus, king of
  Sweden, 26
African Art in Motion, 238
Agassiz, Louis, 67
Aiton, William, 142, 143
Akeley, Carl E., 56, 68, 245
Albert, prince of England, 88
Albertinum (Dresden), 35
Alcazar (Madrid), 26
Aldrovandi, Ulisse, 55, 86
Alexander, Edward P., ix, 259
Alexander the Great, 2
Allan, Douglas, 2
Alte Pinakothek (Munich), 34

Altes Museum (Berlin), 33, 34
Ambach, Gordon, 180–81, 257
American Academy of Fine Art (New
  York), 63
American Antiquarian Society
  (Worcester, MA), 118, 119
American Art Museum (Washington,
  DC), 250
American Association for State and
  Local History (AASLH), 133, 307,
  318
American Association of Museums
  (AAM): accreditation commission,
  311; collection planning, 195;
  museum accreditation, 208, 308,
  310; museum definition, 2, 169,
  259, 283, 306; objectives, 307;
  publications, 282, 307, 314
American Bison Society, 156
American Museum of Natural
  History (New York):
  establishment, 7, 67–70, 245;
  mentioned, 77
American museums, 6, 36, 61–74,
  268, 284, 318
America on the Move, 120
Ames, Kenneth, 238, 240

Ames, Michael, 12, 53, 75
Anacostia Neighborhood Museum
(Washington, DC), 287. *See also*
Smithsonian Institution
Anderson, Thomas, 147
"andragogy," 273
Andrews, Roy Chapman, 68
Angerstein, John Julius, 33
Anguillara, Luigi (Luigi Squalerno),
141
anthropological museums, 71–74
Appleton, William Sumner, 27
Appolonius of Perga, 4
Apsley House, 31
aquariums, 140, 156
arboretums, 140
archaeological museums and
expeditions: for collection
purposes, 38, 39, 191;
environmental problems, 231;
illicit art trade and, 202, 210
Archimedes, 24
architectural history, 97, 127, 128, 258
Ardier, Paul, 115
Arizona-Sonora Desert Museum
(Tucson, AZ), 158
Arnold Arboretum (Jamaica Plain,
MA), 149
Art Institute of Chicago, 36
art museums: American, 42;
blockbusters, 44; challenges, 42;
collection function, 43, 193;
disposal procedures, 208;
educational purpose, 42; exhibits,
189, 246; illicit trade, 43;
mentioned, 41. *See also* modern
art; *specific art museums*
Ashmole, Elias, 57
Ashmolean Museum (Oxford,
England), 5, 28, 57, 58
Asian Art Museum (San Francisco,
CA), 245
Association of Art Museum Directors
(AAMD), 203, 307

Association of Children's Museums
(ACM), 174, 307
Association of Science Museum
Directors, 307
Association of Science-Technology
Centers (ASTC), 99, 126, 271
Athenaeum (Boston, MA), 36, 191
attendance, at museums, 2, 14, 46, 92,
100, 105, 154, 252, 269. *See also*
audiences
auctions, 44, 198, 204, 207, 316;
Internet, 131, 191
audiences: participation and
interactive exhibits, 90, 93, 129;
research and reactions, 243, 264.
See also interpretation
(educational) function
audiovisual materials, 123, 243, 268,
269. *See also* multimedia
(audiovisual) exhibits;
publications
August I (Dresden), 86
Augustus the Strong, king of Poland,
34
authenticity: determination of, for
museum holdings, 123, 132, 199,
200, 263, 299, 318. *See also* fakes
and frauds
authority, 15, 249, 276, 299
Ayer, Edward E., 70

Baird, Spencer Fullerton, 66–67
Baker, Samuel, 198
Balfour, Isaac Bailey, 145
Balfour, John Hutton, 145
Ballou, J. de, 61
Banks, Joseph, 59, 143
Barbier, Luc, 29
Barclay, R. J., 230
Barker, Robert, 116
Barnard, George Gray, 38
Barnum, Phineas T., 60, 63
Barnum's American Museum (New
York), 64

Barr, Alfred H., Jr., 39
Bartram, John, 148
Bator, Paul, 205
Bauhaus School, 39
Bavarian National Museum
    (Munich), 91, 118
Beaubourg, 35
Beaumont, George, 33
Belcher, Michael, 252, 261
Belmont Report, 259
Belvedere botanical gardens
    (Vienna), 145
Belvedere Palace, 27
Benchley, Belle J., 157
Berenson, Bernard, 198
Berlin-Dahlem Botanical Museum,
    145
Berry, duc de. *See* France, Jean de
Between a Rock and a Hard Place, 132,
    249
Beuningen, D. G. van, 199
Bibliotheque Nationale (Paris), 30
Bickmore, Albert S., 67
Bigelow, William Sturgis, 38
Black Paintings of Goya, 200
Blair, Reed, 156
Bliss, Lizzie, 39
blockbusters, 44, 250
Boas, Franz, 11
Bode, Wilhelm von, 33, 198
Bode Museum (Berlin), 33, 34
Boerhaave, Hermann, 141
Bonacolsi, Rinaldo, 54
Bonafede, Francisco, 141
Bonaparte, Joseph, king of Spain, 31
Bonaparte, Napoleon: art
    confiscations and museum
    system, 26, 29–32
botanical gardens: American, 142,
    148; challenges, 151; children's
    gardens, 150; economic and
    medicinal basis for, 5; educational
    purpose, 140; European, 141;
    historic background, 5, 140–56;

physic gardens, 5, 141; seed
banks, 143, 144, 220, 221;
worldwide, 146, 152. *See also*
specific botanical gardens
Bouton, Charles Marie, 116
Boymans Museum (Rotterdam), 199
Brademas, John, 311
Brera Gallery (Milan), 31
British Museum (London):
    establishment, 28, 58–59
British Museum (Natural History),
    58
British museums and collections, 32,
    117. *See also specific museums and*
    collections
Brodie, Neil, 210
Bronx Zoo, 155–56
Brooklyn Botanic Garden, 150
Brooklyn Children's Museum, 7, 167,
    169–72; KidsCrew program, 171;
    MUSE community project, 170, 288
Brooklyn Museum, 36, 250, 283
Browere, John H. I., 115
Brown, Lancelot "Capability," 143
Bruchium (Alexandria), 2
Bryan, Thomas J., 36
Buckingham Palace, 33
Bullock, William, 56, 60
Bunch, Lonnie, 132, 249
Burcaw, Ellis, 114
Burns, Ken, 269
Burt, Nicholas, 14
Bussy-Rabutin, Roger de, 115

cabinet (*gabinetto, Wunderkammer*), 5
Cameron, Duncan, 11, 282, 290, 318
Capitoline Museum, 25
Carey, Mary Stewart, 175
Carmichael, Leonard, 94
Carnes, Alice, 85
Cary Arboretum (Millbrook, NY),
    149
Catherine de Medici, queen of
    France, 115

Catherine the Great, 27, 28, 35, 115
Center for Information about
    Natural Science and Modern
    Technology, 103
Centre Georges Pompidou, 35
ceramics: conservation of, 220
Cesalpino, Andrea, 141
Cesnola, Louis P. di, 37
Cezanne, 44, 238
Chalco, 141
Chambers, William, 143
Charles of Bourbon, king of the Two
    Sicilies, 27
Charles I, king of England, 25
Charles V, Holy Roman Emperor, 26
Charles VI, Holy Roman Emperor,
    27
Charleston Historic District (SC),
    128
Charleston Library Society (SC), 61
Charleston Museum (SC), 6, 62
Chelsea Physic Garden, 142
Chicago Historical Society, 238
children's activities. *See* youth
    activities and programs
Children's Adventure Garden
    (Boston, MA), 180
Children's Museum (Boston, MA),
    172, 241, 246, 289; MATCHBOX
    program, 173, 174
children's museums, 167–83, 239,
    244; development, 176–79;
    galleries, 168; history, 168;
    impact, 178. *See also* museums;
    specific museums
Chinatown History Museum (New
    York), 13
Choate, Joseph C., 36
Christian V, king of Denmark, 55, 87
Christie, James, 198
Christina, queen of Sweden, 26
Chute, Mary, 187
Cincinnati Arts Center, 13, 40
Cite des Sciences et de l'Industrie
    (Paris), 101, 103, 296

Clark, Kenneth, 8
Clavir, Miriam, 209, 217, 230
Clement XIV, pope, 27
Cleveland Museum of Art, 11, 36
Climatron (St. Louis, MO), 149
Clusius, Carolus (Charles de
    l'Ecluse), 141
codes of ethics, 206, 309–10
Colbert, Jean Baptiste, 26
Cole, Henry, 88
Cole, Thomas, 36
Coleman, Laurence Vail, 169, 307
collecting and collections, 8, 15, 187,
    299; acquisition methods and
    ethics, 190, 200, 202; artificial
    curiosities, 86; contemporary
    materials, 194; dealers, 191, 197;
    disposal procedures, 205;
    donations to museums, 190, 196;
    educational value, 190; field work
    and expeditions, 191; loans and
    exchanges, 191, 196; management,
    201; as museum function, 8;
    planning, 192, 194; protecting in
    wartime, 210; purposes, 189;
    records, 195, 200; unrestricted
    ownership, 196, 209. *See also* fakes
    and frauds; objects
College Art Association, 307
Colonial Williamsburg (VA), 123, 264,
    269
Columbia (CA): outdoor mining
    museum, 123
Common Agenda for History
    Museums, 133, 333
community (neighborhood)
    museums, 287
computerization, 209, 262
computerized documentation, 209
computers, 88, 176, 243, 261, 262;
    games, 181; home, 90, 268;
    networks, 72, 202, 209; virtual
    display, 244, 246
Conisbee, Philip, 209
Conn, Steven, 124

Conner Prairie (IN), 123
conservation (preservation):
cleaning, 8; conjecture dangers,
227; conservator duties and
training, 218, 227, 228; cost, 222;
curator role, 220; environmental
factors, 221–23; examination of
objects, 226; historical methods,
226–28; metals, 220; as a museum
function, 8, 217, 229; objects, 219;
organic materials, 219; packing
and shipping, 225; paintings, 220;
physical nature of records, 200,
226, 227, 229; preventive methods,
8, 227; publications on, 219, 256;
rebacking (relining), 8; restoration,
226; reversibility, 227; stone,
ceramics, and glass (siliceous
materials), 220; storage, 221,
222–23; textiles, 219. *See also*
historic structures and districts;
specific types of museums
Conservatoire National des Arts et
Metiers (Paris), 87
Constructivist Museum, 277
Convention on the Means of
Protecting and Preventing the
Illicit Export, Import and Transfer
of Ownership of Cultural
Property, 314
Cook, James, 59, 143
Cooper, Karen Coody, 290
Corcoran Gallery of Art
(Washington, DC), 36, 65
Cospi, Ferdinando, 55, 86
costume museums, 38, 313
creationism, 77
Crew, Spencer, 132, 249
Croke, Vicki, 139
Crook, J. Mordaunt, 5
Crusades: and acquisition of art
objects, 5
Crystal Palace Exhibition (Great
Exhibition of the Industry of all
Nations, London), 10, 88

cultural cleansing, 210
cultural function: of museums, 10;
social events, 10
cultural tourism, 300
culture-history arrangements, 117
Cunningham, Ann Pamela, 126
curator (museum): collection role,
191; conservation responsibility,
220; exhibition responsibility, 192,
224; training, 306, 399. *See also*
museum profession; museums
cyberspace, 106
cycloramas, 116, 117

Daguerre, Louis J. M., 116
Dana, John Cotton, 42, 170, 257, 282,
284, 316
d'Angiviller, Count, 28
Darwin, Charles, 54, 77
deaccession, 44, 195, 205, 310. *See
also* disposal policies and
procedures
dealers: in art objects and museum
collectibles, 197. *See also*
acquisition methods; museums
decorative art, 34, 117, 193
Deetz, James, 125
de Forest, Robert W., 38
Delta Plan, 229
Den Gamle By (Old Town,
Denmark), 123
Descartes, René, 87
Desmarais, Charles, 13
d'Estaing, Girard, president of
France, 101
Detroit Children's Museum, 174
Detroit Historical Museum, 210
Detroit Institute of Art, 36
Detroit Museum of Art, 175
Deutsches Museum (Munich), 91–93,
103, 262
Dewey, John, 168
Dia Foundation, 40
Dierking, Lynn, 179, 264
dioramas, 56, 244

Directors of Systematic Collections, 307
Discovery Rooms, 179, 239
Disney, Walt, 129, 239
Disneyland, 129, 239
displays. *See* exhibitions
disposal policies and procedures, 44, 192, 205–8, 310. *See also* collecting and collections; deaccession
docents, 7, 42, 275, 286. *See also* guides
Douglas, Charles J., 172
Draper, Lyman Copeland, 116
Dresden museums, 34
Dubin, Steven, 249
Duncan, Carol, 12, 297
Du Pont, Henry Francis, 38
Du Pont, Pierre S., 150
Duran-Ruel, Paul, 198
Duveen, Joseph, 188, 198

eBay, 131, 191
ecomuseums, 125, 128, 158
Eden Project, 277, 294
Edison, Thomas Alva, 97
educational function. *See* interpretation (educational) function
Elgin Botanic Garden (New York), 148
Engelmann, George, 148
Enola Gay, 131, 249
environmental factors, 8, 195, 218, 221–24, 294
Eratosthenes, 4
Erhard, Ludwig, 93
Escorial (Madrid), 26
ethnic museums, 288, 298
ethnological museums, 72
evaluation, 46, 239, 241
evolution, 77
Excellence and Equity (report), 259, 260, 283, 309, 395

exhibitions (arrangements, displays): audience reaction, 236, 237, 240, 247, 248; blockbusters, 44, 237; care, 224; cases, 225, 238, 244; definition, 236; demonstrations and activities, 245, 263; design techniques, 244, 251; development, 239, 242; dioramas, 244; functional arrangement, 237; guidelines, 240; habitat groups, 56, 68, 245; history, 9–10; influences on, 236; labeling, 247; lighting, 222, 245; mentioned, 44; multimedia programs, 245; objects, 242; organization, 241; orientation program, 261, 269; packing and shipping, 225–26; publications, 266–69; research and, 242, 251; sensory approach, 238; special (temporary), 237–38; teams, 240–42; tours, 261; types, 8, 237
exhibitions by title: *African Art in Motion*, 238; *America on the Move*, 120; *Between a Rock and a Hard Place*, 131, 132, 249; *Cezanne*, 44, 238; *Gaelic Gotham*, 131, 250; *Into the Heart of Africa*, 249; *The Last Act*, 249; *A Question of Truth*, 250; *Sensation*, 45, 250; *The Splendors of Dresden*, 243–44; *Treasures of Tutankhamen* (*King Tut*), 237; *Van Gogh's Van Goghs*, 237; *The West as America*, 45, 250; *We the People*, 238; *Within These Walls*, 246
Experimentarium (Denmark), 103
Exploratorium (San Francisco), 13, 92, 100, 106, 270, 297

Fairchild Tropical Garden (Miami), 151
fakes and frauds, 96, 199, 202
Falk, John, 179, 264
Farmelo, Graham, 105

Farmers Museum (Cooperstown, NY), 124
Farnese, Cardinal (Pope Paul III), 27
fatigue, museum: avoidance methods, 244, 247. *See also* audiences: research and reactions
Fenollosa, Ernest, 38
Field family: as patrons, 70
Field Museum of Natural History (Chicago), 70–71, 96, 290, 298
Flower, William, 59
Fogg Art Museum (Cambridge, MA), 316
folk museums, 125. *See also* outdoor (open-air) museums; *specific museums*
Foner, Eric, 133
Force, Juliana, 40
Ford, Henry, 92, 97, 100, 124, 272
forgeries. *See* fakes and frauds
Forrest, George, 145
Fortune, Robert, 147
Fort Worth Museum of Science and History, 176
France: royal art collection, 25, 26. *See also* Bonaparte, Napoleon; *specific museums and cities*
France, Jean de, 24, 86
Francis I, Holy Roman Emperor, 61, 92, 153, 200
Franco, Barbara, 192
Franklin Institute Science Museum and Planetarium (Philadelphia, PA), 93
Frilandsmuseet (Copenhagen), 122
Fuller, Buckminster, 149
funding: for art museums, 45; children's museums, 178; federal, 204, 308; for science and technological museums, 90, 91
Futter, Ellen, 69

Gaelic Gotham, 131, 250
Gager, C. Stuart, 150

Gaither, Edmund Barry, 3
gallery (galleria), 5
Gallup, Anna Billings, 167, 169, 170, 171
gardens. *See* botanical gardens
Gardner, Howard, 272, 274
Gardner, James, 245
George III, king of England, 143
Germanisches Museum (Nuremberg), 118
Gesner, Conrad, 55
Getty Museum, 203
Gettysburg National Historical Park panorama, 117, 193
Ghini, Luca, 141
Gillmore, Gertrude A., 175
Gilman, Benjamin Ives, 7, 23, 42, 257
Gilpin, William, 25
Giovio, Paolo, 114
glass: conservation of, 220
Glass, Brent, 113
globalism, 296
Glyptothek (Munich), 34
Goethe, Johann Wolfgang von, 141
Goethe's Palm, 141
Gonzaga collection, 25, 54, 115
Goode, George Brown: on educational function, 284; on labels, 248; Smithsonian career, 6, 66
Goodman, Nelson, 305
Goodwin, W. A. R., 123
Goodyear, William Henry, 169
Goya, Francisco Jose de, 31, 200
Goya's Black Paintings, 200
Grand Rapids Public Museum (MI), 120
Grant, Ulysses S., 94
Gray, Asa, 148
Greek collections, 4, 24, 32, 35, 39, 59; menageries, 153
Greenfield Village (Dearborn, MI), 97, 124. *See also* Henry Ford Museum

Guggenheim, Solomon B., 40
Guggenheim Museum (New York),
    40, 296
guides: mentioned, 7, 131, 262; role-
    playing, 121, 123, 295, 263;
    volunteers, 275
Gulag Museum (Russia), 128
Gunston Hall (VA), 127
Gurian, Elaine Heumann, 12, 172,
    180, 281, 290
Guthe, Carl E., 192

habitat groups, 56, 68, 245
Hadrian, Emperor, 4
Hagenbeck, Carl, 154
Hague Convention for the Protection
    of Cultural Property in the Event
    of Armed Conflict, 314
Hamlin, Chauncey L., 313
Hapsburg collections, 26
Harris, Neil, 15
Harvard University, 67, 70, 148, 272,
    316
Hasbrouck House (Newburgh, NY),
    126
Hatshepsut, queen of Egypt, 153
Hayden Planetarium, 69
Hazelius, Artur, 10, 120–22
Hein, George, 274, 277, 297
Heine, Albert, 167
Hennes, Tom, 246, 297
Henry, Joseph, 65
Henry Ford Museum (Dearborn, MI),
    92, 97, 272
Heritage Health Index, 218, 222, 249,
    299
Hermitage (Leningrad), 27, 35
Hermitage (Nashville), 127
Hertrich, William, 150
Heureka (Finland), 13, 102
Hezekiah, Lloyd, 288
Hindle, Brooke, 85
historical societies. See specific
    societies

Historic Deerfield (MA), 123
historic house museums, 126–28, 132.
    See also historic structures and
    districts
Historic New England, 127
historic preservation. See historic
    structures and districts
Historic Preservation Act of 1966,
    128
Historic Sites Act of 1935, 128
historic structures and districts, 126;
    adaptive uses, 127–28;
    international preservation
    organizations, 128; mentioned,
    123
history museums, 113–38;
    background, 114; challenges of,
    130, 193; collection function of,
    122, 130, 189, 193; culture history
    arrangement, 117; educational
    function, 132, 133; exhibition
    function, 125, 132; of historical
    societies, 118–20; panoramas and
    dioramas, 116; portrait galleries,
    64. See also guides; historic
    structures and districts; outdoor
    (open-air) museums; specific
    history museums
Hitler, Adolf, 34
Holburn Physic Garden (London),
    140
Holm, Peter, 123
Hooker, Joseph Dalton, 144, 148
Hooker, William Jackson, 143
Hopps, Walter, 237
Hornaday, William Temple, 155, 245
Horta, Maria de Lourdes, 299
Hortus Botanicus (Leiden), 141
Hosack, David, 148
house museums. See historic
    structures and districts
Hoving, Thomas P. F., 2
Howard, Thomas, earl of Arundel, 25
Hradcany Castle (Prague), 26

Hudson, Kenneth, 104, 205
Humboldt, Alexander von, 146
Hunter, John, 60
Hunter, William, 60
Huntington Botanical Gardens (San Marino, CA), 150

Illicit Antiquities Research Centre (Cambridge, UK), 210
illicit art trade, 202. *See also* fakes and frauds
Imperati, Ferrante, 55, 56
Imperati, Francesco, 55, 56
Indian (American) museums, 13, 74, 75, 297
Indianapolis Children's Museum, 175, 179
Indian Botanic Garden (Calcutta), 146
industrial arts museums, 88, 90, 93, 97, 202, 112, 117, 190
Industrial Revolution: effect on museums, 8, 86, 121
industry and company exhibits and museums, 93, 97, 112, 263
Institute of Museum and Library Services, 308, 318
Institute of Museum Services, 308, 312
Instituto delle Scienze of the Conte de Luigi Ferdinando Marsigli, 55
international art trade, illicit, 202
International Centre for the Study of Preservation and Restoration of Cultural Property (Rome Centre), 313
International Coalition of Historic Site Museums of Conscience, 128, 292
International Council of Monuments and Sites (ICOMOS), 314
International Council of Museums (ICOM), 2, 206, 260, 283, 299, 306, 312–15

Internet, 103, 106, 131, 142, 218, 246, 268, 297. *See also* computers
interpretation (educational) function: audience approach, 264, 270; definition of, 258; demonstration and activities, 262; of museums, 2, 8, 10, 257; orientation programs, 261, 269; publications and audiovisual projects, 266–69; tours and guides, 261–65
Into the Heart of Africa, 249
Istapalan, 140

Jabach, Everhard, 26
Jardin des Plantes (Paris), 30, 60, 145, 153
Jardin Gabrielle, 148
Java botanical garden (Bogor), 147
Jelinek, Jan, 281
Jesup, Morris K., 68
John Savage's City Museum, 63
John IV, prince regent of Portugal, 148
Jorvik Center (York), 129
Joseph, Franz, emperor, 92
J. Paul Getty Museum, 203
Junquera, Juan Jose, 200
Justi, Ludwig, 34

Kaiser Wilhelm Museum of Western Art (Berlin), 33, 34
Karnak, Temple of, 140
Keck, Caroline, 225
Kellogg Foundation, 241
Kent, Henry Watson, 41
Kent, William, 143
Kerr, William, 147
Kew. *See* Royal Botanic Gardens at Kew
Kimmelman, Michael, 252
Kinard, John R., 287
King, George, 147
Kircher, Athanasius, 55, 87
Kircheriano museum (Rome), 55–56

"kitchen conversations," 292
Knell, Stephen, 104, 295
Knoedler, Michel, 198
Knowles, Malcolm, 273
Komarov Botanical Institute (St. Petersburg), 146
Koninklijk Museum (Amsterdam), 31
Krens, Thomas, 291
Kyd, Robert, 146

labels, 236, 242, 247
La Caze, Louis, 32
Landesmuseum (Zurich), 118
Lang, Jack, 125
Langley, Samuel P., 95, 157, 168
Lascaux caves, 23, 232, 300
La Specola (zoological museum, Florence, Italy), 61
Last Act, The (Enola Gay), 131, 249
La Villette, 101, 103
LeClerc, Georges-Louis, comte de Buffon, 60, 145
l'Ecluse, Charles de (Carolus Clusius), 141
lectures, forums, and seminars, 265, 266, 274, 284, 307
Leopold, Peter, grand duke of Italy, 61
Leopold-Wilhelm, archduke, 26
Lever, Ashton, 60
Lewis, Henry, 117
lighting. See exhibitions: lighting
Lincoln, Abraham, 129
Link, Heinrich Friedrich, 146
Linnaean Botanic Garden, 148
Linnaeus, Carl, 141
Lion Country Safari (West Palm Beach, FL), 159
loans and exchanges: as acquisition methods, 44, 196–97; among museums, 201, 224, 237, 286; packing and shipping of, 225–26; unrestricted ownership, 196

Loewen, James, 131
Lohr, Lenox R., 96
Longleat estate, 159
Longwood Gardens (Kennett Square, PA), 150
Los Angeles County Museum of Art, 237
Louis I of Bavaria, 34
Louis XIV, king of France, 26, 28
Louis XV, king of France, 28
Loutherbourg, Philippe de, 117
Louvre Museum (Paris): decorative arts, 35; establishment and growth of, 6, 28, 29–32, 41, 58, 72; mentioned, 41
Low, Theodore L., 282, 284
Lowenthal, David, 131
Lower East Side Tenement Museum (New York), 128, 292
Lubow, Arthur, 200
Luke, Timothy W., 235
Luxembourg Palace (Paris), 35

MacBeth, William, 198
Macintyre, Robert, 198
Maihaugen (Lillehammer, Norway), 122, 130
Malaro, Marie, 204, 205
Maleuvre, Didier, 4
Marsh, Othniel C., 67
Marshall, Humphrey, 148
Marum, Martin van, 87
Marzio, Peter, 180, 181
Massachusetts Historical Society (Boston, MA), 119
Massachusetts Museum of Contemporary Art (MassMOCA, North Adams, MA), 40, 291
Mauritius botanical garden, 146
Mazarin, Cardinal, 26
McNab, James, 145
McNab, William, 145
Mead, Margaret, 69
Mechel, Chretien de, 28

Medici (Riccardi) Palace (Florence), 25
Medici, Marie de, queen of France, 25
Medici collections, 24, 27, 55, 86
Meegeren, Han van, 199
Melbourne botanical garden, 147
Mellon, Andrew W., 39, 188
Melton, Arthur W., 272
Menagerie du Parc (Versailles), 153
menageries. *See* zoos
metals, conservation of, 220
Metropolitan Museum of Art (New York), 67, 237; acquisition case, 203; American Wing, 38; children's galleries, 168; Cloisters, 38; Costume Institute, 38; disposal procedures, 207; educational programs, 41; establishment of, 7, 36–39; Greek calyx krater, 203; purpose, 36
Middle Ages, 5, 197
Millennium Seedbank Project, 144
Miller, Oskar von, 91, 100
Miller, Philip, 142
Miller, Stephen H., 187
minority groups, 42
Missouri Botanical Garden (St. Louis, MO), 148
mobile (traveling) museums: mentioned, 237; risks, 224, 225; for schools, 41
modern art: audience reaction, 34, 44; museums, 44, 193
Montebello, Philippe de, 38, 44, 203
Montgomery, Robert A., 151
Montpellier (France) botanical garden, 5, 142
Moon, Alexander, 147
Morgan, J. P., 37
Morison, Robert, 142
Morley, Grace L. McCann, 313
Moroni, Giovanni, 141
Morse, Edward S., 38

Mount Vernon (VA), 126
Mouseion at Alexandria, 3, 28, 140, 153
multimedia (audiovisual) exhibits, 40, 76, 236, 245, 262, 271, 294. *See also* exhibitions
Mumford, Lewis, 188
murals, 29, 220
Murton, Henry James, 147
MUSE community project (Brooklyn, NY), 170, 288
Musee de l'Homme (Paris), 72, 125
Musee du Quai Branly, 75, 298
Musee Napoleon, 31
Musee Napoleon III, 32
Museo Kircheriano (Rome), 55–56
museum accreditation. *See* accreditation, museum
Museum Assessment Program (MAP), 312
Museum Dahlem (Berlin), 145
Museum fur Volkerkunde, 61
Museum Island (Berlin), 33, 34
Museum Jovianum (Como, Italy), 114
Museum National d'Histoire Naturelle (Paris), 60, 72
Museum of American History, 131
Museum of Comparative Zoology (Harvard), 67
Museum of Fine Arts (Boston): docents, 7; dual arrangement, 196; educational program, 41; establishment of, 7, 36–39
Museum of Florida History, 241
Museum of History and Technology (Washington, DC), 120
Museum of Modern Art (MOMA, New York): disposal procedures, 207; founded, 39; mentioned, 40
Museum of Scandinavian Folklore (Nordiska Museet, Stockholm), 121
Museum of Science and Industry (Chicago), 92, 96–97

Museum of the City of New York, 131, 240, 289
Museum of the National Center of African American Artists, 3
Museum of World Culture (Sweden), 298
museum profession, 305; ethics code, 310; mentioned, 235; objectives, 306; statistics, 282
museums: acquisitions methods of, 44, 196; audience reaction, 122, 177, 275, 281; blockbusters, 44, 237, 250, 275; challenges, 14, 250, 275; collection planning, 194; as cultural centers, 282; deaccessions, 44, 205; dealers in art objects, 197; definitions of, 2, 11–13, 189, 283, 311; disposal procedures of, 205; educational purpose, 40, 259; history of, 3–7, 27, 53–74; learning in, 272; outreach, 288; performing arts, 286; post-colonial, 297; publications, 269, 314; record-keeping, 200; research, 275, 298; social events, 286; studies, 316
museums, outdoor. See outdoor (open-air) museums
museums, specialized. See under specific fields of specialization
Museums Association of Great Britain, 315
Museums for a New Century, 309, 315
music: mood creation, 117, 121, 123, 294; programs, 72, 151, 175, 286, 288
Mystic Seaport (CT), 124

Napoleon. See Bonaparte, Napoleon
Napoleon, Louis, king of Holland, 31
Napoleon III, emperor of France, 32

Nationaal Herbarium Nederland (Netherlands), 141
National Air and Space Museum (Washington, DC), 95, 131. See also Smithsonian Institution
National Endowment for the Arts, 241
National Endowment for the Humanities, 133, 178, 241
Nationalgalerie (Berlin), 33, 34
National Gallery (London), 32, 33
National Gallery of Art (Washington, DC), 36, 39, 209, 238. See also Smithsonian Institution
National Gallery of British Art (London). See Tate Britain Gallery
National Great Blacks in Wax Museum (Baltimore, MD), 271
National Herbarium (St. Petersburg, Russia), 146
National Museum (Denmark), 122
National Museum (Naples), 27
National Museum Act, 308
National Museum of American History (Washington, DC), 120, 133, 229, 246, 249, 251, 269
National Museum of Anthropology (Mexico City), 72, 73
National Museum of Ethnology (Rijksmuseum voor Volkenkunde, Leiden), 72
National Museum of History and Technology (Washington, DC), 120; audience survey, 246; exhibits, 246, 249. See also Smithsonian Institution
National Museum of Modern Art (Paris), 35
National Museum of Natural History (Washington, DC), 56, 66, 74, 239. See also Smithsonian Institution
National Museum of Photography, Film and Television, 90, 103

National Museum of Science and Industry (London), 88–91, 103
National Museum of the American Indian (Washington, DC), 297
National Park Service, 128, 195, 257
National Portrait Gallery (Washington, DC), 116, 192. *See also* Smithsonian Institution
National Railway Museum (York), 90, 103
National Science Foundation, 308
National Trust for Historic Preservation (Washington, DC), 129
National Zoological Park, 157. *See also* Smithsonian Institution
Native American Graves Protection and Repatriation Act, 204
Natural History Museum (Basel), 55
natural history museums, 53–84; American, 61; anthropological museums, 53; arrangements of habitat groups, 56, 68, 245; audience reaction, 56; British and continental, 60; collection function and methods, 55, 190, 194; collections of curiosities, 54, 74; history, 53, 56. *See also specific natural history museums*
natural science museums. *See* natural history museums
Naturhistoriches Museum (Vienna), 61
Nazis and art, 203
Neickel, Caspar F., 55
neighborhood museums. *See* community (neighborhood) museums
Neue Pinakothek (Munich), 34, 35
Neues Museum (Berlin), 33, 34
Newark (NJ) Museum, 42, 170, 282, 315, 316; audience survey, 170
Newhouse, Victoria, 43, 237, 244

New Orleans historic district, 128
New Thing Art and Architecture Center (Washington, DC), 288
New York Botanical Garden, 149
New-York Historical Society, 63, 119
New York State Historical Association (Cooperstown), 116
New York Zoological Society (Bronx Zoo), 155
Noble, Joseph Veach, 305
Nordiska Museet (Stockholm), 121
Norsk Folkemuseum (Oslo), 122

objects: authentication, 195; exhibits, 224, 242; importance, 188, 191, 242; in museum definition, 188, 189; physical nature, 219; research, 201; types, 219; value guidelines, 193. *See also* collecting and collections
Old Salem (Winston-Salem, NC), 123
Old Sturbridge Village (MA), 124, 273
Old Town (Den Gamle By, Denmark), 123
Old World Wisconsin, 124
Ole Worm Museum (Copenhagen), 55
Olmstead, Frederick Law, 149, 150, 157
Olsen, Bernhard, 122
Ontario Science Centre (Toronto), 100, 277, 293, 298
open-air museums. *See* outdoor (open-air) museums
Oppenheimer, Frank, 85, 101
organic materials, conservation of, 219
Osborn, Fairfield, 156
Osborn, Henry Fairfield, 68, 156
Otto, Judy, 167
outdoor (open-air) museums, 123; American, 97, 123, 125; ancient, 5,

120; audiences, 123, 263; education function, 118, 119, 123, 125; exhibits, 73, 123; guides, 263; mentioned, 114, 121, 313; research and, 123
outreach programs (community services): mentioned, 119, 241; as museum aim, 289–91, 314. *See also* audiences; community (neighborhood) museums
Oxford Botanical Garden, 142

Packer, Jan, 265
packing and shipping, 225–26
Padua botanical garden, 141
Palais Cardinal, 26
Palais de la Découverte (Paris), 99, 263
Palais Royal, 26
Paludanus, Bernhardus, 55
panorama, 116–17
Paris World's Fair, 121
Parke Bernet, 198
Parker, Arthur, 10
Parker, Arthur C., 113
Parr, Albert E., 306
Parson, Beatrice, 175
Patchen, Jeff, 179
Patterson, Joseph Allen, 308
Peabody Museum (Harvard), 70
Peabody Museum (Yale), 67
Peale, Charles Willson, 6, 36, 54, 56, 62, 116, 129, 226
Peale Museum, 6, 62. *See also* Philadelphia Museum
Pearson, Harold Welch, 147
Peate, Iorwerth C., 122
Pedro II, Don, emperor of Brazil, 94
Pennsylvania Academy of Fine Arts, 36, 286
Pergamon Museum (Berlin), 33, 34
Peter the Great, 27
Philadelphia Museum, 62, 155, 130. *See also* Peale Museum

Philadelphia Museum of Art, 36, 44, 237
Philadelphia Zoological Garden, 155
Phillip II, Holy Roman Emperor, 26
Phillip V, Holy Roman Emperor, 26
Pio-Clementine Museum (Rome), 27
Pisa botanical garden, 141
Pittman, Bonnie, 284
Platter, Felix, 55
Plenderleith, Harold J., 219
Plimoth Plantation (MA), 125, 264
Plot, Robert, 57
Prado (Madrid), 26
Preservation of Industrial and Scientific Materials (PRISM), 90
Prince, Robert, 148
Prince, William, 148
Pring, George H., 149
provenance, 200
Ptolemy Soter, 3
publications, 219, 256, 266–69, 307, 314
publicity, 131, 252, 266
Putnam, Frederick Ward, 70

Question of Truth, A, 250
Quin, Melanie, 86, 106

Raffles, Thomas Stamford, 153
Ramirez, Jan, 249, 299
Raphael, 25
Ravenel, Gaillard E., 235, 243
Rebay, Hilla, baroness von Ehrenwiesen, 40
record systems, 200
recreational aspects, of museums, 157, 159
Reed, Luman, 36
research: in ancient period, 9; computerization and, 208; mentioned, 15, 101, 251, 275, 307, 317
restaurants, museum, 44, 176, 238

restoration techniques, 8, 34, 226, 227. *See also* conservation; historic structures and districts
Rhodes, Cecil, 147
Richelieu, Cardinal, 25
Rijksmuseum (Amsterdam), 31
Rijksmuseum voor Volkenkunde (Leiden), 121
Rinker, H. Bruce, 139
Rio de Janeiro Botanic Garden, 148
Ripley, S. Dillon, 2
Rittenhouse, David, 61
Rivet, Paul, 72
Riviere, Georges-Henri, 53, 125
Robert, Hubert, 28, 29
Roberts, Lisa C., 235, 257
Robinson, Edward S., 272
Robinson, Franklin, 45
Rockefeller, John D., Jr., 38, 123
Rockefeller, Mrs. John D., Jr., 39
Rodriguez, Joao Barbosa, 148
Rome: ancient collections and menageries, 25; Vatican museums, 27
Rose, Carolyn, 231
Rosenwald, Julius, 96, 100
Rosenzweig, Roy, 133
Ross, James, 144
Rothfels, Nigel, 139
Roxburgh, William, 146
Royal Academy (London), 32
Royal Botanic Garden (Edinburgh), 145
Royal Botanic Gardens at Kew (London), 143, 157
Royal Ontario Museum (Toronto), 249
Royal Scottish Museum (Edinburgh), 2
Royal Society of Arts (London), 87
Rubens, Peter Paul, 25, 26, 197
Rudolph II, Holy Roman Emperor, 26

Russian museums and collections, 146, 296
Russian State Hermitage, 296
Ruysch, Frederick, 55

Sachs, Paul J., 316
Sacramento, Frie do, 148
safari and wild animal parks, 159
Saint Gall, 140
Salles, Georges, 313
Sandburg, Mark, 178
San Diego Wild Animal Park, 158
San Diego Zoological Garden, 157
Sandvig, Anders, 122, 130
Sargent, Charles Sprague, 149
Saxe-Gotha, Augusta, 143
Schlereth, Thomas, 189
Schonbrunn (Vienna), 145
schools and museums: educational programs, 41, 156, 168, 259, 270; mentioned, 7, 41; in neighborhood museum, 169, 271; performing arts programs, 10; traveling museums, 237
science and technology museums, 85–112, 244; audience reaction, 103, 105, 107; challenges, 104; dual arrangement, 196; educational function, 99; exhibitions, 103; history, 85, 99; industry museums and exhibits, 93, 97, 112, 263. *See also specific science and technology museums*
Science Museum (Boston), 98
Science Museum (London), 103
Scudder, John, 63
Seattle World's Fair, 99
Seba, Albert, 55
Seligman, Germain, 198
Seligman, Jacques, 198
Semper, Robert, 106
Sensation, 45, 250
Serrell, Beverly, 248

Settala, Ludovico, 87
Settala, Manfredo, 87
Shaw, Henry, 148
Shelburne (VT) Museum, 124
Shen Nung, emperor, 140
shipping. *See* packing and shipping
Siebold, F. B. von, 72
Silver, Adele, 11
Simitiere, Pierre Eugene du, 36, 62, 115
Singapore botanical garden, 147
Skansen outdoor museum (Stockholm), 10
Skiff, Frederick J. V., 70
Slave House Museum (Senegal), 128
Sloane, Hans, 28, 58, 142
Smirke, Robert, 59
Smith, David Hugh, 217
Smithson, James, 6, 39, 64
Smithsonian Institution (Washington, DC): American Art Museum, 250; Anacostia Neighborhood Museum, 287; children's gallery, 168; founded, 6, 39, 64–67, 74, 92; funding, 64; mentioned, 3, 168; Museum of History and Technology, 120; National Air and Space Museum, 95; National Gallery of Art, 36, 39, 209, 238; National Museum of American History, 120, 131, 269; National Museum of Natural History, 66–67, 74, 239; National Museum of the American Indian, 13, 297; National Portrait Gallery, 116, 192; National Zoological Park, 157
social events: as museum function, 286
Society for the Preservation of New England Antiquities (Boston), 127
Soderstrom, Mary, 139
Solly, Edward, 33
Sonora Desert Museum (Tucson, AZ), 158

Sotheby's, 198
South African National Botanical Garden (Kirstenbosch), 147
South Kensington Museum of Science and Art (London), 89, 117
Spadaccini, James, 106
Species Survival Program (SSP), 156, 221
Splendors of Dresden, The, 243
Spock, Michael, 168, 172, 246
Squalerno, Luigi (Luigi Anguillara), 141
Sri Lanka botanic garden, 147
Starn, Randolph, 113
State Historical Society of Wisconsin (Madison), 116, 119
Stein, Gertrude, 40
Stellingen Zoo (Hamburg, Germany), 154
Sterling, Peter, 179, 181
Stevenson, Sarah Yorke, 316
Stolow, Nathan, 222, 225, 228
stone, ceramics, glass (siliceous materials): conservation of, 220
Stonefield (WI) historic village, 124
storage, 208, 222
Stratford Hall (VA), 127
Strong, Margaret Woodbury, 177
Strong—The National Museum of Play, 177–78
Stuart, John (Lord Bute), 143
Studio Watts (Los Angeles, CA), 288
Sullivan, Mrs. Cornelius J., 39
Swiss Landesmuseum (Zurich), 118
Sydney botanical garden, 147

Tate Britain Gallery (London), 35
Taylor, Francis Henry, 5
Tchen, John Kuo Wei, 13
Technical Museum (Vienna), 92
technology museums. *See* science and technology museums
Tekniska Museet (Stockholm), 102
Teknorama (Stockholm) 102

Temple of Karnak, 140
Teniers, David, the Younger, 26
Terezin Memorial (Czech Republic),
128
textiles: conservation of, 219
Teyler Stichting Foundation
(Haarlem, Netherlands), 87
theft, 8. *See also* international art
trade, illicit
theme parks, 129, 239
Thutmose III, 140
Thwaites, Henry George Kendrick,
147
Thwaites, Reuben Gold, 119
Tilden, Freeman, 258, 270
Titian, 25, 26
Tivoli amusement park
(Copenhagen), 4, 122
Toledo Museum of Art (OH), 36
tourism, 132
tours, 44, 90, 258, 261–63, 265, 270,
274, 288; virtual tours, 258, 269
Towneley, Charles, 59
Tradescant, John, Jr., 57, 87, 142
Tradescant, John, Sr., 57, 87, 142
training courses. *See* museum
profession
traveling exhibitions, 237
Treasures of Tutankhamen (*King Tut*),
237
Trumbull, Colonel John, 36
Tuilleries Gardens (Paris), 30
Tweed, William Marcy ("Boss"), 37
Tyson, Neil deGrasse, 77

Uffizi Palace (Florence), 27
United Nations Educational,
Scientific, and Cultural
Organization (UNESCO), 202, 306,
313
United States Department of Health,
Education, and Welfare, 308
United States Department of the
Interior, 128

United States Holocaust Memorial
Museum (Washington, DC), 240
University Museum (Basel), 5, 28
"unmuseum," 13, 40
Uppsala University (Sweden)
botanical garden, 146

Vaccaro, Alessandra Malucco, 231
Valentine, Mann, II, 120
Valentine Museum (Richmond, VA),
120
Valentiner, W. R., 198
Valley Forge (PA), 127
Van Gogh's Van Goghs, 237
Vasa (Stockholm), 275
Vatican museums (Rome), 6, 27
Vaucanson, Jacques, 87
Vaux, Calvert, 150
Veblen, Thorstein, 8
Velazquez, Diego, 25, 26, 207
Versailles: Historical Museum, 132;
Palace, 28, 151, 153
Victoria, queen of England, 33
Victoria and Albert Museum
(London), 35, 117, 168, 270
Villiers, George Francis, duke of
Buckingham, 25
virtual exhibits and museums, 2, 9,
77, 89, 99, 246, 258, 271, 297, 299
Vivant-Denon, Dominique, 30
volunteer personnel, 43, 161, 260,
275, 319
Vose, Robert C., 198

Waagen, Gustav, 35
Wadsworth Atheneum (Hartford,
CT), 36
Wakehurst garden (Ardingly,
Sussex), 144
Walcott, Charles D., 95
Walker Art Center (Minneapolis,
MN), 40
Walters Art Gallery (Baltimore, MD),
223

Ward, Nathaniel Bagshaw, 56, 142
Ward, Philip R., 217
Washington's headquarters
    (Newburgh, NY), 126, 136
Wedgeforth, Harry M., 157
Weil, Stephen E., 10, 12, 284, 319
Wellington Museum (London), 31
Welsh Folk Museum, 122
Werner, A. E. A., 219
West, W. Richard, 13
West as America, The, 45, 250
We the People, 238
Whitney, Gertrude Vanderbilt, 40
Whitney Museum of American Art
    (New York), 40
Wildlife Conservation Society, 156
Wilhelm, Landgrave, IV, 86
Wilkes, John, 28
Willdenow, Carl Ludwig, 146
Williams, Stephen L., 15, 319
Wilson-Bareau, Juliet, 200
Winterthur Museum (DE), 38, 227
Within These Walls, 246
Wittlin, Alma S., 9, 18, 189, 198, 235,
    264
Wittman, Otto, 286
Woodcroft, Bennet, 89

World's Columbian Exposition of
    1893 (Chicago), 70, 96
Worm, Ole, 55, 56
Wright Brothers, 95

Yale University (New Haven, CT),
    36, 37
Yanni, Carol, 76
Young at Art, 180
youth activities and programs, 171,
    180, 270; and botanical gardens,
    150; inquiry approach to, 271;
    and museums, 271; and zoos,
    158. See also schools and
    museums
Youth ALIVE! program, 171, 271

Zoological Society (London), 153
Zoological Society (San Diego), 157
zoos: American, 155; audiences, 161;
    challenges, 160; conservation
    purpose, 139, 140, 154, 156, 160;
    historical background
    (menageries), 153–61; purpose,
    139, 154; safari and wild animal
    parks, 159. See also specific zoos
Zwinger Palace (Dresden), 35

About the Authors

Edward Porter Alexander

Edward Porter Alexander served as director of the New York State Historical Association (1934–1941), director for the Historical Society of Wisconsin (1941–1946), Vice President for Interpretation, Colonial Williamsburg (1946–1972), and founder and professor of Museum Studies, University of Delaware (1972–1978).

He earned his B.A. at Drake University, M.A. at the University of Iowa, and Ph.D. at Columbia University.

His honors include Phi Beta Kappa, Katherine Coffey Award (Northeast Museums Conference), Award of Distinction (American Association for State and Local History), and Distinguished Service Award (American Association of Museums), and in 2006 he was listed on the AAM's Centennial Honor Roll.

His publications are *James Duane, Revolutionary Conservative*; *Museums in Motion: An Introduction to the History and Functions of Museums*; *Museum Masters: Their Museums and Their Influence*; and *The Museum in America: Innovators and Pioneers*.

Mary Alexander

Mary Alexander has been a museum educator and administrator in Washington, D.C., area since 1970. She has worked for the George

Washington Bicentennial Center, National Archives and Records Administration, Mount Vernon Ladies' Association, and Hillwood Museum. She coordinated the American Association for State and Local History's Common Agenda for History Museums and directs the Museum Advancement Program at the Maryland Historical Trust. Her honors include the Katherine Coffey Award for Distinguished Service (Mid-Atlantic Association of Museums).

She earned her B.A. at Beloit College and M.A. at the University of Connecticut. She was associate editor for *A Museum Education Anthology* (1984) and coauthored *Museums: Places of Learning* (1998) with George E. Hein.